WOMEN, MIGRATION AND CITIZENSHIP

Gender in a Global/Local World

Series Editors: Jane Parpart, Pauline Gardiner Barber
and Marianne H. Marchand

Gender in a Global/Local World critically explores the uneven and often contradictory ways in which global processes and local identities come together. Much has been and is being written about globalization and responses to it but rarely from a critical, historical, gendered perspective. Yet, these processes are profoundly gendered albeit in different ways in particular contexts and times. The changes in social, cultural, economic and political institutions and practices alter the conditions under which women and men make and remake their lives. New spaces have been created – economic, political, social – and previously silent voices are being heard. North-South dichotomies are being undermined as increasing numbers of people and communities are exposed to international processes through migration, travel and communication, even as marginalization and poverty intensify for many in all parts of the world. The series features monographs and collections which explore the tensions in a 'global/local world', and includes contributions from all disciplines in recognition that no single approach can capture these complex processes.

Also in the series

Women, Migration and Citizenship

Making Local, National and Transnational Connections

Edited by
EVANGELIA TASTSOGLOU
ALEXANDRA DOBROWOLSKY
Saint Mary's University, Canada

ASHGATE

#62408723

Published by
Ashgate Publishing Limited
Gower House
Croft Road
Aldershot
Hampshire GU11 3HR
England

Ashgate Publishing Company
Suite 420
101 Cherry Street
Burlington, VT 05401-4405
USA

Ashgate website: http://www.ashgate.com

British Library Cataloguing in Publication Data
Women, migration and citizenship : making local, national
    and transnational connections. - (Gender in a global/local
    world)
    1. Women immigrants - Western countries - Social conditions
    2. Citizenship 3. Women immigrants - Canada - Social
    conditions 4. Citizenship - Canada
    I. Tastsoglou, Evangelia II. Dobrowolsky, Alexandra Z.
    (Alexandra Zorianna), 1964-
    305.4'896912

Library of Congress Cataloging-in-Publication Data
Women, migration, and citizenship : making local, national, and transnational
connections / edited by Evangelia Tastsoglou and Alexandra Dobrowolsky.
        p. cm. -- (Gender in a global/local world)
    Includes bibliographical references and index.
    ISBN 0-7546-4379-4
    1. Women immigrants. 2. Alien labor. 3. Women refugees. 4. Emigration and
    immigration--Social aspects. 5. Citizenship. 6. Marginality, Social. I. Tastsoglou,
    Evangelia. II. Dobrowolsky, Alexandra Z. (Alexandra Zorianna), 1964- III. Series.

    HQ1155.W67 2006
    305.48'96914090511--dc22

                                                                        2005034910

ISBN-10: 0 7546 4379 4

Printed and bound in Great Britain by Antony Rowe Ltd, Chippenham, Wiltshire.

Contents

Notes on Contributors

Awa Mohamed Abdi is a Somali-Canadian scholar currently completing a PhD in the department of Sociology at the University of Sussex. Her thesis entitled: 'Continuity and Change: Somali Diasporic Gender relations' builds on her previous work with Somali refugees in the Horn of Africa and in North America, and explores the impact of forced displacement on gender relations. Her latest publication, 'In Limbo: Dependency, Insecurity, and Identity amongst Somali Refugees in Dadaab Camps,' was published in the journal, *Refuge*. In addition to her academic work, she has worked as a consultant for national and international bodies including CARE Canada and the UK Home Office.

Pauline Gardiner Barber is a Social Anthropologist and Associate Professor at Dalhousie University. Her research explores the changing dynamics of Philippine migration, development and citizenship and is published in such journals as *International Women's Studies Forum*, *Asia Pacific Viewpoint*, and *Anthropologica*, as well in edited volumes with Routledge, SUNY Press, Broadview Press and Berghahn Books. She is a domain leader in the Atlantic Metropolis Centre and a co-editor for Ashgate's *Gender in a Global/Local World* series.

Ann Denis is a Professor in the Département de sociologie, Université d'Ottawa and has been Visiting Researcher and Visiting Professor at the Centre for Gender and Development Studies, University of the West Indies, Barbados. Her current research interests include the study, in both Canada and the Caribbean, of the impact of state policies on women's work and of the gendered use of the Internet by minority students, and also women's retention in engineering in Canadian universities.

Alexandra Dobrowolsky is an Associate Professor in Political Science at Saint Mary's University. She has published *The Politics of Pragmatism: Women, Representation and Constitutionalism in Canada* (with Oxford, 2000) and co-edited (with Vivien Hart) *Women Making Constitutions: New Politics and Comparative Perspectives* (with Palgrave, 2003). Her recent work appears in various journals including: *Commonwealth and Comparative Politics*; *Social Politics*; *Review of Constitutional Studies*; and *Studies in Political Economy* as well as in edited volumes with The Policy Press and Cambridge University, University of British Columbia, and University of Toronto Presses. Her research interests revolve around issues of social policy, democracy and citizenship. She is currently working on im/migration and security concerns.

Arent Greve is a Professor of organization theory at the Norwegian School of Economics and Business Administration and adjunct professor at the Department of Sociology, University of Toronto. His main research interests are topics related to social capital. He applies the concept to a variety of theoretical and empirical settings using social network analysis. Greve's research covers both organizational as well as individual networks looking at knowledge networks, technology, telework, labour markets for immigrant professionals, and entrepreneurship. His main theoretical point of departure is institutional theory of organizations.

Luz María Hermoso Santamaría is a Faculty Member in the Area of Social Sciences at the Universidad Autónoma Chapingo in Mexico, on leave to pursue a PhD at the University of Guelph in Canada. Her research interests focus on International Relations, Gender and Migration. She has lived and conducted research in Canada, Hungary, and the US. At present Luz María is studying the Mexican Seasonal Agricultural Workers Program between Mexico and Canada.

Wendy Larner is a Professor of Human Geography and Sociology at the University of Bristol, United Kingdom, having recently moved from the University of Auckland, New Zealand. She is co-editor (with William Walters) of *Global Governmentality* (Routledge, 2004) and author of a wide range of journal articles and book chapters. Her research interests include political economy, governmentality, economic geography and social policy.

Ruth Lister is a Professor of Social Policy in the Department of Social Sciences, Loughborough University. She is a former Director of the Child Poverty Action Group. She has published widely around poverty, gender and citizenship. Her latest books are *Citizenship: Feminist Perspectives* (2nd edition) (with Palgrave, 2003) and *Poverty* (with Polity, 2004).

Kerry Preibisch is a rural sociologist in the Department of Sociology and Anthropology at the University of Guelph. She is a Canadian scholar who has conducted research in Latin America, primarily Mexico, on issues of gender and rural development. Her research interests include gender, citizenship, and migration; foreign workers and the global restructuring of agro-food systems; and rural livelihood diversification. She has published in both English and Spanish, including a recent article in the Canadian Journal of Latin American and Caribbean Studies.

Helen Ralston is a Professor Emerita of Sociology, Saint Mary's University, Canada. Her current research includes a comparative study of immigration, refugee, multicultural and settlement policies; citizenship, identity construction, experience, and agency of immigrant mothers and daughters of South Asian origin. Her present focus is on transnational identity construction in multi-racial and multi-religious local, national, and global diaspora space.

Janet Salaff is a Professor of Sociology, University of Toronto, and Honorary Research Fellow at the Centre of Asian Studies, University of Hong Kong. Throughout her work she has been interested gaining a better understanding of the Chinese family economy. Her current research, on Chinese family immigration, leads her into institutional analyses of the social resources of new immigrants. She is especially interested in how employment, political and family structures can assist women to achieve their goals.

Evangelia Tastsoglou is an Associate Professor of Sociology at the Department of Sociology and Criminology, Saint Mary's University, Canada. Her research interests are in the areas of gender and migration; immigrant women's labour market experiences; immigrant women and community development; ethnicity and race; diasporas and diasporic identities. Her publications appear in the *Canadian Journal of Sociology, Studies in Political Economy, Atlantis, Affilia, Advances in Gender Research, Canadian Ethnic Studies*, among other venues. She is currently the principle investigator in a three-year project on 'Security and Immigration, Changes and Challenges: Immigrant and Ethnic Communities in Atlantic Canada, Presumed Guilty?'

Series Editor's Preface

Women, Migration and Citizenship, edited by Evie Tastsoglou and Alexandra Dobrowolsky, is the eighth title to appear in the Ashgate series "Gender in a Global/ Local World." The series takes advantage of critically engaged new feminist and gender studies scholarship in the turn towards the global. This turn has produced an increased concern with the (gendered) impacts of globalization and contingent international processes. All volumes in this interdisciplinary series pose alternative, gendered questions to mainstream discussion of global processes and local responses.

This volume is no exception. *Women, Migration and Citizenship* examines the experiences of migrant women moving across local, national and transnational borders in a world that, while nominally supportive of more inclusive, cosmopolitan ideals, is actually witnessing a tightening of citizenship rights and opportunities for migrants. The focus on women reflects a growing awareness that over half of global immigrants are women, and that this phenomenon requires a feminist analysis which pays attention to both global and local factors. Drawing on the work of various disciplines, and combining theory and grounded empirical research, the authors in this path-breaking volume seek to analyze both the often daunting and deplorable conditions facing migrant women and the many ingenious ways they are taking up these challenges and transforming them into opportunities. The chapters also pay attention to the differences among migrant women – some are refugees, some asylum seekers, some economic migrants, but often their experiences cross the lines between these "categories". Challenging the stereotype of women migrants as simply dependents of men, the authors demonstrate that while some women migrate as wives, many have their own agendas. Moreover, migrant women increasingly migrate independently, as care givers, skilled professionals, sex workers and asylum seekers. Indeed, migrant women emerge as complex subjects, whose autonomous action and agency, even under the most difficult circumstances, can be amply demonstrated. They enter not only highly feminized labour markets, but also some masculinized (and racialized) occupations, at all levels. Moreover, by making cultural identifications and connections across borders, and conceiving of 'home' as multi-local, immigrant women challenge and contest existing, nation-state based notions of membership and make identity-based claims aiming at a richer and more multi-layered notion of citizenship. Thus, despite many constraints, some women and men have been able to use migration as a means to challenge both gender roles and citizenship practices. The authors examine the experiences of women migrants from the Caribbean, China and Mexico, to the Phillipines and Somalia and of women immigrants in a number of sites, including Canada, Britain, Australia, and New Zealand in a variety of occupations, including seasonal agricultural migrants, domestic workers as well as skilled professionals. Overall, the book highlights the important contributions that gendered processes of migration and citizenship offer, both for rethinking global citizenship and for designing ways to improve the immigrant experience, especially for women.

Jane Parpart
Marianne Marchand
Pauline Gardiner Barber

Acknowledgements

Our sincere thanks first of all to the women who have inspired this research and to all our authors who contributed to this collection. In addition, we would like to acknowledge Jane Parpart, editor of Gender in a Global/Local World series, and Kirstin Howgate, Publisher, Politics and International Relations at Ashgate for their belief in us, patience, encouragement and support throughout this process. Special thanks to Maureen Mansell-Ward, Desk Editor, Carolyn Court Editorial Administrator – Social Science, and the entire team at Ashgate Publishing for their excellent editorial and administrative skills. We are extremely grateful for the wide-ranging assistance (from research to typo hunting and page formatting) of Stephanie Fletcher, Lori Root and Kristel vom Scheidt, graduate students at Saint Mary's University. A special acknowledgement to Susan Rolston for her work on our index and to the small grants provided by the Faculty of Graduate Studies and Research of Saint Mary's University.

Evie would like to acknowledge the unconditional affection and delightful messiness in her life caused by Athena, Aristides and Evangelos Milios as well as her family of origin in her native Greece. Evie dedicates this book to her three mothers, Adamantia Tastsoglou, Ntoula and Nina Louka, whose own numerous border crossings, despite distances and aging, have enabled her to complete this book.

Alexandra would like to acknowledge the unwaivering support of Richard Devlin as well as his dogged attempts to provide more balance in her life. Alexandra dedicates this book to her mother, Halyna Dobrowolsky, who emigrated to Canada to ensure better lives for her future children and grandchildren.

Chapter 1

Crossing Boundaries and Making Connections

Alexandra Dobrowolsky and Evangelia Tastsoglou

From the Post-War to the Post 9/11 Period

> As a woman I have no country, as a woman I want no country, as a woman my country is the whole world.

Virginia Woolf articulated these sentiments at the start of the twentieth century, at a time – in between two devastating World Wars – when the world was rife with rising nationalisms, boundary disputes were deadly and exclusions were rampant (Stolcke 1997: 77). Today, Woolf's aspirations fit remarkably well with certain theoretical trends that trace the development of a new cosmopolitanism and the formation of a fledgling, universal citizenship (Soysal 1994; Held 1995; Kymlicka 2001). These advocates of transnationalism in a postmodern, global world envision an enhanced, borderless citizenship based on political models where the exclusions of the traditional nation-state no longer exist.

To be sure, new global formations, exemplified by 'post-national' types of membership/citizenship (Soysal 2000), increasingly internationalized professional labour markets (Iredale 2001; Ball 2004), 'imagined (global) communities' that transgress the nation-state (Parreñas 2001), and the dynamic nature of migrants certainly 'challenge any notion that the state and individual are hermetically sealed' (Kapur 2003: 12). Ratna Kapur explains:

> The inability to distinguish those who constitute national subjects from those who are alien or foreign is blurred reflecting the uneasy location of a distinct national entity with distinct borders and a distinct, clearly delineated national subject. The legitimizing tools of cohesion, unity and sovereignty become blunt in the face of a more complex and integrated world and global economy and the challenges posed by the transnational subaltern subject. (Kapur 2003: 12)

Nevertheless, as Verena Stolcke cautions:

> Although it is nowadays commonplace to prophesy the end of the nation-state, the powerful ideological logic of the nation-state in reality appears to be far from fading away. Instead, progressively tighter nationality laws control the freedom of movement in

particular of certain peoples despite or precisely because of ever more intense globalized economic competition (Stolcke 1997: 77).

And so, even in the twenty-first century, and despite creative, cosmopolitan ideals and dreams of citizenship reforms in a progressively inclusive world, Woolf's proposition continues to prove to be more fiction than fact. States and citizenship still matter, greatly (Pettman 1999: 214) because we are witnessing, particularly in Canada and the United States, what some have described as the 'tightening of citizenship' (Joppke and Morawska 2003: 16) with more restrictions on access to citizenship, and even the scaling back of citizenship rights with changing citizenship regimes (Jenson and Phillips 1996; Ball 2004; Maher 2004; Dobrowolsky and Jenson 2004).

To be sure, a degree of broadening and de-ethnicization of citizenship has taken place in the European Union (EU). We see, for example, the inclusion of *jus soli* regulations on the acquisition of citizenship, greater tolerance of dual citizenship, and more relaxed attitudes toward minority identities within states. Yet the evidence is ambiguous. For example, in many European states, despite human rights discourses, right-wing parties with anti-immigration platforms have gained political strength (Maher 2004: 138). Moreover, EU member states are not immune from reverting to more exclusionary practices, particularly towards migrants. This is clearly illustrated in this volume in the British case study vis-à-vis asylum seekers (see Dobrowolsky with Lister). Consequently, the importance of citizenship is on the increase in the EU, as well as in North America.

Furthermore, as Pauline Gardiner Barber argues in this collection, there seems to be a growing disjuncture between critical traditions of research regarding citizenship in theory, and the narrowing definitions of citizenship in practice. While the former seeks to address *political and social exclusion* philosophically, the latter refers to states using the rhetoric of *social inclusion* and *social cohesion*, but adopting policies that are more exclusive than inclusive, thereby, concretely, circumscribing their citizenship norms and processes (see Dobrowolsky with Lister in this volume).

Globalization complicates matters, no doubt, but in spite of, and sometimes as a reaction to new challenges from 'above' and 'below,' states still have the capacity to set and enforce an array of laws and limitations. While some walls and fences have come down, literally and figuratively, state actors may also resurrect, or reinstate, and clearly regulate and reinforce others. For instance, despite the increasing internationalization of professional labour markets (e.g. the IT industry), and state competition for professional skill, the global trend is toward temporary skilled labour migration with all kinds of inequalities and contradictions in the treatment of temporary and permanent migrants within states (Iredale 2001: 20-21). As Preibisch and Santamaría in this volume illustrate, the state can grant, and withhold, citizenship rights, and given its access to various regulatory mechanisms, the state can exert its hegemonic authority.

With shrinking opportunities for male employment for many countries in the South, reduced opportunities for traditional forms of profit making, and the fall of government revenues (partly linked to the burden of debt-servicing), the task of ensuring family and community survival has increasingly fallen on women's shoulders. Sassen calls this phenomenon the 'feminization of survival' (2000: 506). In an era of globalization, the consequences of the feminization of survival involve the increasing incorporation of migrants and women from the South, as the global world's newest proletariat, into the global capitalist activities of the North, all under severely diminished citizenship regimes.

Women are disproportionately found in these low-paid, formal right-restricted 'serving classes.' Assuming globalized social reproductive labour, women work not just as nannies and domestic workers (Maher 2004; Ehrenreich and Hochschild 2002; Parreñas 2002, 2000; Sassen 2000, 2002) but also in the whole 'transnational care services sector' (Yeates 2004b). We also find them engaged in other low-wage, precarious work of various kinds, from clerical and blue-collar work to work in the sex trade. And of course, we must also consider here the plight of undocumented, trafficked women who can live in the most extreme conditions of bondage and abuse (Sassen 2000: 510, 518 and 2002: 273).

There are, then, important gendered and racialized 'tie-ins' (Sassen 2000: 519) and synergies on multiple levels between and within states of the North (in terms of labour markets, immigration policies, welfare regimes and so forth) and states of the South (in terms of emigration policies, development policies, labour markets, welfare regimes and forms of patriarchy), international organizations (e.g. IMF, World Bank), SAPS, development policies, migration agencies and networks, and 'alternative global circuits' (or alternative 'survival circuits,' Sassen 2000: 523 and 2002: 267).

At the same time, alongside these intense, and complex, globalized, migration patterns, we see an anti-(im)migrant backlash reinforced by a security/global (im)migration nexus. The growing calls, especially on the part of states of the North, for security and a law and order agenda have resulted in the securitization of migration. This security/(im)migration association is in evidence in various state-sanctioned restrictive and coercive measures, especially in wealthier immigration countries around the world (Brouwer 2002; Faist 2002; Humphrey 2003; Robin-Olivier 2005). For example, post-9/11 immigration policies in North America are now linked to security concerns (see Daniels, Macklem and Roach 2001; Macklin 2001; Abu-Laban and Gabriel 2003; Roach 2003; Drache 2004; Whitaker 2004). As states have increasingly transformed international migration issues and ethnic differences into security issues, attitudes and policies have hardened. We see this in the form of amplified border controls in North America, along with various 'crack downs' on migration violations, and tougher policies on immigration and asylum, more broadly.

Even though states all over Western Europe, North America and Australasia are beefing up external controls as well as internal controls, especially of non-citizens, both citizens and non-citizens alike are feeling more insecure (Crocker, Dobrowolsky, Keeble and Tastsoglou 2005). For migrants the situation is particularly precarious. Engin Isin and Patricia Wood explain, after migrating, for many 'the place to which they have escaped is no more secure than that which they left. Even in a more peaceful haven, their legal status or that of any family they have left behind may remain unresolved for years' (Isin and Wood: 1999: 51). And now, in a tightened security environment where targeting of 'the Other' becomes more explicit, it is not surprising that we see heightened levels of insecurity on the part of migrants. As recent research illustrates (Crocker et al. 2005) women (im)migrants, and especially those whose 'Otherness' is visible, those who wear headscarves for instance, feel highly exposed and at risk. These changes and others indicate a clear change in citizenship regimes and practices across the western world.

Despite the rise of this security state, heightened levels of insecurity, and the changing context vis-à-vis citizenship, individuals and groups continue to contest and transgress such limitations, and others. As we shall see, migration levels are growing and these gendered and racialized cross-border movements do challenge and can even reconfigure typical boundaries of inclusion and exclusion. As Sassen (2000: 509) argues, an important new area of scholarship focuses on 'new forms of cross border solidarity and experiences of membership and identity formation that represents new subjectivities, including feminist subjectivities.' In an increasingly volatile terrain, and as a result of contested claims-making, new citizenship practices are unfolding. And here, as Wendy Larner observes in her chapter in this book, minority and (im)migrant women especially find themselves 'on the front line.' Consequently, the paradoxes of citizenship persist, continue to perplex and provoke, presenting both obstacles and opportunities. These are the very concerns that this book sets out to address.

Goals, Objectives and Scope

This collection is all about women crossing, contesting and reconfiguring various boundaries. It sheds light on why and how migrant women are navigating political, social, economic and psychological spaces and negotiating global, regional, national and local dimensions of belonging, in contexts of both opportunity and constraint. The contributors to this volume explore continuities and changes, given complicated contemporary global realities that stem from the intricate interplay of gender, migration and citizenship, and the inclusions and exclusions that result under specific conditions. This book, in a nutshell, seeks to cross boundaries and strives to make connections.

At its most straightforward level, the volume is about (im)migrant women moving across local, national and transnational borders, and what happens to them when doing so. More profoundly, it explores how, as active human agents, they take up challenges and often transform them into opportunities and what the significance of this is for women's citizenship. In so doing, the book plumbs the interrelations between gender, migration and citizenship and details how they concretely and complexly play out.

On one hand, contributors strive to ground abstract theorizing on these contested issues. The volume's empirical studies add sociological substance to current philosophical treatments on citizenship and migration. On the other hand, the chapters are careful to avoid 'crude empiricism' that can also distinguish these areas of study (Ackers 1998: 22). Here theoretical propositions are advanced and insights are provided that connect gender, migration and citizenship. The aim then is to examine the interplay of theories of migration and citizenship with feminist analyses and women (im)migrants' real-life experiences.

Women comprise an absolute majority around the world and constitute ever-larger numbers of (im)migrants. Globally, women migrate at approximately the same rate as men, but men constitute a higher proportion of migrants to 'developing countries' whereas women comprise a majority of migrants to many 'developed' countries (DeLaet 1999: 2). For example, on a yearly basis, approximately 75,000 women leave South and South East Asia to work as nurses, domestic and service industry workers in Australia, Canada, the United States and Western Europe. By the late 1990s over 1 million (nearly 1.5 million) Asian women were working elsewhere in Asia and in the Middle East as foreign domestic workers alone (Seager 2003). It is also frequently suggested that the majority of refugees are women and children. As DeLaet points out, such presumptions can be based on stereotypical portrayals (1999: 9); however, there is no denying that, women and children comprise substantial numbers of refugees, and that overall, the position of refugee women is even more uncertain than that of men, given their weaker political, social and economic status (Yuval-Davis 1997: 109).

The numbers of women (im)migrants are on the rise and the conditions that they face and live through can be daunting and often deplorable. Many are forced to leave their countries of origin given conditions of disadvantage and exclusion only to face similar situations in their host countries. Of course, there are various degrees of marginalization at play. For example, some women struggle for their very existence, others with 'absolute or subsistence poverty' and still others fight for 'social and territorial justice; notions of need, welfare and social status' (Ackers 1998: 26). There are obviously many differences between women and yet there are also points of commonality. For example, while not all women are poor, 'nowhere are women as well off or well paid as men are' (Pettman 1999: 214). Despite women's multiple, intersecting identities (such as race, ethnicity, class, ability, sexual orientation, age, religion and so on) they all experience elements of exclusion unique to their gender at some level (Kofman et al. 2000: 83-84; Raghuram and Kofman 2004: 97). All this is compounded by the fact that women (im)migrants frequently find themselves in citizenship limbo, or with various kinds of 'partial citizenship' as is the case for temporary workers (Parreñas 2001), with very few if any rights to draw upon. This, in turn, can lead to further deprivation and impoverishment, and an array of abuses or forms of exploitation.

Yet, while (im)migrant women can and do put their lives on the line, they should not be cast as victims, as they are by no means passive. This has been a problematic feature of the literature on migrants which has tended to portray women unidimensionally as 'unskilled, weak and lacking the ability to shape their own fate or to defend themselves against exploitation or the marginality of secondary or reserve army of labor status' (Ip and Lever-Tracy 1999: 59). In contrast, more recent studies indicate that women can be, and often are, the primary movers (principal applicants) in the migration of their families, for certain types of migration, especially among the highly skilled (Raghuram 2004), beyond having been primary movers historically in feminized, care-oriented occupations (e.g. nursing, domestic work) that have been in demand at different times (Yeates 2004a).

In our collection, (im)migrant women are shown to be complex subjects whose autonomous action, and agency even under the most dire circumstances (as in refugee camps, see Abdi in this volume), should not be underplayed. They are affected by structural processes (global, transnational, national and local) as they seek safe passage across borders, or eke out an existence in borderlands, or struggle to re-establish professional careers in new contexts when immigration regulations construct them as dependents on a male breadwinner. Yet, out of necessity and with ingenuity, women migrants take action and empower themselves, refusing to be victims of circumstance (Anthias and Lazaridis 2000; Raghuram and Kofman 2004; as well as Ralston and Tastsoglou in this volume).

Still, because the rights and political activism of (im)migrant women (especially in light of what is often their 'non-citizen' status) are constrained, their agency can be easily obscured. Recent scholarly efforts, however, uncover more of a multi-layered existence. Here the borderland literature is instructive. Borderlands are spaces typically, but not only, found at national borders that experience intensive 'economic, social and cultural exchange' (Isin and Wood 1999: 18). Border residents come from households of 'migration mosaics containing people who range from native born to naturalized and citizen children to permanent residents ... and those without "papers"' (Studt 1999: 26). Countries of the North and South, 'are pockmarked with these global borderlands and their alien inhabitants are practically invisible to those who reside in and manage the business and defence of homelands' (Kapur 2003: 7). Nonetheless, in these physical spaces, women problematize common categories of identity in terms of gender, race, ethnicity, and nation, and develop extended forms of identification and networking across multiple borders as Tastsoglou's research in this volume attests. By making cultural identifications and connections across borders, and conceiving of 'home' as multi-local, immigrant women challenge and contest existing, nation-state based notions of membership and make identity-based claims aiming at a richer and more multi-layered citizenship (Isin and Wood 1999).

This borderland experience parallels the plight of temporary workers, from nannies and care workers in traditional, feminized and racialized occupations (Parreñas 2002, 2001, 2000; Ball 2004; Yeates 2004a, 2004b) to less common categories of temporary agricultural workers in Canada as outlined in this volume by Preibisch and Santamaría. Here we see the challenges but also the politics of resistance and work of coalition building across ethnic, gender and national boundaries. Again, as with Abdi's chapter, it becomes evident that even the most sequestered, disenfranchised and seemingly vulnerable women migrants can and do politically engage and mobilize to make change for themselves, their families and their communities.

In short, a consideration of both agency and identity is central to this collection. Through both careful empirical studies as well as theoretical propositions, we highlight women crossing various boundaries and making connections at both concrete as well as abstract levels. Throughout we see women working to build cultures of resistance and broaden solidarities cross-nationally. The notion of citizenship as practice, and as a *process,* is underscored as the chapters detail the multiple restrictions involved all the while showing that these women are active agents in their own lives. Women (im)migrants cross, contest and reconfigure borders problematizing not only legal and political dimensions of citizenship, but also social, economic and psychological ones (i.e. in terms of cultural belonging). We see then how citizenship rights and entitlements are not bestowed, nor permanent; they are actively claimed, contested, fought over, locally, nationally and transnationally (Stasiulis and Bakan 2000).

This book traverses borders and broadens boundaries on several other dimensions as well. We see, for instance, how women (im)migrants' experiences extend the boundaries of both politics and civil society, blurring the distinction between public and private. For example, Gardiner Barber's work points to how foreign domestic workers publicize the private sphere, rendering it more of a public space given not only the paid work done there, but also due to the political activism of domestic workers. Tastsoglou's detailing of the formation of multi-local identity practices illustrates how such practices cut across private and public spheres.

Problematizing the private/public divide is crucial. Any citizenship gains that women have made historically have been as a result of them entering public space, either as voters, or workers. Yet women have also politicized the private realm. Nevertheless, making private spaces public, thus increasing state regulation and codification of activities in those areas, denies the complexity and reality of most men's and women's everyday lives. It is one thing to intervene in the private sphere to protect women from violence, and quite another to codify this sphere of social life (Isin and Wood 1999: 80). Blurring the distinction across genders, i.e. disrupting the divide's gendered meaning might be the only solution. As Lister argues: 'the rearticulation of this public-private divide provides one of the keys to challenging women's exclusion at the level of both theory and practice' and central to this rearticulation would be the 'disruption of the divide's gendered meaning' (Lister 1997b: 22).

Furthermore, the volume deals with women working across a range of occupational categories and traversing not only spatial but also gender boundaries when it comes to certain kinds of employment outside their country of origin. When immigration researchers have paid attention to gender, they invariably turn to feminized occupations (e.g. domestic workers, nannies). In contrast, contributors to this volume study not only highly feminized but also masculinized (and racialized) occupations, with the latter particularly evident in the analysis of foreign workers in agriculture.

In addition, the experience of migrant women workers in 'unskilled' (perhaps more aptly deemed non-professionalized), low-wage labour has tended to be a preoccupation of gendered migration studies (DeLaet 1999: 6). While this is an important consideration given the inequitable patterns of global restructuring, and one that is assessed in several chapters in this volume, it is not the exclusive focus. Contributors also study what happens to woman (im)migrants with professional degrees and skills (Salaff and Greve in this volume), nurses, doctors, educators and engineers who have the potential for higher waged work. In sum, the collection provides insights into women's experience across various spheres, sectors and employment categories in the global economy.

The book embraces the complexity of women (im)migrants' present day realities in countries of the Global North and the Global South and how they grapple with moving between and connecting often disparate worlds. Chapters illuminate women (im)migrants' experiences in Africa, Australasia, Britain and Canada, as well as those who come from specific national origins, such as the Philippines, Mexico, South Asia, the Caribbean and China, to Canada.

While global connections are integral to the volume, there is also a notable Canadian component given that the contributors are largely based, or have worked for a time, in Canada. We believe that this point of reference is useful given that Canada, an infamous 'white settler nation,' (Abu-Laban and Gabriel 2002; Stasiulis and Abu-Laban 2004), is also renowned for its immigrant receiving past and present. Moreover, Canadian theorists have broken ground with their analyses of multiculturalism, identity, difference and diversity (see for example, Taylor 1994; Kymlicka 1995, 2001). And, of course, the Canadian state's efforts at: formulating and implementing a multicultural policy (1970s); enshrining multiculturalism in Canada's new Charter of Rights and Freedoms (1982); and reinforcing it through a Multicultural Act (1988), have provided a template to emulate, or a target to deride, for both states and scholars at home and abroad. At the same time, we can also learn from actions that serve to tarnish Canada's reputation for dealing with (im)migration and diversity. Most recently, we see this with the Canadian state's move away from permanent (im)migrant settlement to an increasing reliance on temporary workers (Macklin 2002; Preibisch and Santamaría in this volume), and with its current security preoccupations and related citizenship preclusions (Whitaker 2004; Gabriel 2005: 127-28; Crocker et al. 2005).

Ultimately, the book makes connections by drawing from several scholarly disciplines and from different literatures therein. We, as the editors, work in Departments of Sociology (Tastsoglou) and Political Science (Dobrowolsky) and attempt not only to cross these disciplinary divides but also forge broader connections (e.g. with fields such as Anthropology and Law) in this collection. We embrace multi-disciplinarity as well as cross-disciplinarity through our mutual commitment to Women's Studies and our affiliation with an inter-disciplinary, inter-university Women's Studies programme.

The genesis of this book can be traced to a series of panels organized by Evangelia Tastsoglou on the theme of 'Gender, Migration and Citizenship: Linking the Local, the National and the Transnational' at the Canadian Sociology and Anthropology Association's annual meetings in the summer of 2003 and at the Canadian Ethnic Studies Biennial meeting in the fall of 2003. Beyond this effort, selected feminist academics working in Political and Social Science subsequently were contacted by both editors and asked to contribute chapters. As a result, this volume will be of interest to those who work in and across the aforementioned disciplines, as well as in other areas and sub fields concerned with gender, migration and citizenship: from Philosophy to International Relations and Public Policy.

Because this book crosses conceptual boundaries by: first, challenging common assumptions and filling in gaps when it comes to gender in both the citizenship and migration literatures; and second, striving to break ground by making connections between the two, a brief review of each is in order. We will then discuss their intersections and conclude by indicating how they play out in the chapters of this volume.

Women and Citizenship

Practices and Problems, Past and Present

As is well-known, the origins of citizenship can be traced back to the ancient Greek city-state of Athens. But there, the privileges of citizenship were granted to only a select few. Early ideas and practices of citizenship were developed on the premise that women should be denied the basic rights of citizens because they could not perform particular duties but, together with artisans, servants, and minors earned their living, food and protection 'under the orders of others' (Kant, cited in Stolcke 1997). Given that women were to be the mothers, wives and daughters of male citizens, they should not be granted rights like the vote. This logic persisted as nation-states developed, and with time, for old and new states alike.

Consequently, feminist scholars have illustrated that, 'Citizenship constructs a public status and identity – long presumed to be male – that rests in ambiguous ways on the private support world of family, home and women' (Pettman 1999: 207). The exclusion of women from citizenship was 'an intrinsic feature of their naturalization as embodiments of the private, the familial and the emotional. It was thus essential to the construction of the public sphere as masculine, rational, responsible and respectable' (Werbner and Yuval-Davis 1999: 6). In practice, and over centuries, women challenged these roles and mobilized for more inclusive discourses and processes. But even in contemporary theorizations these public and private assumptions are often not sufficiently interrogated. For example, Sylvia Walby (1994) critiques Bryan Turner's (1990) framework of citizenship for its portrayal of the family as a space of autonomy beyond state intervention, when this has not been the experience for many women (on this issue see Werbner and Yuval-Davis 1999: 16).

As has been widely discussed and well-documented, national identity, nationality and citizenship are not only about unequal power relations between women and men, but among groups variously involving conquest, colonization, and (im)migration along with other exclusionary practices. For instance, at Canada's inception, with Confederation in 1867, only propertied white men held citizenship rights such as the vote. Through political struggle this basic right was progressively extended to different groups over time (and sometimes retracted, as in war time, for those with origins in 'enemy alien' countries). Still the vote was only granted to Aboriginal women and men in Canada in 1960 and was made practically feasible for many Canadians with disabilities in 1992 (Bonnett 2003: 157).

European nation-states were historically created to define and defend a cultural and political community. In so doing, in numerous ways, through discourses and practices, nation-states created the 'Other' (Castles and Davidson 2000: 81-82). The rise of the nation-state, and along with it nationalism and citizenship, then, creates insiders and outsiders, and sets up differences between people. These exclusions have ranged historically from colonial subjects to women, particular classes and racialized minorities, to people with different sexualities and abilities (on 'dis-citizenship' see Devlin and Pothier 2004).

Yet the contradictions and tensions are multiple. For example, even though women were excluded from citizenship, they were linked to the nation, and nationalist imaginaries (Yuval-Davis and Anthias 1989; Yuval-Davis 1997). Women in nationalist discourses are portrayed as 'mothers of the nation' and take both symbolic and active roles in nationalist projects, often as the 'bearers of culture' and tradition (see Larner in this volume). Moreover, as Castles and Davidson write: 'Just as women become signifiers of the nation, ethnic minority women may become signifiers of the ethnic community' (Castles and Davidson 2000: 123-24). This may manifest itself in several ways and have widely divergent consequences. For instance, reverting to traditional values may provide greater limitations on women's roles, or alternatively, can offer women some room to negotiate (Fiske 1999; Dobrowolsky 2002) by, for instance, working as a form of resistance to widespread racism against the ethnic community in question (Pessar 1995).

When it comes to citizenship, gender, racialization and class are intertwined with political, social, cultural, psychological and economic repercussions. As Larner recounts, despite the political gains, cultural recognition and psychological affirmation of Maori in New Zealand, socio-economic gaps between Maori and non-Maori persist with deleterious effects. For Maori women, longstanding inequitable labour force patterns worsen the matter, and contribute to their subordination. This example also underscores the fact that 'women cannot become full citizens simply by achieving formal equality, because this will not in itself overcome the sexism and racism that are deeply rooted in western societies' resulting in their 'incomplete citizenship' (Arat-Koc 1992). Minority women, especially, need specific 'group-differentiated' rights (Kymlicka 1995: 34-35); that is, 'specific sets of rights which recognize these historical forms in which their oppression and exclusion have been constructed' (Castles and Davidson 2000: 122-23).

The foregoing flags several other issues as well. These range from the question of how formal equality must be counterbalanced by substantive equality, to the question of the extent to which citizenship goes beyond individual rights to include collective identity and forms of group-based recognition. Such dilemmas arise because of the way in which citizenship has been theorized and operationalized in terms of various binaries. These include but are not limited to the following: equality of opportunity versus equality of end result; a masculinized public defined by rationality versus a feminized private defined by care; individualism versus collectivism; individual liberal 'rights' versus civic republicanism or communitarian 'responsibilities;' negative rights versus positive entitlements; identity versus difference and diversity, and the list continues (Lister 2003).

Contemporary theorists, with feminists leading the way, have challenged these and other either/or formulations (Fraser 1995, 1997; Young 1997; Isin and Wood 1999). Ruth Lister calls for a dialectal model of citizenship that moves between these false dichotomies. With her concept of 'differentiated univeralism' (Lister 1997a), or with Nira Yuval-Davis' (Yuval-Davis 1997; Werbner and Yuval-Davis 1999) 'transversal dialogue' attempts have been made to move beyond such stark alternatives. Similarly, in this volume, by challenging the structure versus agency dichotomy, the nuances involved with new citizenship practices become ever more apparent. For example, despite the weight of structural forces, in the context of Aotearoa New Zealand, Larner argues that women are becoming the 'midwives' of a new conception of citizenship.

Admittedly, the foregoing skims over a number of huge debates. However, to explore these concerns at more length and in more depth, is beyond the scope of this introductory chapter. What is essential for our present purposes is the following: to underline the contested nature of the concept of citizenship; to explore its dimensions as a plural, multi-layered construct; and to emphasize it as a critical process involving not only inclusion and exclusion, but identity, agency, participation/practice, contestation and empowerment, for these are the key ideas that are played out in the chapters that follow.

The Concept of Citizenship and Processes of Construction/Deconstruction

At its most basic level, citizenship is a legal and political *concept*, albeit one that is highly contested (Lister 1997a, 2003). As such, it involves an assortment of duties and rights but also encompasses a series of practices. It becomes a sociological concept as well, going beyond the legal and political relationship between individual and the state, and involving participation in civil society (Kymlicka 1995; Isin and Wood 1999). As a social construct, citizenship therefore includes not only political, but also socio-economic, cultural and psychological dimensions that develop in specific contexts, and that change over space and time. As such, citizenship is fluid and dynamic:

> [it]opens up spaces and arenas of freedom – of conflict, unpredictability, intimacy, the right to be different, while restricting and structuring these spaces by procedural hedges about limits. It orders conflict, channels and tames it; it labels and classifies collective difference;

it determines how, where and when difference may be legitimately 'represented,' and who counts as 'different' in the political arena, itself a social construct. (Werbner and Yuval-Davis 1999: 2)

Because it involves shifting statuses and struggles, citizenship must be ultimately conceived of as a *process*. This process implicates and engages individuals and groups in the state, market, family and community (Jenson and Phillips 1996). It is through political struggle, broadly conceived, that the boundaries between state, market, family and community get defined and redefined (Dobrowolsky and Jenson 2004). This process, then, does not necessarily signal inevitable progress, and can involve and gains and losses.

In common parlance, when the notion of citizenship arises, basic rights, the civic status or legal membership in a country, and rights and obligations of citizens come to mind. Citizenship is thought of in terms of holding a certain passport, or being able to participate politically by way of voting in an election. It is often associated with the rights, responsibilities, duties and obligations that come with belonging to a country. However, citizenship encompasses much more, and for several reasons, which will be discussed below, it is crucial to consider its potential scope and its present-day limitations.

Given T. H. Marshall's foundational role in expanding contemporary conceptualizations of citizenship, a brief reflection on his work is in order. For Marshall, citizenship entailed civil rights, such as the freedom of thought or religion; political rights, such as the ability to run for office, but also necessitated social rights, e.g., the right to work or to have a minimum standard of living (1965). Marshall's contribution came with emphasizing the interdependency of rights and that the state had responsibilities in relation to its citizens and should play an active part in ensuring that citizenship encompassed social rights.

There have been numerous critiques of Marshall's work. For a start, many feminists challenged Marshall's analysis for its exclusive class focus, its obliviousness to gender, and its ethnocentrism (Lister 1997a; Yuval-Davis 1997). As discussed above, citizenship entails not only class and economic interest, but the interests and identities of gender, race, ethnicity, sexuality, ability, and religion, and it works across these and other differences (Werbner and Yuval-Davis 1999: 9). Marshall's developmental stages of citizenship suggested more of an ideal than a reality in many places, and for many people. His universal chronology was clearly attuned to a circumscribed British context, in a particular time and space. As Kabeer recounts, 'The forces of socio-economic change [Marshall] describes are those of the industrial revolution in Britain, the exclusions he focuses on are those of property and class and his history of citizenship is that of it white, male working class. It is an account of a society without empire' (Kabeer 2002: 7). Indeed, most notions of citizenship have been constructed in the West with problematic results particularly in post-colonial contexts (Kabeer 2002, passim).

Marshall's rights progression also did not fit with the political reality of women. When Marshall was writing, many women around the world had not achieved the most basic civil or political rights, let alone social rights. In France, although women had struggled for rights as far back as the Revolution (and were beheaded as a result of it), women were not granted the right to vote until 1946. While some Canadian women gained suffrage rights a few decades earlier, they still could not claim independent citizenship until 1947.[1] For decades, other rights restrictions remained. From 1892 to 1967, Canada's *Criminal Code* provisions 'banned the sale, advertisement and distribution of birth control information, procedures and devices' (Trimble 2003: 134) limiting women's right to control their own bodies. Even in the 1980s, laws reflected the fact that women and children were considered to be the property of their husbands.[2] Not only is women's trajectory when it comes to attaining rights different from men's, but also, the basic categories of citizenship have gendered implications which mean that women and men had very different relationships to the rights and obligations of citizenship.

Today, the fundamental rights of citizenship continue to elude women. Women generally, are seen as the biological and cultural reproducers of the 'nation.' As such, they have been provided with some rights regarding protection of their socially approved roles as mothers and educated gendered subjects who will be called upon to educate their children in the national project (Anthias 2000: 32-33). Their social citizenship as far as other areas has been at best tenuous, incomplete and ambiguous. Moreover, (im)migrant women's citizenship, lacking the legitimacy of mothering for the nation or educating future national subjects, can be very limited or even practically absent (Arat-Koc 1992; Yuval-Davis 1993). As Parreñas illustrates, the citizenship of migrant Filipina domestic workers even in the most liberal Western countries is at best 'partial,' so that receiving countries can secure a source of low-wage labour and the Philippine state can ensure the smooth flow of foreign currency into its economy (Parreñas 2001: 1151). In the contemporary context, (im)migrant women's limited citizenship or lack of citizenship rights is often explained by women's lack of 'human capital.' But as the Salaff and Greve chapter in this volume suggests, the story is more complicated. There are other structural explanations from patriarchal and racist attitudes in sending and receiving countries, to culturally specific gender roles and practices, and other socio-politico-economic realities that explain why, for example, highly skilled women (im)migrants are not able to have their qualifications acknowledged and accepted.

Feminist analysts have also underscored the significance of Marshall's argument that civil, political and social rights be viewed as interdependent (Meehan 1993). This interdependence is especially critical for women. For instance, since women are poorer than men and disproportionately rely on social programmes given their

---

1   Before the 1947 Citizenship Act was passed, Canadians were British subjects, and a Canadian woman's citizenship was determined by that of her father or husband. This meant that if a woman married a non-Canadian man she lost her citizenship. Conversely, a man who married a non-Canadian kept his citizenship and transferred it to his wife.

2   In Canada, it was not until 1983 that husbands could be charged with sexual assault against their wives; and the list goes on.

care work in the private sphere, without basic social rights, how can they fully, or even minimally, exercise their political rights? But even when women are more fully 'commodified' through high labour market participation, such as in the Scandinavian model, the combination of work and family pressures leaves them 'time poor' and unable to participate in political activity (Ackers 1998). This is why feminist citizenship scholars 'have long argued that active citizenship requires material conditions which support and enable women's participation in the public/political sphere ... and have insisted on expanded notions of the political' (Pettman 1999: 212). Moreover, active citizenship for women requires their right to participate in public space not in a gender-neutral way (e.g. through the right to vote) but as women, allowing for their gender differences to be recognized as relevant and integral to the constitution of sociality (Isin and Wood 1999; Werbner and Yuval-Davis 1999: 7).

In addition, now, perhaps more than ever before, there is a need to go beyond Marshall's triad. That is, a fight for more rights is necessary. As Castles and Davidson write, 'citizenship has always been about empowerment in and over a baffling and changing world context. It has involved more and more acts, rights and obligations as people have increasingly seen what is necessary in order to be empowered' (2000: 28).

Here we return to the issue of individual versus collective rights. Given the global, increasingly mobile and diverse, world we live in, citizenship must grapple with both individual equality and recognition of collective difference (Young 1990; Taylor 1994; Kymlicka 1995, 2001; Castles and Davidson 2000: ix). Interestingly, Marshall's theory, by treating citizenship primarily as full membership to a collectivity (not only to a state and not necessarily membership of an individual), indirectly provides a framework for allowing for multicultural citizenship and collective rights, i.e. membership to different levels of collectivities, the nation-state being only one of them, or a 'differential multi-tier citizenship that people have in their ethnic community, their local community, the state and, more and more often these days also in supra-national organizations' (Yuval-Davis 1997: 24, 72-73). Yet, this, in turn, translates into much more complex dimensions of citizenship than those conceived of by Marshall.

For instance, recent citizenship scholarship highlights the cultural aspects of citizenship. Here citizenship is understood to encompass more than rights, but also includes membership in a community encompassing social, symbolic, and even emotional/psychological dimensions. Feelings of belonging, values, principles, stories, myths, real and imagined communities, as well as personal and state-societal connections are critical to citizenship (Carens 2000; Castles and Davidson 2000; Barber 2003; Wilkinson and Hebert 2003; Tastsoglou in this volume).

And yet, paradoxically, as theories and demands of citizenship expand, the practices of citizenship appear to be contracting. This underscores the fact that nowhere is Marshall's rights progression inevitable. Indeed there can be backsliding when it comes to what were once considered set markers of citizenship (Castles and Davidson 2000; Stasiulis and Bakan 2000). To illustrate, in places like Britain, Canada and the United States, social rights have fallen by the wayside with the rise of neo-liberalism, welfare state retrenchment, decline of state employment, and the rising gap between rich and poor (Bashevkin 2002). And of course, much of this re-structuring has come on the backs of women (Brodie 1995; Bakker 1996; Banaszak, Beckwith and Rucht 2003; Dobrowolsky and Jenson 2004; Dobrowolsky 2004). As Pettman contends:

> Women are disproportionately represented among state workers in those areas most under attack, like health and education; moreover, women in their domestic and reproductive roles must compensate for state retreat, or for state failure to provide social infrastructure and support. (Pettman 1999: 212)

Cutting back on the state and public provision has meant that women have had to pick up the slack, caring for children, the sick and the elderly. Feminist gains, in many countries around the world, are in question given the influence of neo-liberal state ideologies, or in light of global deregulation, restructuring and (re)privatization (Cossman and Fudge 2002).

At the same time, cuts to welfare also go hand in hand with the 'intensification of racialization' (Castles and Davidson 2000: 118) or the creation of 'racialized rights,' as in the case of Filipina nurses overseas (Ball 2004: 130-31). Consider here the welfare backlash directed toward migrants (Dobrowolsky with Lister in this volume). And yet, the effects of shrinking welfare provision on migrants are devastating. The 'combination of only partial incorporation into mainstream economic and social systems with continuing processes of racialization makes ... [migrants even more] vulnerable to social exclusion' (Castles and Davidson 2000: 118).

Granted, over time, there have been moves toward more democratic citizenship and even some citizenship openings in areas like the EU, particularly for more privileged states. Nonetheless, the point here is that even in the more privileged states these rights are not secure. As alluded to at the start of this chapter, in an era of globalization and rising security concerns, even basic citizenship rights are tenuous. For instance, in North America, we are seeing more border restrictions and less civil rights. Recent moves to close borders in the U.S. and Canada are justified in terms of guaranteeing public security, i.e., this closure would help with citizens' civil rights (see Bader 1997: 43). Yet, the converse appears to be taking place.

Nevertheless, women, people of colour, (im)migrants and other disadvantaged or oppressed groups have been and remain instrumental in pointing out how citizenship produces and affects insiders and outsiders; how it engages the included as well as the excluded; and how it can work towards a society that respects and accommodates people of all origins. Therefore, they continue their struggles over citizenship, a historical and contemporary fact that Marshall did not account for (Castles and Davidson 2000: 105). All this underscores the fact that citizenship is a critical process in flux.

Citizenship is a *concept* that refers to, at minimum, a legally defined but always politically significant social construction of membership and participation based on gender, age, sexuality, migrant status, class, states, ethnicity/race and other 'nodes' and forms of social division and inequality. Furthermore and perhaps more importantly, it is a *process* that is negotiated and contested by those whose citizenship is incomplete, not simply bestowed by states on people. It has always been and continues to be about inclusion and exclusion but also power, agency, and identity: the power to name and categorize (Jenson 1993), the agency of contestation and resistance, the identities formed on the basis of multiple, shifting intersections of group memberships (Dobrowolsky and Jenson 2004). It cuts across the private/ public dichotomy and is both an individual and a collective concept. As such it involves legal, political, socio-economic, and cultural dimensions including senses of belonging. It is the broad connection of citizenship with women's migration that we are focusing on in this volume and so now a more systematic review migration studies would be beneficial.

Women and Migration

Migration also signifies a dynamic process, but one whereby people geographically move from one country, territory, region or locale to another. Today migration is more often than not considered to be about the global movement of people. Historically, mass migrations did occur as a result of, for instance, natural and human-made disasters, or due to political upheaval. There were also forced migrations that occurred with slavery or colonialism. At present, we continue to see migration due to war and human rights abuses, as a result of civil unrest, ethnic violence and extreme poverty, but also because of globalization. For example, with changes in the global economy, money switches hands at the press of a button, and given this free flow of capital, there is also an economic need for a freer flow of labour which, in turn, accelerates the migration drive. Given globalized communications, more people are aware that life may be better somewhere else, and this also serves as a catalyst for migration. A case in point comes with increases in highly skilled migration (HSM) as a result of changing global labour market demand/supply conditions and, consequently, changing immigration regulations, increasing internationalization of professional labour markets, as well as scientific and professional contexts in leaving and receiving societies (Iredale 2001; Ackers 2004; Couton 2002).

Migration is definitely not a new phenomenon, but what is different today is the number and scale of migrants and their global impact (Castles and Davidson 2000: 9). Today, as many as 150 million migrants are crossing borders (Kapur 2003: 7). The numbers are increasing as result of various political and social phenomena, from fears of ethnic cleansing to new travel opportunities, but also given global economic reconfigurations. It is also important not to lose sight of the fact that global economic trends have societal interrelations. Although an enormously heterogeneous process (Kofman 2004: 644, 654), economic migration is occurring on a large scale because populations continue to be marginalized and dispossessed (Ehrenreich and Hochschild 2002: 6; Parreñas 2002; Sassen 2000, 2002; Ball 2004), enabled, of course, by particular contexts and mediated by a number of factors on various levels.

A wide array of theoretical frameworks have been used to analyze international migration at macro and micro levels, from 'push-pull' and neo-classical human capital approaches to Marxist historical-structural theories (including world systems and dual labour market theory), to institutional analysis and network approaches, to the 'new economics of labour migration', to even 'synthetic approaches' (Castles and Miller 1998; Grieco and Boyd 1998: 3-8), with various degrees of gender sensitivity. But, as Cheng perceives, 'The complexity of the migration process and its multidimensional impact on political, social, economic, cultural and demographic aspects, has rendered no one single theoretical framework adequate' to explain it (1999: 39).

To fully appreciate the intricacies of migration the interaction of macro, meso and micro level factors must be taken into consideration, along with the interplay of structure and agency (Hoerder 1997; Iredale 2001: 9). A number of more recent integrative approaches achieve this with varying degrees of success. They include: transnationalism; structuration theory, and alternative circuits of globalization or circuits of survival (Mahler and Pessar 2001; Sassen 2000, 2002; Kofman 2004). Furthermore, recent work also underscores that different stages in the migration process need to be taken into account (Grieco and Boyd 1998). Finally, examining closely how gender is implicated in processes of migration is a must. Gender differences arise from the subordinate status of women in society which acts as a 'filter,' gendering structural forces and influencing the experiences of men and women differently (Grieco and Boyd 1998: 11). As we shall see, this crucial consideration has often been lacking in leading migration studies.

At the macro-level we see the forces of globalization and the socio-structural economic and geo-political determinants at play. Recall here the gendering of globalized domestic work or globalized social reproduction (Maher 2004), involving the 'extraction of care from the global South to the global North' (Parreñas 2002: 53). Ehrenreich and Hochschild (2002: 8, 11-12) argue that countries of the North take on, broadly speaking, the role of an old-fashioned male, provider and successful in the public sphere but in need of care in every other way, while countries of the South take on the role of the traditional female, caring and nurturing and even sexually available, filling in the 'care deficit' that has emerged in the North.

At meso-level issues such as the demands of segmented labour markets, state and private capital, organizational agencies, but also gendered social networks and extended families are significant explanatory factors. At the micro level, smaller-scale familial pushes and pulls, as well as individual decisions taken are revealing.

Thus, migration involves a range of determinants from economics and demographic to familial catalysts to individual decisions that do not always conform to the pressures and the outside forces of larger socio-structural factors. Most significantly, at each level (macro, meso and micro) there are dynamics involved which are marked by uneven power relations and result, as a consequence, differential impacts on groups (Grieco and Boyd 1998: 28-29; Kofman 2004: 644). Indeed, Veit Bader (1997: 6) defines migration as an: 'interactive balancing process within unequal power relationships'. This interactive process involves changes and redistributive processes in both receiving and immigrant cultures and economies (Hoerder 1997: 82).

Beyond a comprehensive and integrative framework, one that combines various conceptual/analytical and spatial levels (e.g. macro/meso/micro, structure/agency, migration as a process with stages), a feminist analysis of migration is necessary. The differential and unequal social, cultural, political and economic relations of women as compared to men shape and mould (im)migrant women's experiences differently and produce different outcomes in the migration and settlement process than those of men. These distinctive dynamics extend from the sexual (and racialized) division of labour at global and national levels, given, for instance: the concentration of women in gendered occupations; the unequal division of labour in the family, where women (im)migrants continue to do the bulk of the household service and care work; their inferior citizenship claims compared to men based on disparate contributions to the labour market; and their increased 'de-commodification' through their relationship to a male breadwinner (Ackers 1998). Furthermore, (im)migrant women in particular are differentiated from the general population of women, as a result of their 'Otherness' constructed on the basis of language/accent, dress, migrant (legal) status, entry status (independent versus dependent migrants), race/ethnicity, religion, class and so forth and these differences have to be taken into account in the analysis of their citizenship (Kofman et al. 2000: 84; Maher 2004: 136-41).

Unfortunately, the mainstream migration literature has been slow to appreciate the significance of gender. Indeed, women were largely absent from the study of international migration prior to the 1970s and this inattentiveness has been widely criticized in the literature of the 1980s and 1990s (Boyd 1986, 1992, 1995; Cheng 1999: 40; Hondagneu-Sotelo 1999; Pessar 1999; Kofman et al. 2000). While in the 1970s women were gradually incorporated (the 'add-women-and-stir' approach), it was only in the mid-1980s and 1990s that gender, as a set of social relations and a central organizing category affecting decisions, circumstances, institutional processes and outcomes of migration, started gradually taking hold in the migration literature (Hondagneu-Sotelo 1994; Willis and Yeoh 2000; Tastsoglou and Maratou-Alipranti 2003).

Conventionally, men were assumed to be the principal (im)migrants and indeed many immigration rules are still based on such notions. Yet, feminists have worked to expose past and present realities of women migrants, for example, with basic facts illustrating that women have always been migrants. To be sure, aside from specific female movements in the nineteenth and early twentieth centuries and for specific countries during particular periods of time (Kofman 2004: 646), male migrants outnumbered female migrants in international migration streams. This is no longer the case, however. As Pettman observes,

> Globalization of labour and the feminisation of the global division of labour mean that more and more women move across state boundaries in search of work. This places them beyond their state's legal reach, and means they often lack even formal citizenship or legal

rights. This is more so where they enter another state illegally, or become illegals through, for example, overstaying a work of tourist visa. (Pettman 1999: 213-14)

Today, women make up about 45 per cent of international migration and in a few countries, including the United States and Canada, female migrants actually outnumber men (Grieco and Boyd 1998; Kofman 2004). In the new migrations into Southern Europe, the majority of labour migrants from the Philippines, Eastern Europe and Latin America have been female (Anthias and Lazaridis 2000). New research indicates that labour demands in the affluent and newly industrializing countries now call for women workers (Kofman et al. 2000: 25; Kofman 2004: 655-56; Ehrenreich and Hochschild 2002: 1-13; Ball 2004: 125). All this evidence lends support to the claim of the more recent trend of 'feminisation of migration' discussed by Kofman (2004: 646-47), Ehrenreich and Hochschild (2002: 5), Anthias (2000: 20) and Castles and Miller (1998). Indeed, women as independent migrants have been described as 'the new helots' of a changing world order (Alund 1999: 155).

Nonetheless, gendered misperceptions persist due to the predominance of the male breadwinner model. The mainstream migration literature perpetuates this model by reinforcing ideas such as: women simply follow men when it comes to migration; women invariably sacrifice their careers for their family; and women's primary role is that of unpaid carer (Ackers 1998: 8-9). The story typically unfolds as follows: you have an active male pioneer who sets out to a new land and he is then followed by the passive and dependent family that consists of the wife who comes to look after the children and be the caregiver so that the husband can continue to be the breadwinner. There are often racist assumptions embedded in this literature as well, such as the idea that migrant men and women marry their 'own kind.' Heterosexist (reinforcing traditional notions of the family) and able-ist (being active is linked to capacity for paid work) notions also abound. In reality, (im)migrant women's experiences are far more varied and multi-layered.

Women are found in all classifications of migrants, from colonial immigrants and illegal migrant workers, to asylum seekers and indigenous migrants (Castles and Davidson 2000: 71-74 address these particular categories). In other words, women (im)migrants are not just found in family reunification categories (DeLaet 1999: 3-9). While a large number of women do migrate under policies designed to facilitate family reunification (Bechold and Dziewięcka-Bokun 1999: 189), they are nevertheless also present as employment-based migrants (including domestic workers and nurses), refugees and illegal or undocumented migrants (DeLaet 1999: 3-9).

In a clear reversal of earlier patterns, increasing numbers of highly-skilled women are becoming primary labour migrants (principal applicants) bringing spouses along as 'tied migrants' for reasons that have to do with changing migration regulations, specific professional labour market conditions and family decision-making in HSM (Raghuram and Kofman 2004: 96-97). But it is not only female workers from the higher professional echelons of high technology sectors and regulated professions, such as medicine (i.e. HSM) who migrate as principal applicants. Since the late

1990s increasing labour shortages in affluent western countries, coupled with growing emigration and international circulation of certain professional groups from some of these countries (e.g. Canada, the UK) as well as geographical inequalities of service provision in inner city and remote rural areas, have resulted in states officially globalizing their labour markets to meet the shortages, especially in such areas as nursing, education and social work, and relaxing their immigration regulations, including family migration and employment of spouses (Kofman 2004: 655-56; Ball 2004: 125-29).

While no consensus emerges as to why women migrate, studies do show that female migration 'is neither driven exactly by the same determinants as male migration nor do women experience migration in precisely the same way as men' (DeLaet 1999: 2). Kapur elucidates:

> Women move and are moved with or without their consent for a variety of reasons. The insecurity of food and livelihood and the growing economic reliance of households on earnings of women and girls; the erosion of social capital and the break down of traditional societies; the transnationalization of women's labour in sectors which do not comply with labour or human rights standards and often rely on exploitative labour, forced labour and slavery practices. And this movement is rendered vulnerable as a result of several normative assumptions about gender and sexuality ... (Kapur 2003: 8)

What is more, it is also important to consider the gendered impact at different stages of migration. Grieco and Boyd (1998) have constructed a model involving a gender-based analysis that distinguishes between three stages: i) the pre-migration stage (factors of the sending societies); ii) the stage of act of migration itself (interface of factors of sending and receiving societies); and iii) the post-migration stage (factors of the receiving societies). Although their model is analytically very useful in understanding what happens in gendered migration as a process, it leaves out some of the global factors and the 'tie-ins' that have moulded the relationship of sending and receiving societies that Sassen's 'counter-geographies of globalization' tackle.

Starting with a feminist perspective, Sassen (2000, 2002) conceptualizes migration in the context of globalization in such an integrative manner by linking socio-economic fields to actors on various levels (e.g. globalization, states, families, survival circuits, migration agencies and women). Kofman, on the other hand, critiquing earlier integrative models (such as structuration theory, transnationalism and alternative circuits of globalization or circuits of survival), notes a certain reductionism in that they all neglect the socio-economic class of migrants and focus almost exclusive on the 'lesser skilled' female migrants who provide feminized, sexualized and racialized services. Furthermore, she synthesizes existing research on various types of female labour migration and points to the range and rich diversity of lesser, intermediate and highly skilled female migrations (Kofman 2004: 648-54).

Here women's experiences with HSM illustrate the significance of factoring in the stages of migration in the context of globalization, as well as the intersections of gender, race and class. Women who are HSM often find it difficult to gain access to the labour market due to accreditation problems after migration and also difficult to find employment that is commensurate with their qualifications (Couton 2002; Tastsoglou and Preston in press). As Man (2004), and Preston and Man (1999) in the case of the Chinese immigrant women in Canada, and Pratt (1999) in the case of Filipina domestic workers in Vancouver, have demonstrated, the 'brain drain' from developing countries evolves into 'deskilled labour' in the new country (Canada in these studies) and even 'brain waste' in HSM (Raghuram and Kofman 2004: 97; Kofman 2004: 651-54). Gender differentiates the experience of these workers in terms of the private/public nexus first. As Raghuram and Kofman argue:

> The nature and extent of this 'brain waste' is not gender-neutral, and women may be particularly affected due to gender stereotyping ... The collapse of care networks after migration too influence women much more than men. Differences between the ways in which reproductive activities are organized in the countries of immigration and in the sending countries mean that women, who usually have primary responsibility for arranging reproductive activity, may find that they are unable to work in the new country ... (Raghuram and Kofman 2004: 97)

Furthermore, gender interacts with class, race and position of state of origin in the global economy in complex ways. As Cheng argues, 'Although gender is an important element in arranging social relations and organizations, it is also always racialized with distinct class implications' (Cheng 1999: 43). Degrees from non-western countries have been systematically devalued and their holders systematically excluded from the higher echelons of the labour market (Kofman 2004: 654; Parreñas 2000: 566).

> This systemic discrimination operates in a gendered manner since a disproportionate number of the regulated professions, including medicine, have become feminized. (Kofman 2004: 654)

Kofman (2004: 657-58) however implies that this trend in devaluing qualifications is increasingly receding as a result of growing labour shortages in critical fields of the knowledge society that do not necessarily involve the high technology sectors.

At the same time however, labour shortages can result in questionable outcomes, as a different type of globalized migration movement – the movement of female domestic workers – attests. While women have, historically, been migrating to work as foreign domestics, this type of migration has increased enormously in the 1980s and 1990s. Consider the example of the European Union in this regard, where foreign females from countries outside the EU made up only six per cent of all domestic workers in 1984 but had jumped to 52 per cent by 1987 (Ehrenreich and Hochschild 2002: 7). Increasing labour demand in countries of the North has arisen out of a 'care deficit,' precipitated by growing numbers of women joining the labour force, states failing to provide needed care services or outright downsizing (as happened markedly in Canada, the US and Britain, Bashevkin 2002) and husbands failing to assume their share of responsibility for domestic labour. This demand for social reproductive labour, in an era of global markets, has found global channels and powerfully 'pulls' to the North some of the most ambitious and adventurous educated, middle or lower-middle class women of the global South who are often 'pushed' by patriarchal constraints, abusive husbands, generalized poverty and lack of opportunity for themselves and their children in their countries of origin (Ehrenreich and Hochschild 2002: 8-11; Parreñas 2002, 2001, 2000). Filling in the social reproductive needs of the North creates a deficit of care in the South with all kinds of backlash and further victimization of women and their children in the South (Parreñas 2002). Migration movements, again, are not random but follow for the most part well-established historical, military, economic and colonial connections (Parreñas 2000: 565).

In sum, there have been some significant gaps in the migration literature that have only just begun to be filled. Generally, there is now an increased awareness of the importance of gender in migration. In fact, even in recent Canadian legislation, on the basis of mandatory gendered analysis of immigration policy, the 'Immigration and Refugee Protection Act' (IRPA) that came into effect in 2002, includes some accessions to women. With respect to skilled migration in particular, while the previous law designated (mostly) men as principal applicants and relegated women to the status of dependants, devaluing their occupations and qualifications, the new law facilitates women's entry to Canada as principal applicants in the following ways: the number of years of experience was restricted to a maximum of four years, to reflect women's greater likelihood of interrupted careers; spouses/common-law partners' education was included in the number of points collected; a greater emphasis on education than on paid work experience was placed, likely to be advantageous to women; and the lack of points for specific occupations should also help make women's entry as skilled workers more equitable. However, the criticism remains that 'awarding points on the basis of formal education, training and patterns of paid labour force participation does not always take into account barriers that women face in accessing those opportunities in source countries' (Citizenship and Immigration Canada (undated), quoted in Tolley 2003: 6).

Linking Citizenship, Migration and Women: This Volume

At this point, it becomes increasingly apparent that migration and citizenship share numerous commonalities and points of intersection: both are dynamic processes; both are deeply gendered processes; both involve inclusion and exclusion; both are fundamentally about power relations. Migration involves crossing various borders, and can be about settling in a new land, which can eventually lead to acquiring formal legal citizenship. Apart from the legal aspect of citizenship, migrating and settling involves participation in economic, social, civic, and cultural dimensions of the receiving society that is citizenship in the broader sense. Migrants are prospective citizens in the legal as well as broader socio-economic and cultural sense. How a country deals with (im)migrant incorporation (and citizenship) has a great deal to do with the country's institutional and organizational arrangements for membership in its polity (Soysal 1994). Furthermore, it has to do with how nation-states have historically dealt with the integration of their own populations in various economic, social, cultural and civic arenas, how they conceive of themselves, the 'national community,' collective identities and the actual relationship between 'nation' and state (Munch 2001). Regimes of immigrant incorporation and feelings of belonging on the part of (im)migrants influence the nature and claims of citizenship within a country and affect its reputation abroad. Migration also offers women and men the opportunity to transgress gender roles, which is especially important for women who are usually under greater constraints than men (Kofman et al. 2000: 21-22; Maher 2004: 135; Parreñas 2001: 1140). By transgressing, immigrant women may contest and re-negotiate not only gender roles but also women's citizenship limits. The promise for expanding immigrant women's citizenship limits to include the citizenship rights of other 'second-tier' migrant workers in the global economy is there as well.

But migration can also be transnational, involving not a permanent move but several back and forth or consecutive movements, multiple, varying, and shifting over time psychological commitments and affiliations to encountered and imagined collectivities on local, national and transnational spaces, and multiple forms of participation and entitlement on local, national and transnational levels, i.e. transnational forms of citizenship. Gender plays a major role in the different patterns of transnational citizenship practices of migrant women and men, with men being, for example, far more likely to be involved in leading roles in political and social organizations in their country of origin, while migrant women are more likely to be involved in mainstream organizations and social citizenship practices in the country of settlement (Goldring 2000; Jones-Correa 2000). The migration process, like citizenship, therefore, has political, economic, cultural, societal and psychological repercussions that are all gender-based and gender-differentiated throughout.

At the same time, migration and especially forced migration, is a conceptual disruption of citizenship in the historical nation-state system. According to the latter, citizenship is a quality bestowed on citizens, i.e. those who are legitimate members of its national collectivity, leaving aside questions about who defines legitimacy, power relations in the process, and the social construction of the national collectivity. Migrants, even if invited and legal, need to become 'naturalized,' the assumption being that citizens are members of a nation by natural law (Castles and Davidson 2000), i.e. foreign-born can become 'natural' exceptionally and on certain conditions. Consequently, they suffer from a certain lack of legitimacy even in the most liberal democratic and multicultural states, in the sense that their needs and priorities are not on a par with those of the native-born citizens. Kymlicka, for example, although recognizing group-differentiated (i.e. collective rights) for immigrants has a clear hierarchy of rights and groups in his theory of multicultural citizenship, with immigrants ranking low on his pyramid (Kymlicka 1995; Isin and Wood 1999: 60; Carens 2000: 52-87). Yet, migrants make claims to citizenship and by doing so they turn the rule upside down and make citizenship the quality that makes one a citizen

(Castles and Davidson 2000: viii-ix; Joppke 2004: 85-87; Rummens 2004: 39-42), as opposed to an outcome of being a citizen.

As for forced migration, it is especially disruptive of citizenship and the nation-state system because every human being is supposed to be a citizen of a country and enjoy the protection and rights of people in that country. By contrast, refugees and forced migrants are protected neither by the country whose citizenship they presumably carry, nor by the country where they flee which does not consider them its citizens. The UN international refugee system is an attempt to normalize this situation by establishing the conditions under which certain categories of forced migrants come under the protection of the country of asylum but this is a far cry from citizenship. Female migrants and refugees constitute an ever-greater disruption in the nation-state system due to the historical exclusion of women from citizenship (e.g. Yuval-Davis 1997; Hobson and Lister 2002) interacting in complex ways and reinforcing the second class citizenship of migrant and refugee women (Arat-Koc 1992; Abdi in this volume).

A particular form of second class, 'lessened citizenship' (Maher 2004: 144) or 'partial citizenship' (Parreñas 2001) is experienced by domestic migrant workers globally. As Maher demonstrates, domestic workers suffer from special vulnerabilities as migrants from less developed states that afford, at best, reduced protection to their citizens, and by virtue of the 'privatized,' little-regulated, highly gendered and racialized construction of their social reproductive labour and their legal status on temporary work visas under conditions that resemble 'indentured servitude' (Maher 2004: 144). As we have seen, as social reproduction has become globalized, a 'citizenship gap' has emerged between not only female migrant domestic workers and citizens of receiving states (whose citizenship is in fact enhanced politically and economically by the domestic workers' labour) but also between sending and receiving societies, more generally (Maher 2004: 144-47).

Parreñas (2002: 52-53) describes how migrant women from the Philippines doing social reproductive labour in the North suffer from lessened citizenship in the Philippines as well, as a result of their vilification by the state and patriarchal society for 'abandoning' their children, something that migrant men are never accused of. Furthermore, she demonstrates how the transnational social reproductive labour of Filipina migrants contributes to a diminished citizenship for the women on the lowest rank of the global care chain, i.e. those who care in the Philippines for the transnational care providers' own children (Parreñas 2000: 573; on the same point, see Yeates 2004a: 80). Despite the limitations of the 'imagined (global) community' of Filipina domestic workers, Parreñas recognizes its subversive character that is the transgression of the nation-state it represents as well as its revolutionary potential, that is 'the promise of the expansion of this global community to include other groups of secondary-tier migrant workers in the global economy' (Parreñas 2001: 1152).

Not only domestic workers however, but also more skilled yet also feminized occupations in the transnational care service sector (Yeates 2004b: 386), such as nurses, experience a diminished citizenship. As Ball (2004) illustrates, the migration of Filipino nurses in the post-WWII period has been marked by a shift from permanent migration mostly to the U.S. to the globalization of nursing from the Philippines through short-term labour migration throughout the world. 'Brain drain' has not only continued but also intensified in the era of globalization. At the same time however, this contemporary form of brain drain is characterized by a 'weakening of the rights of nurses (as part of a global hierarchy of labour) in their contracted and globalized form' (Ball 2004: 131). In addition to the diminished citizenship of the racialized transnational care service sector migrant workers in receiving societies, other individuals, further down the global care chain fill in the huge care system gaps in sending societies (Yeates 2004a, 2004b) thus becoming second and third-tier citizens in their own societies.

Migration like citizenship is not free of identity politics struggles. Migration involves identities like gender, class, religion, sexual orientation, race and so forth on various levels, local, national and transnational, as does citizenship. Both migration and citizenship are gendered. About half of all migrants are women and girls, and they are more susceptible to human rights violations than men. These bring to the fore concerns of citizenship. Again, as Pettman outlines:

> Women as workers have long been caught between their productive and reproductive roles, in ways that disadvantage them in the labour market. That market is segmented along lines of nationality, race/ethnicity, gender and often age, as well as class. International processes, including colonization and migration, have informed these divisions within states. Now globalization compounds these dis/connections, and makes access or not to citizenship a crucial determination of difference. And globalization of the labour force makes it more likely that workers must negotiate state borders and join transnational flows in search of work. (Pettman 1999: 213)

Yet, as has been noted, this global movement of people has created a hysteria in certain quarters with implications for citizenship regimes. This panic has led to concrete actions: more prevalent discourses and policies about tightening immigration; the strengthening border controls and limiting cross-border movements; and criminalizing and deporting migrants. All of these reactions are gender-differentiated and all have specific gender-based consequences for immigrant and racialized women's collective rights, citizenship practices and economic livelihoods. Although the new trends in citizenship may not be the same everywhere, there is a clear movement away from post-nationalism and even multiculturalism and a renewed emphasis on assimilation and cohesion (Joppke and Morawska 2003: 2).

In a rapidly changing global environment, in the context of both acute labour demands, and various forms of migration backlash (from 'Fortress Europe,' and the American 'War on Terror,' to Australasian and Canadian backpeddling when it comes to bi and multiculturalism) gendered, racialized, (see Abu-Laban 2002) and state's cultural norms are being put to the test. Bader succinctly encapsulates the nature of the change. Up until the early 1970s, migrants were either 'wanted and welcome' as official immigrants, or certain forms of refugees, or 'wanted and unwelcome' as with some manual guest workers, or given racialization. Now, however, the bulk of migrants appear to be both 'unwanted and not welcome' (Bader 1997: 1; see also Dobrowolsky with Lister in this volume).

Such changes raise some critical questions when it comes to (im)migrant women. For instance: are women migrants wanted and welcome, wanted and unwelcome, or unwanted and not welcome? How does each tendency affect women's ability to make connections in all the ways we have outlined above? How does each tendency affect immigrant women's citizenship in all of its dimensions, i.e. socio-economic, political, cultural, and the psychological sense of belonging? Is global migration driven by actors and institutions taking advantage of women who are more socially, economically and political vulnerable than men? How do women respond, negotiate, resist or subvert such attempts, contesting and redefining in the process current citizenship regimes? Does migration provide women with an opportunity to subvert gender roles in their country of origin and/or in the receiving country and what are the implications for citizenship? Are (im)migrant women facing new forms of discrimination, subordination, exploitation and with what kinds of responses or forms of resistance?

To address these questions, this volume consists of nine substantive chapters, for the most part empirically grounded analyses, exploring, calling into question, and identifying the consequences of different dimensions of citizenship for migrant women. Although we have adopted a gender-based analysis throughout, the majority of our chapters focus on the experiences of women and hence the title of the volume. The women involved encompass seasonal agricultural migrants (Preibisch and Santamaría) and domestic workers (Denis, Gardiner Barber), industrial migrants and skilled professionals (Salaff and Greve), women and children refugees and asylum seekers (Dobrowolsky with Lister), refugee women in camps (Abdi), as well as 'associational' female migrants of South Asian origins (Ralston), and they are on the move for a whole host of reasons. They also engage in intricate inter and intra-racial and ethnic group relations and they deconstruct and reconstruct various gender, racial, ethnic power dynamics. For example, Tastsoglou in this volume illustrates how the territorial, spatial border lines, define physical locations, but also the cultural boundaries that (im)migrants have to cross over are rendered more complex by gender. In fact, each group and every individual is moving across shifting cultural, racial, ethnic, religious and linguistic and gendered boundaries. To a certain extent, (im)migrant women may call on different identities at different moments, depending on the politics in play under given sets of circumstances.

The dimensions of citizenship, are inspired by, but build on, T. H. Marshall's categories of rights, and are interdependent. They are interlocking, in the sense that clear-cut conceptual distinctions among them are hard to make.

Nonetheless, we start our exposition with Ann Denis' feminist re-conceptualization of citizenship which she uses to assess the meaning and experience of citizenship for domestic workers in Canada, focusing on live-in caregivers from the Caribbean and using as reference points other immigrant women and women in general. Denis identifies further conceptual challenges of the Marshallian framework, as she is trying to refine it to take into account women's various affiliations to dominant and subordinate groups, including their membership in sub-, cross- and supra-national collectivities as well as in one or more states.

Gardiner Barber's chapter adds to this initial framework the transnational level of analysis: it is an empirically grounded exploration of the meaning of citizenship both as policy and as lived experience for gendered social subjects in the case of Philippine labour migration. The scale of the migration flows and resulting diaspora has encouraged debates over the meanings and locations of Philippine citizenship and the transnational implications of dual citizenship. Gardiner Barber ponders the implications of the unlocking of people and place for citizenship and in particular whether our vocabularies of citizenship distract attention from the ever-present processes of class, gender and racialized differentiation that attend migration, both in migrant sending and receiving contexts.

The socio-economic dimensions of citizenship is next explored through two highly nuanced case studies discussing gendered processes and outcomes in the labour market in the migration of skilled women and men emigrating from China to Canada (Salaff and Greve) and in the temporary labour migration of foreign – primarily Mexican – workers in Canadian agriculture (Preibisch and Santamaría). The authors outline and analyze in captivating detail complex labour market processes that are par excellence social, racialized, class-based and gendered and that, although with local impact, cut across the sending and receiving societies, i.e. transnational processes. The consequences are the professional de-skilling of immigrant female professionals from China and the continuous supply of a disciplined, low-cost and indentured labour to a geographically immobile sector of the economy, ensuring competitiveness in global markets, circumventing and compromising the social, economic and even legal dimensions (in the case of foreign agricultural workers under temporary employment authorization) of citizenship.

The next two chapters transport us to two geographically opposite, though in many important ways culturally and historically related sites of the globe, New Zealand and Britain. Both provide accounts of the changing political climates under neo-liberal and post-neo-liberal regimes. Both detail the reactions to neo-liberalism's legacy with respect to immigrant and minority women's social citizenship claims, as well as assessments of these changes, in the respective countries. Larner discusses in depth the gendered implications, for both Maori and Pacific communities but also migrant and refugee ones, of shifting relationships between neo-liberalism, biculturalism and multiculturalism in Aotearoa New Zealand. At the other end of the globe, focusing on recent welfare restructuring and immigration and asylum policies, Dobrowolsky with Lister, tease out the current state of citizenship in Britain in light of the rise of political discourses and practices that seek to remedy social exclusions in the 'third way' of the Labour government of Tony Blair. They expose the limited ways in which such policies and practices address social exclusion and citizenship when it comes to women, racial and ethnic minorities, (im)migrants, refugees and asylum seekers and their children.

This is followed by two empirically grounded sociological studies that explore and interrogate immigrant women's participation in organizations, i.e. the practice of citizenship and its implications for identity-reconstruction, agency and resistance. Ralston's chapter focuses on citizenship as the practice of participation in voluntary organizations, both service – and advocacy-oriented, identity construction, agency and resistance among Canadian and Australian immigrant women of South Asian origin, illustrating the interconnections among these concepts. Organizational participation in voluntary associations and activism consist of involvement in the 'political,' broadly defined, dimension of citizenship. Although Tastsoglou also examines issues of organizational participation, she focuses on immigrant women's sense of belonging, i.e. the psychological/cultural dimension of their citizenship, the social processes by which they construct new spaces for themselves on 'borderlands' and the identity shifts they experience as a result. Issues of transnational identity emerge as a result of the 'politics of belonging' that further expand our understanding of citizenship.

Finally, Abdi in the last chapter focuses on the plight of Somali refugee women in Dadaab camps in Kenya who have fled ongoing civil war in their homeland only to find themselves exposed to gender-based violence in the camps: their strategies of resistance demonstrating their agency in the context of highly limiting circumstances. This is a case study of the gaps and the challenges to the traditional notion of citizenship based on the nation-state system, an illustration of the human rights violations and gender specific crimes in conflict zones associated with an unfortunately frequent 'disruption' of that model. We consider this area of investigation falling under the legal dimension of citizenship, though in a negative way illustrating what happens when the legal breaks down. The absence of the legal protections of citizenship is of course at the same time a political failure of the citizenship model associated with the nation-state system and has social, cultural, psychological and economic implications for refugee women.

In the end, then, even though Virginia Woolf's vision that begins this chapter is far from realized, the chapters that follow point to potential opportunities as well as old (and new) constraints. Above all, the contributors to this volume illustrate that the trials and tribulations that come with gendered processes of migration and citizenship constitute an ongoing struggle, in theory and in practice.

References

Abu-Laban, Y. (2002), 'Liberalism, Multiculturalism and the Problem of Essentialism,' *Citizenship Studies*, Vol. 6(4), pp. 459-82.

Abu-Laban, Y. and Gabriel, C. (2003), 'Security, Immigration and Post-September 11 Canada,' in J. Brodie and L. Trimble (eds), *Reinventing Canada: Politics of the 21st Century*, Prentice Hall, Toronto, pp. 290-306.

Abu-Laban, Y. and Gabriel, C. (2002), *Selling Diversity: Immigration, Multiculturalism, Employment Equity and Globalization*, Broadview Press, Peterborough.

Ackers, L. (1998), *Shifting Spaces: Women, Citizenship and Migration Within the*

European Union, The Policy Press, Bristol.

Ackers, L. (2004), 'Moving People and Knowledge: The Mobility of Scientists within the European Union,' (http://www.liv.ac.uk/ewc/docs/Migration%20workshop/Ackers-paper03.2004.pdf). Accessed 10 June 2005.

Alund, A. (1999), 'Feminism, Multiculturalism, Essentialism,' in N. Yuval-Davis and P. Werbner (eds), *Women, Citizenship and Difference*, Zed Books, London, New York, pp. 147-61.

Anthias, F. (2000), 'Metaphors of Home: Gendering New Migrations to Southern Europe,' in F. Anthias and G. Lazaridis (eds), *Gender and Migration in Southern Europe*, Berg, Oxford, New York, pp. 15-47.

Anthias, F. and Lazaridis, G. (eds) (2000), *Gender and Migration in Southern Europe*, Berg, Oxford, New York.

Arat-Koc, S. (1992), 'Immigration Policies, Migrant Domestic Workers and the Definition of Citizenship in Canada,' in V. Satzewich (ed.), *Deconstructing a Nation: Immigration, Multiculturalism and Racism in '90s Canada*, Fernwood, Halifax, pp. 229-42.

Bader, V. (1997), 'Fairly Open Borders,' in V. Bader (ed.), *Citizenship and Exclusion*. St. Martin's Press, New York, pp. 28-60.

Ball, R. E. (2004), 'Divergent Development, Racialized Rights: Globalised Labour Markets and the Trade of Nurses – The Case of the Philippines,' *Women's Studies International Forum*, Vol. 27: 119-33.

Bakker, I. (1996), *Rethinking Restructuring*, University of Toronto Press, Toronto.

Banaszak, L., Beckwith, K., and Rucht, D. (2003), *Women's Movements Facing the Reconfigured State*, Cambridge University Press, Cambridge.

Barber, P. G. (2003), 'Citizenship and Attachment Across Borders? A Transnational and Anthropological Research Agenda,' *Canadian Diversity*, Vol. 2(1), Spring, pp. 45-46.

Bashevkin, S. (2002), *Welfare Hot Buttons: Women, Work and Social Policy Reform*, University of Toronto Press, Toronto.

Bechold, B. H. and Dziewięcka-Bokun, L. (1999), 'Social Services for Immigrant Women in European Nations Including Lessons from the Council of Europe's Project on Human Dignity and Social Exclusion,' in G. A. Kelson and D. L. DeLaet (eds), *Gender and Immigration*, New York University Press, New York, pp. 186-206.

Bonnett, L. (2003), 'Citizenship and People with Disabilities,' in J. Brodie and L. Trimble (eds), *Reinventing Canada: Politics of the 21st Century*, Prentice Hall, Toronto, pp. 151-63.

Boyd, M. (1995), 'Migration Regulations and Sex Selective Outcomes in Developed Countries,' in *International Migration Policies and the Status of Female Migrants*, United Nations Department for Economic and Social Information and Policy Analysis, Population Division, New York.

Boyd, M. (1992), 'Gender Issues in Immigration and Language Fluency,' in B. Chiswick (ed.), *Immigration, Language and Ethnicity*, AEI Press, Washington,

D.C.

Boyd, M. (1986), 'Immigrant Women in Canada,' in R. Simon and C. Brettell (eds), *International Migration: The Female Experience*, Rowman and Allanheld, Totowa, New Jersey.

Brodie, J. (1995), *Politics on the Margins: Restructuring and the Canadian Women's Movement*, Fernwood, Halifax.

Brouwer, E. (2002), 'Immigration, Asylum and Terrorism: A Changing Dynamic, Legal and Practical Developments in the EU in Response to the Terrorist Attacks of 11.09,' *European Journal of Migration & Law*, Vol. 4(4), pp. 399-424.

Carens, J. H. (2000), *Culture, Citizenship, and Community*, Oxford University Press, Oxford.

Castles, S. and Davidson, A. (2000), *Citizenship and Migration: Globalization and the Politics of Belonging*, Routledge, New York.

Castles, S. and Miller, M. (1998), *The Age of Migration*, The Guilford Press, New York.

Cheng, S. A. (1999), 'Labor Migration and International Sexual Division of Labor: A Feminist Perspective,' in G. Kelson and D. DeLaet (eds), *Gender and Immigration*, New York University Press, New York, pp. 38-58.

Cossman, B. and Fudge, J. (2002), *Privatization, Law, and the Challenge to Feminism*, University of Toronto Press, Toronto.

Couton, P. (2002), 'Highly Skilled Immigrants. Recent Trends and Issues,' *Canadian Journal of Policy Research*. Vol. 3(2), Fall, pp. 114-23.

Crocker, D., Dobrowolsky, A., Keeble, E. and Tastsoglou, E. (2005), *Security and Immigration, Changes and Challenges: Immigrant and Ethnic Communities in Atlantic Canada, Presumed Guilty?*, Final Research Report to Status of Women Canada, Policy Research Fund.

Daniels, R. J., Macklem, P. and Roach, K. (2001), *The Security of Freedom: Essays on Canada's Anti-Terrorism Bill*, University of Toronto Press, Toronto.

DeLaet, D. L. (1999), 'Introduction: The Invisibility of Women in Scholarship on International Migration,' in G. A. Kelson and D. L. DeLaet (eds), *Gender and Immigration*, New York University Press, New York, pp. 1-17.

Devlin, R. and Pothier, D. (2006), 'Dis-citizenship,' a report prepared for the Law Commission of Canada (forthcoming).

Dobrowolsky, A. (2004), 'The Chrétien Liberal Legacy and Women: Changing Policy Priorities with Little Cause for Celebration,' *Review of Constitutional Studies*, Vol. 9(1-2), pp. 171-98.

Dobrowolsky, A. (2002), 'Identity and Rights Reclaimed: Appreciating and Assessing Aboriginal Women's Interventions in Canada,' *Social Theory*, Vol. 6, pp. 59-84.

Dobrowolsky, A. and Jenson, J. (2004), 'Shifting Representations of Citizenship: Canadian Politics of "Women" and "Children,"' *Social Politics*, Vol. 11(2), pp. 154-80.

Drache, D. (2004), *Borders Matter: Homeland Security and the Search for North America*, Fernwood, Halifax.

Ehrenreich, B. and Hochschild, A. R. (2002), 'Introduction,' in B. Ehrenreich and

A. R. Hochschild (eds), *Global Woman*, Metropolitan Books, Henry Holt and Company, New York.

Faist, T. (2002), '"Extension du domaine de la lutte:" International Migration and Security before and after September 11, 2001,' *International Migration Review*, Vol. 36(1), pp. 53-58.

Fiske, J. (1999), 'The Womb is to the Nation as the Heart is to the Body: Ethnopolitical Discourses of the Canadian Indigenous Women's Movement,' in P. Armstrong and M. P. Connelly (eds), *Feminism, Political Economy and the State: A Contested Terrain*, Canadian Scholars Press, Toronto, pp. 293-325.

Fraser, N. (1997), *Justice Interruptus*, Routledge, London.

Fraser, N. (1995), 'From Redistribution to Recognition? Dilemmas of Justice in a "Post Socialist" Age,' *New Left Review*, Vol. 212, pp. 68-93.

Gabriel, C. (2005), 'Citizens and Citizenship,' in J. Brodie and S. Rein (eds), *Critical Concepts: An Introduction to Politics*, Pearson Prentice Hall, Toronto, pp. 122-34.

Goldring, L. (2000), 'The Gender and Geography of Citizenship in Mexico-U.S. Transnational Spaces,' *Identities*, Vol. 1(1), pp. 1-37.

Grieco, E. and Boyd, M. (1998), 'Women and Migration: Incorporating Gender into International Migration Theory,' Working Paper, Center for the Study of Population, Florida State University, Florida, WPS 98-139 0740-9095.

Held, D. (1995), *Democracy and the Global Order*, Polity Press, Cambridge.

Hobson, B. and Lister, R. (2002), 'Citizenship,' in B. Hobson, J. Lewis and B. Siim (eds), *Contested Concepts in Gendered Social Politics*, Edward Elgar, Cheltenham, pp. 23-54.

Hoerder, D. (1997), 'Segmented Macrosystems, Networking Individuals, Cultural Change: Balancing Processes and Interactive Change in Migration,' in V. Bader (ed.), *Citizenship and Exclusion*. St. Martin's Press, New York, pp. 81-95.

Hondagneu-Sotelo, P. (1999), 'Introduction: Gender and Contemporary U.S. Immigration,' *The American Behavioral Scientist*, Vol. 42(4), pp. 565-76.

Hondagneu-Sotelo, P. (1994), *Gendered Transitions: Mexican Experiences of Immigration*, University of California Press, Berkeley.

Humphrey, M. (2003), 'Refugees an endangered species?,' *Journal of Sociology*, Vol. 39(1), pp. 31-43.

Ip, D. and Lever-Tracy, C. (1999), 'Asian Women in Business in Australia,' in G. A. Kelson and D. L. DeLaet (eds), *Gender and Immigration*, New York University Press, New York, pp. 59-81.

Iredale, R. (2001), 'The Migration of Professionals: Theories and Typologies,' *International Migration*, Vol. 39(5), pp. 9-24.

Isin, E. and Wood, P. (1999), *Citizenship and Identity*, Sage Publications, London.

Jenson, J. (1993), 'Naming Nations: Making Nationalist Claims in Canadian Public Discourse,' *Canadian Review of Sociology and Anthropology*, Vol. 30(2), pp. 337-58.

Jenson, J. and Phillips, S. D. (1996), 'Regime Shift: New Citizenship Practices in

Canada,' *International Journal of Canadian Studies*, Vol. 14, Fall, pp. 111-35.

Jones-Correa, M. (2000), 'Different Paths: Gender, Immigration and Political Participation,' in K. Willis and B. Yeoh (eds), *Gender and Migration*, An Elgar Reference Collection, Cheltenham, U.K., pp. 357-80.

Joppke, C. (2004), 'Citizenship Without Identity,' *Canadian Diversity*, Vol. 3(2), Spring, pp. 85-87.

Joppke, C. and Morawska, E. (2003), 'Integrating Immigrants in Liberal Nation States: Policies and Practices,' in C. Joppke and E. Morawska (eds), *Toward Assimilation and Citizenship: Immigrants in Liberal Nation States*, Palgrave Macmillan, Houndmills, London, pp. 1-36.

Kabeer, N. (2002), 'Citizenship and the Boundaries of the Acknowledged Community: Identity, Affiliation and Exclusion,' Working Paper 171, Institute of Development Studies, Brighton, Sussex.

Kapur, R. (2003), 'The "Other" Side of Globalization: The Legal Regulation of Cross Border Movements,' *Canadian Woman Studies*, Vol. 22(3-4), pp. 6-15.

Kofman, E. (2004), 'Gendered Global Migrations,' *International Feminist Journal of Politics,* Vol. 6(4), December, pp. 643-65.

Kofman, E., Phizacklea, A., Raghuram, P. and Sales, R. (2000), *Gender and International Migration in Europe*, Routledge, London, New York.

Kymlicka, W. (2001), *Politics in the Vernacular: Nationalism, Multiculturalism and Citizenship*, Oxford University Press, Oxford.

Kymlicka, W. (1995), *Multicultural Citizenship: A Liberal Theory of Minority Rights*, Oxford University Press, Oxford.

Lister, R. (2003), *Citizenship: Feminist Perspectives* (2nd edition), New York University Press, New York.

Lister, R. (1997a), 'Citizenship: Towards a Feminist Synthesis,' *Feminist Review*, Vol. 57, pp. 28-48.

Lister, R. (1997b), 'Dialectics of Citizenship,' *Hypatia*, Vol. 12(4), pp. 6-26.

Macklin, A. (2002), 'Public Entrance/Private Member,' in B. Cossman and J. Fudge (eds), *Privatization, Law, and the Challenge to Feminism*, University of Toronto Press, Toronto, pp. 218-64.

Macklin, A. (2001), 'Borderline Security,' in R. J. Daniels, P. Macklem and K. Roach (eds), *The Security of Freedom: Essays on Canada's Anti-Terrorism Bill*, University of Toronto Press, Toronto, pp. 383-404.

Maher, K. H. (2004), 'Globalized Social Reproduction,' in A. Brysk and G. Shafir (eds), *People Out of Place*, Routledge, New York and London, pp. 131-51.

Mahler, S. and Pessar, P. (2001), 'Gendered Geographies of Power. Analyzing Gender across Transnational Spaces,' *Identities,* Vol. 7(4), 441-59.

Man, G. (2004), 'Gender, Work and Migration: Deskilling Chinese Immigrant Women in Canada,' *Women's Studies International Forum,* Vol. 27, pp. 135-48.

Marshall, T.H. (1965), *Class, Citizenship, and Social Development: Essays*, Anchor Books, Garden City, New York.

Meehan, E. (1993), *Citizenship and the European Community*, Sage, London.

Munch, R. (2001), *Nation and Citizenship in the Global Age: From National to Transnational Ties and Identities*, Palgrave, Houndmills, Basingstoke, Hampshire.

Parreñas, R. S. (2002), 'The Care Crisis in the Philippines: Children and Transnational Families in the New Global Economy,' in B. Ehrenreich and A. R. Hochschild (eds) *Global Woman*, A Metropolitan/Owl Book, Henry Holt and Company, New York, pp. 39-54.

Parreñas, R. S. (2001), 'Transgressing the Nation-State: The Partial Citizenship and "Imagined (Global) Community" of Migrant Filipina Domestic Workers,' *Signs*, Vol. 26(4), pp. 1129-54.

Parreñas, R. S. (2000), 'Migrant Filipina Domestic Workers and the International Division of Reproductive Labor,' *Gender and Society*, Vol. 14(4), pp. 560-80.

Pessar, P. (1999), 'Engendering Migration Studies: The Case of New Immigrants in the United States,' *The American Behavioral Scientist*, Vol. 42(4), pp. 577-600.

Pessar, P. (1995), 'On the Homefront and in the Workplace: Integrating Immigrant Women into Feminist Discourse,' *Anthropological Quarterly*, Vol. 68(1), pp. 37-47.

Pettman, J.J. (1999), 'Globalisation and the Gendered Politics of Citizenship,' in N. Yuval-Davis and P. Werbner (eds), *Women, Citizenship and Difference*, Zed, London, pp. 207-20.

Pratt, G. (1999), 'From Registered Nurse to Registered Nanny: Discursive Geographies of Filipina Domestic Workers in Vancouver, B.C.,' *Economic Geography*, Vol. 75(3), pp. 215-36.

Preston, V. and Man, G. (1999), 'Employment Experiences of Chinese Immigrant Women An Exploration of Diversity,' *Canadian Woman Studies*, Vol. 19(3), pp. 116-23.

Raghuram, P. (2004), 'The Difference that Skills Make: Gender, Family Migration Strategies and Regulated Labour Markets,' *Journal of Ethnic and Migration Studies*, Vol. 30(2), pp. 303-21.

Raghuram, P. and Kofman, E. (2004), 'Out of Asia: Skilling, Re-Skilling and Deskilling of Female Migrants,' *Women's Studies International Forum*, Vol. 27, pp. 95-100.

Roach, K. (2003), *September 11: Consequences for Canada*, McGill-Queen's University Press, Montreal, Kingston.

Robin-Olivier, S. (2005), 'Citizens and Noncitizens in Europe: European Union Measures against terrorism after September 11,' *Boston College Third World Law Journal*, Vol. 25(1), pp. 197-220.

Rummens, J. A. (2004), 'Diversity, Identity and Belonging,' *Canadian Diversity*, Vol. 3(2), Spring, pp. 39-42.

Sassen, S. (2002), 'Global Cities and Survival Circuits,' in B. Ehrenreich and A. R. Hochschild (eds), *Global Woman*, A Metropolitan/Owl Book, Henry Holt and Company, New York, pp. 254-74.

Sassen, S. (2000), 'Women's Burden: Counter-geographies of Globalization and the Feminization of Survival,' *Journal of International Affairs*, Vol. 53(2), Spring, pp. 503-24.

Seager, J. (2003), *The Penguin Atlas of Women in the World, Canadian Woman Studies*, Vol. 22(3-4), p. 46.

Soysal, Y. N. (2000), 'Citizenship and Identity: Living in Diasporas in Post War Europe?,' *Ethnic and Racial Studies*, Vol. 23(1), pp. 1-15.

Soysal, Y. N. (1994), *The Limits of Citizenship: Migrants and Post-National Membership in Europe*, University of Chicago Press, Chicago, London.

Stasiulis, D. and Abu-Laban, Y. (2004), 'Unequal Relations and the Struggle for Equality: Race and Ethnicity in Canadian Politics,' in G. Williams and M. S. Whittington (eds), *Canadian Politics in the 21st Century*, Nelson Thomson, Scarborough, pp. 371-97.

Stasiulis, D. and Bakan, A. B. (2000), 'Negotiating Citizenship: The Case of Foreign Domestic Workers in Canada,' in K. Willis and B. Yeoh (eds), *Gender and Migration*, An Elgar Reference Collection, Cheltenham, U.K., pp. 383-410 (original publication date of article: 1997).

Stolcke, V. (1997), 'The "Nature" of Nationality,' in V. Bader (ed.), *Citizenship and Exclusion*, Macmillan Press, Houndmills, London, pp. 61-80.

Studt, K. (1999), 'Seeds for Self Sufficiency? Policy Contradictions at the US-Mexico Border,' in G. A. Kelson and D. L. DeLaet (eds), *Gender and Immigration*, New York University Press, New York, pp. 21-37.

Tastsoglou, E. and Maratou-Alipranti, L. (2003), 'Gender and International Migration: Conceptual, Substantive and Methodological Issues,' in E. Tastsoglou and L. Maratou-Alipranti (eds), *Gender and International Migration: Focus on Greece,* special volume of the *Greek Review of Social Research*, National Centre for Social Research, Athens, Vol. 110 (A), pp. 5-22.

Tastsoglou, E. and Preston, V. (in press), 'Gender, Immigration and Employment Integration: Where We Are and What We Still Need to Know,' *Atlantis: A Women's Studies Journal.*

Taylor, C. (1994), 'The Politics of Recognition,' in A. Gutmann (ed.), *Multiculturalism: Examining the Politics of Recognition*, Princeton University Press, Princeton, pp. 25-73.

Tolley, E. (2003), 'The Skilled Worker Class,' *Metropolis Policy Brief*, No. 1, January.

Trimble, L. (2003), 'Women and Citizenship,' in J. Brodie and L. Trimble (eds), *Reinventing Canada: Politics of the 21st Century*, Prentice Hall, Toronto, pp. 131-50.

Turner, B. (1990), 'Outline of a Theory on Citizenship,' *Sociology*, Vol. 24(2), pp. 189-218.

Walby, S. (1994), 'Is Citizenship Gendered?,' *Sociology*, Vol. 28(2), pp. 379-95.

Werbner, P. and Yuval-Davis, N. (1999), 'Introduction: Women and the New Discourse of Citizenship,' in N. Yuval-Davis and P. Werbner (eds), *Women, Citizenship and Difference*, Zed Books, London, New York, pp. 1-38.

Whitaker, R. (2004), 'The Security State,' in J. Bickerton and A. G. Gagnon (eds),

Canadian Politics (4th edition), Broadview Press, Peterborough, pp. 223-36.

Wilkinson L. and Hebert, Y. (2003), 'The Values Debate, Citizenship Policy and Education in Canada,' *Canadian Diversity*, Vol. 2(1), Spring, pp. 39-41.

Willis, K. and Yeoh, B. (eds) (2000), *Gender and Migration*, An Elgar Reference Collection, Cheltenham, UK and Northampton, MA, USA.

Yeates, N. (2004a), 'A Dialogue with "Global Care Chain" Analysis: Nurse Migration in the Irish Context,' *Feminist Review*, Vol. 77, pp. 79-95.

Yeates, N. (2004b), 'Global Care Chains,' *International Feminist Journal of Politics*, Vol. 63, pp. 369-91.

Young, I. M. (1997), 'A Multicultural Continuum: A Critique of Will Kymlicka's Ethnic Nation Dichotomy,' *Constellations*, Vol. 4(1), pp. 48-53.

Young, I. M. (1990), *Justice and the Politics of Difference*, Princeton University Press, Princeton.

Yuval-Davis, N. (1997), *Gender and Nation*, Sage, London.

Yuval-Davis, N. (1993), 'Gender and Nation,' *Ethnic and Racial Studies*, Vol. 16(4), pp. 621-32.

Yuval-Davis, N. and Anthias, F. (1989), *Women-Nation State*, Macmillan, London.

Chapter 2

Developing a Feminist Analysis of Citizenship of Caribbean Immigrant Women in Canada: Key Dimensions and Conceptual Challenges

Ann Denis

Introduction

This chapter sketches a framework I am developing, both in collaboration with Eudine Barriteau for a feminist analysis of citizenship in the Commonwealth Caribbean (Barriteau and Denis 2001), and independently, for a feminist analysis of citizenship of Caribbean immigrant women in Canada. The analysis is informed by the concept of gender system which Barriteau has developed with reference to the Commonwealth Caribbean (2001, especially pp. 20-44), which I think is also pertinent in the present analysis about Canada. The theorizing of citizenship in relation to Caribbean immigrant women in Canada highlights the importance of developing a *gendered* analysis, and one that incorporates the possibility of continuing boundary crossings and multiple identities. It is informed by T.H. Marshall's concept of citizenship (Marshall 1992 [1950]: 18), a 'status bestowed on those who are full members of a community ... equal with respect to the rights and duties with which the status is endowed' (p. 18). In order to avoid the justified criticisms of ethnocentrism and gender blindness which have been levelled against Marshall, it is also informed by literature on the gendering of citizenship, and on multicultural citizenship.

The point of departure is the question of what would be required for the interests and rights of immigrant women from the Caribbean to be fully included in a concept of citizenship. After outlining Barriteau's concept of gender system and her application of it to the Commonwealth Caribbean, I will discuss its relevance to Canada, arguing as Juteau (2003) does, for the importance of considering both the material and the non-material in the analysis of gender, ethnicity/race and other bases of social differentiation. I will then highlight key tenets of and debates associated with the dimensions of citizenship distinguished by Marshall and selected re-conceptualizations that have been proposed in order to incorporate considerations of gender and multiculturalism. Next, I will present what Barriteau and I have posited is an 'irreducible core' of the concept of citizenship for women. Turning then to the Canadian situation, after an overview of ethnic relations, immigration and multiculturalism focussing on issues of relevance to immigrants from the Caribbean, I will delineate schematically variables which are encompassed in (and can operationalize) what we have proposed as the key dimensions of citizenship – civil, political, social, and economic.[1] This is combined with a preliminary examination of how some of these variables are gendered and/or differentially experienced in terms of race/ethnicity, marital status and class[2] by women in Canada, with specifications, regarding women who are immigrants from the Caribbean.[3]

The Material and the Ideological: Barriteau and Juteau

Barriteau defines a gender system as

> comprising a network of power relations with two principal dimensions: one ideological and the other material ... The material dimension reveals access to and the allocation of power, status and resources within a given community or society ... The ideological dimension ... indicates how a given society's notion of masculinity and femininity are constructed and maintained ... [This reveals] the gender ideologies operating in the state and society, [that is] what is appropriate or expected of the socially constructed beings 'women' and 'men' ... The interactions and operations of gender systems are messy, contingent and are continually contested and negotiated. (Barriteau 2001: 30-2)

In the case of the Commonwealth Caribbean, Barriteau (2001: 33) argues that measures introduced by post-independence governments have given women access to public resources, thus altering material aspects of gender relations, 'while de-emphasizing the ideological aspects and the interconnectedness of both'.

Similarly, it is useful, in the Canadian case, to consider possible unevenness in rates of change relative to gender in the material and the ideological, and the effects of such unevenness. Such analysis can be extended to other (potentially interdependent) bases of social differentiation, including race/ethnicity (Juteau 2003; Abu-Laban and Gabriel 2002; Li 2003).

---

1   Although Marshall includes 'economic' within 'civil,' I feel that it is important to treat it separately because of its importance and its more problematic nature for women.

2   This is not to deny other bases of difference, but simply to circumscribe the task I am undertaking.

3   Although some of the variables also apply to male immigrants, the analysis of men's experiences is not the priority of the present research.

Marshall on Citizenship

Marshall (1992 [1950]) distinguished three elements of citizenship – the civil, the political and the social. The civil is played out through the legal institutions, for instance in laws and in the exercise of justice through the courts. Marshall defined it as 'composed of the rights necessary for individual freedom' (Marshall (1992 [1950]: 8). The political dimension refers to 'the right to participate in the exercise of political power' (Marshall (1992 [1950]: 8), by voting or holding an elected or appointed political office. The social element refers to 'the whole range from the right to a modicum of economic welfare and security to the right to share to the full in the social heritage and to live the life of a civilized being according to the standards prevailing in the society' (Marshall (1992 [1950]: 8).

Marshall showed how social inequality has constrained the exercise of citizenship rights, and, more recently, how citizenship has reduced social inequality. He concluded that 'there is a kind of basic human equality, associated with full community citizenship, which is not inconsistent with a superstructure of economic inequality' (Marshall (1992 [1950]: 45). That citizenship, which involves sharing a unified (middle class) civilization, serves as a unifying force within the national community. Equality through full citizenship is legitimized by social justice, while the economic system is governed by a 'combination of social justice and economic necessity' (Marshall (1992 [1950]: 47).

Although Marshall acknowledged the inaccuracy of his analysis for women, he made no serious attempt to rectify this inadequacy. Moreover he was clearly assuming universal principles based on a shared (English middle class) 'civilization,' within an ethnically homogeneous community. It is, however, noteworthy that Marshall's definition, despite its limitations, does not refer to *state* membership, but to society and community. Yuval-Davis (1997), Hobson and Lister (2002) and Juteau (2003) argue that his definition also allows for consideration of both individual *and* collective rights. The latter refer to rights based on membership in particular collectivities, and, as Dobrowolsky (2001: 82) suggests, discourses related to such rights claims 'may be based on entitlements, needs and interactions with others.'

Addressing Gender and Multiculturalism in Citizenship Analyses

A challenge Marshall's feminist critics have faced is attempting to reconcile universalist principles with the need to eliminate gender inequality (for example: Yuval-Davis 1997; Lister 1995, 1997; Voet 1998). Hobson and Lister (2002: 36-40) summarize the resulting conceptualizations as the gender-neutral citizen, the gender-differentiated citizen and the gender-pluralist citizen. Gender-pluralism is the most promising: it acknowledges the intersection of gender with other variables defining social location. It also stresses the importance of citizens' agency, that is, their autonomy and conscious engagement with fellow citizens (Werbner and Yuval-Davis 1999).

Claims of citizenship rights by members of minority ethnic groups in multicultural states pose another challenge to universalistic principles of citizenship in communities whose ethnic/racial heterogeneity and inequality is acknowledged. Kymlicka (1995) argues that in situations of ethno-cultural diversity, cultural pluralism for minority ethnic groups contributes to overall integration. National minorities, he contends, have a legitimate claim to structural as well as cultural pluralism, but ethnic groups do not. In the absence of structural pluralism, however, cultural pluralism tends only to support diversity in the short term (van den Berghe 1978). Thus Kymlicka's concept of societal culture masks dominant cultural hegemonies. In fact, his vision of a multicultural society is one based on an (ethnically defined) hierarchy of citizens. While critiquing Kymlicka's concepts of 'societal culture,' 'national minority' and 'ethnic groups' (who are, effectively, immigrants), Carens (2000) argues for 'even-handed justice'.This takes account of socio-historic context in discussing the rights of ethnic minorities (and women) in multicultural societies, notably Canada. Both he and Yuval-Davis (1997) point to the increasing complexities of identity and citizenship which involve dual (or multiple) citizenship and supra-national political bodies.

Analysis of both gender and ethnicity challenge the clear dichotomy between the public and the private, whether the latter refers to the market, the domestic sphere and/or voluntary activities. These boundaries are often permeable and are certainly not static (Smith 1999). Thus, a more inclusive definition of citizenship is required in order to encompass recognition of women and of ethnic minorities. It must develop a common standard which still manages to incorporate diversity. As Werbner and Yuval-Davis (1999: 4, cited in Hobson and Lister 2002: 23) argue, it involves conceptualizing citizenship as 'a more total relationship, inflected by identity, social positioning, cultural assumptions, institutional practices and a sense of belonging'.

The 'Irreducible' Core of Citizenship – for Women

Foundational assumptions of feminism are that women are disadvantaged relative to men in societies and that therefore political action to eliminate this disadvantage should be identified and undertaken. The nature of this disadvantage and appropriate remedial measures vary with the feminist framework adopted. What, then, is the core that would allow women to exercise the full and equal social and political participation within a community that citizenship entails? Like men, women would have to be defined as *individuals* (not, for instance, as someone's spouse or mother), and they would have to have as an individual right – regardless of gender, race/ethnicity or social class – the realistic possibility of both enjoying access to the rights and fulfilling the obligations that would allow them to exist in a situation of relative individual autonomy within the community. These core elements enable (and legitimize) other elements that take account of interaction between history and culture without contradicting the foundational principles. This acknowledges the constraints and obligations that being part of a community place on individual freedom, while arguing that, in general, these constraints and obligations should not be differentiated on the basis of the individual's social location or intersecting statuses. Furthermore, stressing that women should have the right to be defined as individuals does not negate the fact that their various social locations (in terms of gender, race/ethnicity, class, etc.) may result in their experiencing constraints (or advantages) as members of the resulting collectivities. Equally they may claim rights as members of these collectivities: such claims can be a mechanism to obviate constraints from gender (and ethnic) ideologies and/or systemic discrimination related to being in specific social locations. It may be by identifying with these collectivities that they experience a sense of belonging, even if the same collectivities can also be sources of disadvantage against which they collectively fight.

This concept of citizenship is necessarily gendered, attending to the differential power relations – both material and ideological – experienced by women and men. It also takes into account women's (and men's) affiliation to cross-cutting dominant or subordinate groups or collectivities, based, for instance, on class, race/ethnicity, and (dual) nationality, recognizing that both citizenship and individuals' social locations are dynamic rather than static concepts (Yuval-Davis 1997). Following Marshall (1992 [1950]) and, especially, the new citizenship literature (Turner 1990; Yuval-Davis 1997; Yuval-Davis and Werbner 1999, for instance), this concept of citizenship includes civil, political, social and economic dimensions of rights and obligations, but without positing that these dimensions occur on the basis of a universal chronology. Adding an economic dimension to the discussion of citizenship addresses more directly than Marshall did some of the bases of socio-economic differentiation, whether in terms of social class, race/ethnicity or gender. Furthermore, as supra-national entities, whether international organizations (such as UN organizations or the WTO) or trans-national corporations, to some extent limit the autonomy of the state by taking on regulatory economic roles in this new era of globalization, it seems important to ensure that the economic dimension is highlighted in a discussion of citizenship.

Following Marshall (1992 [1950]) and Yuval-Davis (1997) citizenship refers to relations with the community – a multi-layered concept that may refer to the state, but also to local levels of community, to communities based on such criteria as ethnicity/race, gender or social class, to supra-national communities, such as the Caribbean diaspora or, for those within the Caribbean diaspora, the community within their country of origin. For those immigrants to Canada who have maintained dual citizenship, this entails concurrent relations with two nation state communities of which they are formally a part. Both human rights considerations and the 'imperatives' for capital of having an internationally mobile labour force are adding new dimensions to these complex relations of citizenship.

Caribbean Immigrants in Canada: Ethnic Relations, Immigration and Multiculturalism

Ethnic Relations and Immigration Policy

As a settler society, Canada has premised its policies about who will be admitted on the expectation of applicants becoming citizens, or at least long term residents. Admission on the basis of a temporary work permit has been exceptional. Until the 1960s, preference for admission was based on national origin, due to its purported association with the capacity to assimilate: Anglo-conformity was effectively the goal (Abu-Laban and Gabriel 2002; Hawkins 1988). Systemic discrimination based on national origin resulted in the almost total exclusion of Afro-Caribbeans, although the Immigration Act of 1952 included provisions that allowed for agreements with Caribbean territories for the admission of an annual quota of (female) residential domestic workers from the region (Anderson 1993).

Independent Immigrants

A significant change in Canadian immigration policy began with the introduction of the 'points system' in 1962,[4] formalized in 1967 in a revised Immigration Act. The 'points system' replaced 'preferential treatment' criteria based on national origin by criteria related to employment skills for *independent* immigrants. Although the specifics, including relative weight, have varied over time, the key criteria relate to education, other training, occupation, work experience, knowledge of one of Canada's two official languages, and age. 'Investors,' a subsequently added sub-category of independent immigrants (Abu-Laban and Gabriel 2002; Hawkins 1988), has not been salient for Caribbean women.

Workers on Temporary Employment Authorizations

Despite the continuing demand for residential domestic workers, nannies, and care-givers (normally women), these occupations were never given additional points as occupations in which there was a shortage (Bakan and Stasiulis 1997; Calliste 1991; Daenzer 1993). Rather, the points accorded have actually diminished since 1968[5] (Arat-Koc 1999a). A sexist, racist and classist consequence is that most applicants are not admitted as independent immigrants, but in a category of *temporary* employment authorization. Although, as a result of lobbying, the constraints on these workers

---

4   Opinion is divided about how significant the change was. Whereas Hawkins (1988) argues that it was a significant change, Satzewich (1989) contends that the policies and their implementation with regard to Caribbean immigrants remained racialized, and Aroc-Koc (1999a) considers that the change corresponds with a shift from conceptualizing immigrants as nation builders to the commodification of immigrants.

5   Except for nannies, who are predominately from Britain where specialized training for this occupation exists.

have lessened, their employment authorizations continue to deny them the freedom to choose their place of residence or change their occupation, and, for part of the period, denied them the freedom to change their employer. During the 1960s, after completion of the year's contract, the individual could apply, from within Canada, for landed immigrant status with a good chance of success.[6] From the 1970s until 1981 it was necessary to leave Canada at the end of the temporary employment authorization in order to apply for landed immigrant status. What is now an obligatory period of two years' employment as a residential worker cannot be counted towards the years required before applying for citizenship. From 1981-1992 a criterion for subsequent admission as an independent immigrant was the demonstration of participation in educational and community activities during the contract as a residential care-giver (Arat-Koc 1999a; Daenzer 1993). For no other category of immigrants do such additional conditions obtain.

Until recently, women from the Commonwealth Caribbean have constituted a large proportion of these workers: some of the programmes were conceived, in collaboration with governments in the Caribbean, specifically for women from that region. From 1955 until the late 1960s, annual quotas of Caribbean women were admitted to Canada under this programme, provided they were healthy and had at least a grade eight education. After a year's domestic service, the individual could apply for landed immigrant status. After five years they could apply for citizenship. As citizens, they could sponsor close relatives. Many unmarried women who were teachers, nurses, secretaries or clerks used this programme as a means of immigration (Satzewich 1989). While it is true that for most the programme (especially prior to the 1970s) offered better opportunities for employment and social mobility than were available in the Caribbean, for many the denial of civil rights (and the obstacles to the option of political citizenship) tarnished the experiences of Caribbean women who were first admitted on temporary employment authorizations.

Sponsored Immigrants

Sponsored immigrants (financé(e)s, spouses and dependents, usually close relatives such as minor children) are the other main category of immigrants. The parameters for the sponsored categories of immigrants have been both lauded as open ones, encouraging family reunification, and criticized as ethno-centric and heterosexist (because of a narrow definition of 'family') and therefore discriminatory. Some aspects of the application process are also criticized as sexist. Initially by regulation, more recently by practice, only one member of a family (usually the adult male) is evaluated as an independent immigrant.[7] All other family members must come

---

6   Some succeeded in entering other employment, more appropriate to their qualifications, without completing the year's contract, and still were accorded landed immigrant status (Bobb-Smith 2003).

7   Until 1974 a married woman could not enter as an independent immigrant (Boyd 1975).

under that individual's sponsorship (Abu-Laban and Gabriel 2002; Boyd 1997). Although the labour force participation rate of foreign-born wives is higher than that of their Canadian-born counterparts of the same ethnic origin, they are admitted as sponsored family members, and the period of dependency when no claims may be made on such state-supported resources as welfare, is for between three and ten years.[8] Fear of being deported has resulted in some of these women, legally admitted as formal dependents, remaining in abusive relationships (Côté et al. 2001; Arat-Koc 1999a).

Immigrants from the Commonwealth Caribbean

In most national origin categories in Canada, male immigrants are more numerous than women. Immigrants from the Caribbean are, however, atypical, since women are more numerous than men, including, it seems, among independent immigrants.[9] This is possibly the result of women's access under domestic worker/care-giver programmes, and as nurses and teachers (Calliste 1991, 1993). Many have completed at least secondary school. Especially during the 1960s and 1970s, women (and men) who initially entered on university student visas remained, as landed immigrants, once their studies were completed. Among immigrants from the Economic South, those from the Commonwealth Caribbean are also atypical because English is the official language in their country of origin and their education has been in English. Thus, they have the formal advantage, under the points system, of knowing one of Canada's official languages. Depending on their country of origin and social class, however, some Caribbean immigrants are more fluent in 'dialect,' 'creole,' or 'patois' than in 'standard English,' and many experience the same type of discrimination as a result of their 'accent' as Creese and Kambere report African women experiencing (Creese and Kambere 2003; Kelly 1998).

Changes in the distribution of points, in the discourse justifying immigration, and in the relative importance of independent and other classes of immigrants, together with measures introduced following 9/11 suggest the increasing impact of neo-liberal and 'national security' considerations in an age of globalization. This contrasts with greater emphasis on humanitarian considerations between the 1960s and the 1980s (Abu-Laban and Gabriel 2002; Arat-Koc 1999b; Li 2003).

Ethnic Relations and Multiculturalism Policy

Shortly after the points system was introduced, and in part as a result of the wide ranging Royal Commission on Bilingualism and Biculturalism, first a national

8   In 2001 the period of dependency was reduced from ten to three years for spouses. It remains ten years for others who are sponsored (Côté et al. 2001).

9   The fact that much of the published data on immigration groups together as independent both the individual receiving that status and sponsored family members who accompany him/her at the time of immigration complicates the analysis.

policy of official bilingualism (the Official Languages Act of 1969) and then a policy on multiculturalism (1971) were introduced, with the latter leading to the Multiculturalism Act in 1988. Other legislation of significance for ethnic relations includes the Canadian Charter of Rights and Freedoms (1982) and the Employment Equity Act (1986). The latter addresses issues of systemic discrimination in the workplace, but only within federally regulated jurisdictions.[10] The 'designated groups' covered by the Act include women, members of 'visible minorities,' Aboriginals and the disabled. The Act's provisions recognize the need for special provisions to enable these groups to achieve employment equity. Thus, measures based on social location as part of one or more designated collectivities are legitimated as helping to redress past exclusions and continuing inequalities of condition. The effect of these measures has been to confirm English and French as official languages in Canada (for matters under federal jurisdiction), while at the same time affirming that each Canadian may choose to enjoy, enhance and share his or her heritage (providing that so doing is not at odds with individual rights under the Charter). Furthermore, no one should be subject to racism. Canada's signing of United Nations' human rights and anti-discrimination conventions provides additional, formal protections. Most of the rights are, however, individual rather than collective ones, so the onus is on individuals to make representations when they feel their rights have been abused (Henry et al. 2000).

Whether adopting a definition of racism limited to discriminatory behaviour based only on physical appearance, or a broader one which would cover discrimination against any ethnic or 'racial' group, racism has certainly been present in Canada, to a greater or lesser degree, throughout the twentieth century (and before) both in official and popular discourse. Li (2003) summarizes public opinion poll results during the past quarter century, which suggest that Canadian government immigration, multiculturalism and employment equity policies have introduced material changes without associated attitudinal changes having necessarily occurred. Other research confirms continuing experiences of discrimination – and resistance – by Caribbean immigrants (for example: Calliste 1991, 1993; Bobb-Smith 2003; Daenzer 1993; Henry 1994; Henry et al. 2000; Greenaway 2004; Mensah 2002; Silvera 1989; Bakan and Stasiulis 1997; Agnew 1996).

Against this backdrop we turn now to a selective consideration of the various dimensions of citizenship, highlighting their salience for Caribbean women immigrants, whether as women or as members of a particular origin category among (women) immigrants.

The Civil Dimension of Citizenship

According to Marshall (1992 [1950]) civil dimensions of citizenship include 'the rights necessary for individual freedom – liberty of the person, freedom of speech,

---

10   Space considerations preclude an analysis of provincial employment legislation.

thought and faith, the right to own property and to conclude valid contracts, and the right to justice' (p. 8), and 'individual economic freedom' (p. 11). As already noted, economic citizenship will be treated separately because of its importance. Freedom from discrimination could be considered as an additional civil right.

When, as feminists, we consider the variable 'liberty of the person,' we specify some elements which would be unproblematic for (most) men. These include the right to education, the right to livelihood, the control of one's own body and freedom of movement, all of which (along with freedom from discrimination) crosscut the civil and social dimensions of citizenship, with the rights to education, livelihood and freedom from discrimination also crosscutting the economic dimensions. These last three will be discussed in later sections of this article.

Making life choices – including whether, when, how frequently and with whom to enter an intimate relationship, choices about procreation and other aspects of bodily integrity – have been less problematically the right of men than of women, although in Canada and, to a certain extent in the Caribbean (Denis 2003; Pargass and Clarke 2003; Robinson 2003), women have greater access to these rights than in many other societies. Liberty of person also entails freedom of association, choice of one's place of residence, and safe movement in public places. Gender inequality in earning increases women's dependence on public transport (with the constraints on freedom of movement that entails) and limits their housing choices. The average earnings[11] of Caribbean women reflect their disadvantage as women, immigrants and 'visible minorities' (Munihiri-Kagiye 1999; Boyd 1975, 1992). The Canadian practice of only assessing the eligibility of the family head (with the default category being the husband) as an independent immigrant has militated against sponsored immigrant women's autonomous choice of their place of residence (Côté et al. 2001; Ng and Ramirez 1981). More dramatically, as was discussed above, the obligation to live in their place of employment, imposed on women who enter Canada under the residential care-givers or domestic workers programmes, constitutes a clear infringement of this right, which has affected substantial numbers of Caribbean women (Bakan and Stasiulis 1997; Bobb-Smith 2003; Calliste 1991; Silvera 1989; Arat-Koc 1999a).

Racial prejudice and discrimination, whether individual or systemic, affect Caribbean women immigrants, together with men and other women who belong to 'visible minorities.' Exclusion from housing, the (non) recognition of credentials and of professional experience, and differential treatment as customers and clients are the forms of discrimination most frequently directly experienced by Caribbean women (Bobb-Smith 2003; Henry 1994; Henry and Ginzberg 1985; Henry et al. 2000). They are also directly affected by racism in the media and in the schools,[12] and indirectly, by racism in policing. Like other women in Canada, they are also affected by sexism in the media.

---

11   When controls for education and occupation are introduced in analysis.
12   See the discussion of education in the section on social rights below.

Finally, there is the right to justice. An aspect that remains problematic for women in Canada is the right to justice when a victim of male violence, whether spousal assault, sexual harassment or rape, to name only three possibilities. It is as if women are conceived of as 'really wanting' such attention or that men have the right to sexually use their wives – their chattels – as they see fit and, to a slightly lesser extent, any other women. These issues have been contested in Canada since the 1970s. Within the Caribbean, 'violence against women is embedded in the context of cultural, socio-economic and political power relations with male domination reducing women to economic and emotional dependency' (Pargass and Clarke 2003: 39-40). Legal reform acknowledging it largely dates from the 1990s, (Pargass and Clarke 2003; Robinson 2003). That violence against women has become a matter of public debate more recently in the Commonwealth Caribbean than in Canada has probably resulted in its legitimacy as an issue remaining even more problematic within the diasporic Caribbean community, for women as well as for men, than it remains in the ideological system of the dominant Canadian society. Their rejection of the perceived anti-male bias (and racism – or at least the lack of engagement with anti-racism) of the Canadian women's movement has limited alliances by feminist immigrants from the Caribbean with the 'main-stream' Canadian women's movement on this issue (Bobb-Smith 2003).

The Political Dimension of Citizenship

Consensus seems greatest about the material manifestations of political citizenship. In Canada, it is the main one which distinguishes the rights of permanent residents[13] from those holding a Canadian passport. It is now possible in Canada to hold two passports, providing this is also permitted in the other society.[14] Materially, political citizenship includes the right to vote independently, to stand for and hold elected political office, and to be named by the government to appointed positions in local, national, regional or international political institutions. By the mid-twentieth century in Canada, the universal franchise existed nationally for all adults, who were citizens by either birth or by application, women as well as men, without differentiation by race, property ownership or literacy.[15]

Yet both material and ideological factors constrain women's standing for office, being elected or being appointed. These factors can partly be traced back to the woman's actual or perceived role as a carer.[16] This role results in a lack of time. There has also been the perceived social unacceptability of its combination with a

---

13   Except for those who are sponsored.

14   Countries of the Commonwealth Caribbean also permit dual citizenship, although it seems that some immigrants from the Caribbean do not realize this, and consequently have not applied for Canadian citizenship (Henry 1994).

15   Except, by 2005, for those who are incarcerated.

16   The expression is used to distinguish a person providing unpaid care-giving work from the one doing the same category of work for pay (a care-giver).

time-consuming political role, especially for women with dependent children. This unacceptability can make the committed backing of a political party more difficult for women to obtain. Their own relative lack of money, often the result of unequal pay, occupational segregation, and the time constraints of their multiple roles, can be a further constraint. Whether due to the perception of women as incapable (because of a lack of knowledge, a lack of rationality or a lack of time, for instance) of fulfilling important positions, and or a lack of awareness by those making the appointments that there are any 'well qualified' women to consider, women, especially those who are not citizens by birth and are not of Northern European origin,[17] have been in the minority of such appointments. Finally male-based informal networks, and profiles of competence based on typical male career paths also militate against women having the opportunity to exercise fully their political citizenship rights and obligations. The net result in Canada has been that less than a quarter of the seats in Parliament are held by women (UNDP 2003: table 23).

Further research is required to determine whether being an immigrant from the Caribbean operates as an additional constraint especially for women, or whether these women have experienced fewer constraints. Despite there having been several notable women in positions of political authority in the post-independence Commonwealth Caribbean, in 1998 women's participation in political decision-making within the Caribbean averaged 28 per cent of the members in the appointed Upper Houses and 12 per cent of the members in the elected Lower Houses (Vassell 2003). In Canada, only a few women of Caribbean origin have served as cabinet ministers federally and provincially, and been appointed to the Senate. Black (2003: 63) reports that there were only two women who were members of visible minorities elected to the House of Commons in 1993, and four in each of the elections in 1997 and 2000. Separate figures for Blacks from the Caribbean are not given.

The Social Dimension of Citizenship

The legitimacy of a social dimension of citizenship, articulated mainly since the mid-twentieth century, has varied across democratic societies, and has recently been the object of severe attacks by the neo-liberal Right, including in Canada. The institutions Marshall identified as most closely connected with this dimension were the educational system and social services. Other authors have since created an equation between the social dimension of citizenship and the welfare state. This equation is only partial, if one wants to include institutions connected with cultural expression within the social dimension: to do so would not be inconsistent with Marshall's including the 'right to share to the full in the social heritage' of the society. In the present analysis, then, the institutions of the welfare state are included, but not just these institutions.

---

17   Especially British.

Education[18] is a key variable which crosscuts the civil, economic and social dimensions of citizenship, and is of crucial importance for women, affording them access to knowledge and the development of various skills, and thus offering them a wider variety of bases for earning a livelihood. At the same time, the literature documents that, due to both material and ideological constraints, women have not had access to as wide a range of education and training as men, in the Commonwealth Caribbean or in Canada. Frequently also it seems that they, to a greater extent than men, have required formal certification in order to have their expertise acknowledged, a fact which makes their access to education all the more important if they are to enjoy full citizenship (Bailey 2003; Coderre et al. 1999). Societal belief systems, with their often unacknowledged, patriarchal foundations no doubt help to explain this difference, and the ghettoization in 'caring' or 'serving' fields that women have experienced until quite recently (Denis et Heap 2000; Denis 2001).

In the case of women who have immigrated to Canada from the Caribbean after early childhood, it is necessary to consider how the ideological and material aspects of the gender system in the country where they spent their childhood will have influenced their access to education. In general, until much more recently than in Canada, there has been less access for girls than for boys to education in the Caribbean. At the same time, education has been highly valued there as a means of social mobility by and for both women and men. There continues to be a gender differentiation in specializations within and beyond secondary school (Bailey 2003; Barriteau 2003). Given the criteria used in the points system, both educational attainment and field of specialization have implications for the ability of Caribbean women to enter Canada as independent immigrants.

The non-recognition or under-valuing of credentials by Canadian employers is a further impediment for Caribbean women (Bobb-Smith 2003; Calliste 1993; Henry 1994), one that they share with their male counterparts and with other immigrants of colour, including some with North American or European credentials (Canada 1984). Differences between educational cultures and (possibly unconscious) racism, including 'othering' have resulted in unduly low expectations of Caribbean children in Canada, an erroneous perception that parents are not interested in their children's academic performance, and difficulties in adaptation to Canadian schools (Kelly 1998; Bobb-Smith 2003; James 2000). Women have been active volunteers in various programmes that the Caribbean-Canadian community has established to counter negative stereotypes and improve student performance. Such activity, including lobbying for the development of anti-racist training for teachers and social service providers, is an example of claims to entitlements for a collectivity. Claims by the Canadian women's movement for the elimination of de facto sexism within

---

18   Although in modern, (post) industrial society, it is formal education, training (including apprenticeships) and certification that play a crucial role, in both developing and developed societies, informal education can also be key. Access to both are among the means of gate-keeping that can determine to what extent the theoretical right to the exercise of full citizenship can also be an actual right.

the ostensibly gender neutral school also reflect claims as a collectivity rather than as individuals.

The right to a livelihood is another variable that crosscuts the civil, the social and the economic dimensions. To fully enjoy liberty of person, including being able to make one's own life choices entails having an autonomous means of livelihood, from some combination of employment, social entitlements, investments and inheritance, which one is accorded as an individual, not as a socially defined appendage (for instance as the economic dependent of a male partner). Otherwise we are assuming that the family is a homogeneous entity whose members share equally the rights and obligations relative to its resources and also share equally in decision-making regarding their allocation. This is patently not the case. Within welfare states, including Canada, the right to livelihood is acknowledged, providing, in theory, the right to not be financially dependent. In practice, however, in Canada entitlements, such as old age security, tax credits for dependents, and welfare payments, have become increasingly dependent on *family* income. Exclusions from entitlements, to which family class immigrants (often women) are subject for up to ten years, have already been mentioned.

If one is expected to support others (such as, but not limited to, one's children), then citizenship could entail receiving additional entitlements on their behalf. However, when the expectation of providing support relates to those who are themselves not citizens within Canada,[19] the added costs do not entail added entitlements. This can increase the costs experienced by women immigrants from the Caribbean, since sending home remittances (in cash or kind), whether to support children still resident in the Caribbean or to assist other relatives, remains an important expectation of the diasporic community.

A number of the (more lucrative) entitlements within the Canadian welfare state are based on financial contributions to the relevant funds – workers' compensation, disability benefits, and contributory pensions. Consequently, those providing unpaid labour in the community, for instance as carers or volunteers of other sorts, are ineligible, despite the social contributions they are making. Some theorists therefore argue that the right to benefits should not be dependent at all on having made financial contributions, a position which proponents of neo-liberalism vigorously reject, stressing, instead, individual self-sufficiency.

If it is accepted that children are a social, not an individual good, then having a coherent and inclusive child care policy implemented through appropriate, and adequately funded child care institutions should be a necessary component of the welfare state that allows all citizens the right to an autonomous livelihood, in this case by facilitating the participation of women as well as men in the labour market. Furthermore, already having dependent children should not be a basis for exclusion,

---

19 I am thinking here both of remittances and support for those one has sponsored during the three to ten years of their financial dependency. Until it ends, they cannot access the financial entitlements enjoyed by those not subject to sponsorship agreements (for example: pensions, some types of social or health services).

as has been the case in some of the programmes of temporary authorization for domestic workers from the Caribbean (Daenzer 1993). Social citizenship rights of mothers are being threatened by neo-liberal 'workfare' policies being introduced in Canada: extending to all but the mothers of very young children the obligation of employment or study in order to receive welfare benefits seems to deny the contributions to society of mothering.

A further right of citizens is the right to health, as access both to medical services in the case of illness, and to the resources needed to promote wellness: immunization, good nutrition, exercise. In keeping with the principles enunciated at the World Population Conference at Cairo in 1994 (see www.iisd.ca/cairo.html), for women, health also involves the right to make choices about biological reproduction within a safe, healthy environment for the foetus, the mother and the infant, something that is becoming threatened in Canada. While feminists in the Caribbean actively supported these same principles at the World Population Conference, the extent to which Caribbean women enjoy them, whether by law or in practice, varies among the islands: values on the relevant indicators range from levels similar to those for Canada to ones that are much lower (UNDP 2003).

Turning, finally, to cultural aspects of social citizenship, it can be argued that the Canadian multiculturalism policy has supported the maintenance of forms of artistic expression from immigrants' countries of origin, even when immigration policies subvert other cultural traditions, such as the multi-generational female support networks widely found in the Caribbean (Barrow 1996). Changes from core to project funding, and a re-orientation of the latter to stress communication to other parts of the Canadian community about the 'minority' culture now tie state funding, however, to a reference community that is broader than those sharing common ethnic origins. I am not aware of research that has examined the dynamics for the defining and implementing of within-community objectives. Such studies will be necessary in order to evaluate the impact of multicultural policy on this aspect of social citizenship of Caribbean women.

The Economic Dimension of Citizenship

Marshall did not distinguish an economic dimension of citizenship. Perhaps in the case of men this was in some way taken for granted, with the social dimension offering alternative means of livelihood when employment was not available. His lack of attention to this dimension may also reflect Turner's (1990) criticism that Marshall did not really address social and, especially, economic inequalities and their contradictions with the formal political equality of having the franchise. For women, however, the economic dimension of citizenship is crucial, both because it is one means of obtaining a livelihood and because it has been the site of so much exclusion and inequity for women. The institutions of most relevance to this dimension are those in which people work for pay or profit in the public, the para-public, the private and the not-for-profit sectors. The constituents of this dimension of citizenship are often hotly contested, when they are not simply ignored. In her useful discussion of ECONSOC rights (economic, cultural and social rights related to work), Rosemarie Antoine (1997) distinguishes three components: the right to work, the right to just remuneration and the right to safe and healthy working conditions. An additional right, I would suggest, is the right to organize (and, by extension, to strike).

This right of association is an extension of the civil right of freedom of speech, thought, and faith. It enables workers to become informed about their rights (especially since these are not always respected), and about national and international practices, including discrepancies between the treatment – in terms of wages, benefits, working conditions and opportunities for training and advancement – of different groups. It also enables workers to reduce the power imbalance between themselves and their employers by collective negotiation. It is particularly important for immigrants, due to their initial lack of familiarity with the laws and norms of the new country. It is also hard to implement in the case of such geographically dispersed workers as live-in domestic workers (Daenzer 1993; Li 2003), an important occupational category for Caribbean women until the 1990s (Calliste 1991). Although not an accredited union, INTERCEDE has been an important NGO of live-in domestic workers. With the support of solidary Canadian feminists, it has effectively lobbied against some of the more discriminatory legislation related to temporary domestic workers (Daenzer 1993; Agnew 1996; Bakan and Stasiulis 1997).

The right to work, Antoine argues (1997), entails equal access to employment, without discrimination based on gender or other characteristics such as race/ethnicity or marital status, or childbearing, actual or potential. Statistics documenting the greater occupational segregation of women than of men, and the differential occupational distribution of women on the basis of birthplace and ethnicity/race, and qualitative material demonstrate that this has been a particular problem for women, including women who have emigrated from the Caribbean (Armstrong and Armstrong 1994; Bobb-Smith 2003; Denis and Heap 2000; Munihiri-Kagiye 1999).

Exclusions can be materially based, though premised on an ideology regarding gender relations within marriage, which implies that the responsibilities of being a wife preclude the execution of a demanding paid position, or on ideological assumptions regarding the need to protect women's morality and their person. It is interesting that these exclusions have typically applied in situations where women would be in competition with men for the job and in situations where the jobs are more desirable ones. Their absence regarding live-in domestic or care-giving work, which can be (and is) a threatening work environment has been interpreted as providing the means to meet the needs of privileged Canadians, both women and men (Arat-Koc 1999a; Silvera 1989).

Discriminatory exclusion can also take a less official, but no less effective form, when it is effected by means of the transmission of attitudes which define certain occupations as 'unwomanly' so that most women simply do not consider entering them, or as unsuitable for those of specific ethnic/racial origins, or as the only ones suitable for women of a particular ethnic origin (Denis and Heap 2000). Originally defined as 'naturally' warm care-givers, for instance, Caribbean women have more recently been defined as 'too uppity' to be desirable domestic employees (Calliste 1991). Calliste's research has also documented that whereas the admission of nurses from the Caribbean was initially justified by their being women of 'exceptional merit,' in fact they have tended to be consigned to the most arduous and least desirable jobs in the hospitals where they are employed (Calliste 1993).

The right to work, Antoine continues, entails not only obtaining initial access to employment, but also not experiencing discrimination in relation to job opportunities and not being under-employed (Bobb-Smith 2003). The right to work also includes the right not to be prevented from having full-time employment. It is more likely to generate the means for an adequate livelihood than are part-time or other non-standard forms of employment. Formal or informal exclusion from it suggests that the assumption of a male breadwinner model is informing both community attitudes and practices, to the disadvantage of women, especially since employment benefits and opportunities for advancement are often limited to those with full-time standard positions. And much of the non-standard work is involuntary, not freely chosen. Analysis of non-standard work has not, to date, differentiated among women in terms of ethnicity and immigration status, so that the particular positioning of Caribbean immigrant women remains unexamined.

The right to just remuneration also involves several component parts. Most fundamentally – and probably most contentiously – there is the right to equal pay for work of equal value. Women in Canada do not enjoy this right, and immigrant women from the Caribbean fare worse than their male counterparts and non-Black Canadian-born women (Munihiri-Kagiye 1999). Just remuneration also includes job-related benefits, such as parental leave, health care benefits for self, partner and dependants, pension, survivors' benefits, leave benefits for self, partner and dependants. Of these, maternity/paternity leave is really the only one for which differential treatment of men and women could be justified, due to the demands on women associated with pregnancy, birth and nursing. That paternity leave is virtually unrecognized as an economic right clearly indicates the ideological exclusion of men from the responsibilities of the carer (as distinct from the economic) role of parenting. For women, provisions related to maternity leave cannot only be conceptualized as a job-related benefit, but also as part of equal access to employment, as part of safe and healthy working conditions (the next variable in the economic dimension to be discussed), and as a variable within the social right to health, one aspect of the social dimension of citizenship already discussed. Arguments supporting the right to maternity benefits recognize that child bearing makes a contribution to the community or society as well as one to the individual, without, however, positing that bearing children is an obligation for all women.

A final set of variables are those related to the right to safe and healthy working conditions. These can include the right to holidays, rest days, and rest periods during the working day, with appropriate installations at the work place for eating and rest periods. As already mentioned, it implies the right of maternity leave. Finally, it includes the right to protection from work-related disease and hazards. This last is a contentious point for feminists, since the 'need' for protective legislation for women has been used as a justification for excluding women from particular (often relatively remunerative) types of jobs. When invoked in the case of women, protective legislation has usually related to their child-bearing capacity: this definition of them as a child-bearing vessel that must be protected, rather than as a human being whose health might be endangered by particular working conditions, explains why protective legislation has been contested. It reflects a social definition of women that does not conceive of them as autonomous beings, who can be citizens in their own right.

In Canada the public sector, which is subject to state control, has been the pioneer in extending economic citizenship rights to women. Even in it, however, these rights have not been fully and consistently extended to women or to members of 'visible minorities' and other designated groups under employment equity legislation (Abella 1984; Canada 1984). Access to employment, training, promotion, and equal pay continue to be contentious issues. That some of these economic rights for women remain problematic in the public sector and are even more so in the private sector implies that the male breadwinner/female housewife and carer model remains ideologically strong, however little it is reflected in day-to-day material reality.

What requires further analysis, though, are the effects of the intersection of this ideology with that of the Afro-Caribbean woman as an economically autonomous being. Has the impact of the latter ideology been the same for Afro-Caribbean immigrant women of different social classes in Canada, despite the fact that 'housewifeization' (Mies 1986) became a dominant ideology in the Caribbean from the late 1930s through the 1960s and 1970s, – an ideal for all, although attainable mainly by the middle class of all races (Denis 2001; Barriteau 2001)? Has this ideology affected the experiences of Afro-Caribbean immigrant women as distinct from immigrant women of other origins? Unfortunately there are presently more questions than answers. Certainly their labour force participation rates have been among the highest for women of any ethnic/birthplace groups (for example, Statistics Canada, n.d.). Most are employees, rather than self-employed (unless, as is not uncommon in the Caribbean (Freeman 2000), their main occupation is waged, but they also have, as a secondary source of livelihood, a micro or small business). My preliminary analyses of census data since 1961 indicate that Caribbean immigrant women[20] have consistently been underrepresented, compared with the female labour force as a whole, in agriculture and in manufacturing. They have been overrepresented in service and professional occupations, although by 1996[21] in both of these and in clerical occupations their representation has become similar to that of the overall Canadian female labour force. It is only when qualitative research complements what can be learned from the Census and the Statistics Canada Ethnic

---

20 According to Brand (1999: 89), the majority of Black women in Canada (whatever their place of birth) 'were excluded from the white women's traditional occupations of clerical, secretarial and sales work until the late sixties and seventies'.

21 The PUMF files for the 2001 Census are not yet available.

Diversity Study[22] that it will be possible to begin to answer the questions I have raised. For the moment, with rare exceptions (most notably Calliste 1991, 1993; Bobb-Smith 2003; and some (1994) of Henry's work) it is difficult to tease out what applies specifically to Afro-Caribbean immigrant women, since many studies do not differentiate among the 'visible minority' immigrant women they examine, do not differentiate between Canadian-born and immigrant women of a particular ethnic origin, or have focussed on women of another ethnicity or from another region.

Concluding Remarks

In this first foray into the development of a framework for an analysis of citizenship of Commonwealth Caribbean immigrant women in Canada, I have, implicitly, concentrated on the Canadian nation state as community, although I have pointed out that a community can exist on different levels, from the local to the international (both diasporic and in the country of origin). I have also concentrated on the rights, rather than the obligations of citizenship, defining rights with reference to the capacity for full participation in the community. It is clear, however, that in terms of gender, women do not, at the present, enjoy the possibility of full participation. This raises a vexing concern with regard to obligations: how are they defined, by whom and in terms of what principles? I concur with Barriteau (2001) when I posit that, despite significant material changes, the definition of women is informed by the patriarchal principles which remain strong at the ideological level (Barriteau 2001) and, as I have shown, continue to exert an influence on the material level. A discussion of obligations of citizenship for women would undoubtedly require a re-definition of the obligations of citizenship for men. This assumes that women's (and men's) obligations are to be articulated in terms of their being autonomous individuals, actively involved in their individual and collective citizenship projects, rather than as people who are defined solely or primarily in terms of their relationships with others and the responsibilities that these relationally defined locations entail (Lister 1997).

Turning to ethnic relations, while the State has the right to determine who will be admitted on a temporary or long term basis,[23] the bases on which these decisions are made can be interrogated. The declared national self-interest of a capitalist society, rather than altruism has consistently had primacy in Canada, but within the last decade the definition of this self interest seems to have narrowed, to a much stronger focus on the individual's anticipated economic self-sufficiency and a dilution of humanist and humanitarian considerations. Changing emphases in the discourse about and implementation of multiculturalism reflects the same shift (Abu-Laban and Gabriel 2002; Das Gupta 1999). Furthermore, even if it is not extensive, research on Canadians of Caribbean origin indicates the continuing impact of material and

---

22 The data file from this survey should be released during 2005.

23 As a signatory of United Nations Conventions and of bilateral and multilateral trade agreements, Canada has relinquished some of that authority.

ideological factors (both from Canada and the Caribbean) constraining their full enjoyment of the rights of citizenship, their resistance to these constraints, and the need to explore further the intersection of 'race'/ethnicity and birthplace with such factors as socio-economic status and gender. The impact of possibly contradictory claims resulting from membership in multiple communities – sub-national, cross national and supra-national remains a subject for both theoretical and empirical study.

References

Abella, R. (1984), *Equality in Employment. A Commission Report*, Ministry of Supply and Services, Ottawa.

Abu-Laban, Y. and Gabriel, C. (2002), *Selling Diversity: Immigration, Multiculturalism, Employment Equity and Globalization*, Broadview Press, Peterborough.

Agnew, V. (1996), *Resisting Discrimination: Women from Asia, Africa, and the Caribbean and the Women's Movement*, University of Toronto Press, Toronto.

Anderson, W.W. (1993), *Caribbean Immigrants: A Socio-Demographic Profile*, Scholars' Press, Toronto.

Antoine, R-M. (1997), 'Constructing a Legal Framework for Securing Economic, Social and Cultural Rights for Women Workers, with Particular Reference to Structural Adjustment and the Caribbean,' *Caribbean Law Review*, Vol. 7(2), pp. 534-87.

Arat-Koc, S. (1999a), 'Gender and Race in "Non-discriminatory" Immigration Policies in Canada: 1960s to the Present,' in E. Dua and A. Robertson (eds), *Scratching the Surface: Canadian Anti-Racist Feminist Thought*, Women's Press, Toronto, pp. 207-33.

Arat-Koc, S. (1999b), 'Neo-liberalism, State Restructuring and Immigration Changes in Canada,' *Journal of Canadian Studies*, Vol. 34(2), pp. 31-56.

Armstrong, P. and Armstrong, H. (1994), *The Double Ghetto* (3rd edition), McClelland and Stewart, Toronto.

Bailey, B. (2003), 'The Search for Gender Equity and Empowerment of Caribbean Women: The Role of Education,' in G. Tang Nain and B. Bailey (eds), *Gender Equality in the Caribbean: Reality or Illusion*, Ian Randle Publishers, Kingston, Jamaica, pp. 108-45.

Bakan, A. and Stasiulis, D. (eds) (1997), *Not One of the Family*, University of Toronto Press, Toronto.

Barriteau, E. (2003), 'Requiem for the Male Marginalization Thesis in the Caribbean: Death of a Non-Theory,' in E. Barriteau (ed.), *Confronting Power, Theorizing Gender*, University of the West Indies Press, Kingston, Jamaica, pp. 324-55.

Barriteau, E. (2001), *The Political Economy of Gender in the Twentieth-Century Caribbean*, Palgrave, Basingstoke, England.

Barriteau, E. and Denis, A. (2001), 'A Framework for an Analysis of Citizenship in the Anglophone Caribbean,' International Sociological Association First Regional Conference for Latin America and the Caribbean, Margarita Island, Venezuela.

Barrow, C. (1996), *Family in the Caribbean: Theories and Perspectives*, Ian Randle Publishers and James Currey Publishers, Kingston, Jamaica, Oxford.

Black, J. (2003), 'Differences That Matter: Minority Women MPs, 1993-2000,' in M. Tremblay and L. Trimble (eds), *Women and Electoral Politics in Canada*, Oxford University Press, Don Mills, ON, pp. 59-74

Bobb-Smith, Y. (2003), *I Know Who I Am*, Scholars' Press/Women's Press, Toronto.

Boyd, M. (1997), 'Migration Policy, Female Dependency, and Family Membership: Canada and Germany,' in P. Evans and G. Wekerle (eds), *Women and the Canadian Welfare State: Challenges and Change*, University of Toronto Press, Toronto, pp. 142-69.

Boyd, M. (1992), 'Gender, Visible Minority and Immigrant Earnings Inequality: Assessing an Employment Equity Premise,' in V. Satzewich (ed.), *Deconstructing a Nation: Immigration, Multiculturalism and Racism in the 1990s*, Fernwood, Halifax, pp. 279-34.

Boyd, M. (1975), 'The Status of Immigrant Women in Canada,' *Canadian Review of Sociology and Anthropology*, Vol. 12(4), Part 1, pp. 406-16.

Brand, D. (1999), 'Black Women and Work,' in E. Dua and A. Robertson (eds), *Scratching the Surface: Canadian Anti-Racist Feminist Thought*, Women's Press, Toronto, pp. 83-96.

Calliste, A. (1993), 'Women of "Exceptional Merit:" Immigration of Caribbean Nurses to Canada,' *Canadian Journal of Women and the Law*, Vol. 6(1), pp. 131-48.

Calliste, A. (1991), 'Canada's Immigration Policy and Domestics from the Caribbean: The Second Domestic Scheme' in J. Vorst et al. (eds), *Race, Class and Gender: Bonds and Barriers*, Garamond Press and Society for Socialist Studies, Toronto.

Canada. House of Commons (1984), *Equality Now: Report of the Special Committee on Visible Minorities in Canadian Society*, Ottawa.

Carens, J. (2000), *Culture, Citizenship and Community*, Oxford University Press, Oxford, New York.

Coderre, C., Denis, A. and Andrew, C. (1999), *Femmes de carrière, carrière de femmes: étude des trajectoires familiales, scolaires et professionnelles des gestionnaires québécoises et ontariennes*, Presses de l'Université d'Ottawa, Ottawa.

Côté, A., Kérisit, M., and Côté, M-L. (2001), *Sponsorship ... for Better or for Worse: The Impact of Sponsorship on the Equality Rights of Immigrant Women*, Status of Women Canada, Ottawa.

Creese, G. and Kambere, E. N. (2003), 'What Colour is your English?,' *Canadian Review of Sociology and Anthropology*, Vol. 40(5), pp. 565-73.

Daenzer, P. (1993), *Regulating Class Privilege*, Canadian Scholars' Press, Toronto.

Das Gupta, T. (1999), 'The Politics of Multiculturalism. "Immigrant Women" and the Canadian State,' in E. Dua and A. Robertson (eds), *Scratching the Surface.*

Canadian, Anti-racist, Feminist Thought, Women's Press, Toronto, pp. 187-205.

Denis, A. (2003), 'A Gendered Analysis of the Impact on Women's Work of Changing State Policies in Barbados,' in C. Barrow-Giles and D. Marshall (eds), *Living at the Borderlines*, Ian Randle, Kingston, Jamaica, pp. 165-83.

Denis, A. (2001), 'Whither Work? A Comparative Analysis of Women and Work in the Commonwealth Caribbean and Canada in the New Era of Globalization,' *Working Paper No. 6*, Centre for Gender and Development Studies, University of the West Indies, Cave Hill, Barbados.

Denis, A. and Heap, R. (2000), 'Le corps des femmes dans la construction des savoirs et des savoirs-faire. Éducation et travail rémunéré des femmes au Canada, 19e-20e siècles,' dans sous la direction de S. Frigon et M. Kérisit, *Du corps des femmes*, Collection Études des femmes, Les Presses de l'Université d'Ottawa, Ottawa, pp. 15-56.

Dobrowolsky, A. (2001), 'Identity and Rights Reclaimed: Appreciating and Assessing Aboriginal Women's Interventions in Canada,' *Papers in Social Theory*, Vol. 6, pp. 59-84.

Freeman, C. (2000), *High Tech and High Heels in the Global Economy,* Duke University Press, Durham N.C., London.

Greenaway, N. (2004), '1 in 3 Canadian blacks claims to have faced discrimination,' *The Ottawa Citizen*, March 10: A5.

Hawkins, F. (1988), *Canada and Immigration* (2nd edition), University of Toronto Press, Toronto.

Henry, F. (1994), *The Caribbean Diaspora in Toronto: Learning to Live with Racism*, University of Toronto Press, Toronto.

Henry, F. and Ginzberg, E. (1985), *Who Gets the Work: A Test of Racial Discrimination in Employment*, Social Planning Council and Urban Alliance on Race Relations, Toronto.

Henry, F., Tator, C., Mallis, W. and Rees, T. (2000), *The Colour of Democracy* (2nd edition), Harcourt Canada, Toronto.

Hobson, B. and Lister, R. (2002), 'Citizenship,' in B. Hobson, J. Lewis and B. Siim (eds), *Contested Concepts in Gender and Social Politics*, Edward Elgar, Cheltenham, UK and Northampton, MA, pp. 23-54.

James, C. (ed.) (2000), *Experiencing Difference,* Fernwood, Halifax.

Juteau, D. (ed.) (2003), *Social Differentiation*, University of Toronto Press, Toronto.

Kelly, J. (1998), *Under the Gaze. Learning to be Black in White Society*, Fernwood, Halifax.

Kymlicka, W. (1995), *Multicultural Citizenship*, Clarendon Press, Oxford.

Li, P. (2003), *Destination Canada,* Oxford University Press, Toronto.

Lister, R. (1997), 'Citizenship: Towards a Feminist Synthesis,' *Feminist Review*, Vol. 57, pp. 28-48.

Lister, R. (1995), 'Dilemmas in engendering citizenship,' *Economy and Society*, Vol. 24(1) pp. 1-40.

Marshall, T. H (1992) [1950], 'Citizenship and Social Class,' in T.H. Marshall and

Tom Bottomore, *Citizenship and Social Class*, Pluto Press, London, pp. 3-51.

Mensah, J. (2002), *Black Canadians*, Fernwood, Halifax.

Mies, M. (1986), *Patriarchy and Accumulation on a World Scale*, Zed, London.

Munihiri-Kagiye, G. (1999), *La discrimination systémique en Ontario : le cas des femmes des « minorités visibles » immigrantes*, Université d'Ottawa, these de maîtrise, Ottawa.

Ng, R. and Ramirez, J. (1981), *Immigrant housewives in Canada, A report,* Immigrant Women's Centre, Toronto.

Pargass, G. and Clarke, R. (2003), 'Violence Against Women: A Human Rights Issue. Post Beijing Five Year Review,' in G. Tang Nain and B. Bailey (eds), *Gender Equality in the Caribbean: Reality or Illusion,* Ian Randle Publishers, Kingston, Jamaica, pp. 39-72.

Robinson, T. (2003), 'Beyond the Bill of Rights: Sexing the Citizens,' in E. Barriteau (ed.), *Confronting Power, Theorizing Gender,* University of the West Indies Press, Mona, Jamaica, pp. 231-61.

Satzewich, V. (1989), 'Racism and Canadian Immigration Policy: The Government's View of Caribbean Migration, 1962-1966,' *Canadian Ethnic Studies*, Vol. XXI(1), pp. 77-97.

Silvera, M. (1989), *Silenced* (2nd edition), Sister Vision Press, Toronto.

Smith, C. L. (1999), 'Is Citizenship a Gendered Concept?' in A. Cairns, J. Courtney and P. MacKinnon (eds), *Citizenship, Diversity and Pluralism*, McGill-Queens University Press, Montreal, Kingston, pp. 138-62.

Statistics Canada, n.d., *Census of Canada, 1996.*

Turner, B. (1990), 'Outline of a Theory on Citizenship,' *Sociology*, Vol. 24(2), pp.189-218.

UNDP (2003), *Human Development Report 2003*, Oxford University Press, New York and Oxford.

van den Berghe, P. (1978), *Race and Racism*, John Wiley, New York.

Vassell, L. (2003), 'Women, Power and Decision-Making in CARICOM Countries: Moving Forward from a Post-Beijing Assessment,' in G. Tang Nain and B. Bailey (eds), *Gender Equality in the Caribbean: Reality or Illusion.* Ian Randle Publishers, Kingston, Jamaica, pp. 1-38.

Voet, R. (1998), *Feminism and Citizenship*, Sage, London.

Walby, S. (1994), 'Is Citizenship Gendered?,' *Sociology*, Vol. 28(2), pp. 379-95.

Werbner, P. and Yuval-Davis, N. (1999), 'Women and the New Discourse of Citizenship, Introduction' in N. Yuval-Davis and P. Werbner (eds), *Women, Citizenship and Difference*, Zed Books, London, New York, pp. 1-38.

Yuval-Davis, N. (1997), 'Women, Citizenship and Difference,' *Feminist Review*, Vol. 57: 4-27.

Yuval-Davis, N. and Werbner, P. (eds) (1999), *Women, Citizenship and Difference*, Zed Books, London, New York.

Chapter 3

Locating Gendered Subjects in Vocabularies of Citizenship

Pauline Gardiner Barber

... the neutrality of the state works only when a broad cultural homogeneity among the governed can be assumed. This assumption has indeed underpinned western liberal democracies until recently. Under the new multi-cultural conditions, however, this premise seems less and less valid. (Hall 2000: 228)

Introduction

Citizenship defines the relationship between people, governments and national territory, providing the framework for public status and the foundation for achieving state loyalty. But in pluralist societies, cultural identities and transnational loyalties pose challenges to citizenship regimes. This is especially true given the relative ease, for current generations, of maintaining transnational connections for those ((im)migrants and descendants) whose citizenship entails relations to more than one state. Contemporary citizenship dynamics thus include pressure from subjects living in the diaspora, eager to claim the rights and privileges of citizenship in their countries of origin. Alternatively, states that provide 'homes' and citizenship status to diasporic populations face the challenges of social equity and inclusion, and social cohesion. Hence, multi-cultural policies are crucially linked to citizenship dynamics. They provide one means for immigrant-receiving states to promote democratic principles of citizenship, to encourage social tolerance on the part of established citizens and vibrant civic engagement on the part of newcomers. However, as Stuart Hall (2000) notes in the essay cited by way of introduction to this chapter, contemporary citizenship politics, including multi-cultural politics, become mired in contradiction when analyzed in light of the dynamics of cultural difference and resulting social polarities. Multi-cultural policies also reflect national differences and colonial histories, signalling global inequities in political-economy; some nations are magnets for immigrants while others in the 'global south' export labour (see also Pettman 1999).

Drawing examples from struggles over citizenship politics, this chapter explores the gender implications of various idioms of citizenship both in Canada and the Philippines. Next is a theoretical discussion of 'Concepts for Citizenship' introducing relevant critical perspectives (mainly feminist and post-colonial) on citizenship policies. The section 'Philippine Migration Policies/Citizens Dispatched' provides an overview of Philippine processes. 'Cultural racism' and anthropological approaches to citizenship are then proposed as helpful ways of understanding identity politics and the processes of inequality that surround how (im)migrants (sometimes differentiated by gender, class, etc., sometimes not) are positioned in national societies and international labour markets, including in Canada. The following section 'Whose Social Capital' discusses recent policy debates concerning the integration and loyalty of new Canadian immigrants. In 'Filipino Transnational Identities' I pose questions about multi-cultural regulation using Philippine-identified Canadians as a case study. Then, I return to the Philippines (in the sections on 'Philippine Citizenship Politics' and 'Transnational Citizenship') and some recent moments in the public struggles over entitlements. Such struggles are shaped through the messiness of colonial history and the need to accommodate the concerns of the significant gendered labour diaspora, hence the transnational emphasis. My conclusion pulls together the strands of my analysis and summarizes six key ideas.

My purpose is not to examine the linkages between Canada and Philippine migration as such.[1] Rather, I use the comparison – net labour importing and exporting countries – to reflect critically on the regulation and experience of citizenship, its discourses and technologies, in countries positioned differently in the global political economy. In the case of the Philippines, there remains the promise of transnational citizenship providing space for resistance to globalization's inequities – but also the closure of this possibility in concert with fluctuations in migration levels, labour market conditions at home and abroad, and citizenship policies (see Barber 2004). If, as theorists in the liberal tradition remind us, citizenship policy is constructed in terms of national interest, feminist and post-colonial theorists ask how is national interest understood? What are the underlying perceptions and always, how are they gendered? What social processes are presumed and to what end?

Concepts for Citizenship

As several decades of feminist enquiry reveal, citizenship, constituted through political processes and everyday understandings, is an extremely fluid, indeed an unstable concept (Yuval-Davis and Werbner 1999). A core feature of the facile nature of citizenship discourse is the constant temptation to imagine citizenship in western liberal democracies as proffering a neutral political space, unmarked by inequalities based on difference (such as gender, class and ethnicity, sexuality, or cultural practices and religion). Hence a major contribution to critical interrogations of citizenship by

---

1   Citizenship and Immigration Canada report that, in 2003, citizenship grants were extended to 7,766 new Canadians who had been born in the Philippines. In this year, the Philippines ranked as the third top source country, after China and India, for new Canadian citizens (http://www.cic.gc.ca/english/monitor/issue07/05-citizenship.html). Accessed on 24/01/05.

political theorists (for example, Taylor 1994; Kymlicka 1995) exposes the fallacies associated with the liberal imagining of citizenship and its promise of universality. These theorists map the terrain of citizenship as fundamentally characterized by diversity and difference in creative tension with ideals of universal equality in public status and in law. The resulting politics are characterized by a dynamic of social exclusion and an absence of social cohesion, potentially resolvable through a negotiated common political identity space (Taylor 1999).

One could argue that it is the role of political philosophers to construct nation-building imaginaries containing equality scenarios but the sociological realities described in this volume, as well as citizenship policy reform confound such visions. As Canadian feminist scholarship reveals, recent changes to that country's citizenship regime have diminished the opportunities for women's political contestation for full citizenship rights and had a detrimental effect on women's claims for gender equality. For example, neo-liberal economic policies targeting welfare state programmes placed a disproportionate burden of work on women, particularly working class and immigrant women. And funding cutbacks for women's programmes combined with the rhetoric of partnership, narrowed the possibilities for women's particularized activism (Jenson and Phillips 1996). More recent programme priorities have substituted the rights and needs of women with the prioritizing of a children's agenda (Dobrowolsky 2004; Dobrowolsky and Jenson 2004). Furthermore, universalism, as seen in liberal citizenship discourse, often disguises particularist interests. Stuart Hall (2000), cited above from his discussion of the conceptual muddles surrounding multi-cultural governance in British society, offers an excellent example of this insight:

> The post-Enlightenment, liberal, rational, humanist universalism of western culture looks, not less historically significant but, less universal (sic) by the minute. Many great ideas – liberty, equality, autonomy, democracy – have been honed within the liberal tradition. However, it is now clear that liberalism is not the 'culture that is beyond cultures' but the culture that won: that particularism which successfully universalized and hegemonized itself across the globe. Its triumph in virtually setting the limits to the domain of 'the political' was not, in retrospect, the result of a disinterested mass conversion to the Rule of Universal Reason, but something close to a more earthy, Foucauldian, power-knowledge sort of 'game.' There have been theoretical critiques of the 'dark' sides of the Enlightenment project before, but it is 'the multi-cultural question' which has most effectively blown its contemporary cover. (Hall 2000: 228)

Hall goes on to note that: 'The double demand for equality and difference appears to outrun our existing political vocabularies' (Hall 2000: 228). But appearances can be deceiving. Using Barnor Hesse's concept of 'transruptive effects,' Hall's investigation of multicultural politics, leads him to propose a 'new multi-cultural political logic' within a radically recast liberal framework. Bold as this effort is, and certainly Hall offers a more careful deconstruction of keywords such as racism, ethnicity, and culture than many political theorists writing on citizenship, he fails to substantively examine how gender differences sit within his model.

So it seems hardly surprising that feminist overviews of citizenship debates insist that the analytically challenging work of 'engendering' citizenship is far from completed (Smith 1999; Lister 2000). Much of this work continues the post-modern concern with subjectivities and how gender articulates with various other identifications that are meaningful in people's lives as social subjects and citizens. In terms of the sites for empirical work in citizenship studies, much of the research examines immigrant-receiving national or regional contexts, with the European Union providing an important reference point (Hobson 2000). However, some scholars, such as Pettman (1999), seek to unlock place-tied citizenship to imagine the transformations of gendered citizenship given the economic imperatives and international inequalities of globalization. What happens to citizenship, both in terms of the institutional framing of rights, entitlements, and responsibilities for national subjects and their subjective identification, in a context where labour migration is a critical feature of political economy?

Such is the case in the Philippines where by 2002, over 800,000 documented migrants left the country annually, with the capital of Manila functioning as a 'key node in the global circuit of labour' (Tyner 2002: 65). Approximately 70 per cent of these workers are now women. Here, I engage with recent debates about Canadian multicultural policies and in particular research about immigrant loyalties, by considering Philippine migrants' responses to their transnational circumstances. When reversing the lens, I draw upon multi-sited ethnographic research on Philippine labour migration where the citizenship issues remain extraordinarily complex, not the least because of the sizeable labour diaspora but also the large number of Filipinos (around 36 per cent of a total population of 78.6 million) living below the poverty line. Problems of access to labour markets and gendered cultural practices which encourage women's participation in the economy in 'family friendly' ways leave women as the major contributors to the Philippine 'informal sector' (Bonnin 2004). This sector is huge, providing the main source of livelihood for 72 per cent of Filipinos who are not supported through agriculture (International Labour Organization 2002). So along with their informal sector participation, women's labour migration looms large in the future plans of many Philippine households. Here again women, with or without family encouragement, see overseas contract work as a means of boosting household income to educate children, for housing for themselves and/or their parents, and meeting particular needs of other relatives (Barber 2004). Some women migrants also imagine an independent future, free from familial obligation.

The social inequities underlying Canadian citizenship multi-cultural policies are magnified in comparison to countries of the global south like the Philippines, which is now dependent upon labour export policies. Most Philippine labour migrants do not receive employment commensurate with their education and women migrants, in particular, can end up working in households where their female employers have less education than they do (Constable 1997; Barber 2004).

But I also question the assumptions behind changes to citizenship policies in Canada that reflect heightened concern about (im)migrants sense of belonging in Canada. Such concerns are reflected in recent policies, which more explicitly specify the obligations of citizenship (see Firth 2003 discussed in Note 9). Changes to Canadian citizenship policy and the management of diversity are accompanied by the reworking of the emphasis (the purpose) of Canadian multicultural policy. The shift is away from the retention of immigrant cultural heritage to civic participation and an emergent discourse of 'interculturalism,' partly in response to border security issues (Tolley 2004). It is also well established that immigration policies for western nations are closely tied to national economic goals. Such policies are formulated in accord with globally powerful, indeed hegemonically so, neo-liberal economic policies that seem gender-blind but are extremely disadvantageous to women (Abu-Laban and Gabriel 2002) and to all immigrants from the global south. As Li (2004) argues, also drawing on Stuart Hall's work, Canadian citizenship discourse, pre-occupied as it is with how immigrants perform in Canada, both economically and socially, begs the question of how policies perpetuate a symbolic system of representation that racializes non-European immigrants. In the case of Philippine women immigrants entering Canada with visas to work as care-givers,[2] the symbolic representations that racialize their 'otherness' in Canadian society operate within a citizenship regime that valorizes economically powerful migrants who are typically white European males (Abu-Laban and Gabriel 2002). As we shall see, Philippine-born Canadians, nonetheless constitute 'model' citizens in terms of their bi-national loyalties.

---

2   Philippine women and men who travel to Canada on the care-givers visa programme are considered 'professional' care-givers. The CIC Canada website (in January 2005) states that they must be functional in English or French and have the equivalent of a Canadian high school education plus 6 months of full-time training, or 12 months (6 months of which are continuous) of full-time paid employment in a related field. This experience must be within 3 years prior to application for a work permit. They must secure an employer's written contract and undergo medical tests. Care-givers must also navigate Philippine exit visa requirements. Many submit to training and recruitment agencies who promise ease of employment placement and assistance with visa processing at home and abroad. The various fees charged are high indeed and (im)migrants are usually deeply in debt – often to relatives. Money lenders typically have a repayment ratio of paying one additional unit for every five borrowed. The loan agents present in most migrant sending communities are called 5/6ers – borrow 5,000 pesos, pay back 6,000. But the Philippine state now regulates the industry and attempts to standardize exit processes. Despite regulation, placement fees remain problematic. Even licensed agencies commit fee violations. Within Canada, care-givers are required to live-in with their employers for a minimum of 2 years after which they can apply for permanent Canada residency. They are free to change employers providing the employment remains live-in. The logic for this is that supposedly, there is not a shortage of Canadian residents for care-giver work with no live-in requirement! Some Canadians in these jobs are Philippine-born, graduates from the care-giver programme. Those with Care-giver visas may not take on other employment and several have been deported for moonlighting.

Philippine Migration Policies/Citizens Dispatched

Since President Marcos' commitment to a labour export policy in the 1970s, Philippine gendered labour migration has increased dramatically both in scale and geographic scope. While some migrants (both men and women), particularly professionals and skilled workers, continue to leave permanently, there has been an increase in the volume of Philippine women, Filipina, participating in temporary overseas work (Go 2002: 2) a situation which the Philippine state has increasingly relied upon to solve incipient economic and political problems (Gonzales 1998). Official overseas employment statistics place 7.3 million Filipinos working or living permanently abroad. A sizeable group of these people (1.84 million) are estimated to be irregular migrants in that they have left the Philippines carrying tourist visas to disguise their intention to work abroad. This saves the travellers the costs associated with document processing, and often recruitment fees, but it also makes them vulnerable to exploitation and abuse, without official recourse. The flow of migrants has been relatively consistent over the last 5 years. During this period local employment shrank and from 1994-2001 more Filipinos received jobs overseas than there were new jobs created in their local labour markets (Go 2002).

The last 30 years have also witnessed shifts in the destination labour markets for contract workers. For example during the 1980s and 1990s there was an increase in Southeast Asian jobs for Filipinos and a decline in the previously prominent Middle Eastern destinations, fluctuations related to conditions in the national economies of the host countries. The newly industrializing countries in Asia produced a demand for service sector workers, especially women domestic workers, while demand for unskilled male labour in production, transport, and construction declined, translating into a marked and relatively rapid feminization of most migration streams, but especially from the Philippines (Go 1998). Philippine women are preferentially hired as domestic workers, for example in Hong Kong, because they speak English and are relatively well-educated compared to workers from other Southeast Asian countries. However, Philippine women seeking work abroad take care not to present themselves as over-educated least they be perceived as unwilling to subordinate themselves to their employers (Constable 1997; Barber 2004). Philippine migration circuits now also make a wider global sweep taking in most regions of the world with over 130 (some say over 180) countries receiving Filipino workers (Gonzales 1998: 39). But it is perhaps the significant increase in women's migration during the 1980s which has had the greatest impact upon how migration is understood and responded to within the Philippines and its diaspora (see Abrera-Mangahas 1998 and Tsuda 2003).

Remittances make a sizeable contribution to the Philippine economy. Between 1990 and 2001 the average annual total of remittances recorded by the formal banking system was 4,082 billion US dollars which amount to an average of just over 20 per cent of the country's export earnings (Go 2002). Obviously the size of the amounts remitted is tied to migrants' salaries and national economies.[3] It bears repeating that the majority of migrants are now domestic service workers whose productive efforts reveal the global interdependency of productive and socially reproductive labour. The labour of overseas workers holds great value to the Philippine economy – hence the praise heaped upon them – but it is also grossly undervalued in all the ways feminist theory reminds us (see Eviota 1992; Chant and McIlwaine 1995; and Anderson 2000).

By the mid-1990s, the normalization of migration was coming more clearly into view as were the gendered cultural and familial tensions provoked by such reliance (Chant and McIlwaine 1995; Asis 2001; Parreñas 2002). A changed consciousness (culturally and politically) towards migration is marked by shifts in political discourse seen in the ongoing valorization of migrants' heroic contributions (primarily economic) to their families and the nation. Routine reference to the heroic sacrificial migrant collides with – yet paradoxically reinforces – the prominent theme of victimhood characterizing until very recently, most of the writing about Philippine women migrants (see Barber 1997, 2000).[4] One of the many complex factors underscoring the Philippine readings of national emigration is the deep awareness in the country of the varieties of racism, sexism, and labour exploitation to which Filipinos working abroad are subjected. Cultural racism is one feature of the national experience of international labour markets producing what Rafael (2000: 212) calls 'an economy of pity'.

Cultural Racism

Dislodged from its initial disciplinary locations in law, sociology and political studies, reference to citizenship (and rights) is sliding into the conceptual discourse of a wider array of disciplines. For example, anthropologists concerned about displacement and poverty, adopt the term as a means to bypass the homogenizing and reifying implications of well-used concepts such as ethnicity and culture.[5] To speak of culture and suggest a common experience of norms and beliefs within a given population is problematic. Culture becomes conflated with geography and history (in the singular) as if they are cohesively bound, in time, place and individual

---

3   Go (2002) reviews various policy documents to conclude: 'Thus, from managing the flow, government now seeks to actively promote international labor migration as a growth strategy, especially of the higher skilled, knowledge-based workers' (Go 2002: 5). This latter group can be relied upon for higher rates of remittance.

4   My description of Philippine migration policy in this paper also appears in Barber (2004). My heartfelt thanks to Dr Maruja (Marla) Asis in Manila, for generously taking the time, at very short notice, to provide thoughtful commentary on some of my ideas reproduced here.

5   The 2004 annual meetings of the Canadian Anthropology Association focused on citizenship, broadly defined. Some researchers such as Gerald Sider (2003) link citizenship explicitly to a critique of the destructiveness of capitalist political economy.

biography (see Crehan 2002). With all the increased attention to global migrations, various kinds of diaspora formations (Cohen 1997), and the post-colonial insistence on difference, and hybridity, it is no longer possible to assume cultural coherence, nor a common fit between geography, history and culture. (Hybridity is used here in Homi Bhabha's sense of changing those who travel and those who make contact with those who travel, hence native born and immigrants dialogically change each other).[6] The turn to citizenship is thus sometimes seeking a more neutral terrain for examining social inequality of various kinds and evaluating notions of western liberal democracy's appeal, in theory, to commonly held rights.

Similarly, with regards to ethnicity, it is now widely accepted that the presence of socially articulated ethnicities often occurs in contexts of power imbalance, where there are inequities between ethnicities. Yet the subjective experiencing of an ethnicity is not straightforwardly similar for ethnicized subjects, nor are the identifications shared (Hall 2000). Social divisions and power relations – particularly those based on gender – exist within ethnically defined communities making assumptions of sameness and shared spaces problematic, if for no other reason than the internal differentiation is rendered invisible. Differences of gender, class and age should at least suggest the infrequently asked question in so-called immigrant communities; who speaks for whom and what gender is, ethnicity (or citizenship)? Moreover, no ethnicity is primordial (Wilmsen and McAllister 1996; Hall 2000). The impetus to define groups in accord with ethnicity often reflects a power struggle, with the power to define 'other' ethnicities residing with dominant groups and powerful state institutions. For example, public discourse in Canada is littered with such hyphenated ethnicities as Filipino-Canadians, or Arab-Canadians, hardly ever American-Canadians, or British-Canadians.

The socio-political constitution of ethnicities and cultural identity is also apparent in settings where identities are self-proclaimed and/or appear to be indigenous. For example, consider the labelling politics associated with aboriginal, or First Nations people in Canada where it is no longer publicly acceptable to speak simply of Indians.[7] Some struggles over expressions of identity respond to injustices and power differentials, as is the case when 'ethnic minorities' seek purchase from multicultural policies in pluralistic societies such as Canada. But here again social differentiation within groups is erased by homogenizing descriptors of identity. To speak of the Filipino community in Canada denies differences based on class, gender, sexuality, religion, and, importantly, migration histories. This may be inconsequential or not depending upon the issue and response. Cultural racism (for example, Hall 2000) is present when ethnic, linguistic, or cultural markers are taken to be descriptive of a group of immigrants treated with suspicion in immigrant receiving contests;

6   Brah's (1996) notion of 'diaspora space' is relevant here, as is Clifford's (1997) notion of 'contact zone,' and Bauman's (1998) 'tourists and vagabonds.'
7   Jenson (1993) outlines the structuring of political opportunity and identifies the importance of the naming of collective political actors, including Aboriginal peoples, in Canadian nationalist debates.

European societies are rife with such examples. After the events of 11 September 2001 (and the train bombings in Spain, 11 March 2004) concern over immigration and immigrant integration preoccupy major immigrant receiving states such as Canada, the US, Australia and New Zealand. Concepts of culture and ethnicity, used uncritically, become discursively the terrain of marking and maintaining difference in a manner which privileges dominant groups and masks social differences within ethnic communities regardless of the origins of the labels used to flag the ethnicities. I suggest similar processes are at issue with discourses and practices relating to citizenship.[8] At work are new hegemonies and old problems; immigrant groups, defined by cultural differences are marked as 'other' despite their internal social differences of gender and class, and their individually varying commitments to national and transnational projects.

While a conceptual frame of citizenship rights provides one vehicle to critically compare and reference social inequalities within and across national boundaries, there is a disjunction between much academic research and official state practices seeking to define more tightly what citizenship ought to entail; normative citizenship, if you will. For example in Canada, five Metropolis Project Centres of Excellence are sponsoring major research and policy debates around state articulated citizenship issues. Recent themes explore Canadian/ness on the part of new immigrants (see contributions to Canadian Diversity/é, Spring 2003) and national identity and diversity (Canadian Diversity/é, Spring 2004). Meanwhile, Canadian multicultural policy has shifted from celebrating immigrant diversity to a policy focusing on immigrant integration and civic participation.[9] This shift is described by some observers as evidence of a neo-liberal backlash against the earlier version of multiculturalism (see Garcea 2003). Others, such as George Day (2000) propose that Canadian state multiculturalism proliferates a diversity that, for historical reasons, remains problematic and untameable, regardless of increased state efforts at diversity management.

So it seems there is a growing disconnection between critical traditions of research regarding citizenship as a bundle of entitlements and rights and the narrowing of definitions of citizenship (emphasizing the responsibilities of new

---

8   Indeed, Abu-Laban (1994) makes the argument that Canadian policy reflects the shift from multicultural to citizenship discourse. In citizenship, policy and practice discourses of ethnicity, cultural difference and citizenship are inter-related being differently configured and expressed in different contexts and over time (Hall 2000).

9   Proposed changes to the Citizenship of Canada Act were tabled in Bill C-18 in 2002. The then Director General of the Integration Branch at Citizenship and Immigration Canada (CIC) describes the changes as 'modernizing' Canadian Citizenship legislation 'to reassert the rights and *reinforce the responsibilities that go with being a Canadian citizen'* (my italics) (Firth 2003: 72). Key differences between the Bill and the Act contain seven principle objectives, including 'to require strong attachment to Canada for the acquisition of citizenship' (p. 73). Modernization is always an interesting term and fits within the rubric of disguised interests noted by Hall (2000) cited herein. The issue of demonstrable 'attachment' to Canada is at issue in my critique here.

citizens) on the part of Canadian policy. Examples of the former include research influenced by Charles Taylor's (1994) liberal philosophy on the politics of recognition (for example his critics, Appiah (1994) and Day (2000)). Aligned with this are critical traditions in feminist and progressive social science, noted at the start of the chapter, where research critically examines citizenship and multicultural policies for the means to address injustices arising from neo-liberal ideologies and cut-backs to social programmes.[10] The timing of this policy shift and its apparent turn away from social justice concerns is troublesome. Western states are compelled demographically, if not morally, to plan for economic development which includes significant (im)migration. Moreover, the awarding and acquisition of citizenship is not best imagined as a means–end relationship to be understood in terms of neo-liberal economic priorities that privilege capital over labour despite the essential economic contributions of working people, including women, to national economic growth.

Similarly, many developing nations such as the Philippines are also compelled to rely on migration as a major component of their development policies. Hence a cruel paradox emerges at precisely the time when migration appears to offer some material purchase for immigrants, their kin who anticipate financial and social benefits from remittances, and for their countries of origin. The reworking of discourse and practice in immigrant receiving contexts promises closer scrutiny of the identity politics of immigrant 'others.' Familiar forms of racism based on visible difference are compounded by insidious new forms of cultural racism seen, for example, in controversial border screening processes that reportedly culturally (and racially) profile people from countries suspected of harbouring terrorists. Or, more germane to the Philippine case, given that many care-givers are qualified nurses and teachers, is the exploitation enabled by the non-acceptance of professional immigrant's qualifications. Li (2004) argues that in citizenship policy and practice, Canada's 'immigration problem is represented as [a] problem of too much diversity, and racialized new immigrants are represented as endless intruders to urban and social space' (Li 2004: 27). He also points out that racialized new immigrants are 'multicultural objects' not subjects:

> As multicultural objects, they only bring superficial novelties and add quantity to Canada's diverse population. As objects, they are to make Canada look better as a tolerant society, but not to demand Canada to change for their sake. (Li 2004: 27-28)

The crux of my principal argument expands on this notion of cultural racism. We have two approaches to citizenship in question here. On the one hand there is an apparently progressive body of academic research describing citizenship dynamics as underscoring social inequality and allowing for, being implicated in, a politics of exclusion. On the other hand, the officially produced discourses of citizenship privilege research into the dynamics of social inclusion, but narrowly defined to

---

10 I have in mind here theorists concerned about the effects of globalization, such as Bauman (1998), Harvey (2000) and Sider (2003).

discount material differences and the many forms of discrimination encountered by immigrants. The onus for the acquisition of citizenship and full participation in its entitlements are being discursively constituted (in a Foucauldian governmentality sense) in a manner which risks preserving, even deepening gendered and racialized inequities within and between immigrant sending and receiving nations. It is not my intention to suggest that this is particularly new, nor necessarily surprising. However, scrutiny of Canadian policy debates reveals that equality concerns have become secondary to the ideal (indeed ideology) of immigrant integration promoted in a manner that places the 'moral' force of civic engagement upon new immigrants bringing them on stream as neo-liberal Canadian subjects. In the case of immigrants from the Philippines, the effort to induce civic participation as a means to social integration and commitment to Canada is both redundant and misguided. But let me further explain through the example of recent government-sponsored research on social capital. This will lead me into a discussion of the likelihood of immigrants retaining transnational yet fluid identities that, certainly in the case of Philippine-born Canadians, include demonstrable evidence of commitment to Canada.

Whose Social Capital?

In recent Metropolis research on social capital, the integration of immigrants is assessed in terms of narrowly understood notions of social capital (after Putnam 2000), the logic being that civic participation and democracy are better served when immigrants thicken their social capital networks. Important gender questions attend this prescription, particularly in cases where gender norms privilege male participation in public sites. Voyer (2003: 31) in a Metropolis publication about 'managing social diversity' proposes that integration is more likely to occur when immigrants shift social capital networks from 'bonding relations' (among familial and ethnic groups) to 'bridging' and 'linking' networks. 'Bridging' networks are those which span ethnic and other groups, and 'linking' networks extend vertically through the social hierarchy better integrating holders of immigrant social capital into the social fabric and structures of power. Voyer's question is cast as the generic problems for western states in a post 9/11, neo-liberal political economy framework:

> How do we sustain social development and harmony at a time when our societies are increasingly multi-faith, multi-cultural, and multi-lingual? This is a challenge that Canada, as well as other OECD countries, currently face and will continue to address in the decades to come. Immigrants and their descendants have transformed Canada into not only a country in the world, but also a country of the world. Over 200 ethnic origins were reported in the 2001 Census and more than 18% of the Canadian population was born outside Canada. (Voyer 2003: 31)

There is, however, a debate underway in Canada about the logic of and evidence for the bridging social capital integrative thesis. Jedwab (2004) notes the shift in theoretical discourse away from the concept of social cohesion towards social capital. He then challenges the central thesis of the proponents of the social capital thesis, namely the issue of immigrant bonding (as opposed to bridging), or ethnic exclusivity, as having a significant relationship to immigrant attachments to Canada. The concern with immigrant's attachment to Canada is supposedly tied to issues of social cohesion. Jedwab draws upon a model of intersectional identities to conclude that a strong sense of belonging to one's ethnic group does not result in 'diminished attachment' to national identity. Findings are cited from Statistics Canada's Ethnic Diversity Survey (completed in 2003) which provide 'little support for social capital theorists in this regard as they make quite clear that strong ethnic attachments neither undercut strong Canadian identification nor reduce trust of others' (Jedwab 2004: 19).

Filipino Transnational Identities

The most telling example in the survey relates to Filipinos living in Canada. The survey was developed by Statistics Canada in partnership with the Department of Canadian Heritage (April-August 2002) and administered to 42,500 people aged 15 and over in ten provinces. Filipino immigrants to Canada (along with Portuguese respondents) show a high measure of 85/100 for a sense of belonging to Canada. At 78/100, their strong sense of belonging to an ethnic or cultural group remains equally high-scoring – indeed the highest of all groups. (Portuguese and East Indian respondents are next with 65/100.) For comparative purposes on the measure of Canadian belonging/ness, the highest scoring group is Scottish (88), followed by English (87), then Dutch (86). The group with the lowest score in terms of 'sense of belonging to Canada' was Quebecois(e) at 51.

But the Filipino case remains interesting for its high score on both measures of attachment – to Canada and to being Filipino. I am not surprised by the data indicating Filipinos remained committed to being Filipino but my research reveals variability in what this means for (im)migrants. All of this research described above – the debate – fails to reference gender differences. Such statistical studies, while interesting for the manner in which they lend themselves to different conclusions in public policy debates about multiculturalism and 'managing diversity,' do little to bring us closer to understanding the lived experiences of (im)migration and migrant decision-making. The erasure of differences of gender and class also precludes understandings about the transnational connections in (im)migrants lives and diminishes the complexities of fluctuations in identity tied to shifting conditions in the places called 'home' that (im)migrants feel connected to. This becomes particularly troublesome when gender differences are erased. One major path of entry to Canada for Filipinos is as domestic service workers; women enter Canada under the live-in caregivers programme (see Note 2). Surely women in the various stages of (im)migration, often separated from their families, sometimes hopeful for their reunification, will have differing issues and sets of experiences relative to identity and identification.

Transnational affinities and networks, it would seem from the preoccupations of Canadian policy research into immigrant loyalty, are considered potentially disruptive, hence the recent efforts to focus on integration dynamics. But, at least part of the intention in the conceptual turn to citizenship discourse (rather than cultural politics and ethnicities) for the previously mentioned critical academic researchers[11] arises from efforts to think more globally. The very idea of citizenship seems more neutral and useful sociologically to account for internal differentiation between and amongst so-called ethnic and cultural groups marked as 'other' through the migration process. Many migration researchers have moved far beyond the simplifying equations of migration as precipitated in rupture followed by a clean break. Citizenship needs similar attention for its elasticity: migrants are not simply moved from one national 'container' to another. The situation for many if not most migrants is messier than this both in terms of their acquisition (or not) of requisite travel documents and, upon arrival in new destinations, their disposition to countries of birth contrasted with their new circumstances.

Concepts such as transnationalism and 'long distance nationalism' (Glick Schiller and Fouron 2001) remind us of the multiplicity of boundary crossing attachments and obligations (im)migrants carry with them (economic, political, legal, social, familial, and subjective). Writing about the migration experiences of Haitians living in the United States, Glick Schiller and Fouron reveal a cross-border citizenship, underscored by shifting social, political and economic dynamics in both countries and fuelled by a relentless, uncompromising, indiscriminate racism. Despite their middle-class and professional occupations, subjects in Glick Schiller and Fouron's study remain vulnerable to racist challenges, which fan their longing for family and 'home' in Haiti. Similarly, disappointment about dismal economic opportunities and violent political struggles in Haiti reverse the feelings of commitment. Such fraught commitments and fragmented loyalties are also apparent in my research with Philippine migrants living abroad and in the Philippines where future potential out-migration remains an ever-present possibility (Barber 1997). How might such an unlocking of people and place be applied to a more critical concept of citizenship which is the theoretical promise of the focus upon gendered citizenship?

I am particularly concerned with processes of migration, gender and development, and the question of class. Racism and gender exploitation need to be relentlessly explored for their persistent reworking in the global sites where migrants locate themselves. Do new vocabularies of citizenship – signified by the shift in multicultural policy to explicitly managed diversity, intercultural discourse and civic participation and integration – distract attention from the ever-present processes of class, gender and racialized differentiation that attend migration, both in migrant sending and receiving contexts? What is gained by the reworking and what is obscured?

---

11 Here I rely on examples from my own discipline, anthropology, but even the humanities have taken this turn, for example in discussion of post-colonial fiction and hybrid identities.

Philippine Citizenship Politics

Pettman (1999: 214) suggests home states are often 'unwilling defenders of citizen rights' because of their dependence upon remittances and foreign aid investment from countries that receive their overseas workers. This has been mainly the case for Philippine policy until recently. As Gonzales (1998) notes, the Philippine state relied upon migration to solve brooding economic and political problems. So exporting labour diminishes the political and social effects of labour market deficiencies in home states;, however, this can also prove troublesome to citizenship politics, particularly when the majority of the overseas workers are women. Massive public protests and international outcry over the fate of two Philippine women overseas workers imprisoned by foreign states brought gendered migration and citizenship politics to the forefront of a presidential election. Flor Contemplaçion, married and the mother of four young children, was executed in Singapore.[12] Sara Balabagan, a young teenager, was imprisoned in the United Arab Emirates and threatened with a death sentence. Her release was negotiated. Prior to 1995, migrants, men and women, had experienced legal travesties working abroad but the expressions of concern were less dramatic. Contemplaçion's fate was the 'last straw' for the many Filipinos anxious about the effects of migration on their families and for their nation (Gonzales 1998). The protests threatened President Ramos' ruling coalition and immediate political response was called for (Gonzales 1998).

From this time there have been various policy changes ostensibly directed towards migrant security and, where possible, the standardization of labour contracts. Efforts have been made to initiate various bilateral labour and related agreements, although not with great success (Go 2003). The most recent migration policy modifications (in process during the early 2000s) reveal a slippage from the idea that the acceleration in migration is temporary – in Philippine public discourse 'a stop-gap measure' – to allow for economic development and the creation of new local labour markets. A further effect of the labour export policy is political. Migration, in theory at least, functions as a safety valve to diminish political unrest caused by the continuing high rates of poverty, unemployment, and underemployment experienced by the majority of Filipinos. But the transnational mobility and political involvement in struggles over Philippine citizenship in the labour diaspora does not so much deflect unrest as alter the content and locations for its expression. Moreover, as a result of the political struggles to garner more state support for Philippine labour migrants, the scope of Philippine citizenship is expanding.

Migrant support groups are present in most countries (outside of the Middle East where they are outlawed). Using Hong Kong as my example, such groups work tirelessly to resolve labour disputes. They also challenge cases of abuse. To the degree they are successful they make a significant difference in the lives of individual migrants. Moving up the register of political effort, groups such as United Filipinos in Hong Kong (UNIFIL-HK) and the Asian Migrant Centre (AMC) co-

---

12 See Hilsdon (2000) detailed analysis of 'the Contemplaçion fiasco.'

ordinate political and critical responses to policy. Increasingly they also advocate for migrants from other countries, although Filipinos are by far the largest Hong Kong based group. UNIFIL-HK, with a membership of domestic workers and AMC, an NGO support group, are also concerned about the economic options available to return migrants as citizens participating in Philippine development. In 2002, I witnessed an interesting discussion about what one activist described as a 'rights and root campaign.' There was disagreement about organizing Hong Kong migrants in co-operative investment groups. The nature of the businesses and sources of capital was at issue. The ideas under review represented different visions of citizenship, and economy, class and community in Philippine society. The debate, however, went beyond particularized local concerns to explore transnationally inspired 'spaces of hope' (Harvey 2000).

Nonetheless, despite policy adjustments, basically bringing discourse closer to everyday social practices, the status quo of Philippine dependence on labour export continues (Asis 2001). Ironically, such dependence is strengthened by transnational political activism which has encouraged more explicit accommodation to the needs and concerns of the labour diaspora. Migration is more closely monitored at the Philippine border and the recruitment industry is now more regulated, including the active tracking down of unlicensed recruiters. Public healthcare and pension support for return migrants, intended to reduce the disparities between local and global labour markets, have been promised. Some aspects of the implementation of these policies are contentious and leave NGOs and church groups to fill the gaps by providing assistance to return migrants. Nonetheless measures focusing of the needs of migrants at home and abroad are indicative of the national long-range commitment to migration and in as much as they smooth the journey to overseas work, they also contribute to the routinization of migration as a predominant livelihood strategy for Filipinos, women especially. Border control and regulatory policies also restrict the conditions under which Filipinos obtain overseas work, making it more difficult for the poorest migrants to raise the required capital to follow regular migration channels. In sum, since Corazon Aquino's presidential term (after the dictator Marcos was deposed in 1986) when she was forced to overturn a moratorium on out-migration – ostensibly set in place by her administration to secure bilateral agreements in major Filipino overseas labour markets – Philippine migration politics reflect deep national ambivalence. Mainly in response to the activism of migrant support groups, the state is more active in migration and citizenship policy development. Activism also holds the Philippine state more accountable for what happens to citizens living and working overseas.

Transnational Citizenship

When I visited the Philippines in June 2003, migration politics were focused upon proposed changes to Philippine citizenship. Two bills, one concerning dual citizenship for Filipinos living abroad, the other concerning absentee voting rights, were being processed by a bicameral committee under the close scrutiny of various expatriate communities (see http://www.philippineupdate.com/vote.htm, Accessed 9 May 2004). The most contentious aspect of the changes concerned extending the right to Filipinos living abroad to participate in Philippine elections. By the time of the presidential elections, in May 2004, these policy changes were in place and the contours of this contention became more visible.

In February 2004, the frontrunner in the Presidential campaigning, Fernando Poe, was awaiting Supreme Court ruling on the question of whether, as the 64 year old son of a Filipino father and an American mother he was eligible to stand for election in the 10 May Polls. Lawyers opposed to his candidacy charged that because Poe was 'born out of wedlock' and since there was no evidence that he was acknowledged by his parents, most particularly his father, he continues, they argued, to be an illegitimate child and an American citizen. This argument was used to challenge his eligibility to run for office but he won his case and remained a leading opponent in the 'presidential race.' Poe was another celebrity candidate, much like deposed President Estrada, popular with poor Filipinos as much for his career in film and media, perhaps more so, than the wisdom of his political platforms. Estrada was removed from office three years prior to the elections under discussion. Charged with economic plunder, he continued to insist on his innocence and co-ordinate protests by his supporters. As Estrada's replacement learned, President Gloria Macapagal Arroyo, populist leaders and candidates are prone to inciting unrest and even a military uprising. This happened the previous year (2003) in Manila when troops occupied a building in one of the capital region's central business areas. President Arroyo and her supporters from the military and other factions of the ruling elite were able to maintain her authority on that occasion. Nor did this prevent her candidacy in the 2004 elections although there was much speculation in the media about what her decision would be prior to confirmation of her interest.

So, questions about the role of dual citizens in the Philippine electoral process underscored debates over Philippine transnational citizenship. As the new citizenship regulations moved slowly through the political system, one concern was the potential for the diaspora to undermine Philippine political processes which remain vulnerable to corruption and military interference. Poe was an interesting candidate in this regard. In the Philippines he was considered a candidate most likely to attract poor, uneducated voter constituencies. Some saw him as a candidate liable to manipulation by reactionary factions of wealthy (and diasporic) elites. Indeed, my Filipino correspondents report that Poe had never held any political office, nationally or locally, prior to his candidacy for the presidency. This suggests that much more than personal ambition underlay his decision to run for office. Some Philippine political observers were concerned that Poe's candidacy invited continuing instability. This was evidenced in the street demonstrations that occurred during the time Poe's candidacy was in question, the fear being the potential of the unrest to spark further military uprisings. At that stage Philippine democracy appeared, once again, to be fragile.

While Poe had some support in the labour diaspora, the incumbent President Arroyo, it turned out, had more, as was the case within the Philippines. Arroyo is well educated and reportedly very politically astute. She worked hard to garner overseas worker support. She actually visited Hong Kong to meet with voters among the sizeable Filipino population (over 80 per cent of 180,000 migrant workers in 2002) resident in the city. Opponents to her re-election rallied in Hong Kong to challenge her lack of support for migrant workers. In particular, migrant support groups were angered by the President's failure to take a firm stand when Hong Kong officials proposed to reduce the minimum wage of Filipino domestic workers in Hong Kong by 21.6 per cent, a measure which would have significantly reduced remittances to the Philippines. Instead President Arroyo posed a compromise cut of ten per cent which caused United Filipinos in Hong Kong (UNIFIL-HK) chair Connie Bragas Regalado to describe Arroyo as 'persona non-grata' amongst Filipinos in Hong Kong (Asian Migration News http://www.smc.org.ph/amnews/amn011231htm Accessed 9/11/2004).[13]

But not all diasporic politics are presidential. Nor are political forces always tugging backwards to past scenarios. On 22 March 2004, the BBC News UK Edition (http://news.bbc.co.uk/1/hi/world/asia-pacific/3545989.stm) reported on the Presidential campaign shaping up in Hong Kong, one of the most politically active sites in the Philippine diaspora. In Hong Kong, 90,000 'overseas workers' (out of a reported 317,448 overseas registered voters), mainly women, registered to vote. Along with President Arroyo, at least one other contender, Eddie Villanueva campaigned for the labour diaspora vote in Hong Kong. University Professor Mondejar (HK City University) called Hong Kong '...practically a political appendage of the Philippines electorate ... In no other place in the world are Philippine overseas workers as densely packed as they are in Hong Kong.' These workers are also described as sophisticated, 'middle-class' even, by one Philippine politician quoted in the news.

When thinking about gendered citizenship, by far the most interesting aspect of this report is the discussion of the candidacy of Connie Bragas-Regalado, a domestic worker and UNIFIL-HK activist. She ran for office in the Congressional elections that paralleled the Presidential election. Bragas-Regalado was the candidate selected by the transnational Philippine migrants' rights group, Migrante, 'Connie,' the article says: '...cleans other peoples houses. Like tens of thousands of Filipinos in Hong Kong she works from morning until night, six days a week. But her days of scrubbing and polishing will soon be over. Connie Bragas-Regalado is almost certain to get elected.'[14] She is reported as saying:

---

13   I have been unable to locate data on the gender breakdown of support for the various candidates. However class features strongly in Philippine elections because of poverty and the patronage relations this inspires (see Sidel 1999). Because of this, class may be more germane than gender within the Philippines at least. In the diaspora, the situation is less clear.

14   She was not elected to office. Several parties representing the migrant sector participated in the elections under the 'party list' system which also includes such specialized constituencies as women, youth, the elderly, etc. This system extends the possibilities for voter representation beyond the established political parties. The presence of several migrant parties

Now that I have decided to be in Congress there is no change in the time that I wake up. This is harder than doing domestic work because you are responsible for seeing to it that migrant workers in 186 countries are being protected by law.

One of her supporters told the reporter:

This is the first time that we were given the right to vote. The person who is going to represent us is a migrant who has worked as a domestic helper. From her experience, she knows what we are fighting for and what we need.

This is an extraordinary story of the exercise of transnational citizenship rights, one that is all the more powerful because the constituency in question – predominantly female migrant domestic workers – happens to be one of the most vulnerable, demeaned, undervalued, de-skilled, and super-exploited groups in the global labour market. And yet, from this example of transnational political expression we also learn that this work is associated within the Philippines with sophistication and an emergent middle-class. This is not a definition we can glean from various feminist accounts of the exploitative nature of their labour contracts and conditions, but certainly it accords with my research in Hong Kong. Moreover, in this example we see Filipino migrants exercising their rights to Philippine citizenship and identity in a manner which appears to pose no threat to their host society, nor to their employers.

The conclusion of the May 2004 elections saw President Arroyo re-elected but Poe's camp challenged the initial result claiming electoral fraud.[15] A lengthy recounting of votes confirmed the initial results giving Arroyo a lead of over one million votes. In July 2004, Arroyo acted to solidify her authority when she recalled the small contingent of Filipinos participating in the US-led coalition in Iraq. The recall was in response to the kidnapping of a Filipino driver. This decision, much criticized by the Bush administration and its allies, is better understood in terms of Philippine citizenship and migration politics than global geo-politics. With this gesture, Arroyo courted the loyalty of those supporters of Poe who could imagine themselves as hostages abroad – a sizeable number of Philippine women and men. On the other hand, a subsequent policy banning Filipinos from working in Iraq was not well received by some potential migrants drawn to the idea of work in the region despite the risks.

Philippine migration and citizenship politics remain mired in contradictions and continue to flow along seemingly well grooved circuits. Little change is apparent but for the deepening of commitment to migration as an economic strategy both at the level of individual and household decision-making, and for the nation.

---

indicates that diverse political positions are found within the migrant sector. In addition, all the party list sectors are competitive with each other for voter support.

15   In a strange twist of fate, Fernando Poe was reported dead less than six months after the election results were confirmed. He died on 13 December 2004, following a stroke. He was described as an 'actor-turned politician' and a 'reluctant presidential candidate' on the popular website of contactmusic.com.

Philippine transnationalism, in the brief examples given here, suggests that there is little about commitments to Philippine politics and livelihoods that constitutes a threat to Canadian citizenship and the social dynamics of integration. The more important question to ask about Philippine migration and citizenship politics concerns the question of the longer term commitment to labour migration on the part of Philippine public policy. What are the costs to Philippine social development of an exported labour policy that sees so many increasingly well qualified women (and men) working abroad in degraded (social) reproductive labour that requires considerable education and productive effort? Often it is female kin who contribute to the education and migration preparations as migration circuits are replicated between and across generations. The Philippine example also suggests that Canadian citizenship priorities are misplaced. This applies both to the failure to properly value the educational credentials and professional experience of many care-givers and in policies which seemingly question Philippine-born Canadians' loyalty to Canada. Clearly this example shows transnational loyalties are not incompatible with Canadian citizenship.

Conclusion

In conclusion, I turn to the wisdom of Benedict Anderson's insightful discussion of the pathways for the emergent consciousness of nationalism(s). Anderson has much to teach us about the biographies and technologies of Imagined Communities of nations. Proposing a reading of the 'grammar' of how consciousness is tackled in nation-building projects, he reminds us that citizenship policies are never benign and they require our analytical attention. He identifies '… three institutions of power … the census, the map, and the museum: together, they profoundly shape(d) the way in which the colonial state imagines its dominion – the nature of the human beings it rules, the geography of its domain, and the legitimacy of its ancestry' (Anderson 1983, 1991: 164). Anderson's ideas enable us to constitute 'a grammar' of Canadian citizenship imperatives. The grammar privileges immigrants, typically males, from dominant western nations who are already 'bridged' and 'linked,' to use social capital discourse.

The arguments in the paper have hinged on six key points. I have drawn on feminist and post-colonial critiques in citizenship studies and debates in anthropology to argue: 1) that discourses and technologies of citizenship fail to take account of the fluid and complex nature of identity and cultural politics. Instead they rely on static notions of ethnicity and culture. 2) Statistical categorizations of national groups fail to capture heterogeneity. Similarly, reference to ethnic and cultural groups can reify and homogenize (im)migrants with two main results: internal differentiation and forms of discrimination based on class, gender, age, sexuality, etc are rendered invisible. Such reified categories undermine the dynamic character of individual and national identities, misreading transnational affinities and connections as measures of defaulted commitment to Canada. What passes as data for the measurement of identity are in the first instance not so amenable to quantification, nor are they reliable and hence the knowledge produced from them is at best superficial. 3) There are problems associated with attempts to impress upon newcomers the obligations of citizenship if this means downplaying their rights. Discussion of obligation distracts attention from the actual social, economic, and political inequalities associated with citizenship – most particularly those based on gender but also those relating to the countries of origin. As we have seen, immigrants from the global south are particularly disadvantaged through cultural racism. 4) There has been a narrowing of the definitions of citizenship in Canada, particularly for new immigrants but for other disadvantaged groups of well. Citizenship, I argue, should not be understood in terms of a means-end relationship read off from neo-liberal economic state agendas. 5) The crux of my argument notes that the switch from celebrating to managing diversity in Canadian citizenship and multicultural policy invites the perpetuation of insidious forms of cultural racism in Canada. And, 6) I have insisted on consideration of (im)migrants' transnational frames of reference and that Canadian citizenship needs to be considered in terms of sending and receiving countries. At this historical conjuncture, those who expose and critique the policy and ideological shifts that bolster neo-liberal political and economic dictates certainly have more critical purchase on citizenship discourse than those who stick within the contours of the policy debates. We need to remain vigilant about the new cultural politics of racism along with migration-based divisions of gender and class in global political economy.

References

Abrera-Mangahas, M. (1998), 'Violence Against Women Migrant Workers: The Philippine Experience,' in B. Cariño (ed.), *Filipino Workers on the Move: Trends, Dilemmas and Policy Options*, Philippine Migration Research Network and Philippine Social Science Council, Quezon City, pp. 45-80.

Abu-Laban, Y. (1994), 'The Politics of Race and Ethnicity: Multiculturalism as a Contested Arena,' in J. Bickerton and A. Gagnon (eds), *Canadian Politics*, Broadview Press, Peterborough, pp. 242-63.

Abu-Laban, Y. and Gabriel, C. (2002), *Selling Diversity: Immigration, Multiculturalism, Employment Equity and Globalization*, Broadview Press, Peterborough.

Anderson, B. (2000), *Doing the Dirty Work? The Global Politics of Domestic Labour*, Zed Books, London.

Anderson, B. (1983, 1991), *Imagined Communities: Reflections on the Origin and Spread of Nationalism*, Anvil Publishing, Manila.

Appiah, A. (1994), 'Identity, Authenticity, Survival: Multicultural Societies and Social Reproduction,' in C. Taylor (ed.), *Multiculturalism: Examining the Politics of Recognition*, Princeton University Press, Princeton, pp. 149-63.

Asis, M. (2001), 'The Return Migration of Filipino Women Migrants: Home But Not for Good?,' in C. Wille and B. Passl (eds), *Female Labour Migration in South-East Asia: Change and Continuity*, Asian Research Centre for Migration, Institute for Asian Studies, Chulalongkorn University, Bangkok, pp. 23-93.

Barber, P. Gardiner (2004), 'Contradictions of Class and Consumption when the Commodity is Labour,' *Anthropologica,* Vol. 46(2), pp. 213-18.

Barber, P. Gardiner (2000), 'Agency in Philippine Women's Labour Migration and Provisional Diaspora,' *Women's Studies International Forum*, Vol. 23(4), pp. 399-411.

Barber, P. Gardiner (1997), 'Transnationalism and the Politics of "home" for Philippine Domestic Workers,' *Anthropologica*, Vol. 39, pp. 39-52.

Bauman, Z. (1998), *Globalization: The Human Consequences*, Columbia University Press, New York.

Bhabha, H. (1994), *The Location of Culture*, Routledge, London.

Bonnin, C. (2004), *Windows to the Market: Exploring Women's Strategies and Supports as Home-based Traders in Metro Manila*, unpublished MA thesis, Dalhousie University, Halifax.

Brah, A. (1996), *Cartographies of Diaspora: Contesting Identities*, Routledge, London.

Chant, S. and McIlwaine, C. (1995), *Women of a Lesser Cost: Female Labour, Foreign Exchange and Philippine Development*, Pluto Press, London.

Clifford, J. (1997), *Routes: Travel and Translation in the Late Twentieth Century*, Harvard University Press, Cambridge, Mass.

Cohen, R. (1997), *Global Diasporas: An Introduction*, University of Washington Press, Seattle.

Constable, N. (1997), *Maid to Order in Hong Kong: Stories of Filipina Workers*, Cornell University Press, Ithaca.

Crehan, K. (2002), *Gramsci, Culture and Anthropology*, University of California Press, Berkeley.

Day, R. (2000), *Multiculturalism and the History of Canadian Diversity*, University of Toronto Press, Toronto.

Dobrowolsky, A. (2004), 'The Chrétien Liberal Legacy and Women: Changing Policy Priorities with Little Cause for Celebration,' *Review of Constitutional Studies*, Vol. 9(1-2), pp. 171-98.

Dobrowolsky, A. and Jenson, J. (2004), 'Shifting Representations of Citizenship: Canadian Politics of "Women" and "Children",' *Social Politics*, Vol. 11(2), pp. 154-80.

Eviota, E. (1992), *The Political Economy of Gender: Women and the Sexual Division of Labour in the Philippines*, Zed Books, London.

Firth, R. (2003), 'Citizenship of Canada Act: Strengthening the Value of our Citizenship,' *Canadian Diversity/Diversité*, Vol. 2(1), pp. 72-4.

Garcea, J. (2003), 'The Construction and Constitutionalization of Canada's Citizenship Regime: Reconciliation of Diversity and Equality,' *Canadian Diversity/Diversité*, Vol. 2(1), pp. 59-66.

Glick Schiller, N. and Fouron, G. (2001), *George Woke Up Laughing: Long Distance*

Nationalism and the Search for Home, Duke University Press, Durham, NC.

Go, S. (2003), 'The State and Content of Bilateral Labour and Similar Agreements: The Philippine Case,' unpublished paper prepared for the Seminar on Bilateral Labour Agreements and Other Forms of Recruitment of Foreign Workers, Montreaux, Switzerland, 19-20 June.

Go, S. (2002), 'Remittances and International Labour Migration: Impact on the Philippines,' unpublished paper prepared for the Metropolis Seminar on Immigrants and Homeland, Dubrovnik, Croatia, 9-12 May.

Go, S. (1998), 'Towards the 21st Century: Whither Philippine Labor Migration?,' in B. Cariño (ed.), *Filipino Workers on the Move: Trends, Dilemmas and Policy Options*, Philippine Migration Research Network and Philippine Social Science Council, Quezon City, pp. 9-44.

Gonzales III, J. (1998), *Philippine Labour Migration: Critical Dimensions of Public Policy*, Institute for Southeast Asian Studies and De La Salle University Press, Singapore/Manila.

Hall, S. (2000), 'Conclusion: the Multi-cultural Question,' in B. Hesse (ed.), *Un/Settled Multiculturalisms: Diasporas, Entanglements, 'Transruptions,'* Zed Books, London, pp. 209-41.

Harvey, D. (2000), *Spaces of Hope*, University of California Press, Berkeley.

Hilsdon, A. (2000), 'The Contemplaçion Fiasco: The Hanging of a Filipino Domestic Worker in Singapore,' in A. Hilsdon, M. Macintyre, et al. (eds), *Human Rights and Gender Politics: Asia-Pacific Perspectives*, Routledge, London, pp. 172-92.

Hobson, B. (ed.) (2000), *Gender and Citizenship in Transition*, Macmillan, London & Routledge, New York, pp. 172-92

International Labour Organization (2002), *Women and Men in the Informal Economy: A Statistical Picture, Employment Sector*, International Labour Organization, Geneva.

Jedwab, J. (2004), 'Intersecting Identities and Dissecting Social Capital in Canada,' *Canadian Diversity/Canadienne Diversité*, Vol. 3(1), pp. 17-19.

Jenson, J. (1993), 'Naming Nations: Making Nationalist Claims in Canadian Public Discourse,' *Canadian Review of Sociology and Anthropology*, Vol. 30(2), pp. 337-58.

Jenson, J. and Phillips, S. D. (1996), 'Regime Shift: New Citizenship Practices in Canada,' *International Journal of Canadian Studies*, Vol. 14, Fall, pp. 111-35.

Kymlicka, W. (1995), *Multicultural Citizenship*, Clarendon Press, Oxford.

Li, P. (2004), 'Politics of Difference in Territorial and Social Spaces,' *Canadian Diversity/ Diversité Canadienne*, Vol. 3(2), pp. 23-8.

Lister, R. (2000), 'Dilemmas in Engendering Citizenship,' in B. Hobson (ed.), *Gender and Citizenship in Transition*, Macmillan, London & Routledge, New York, pp. 33-83.

Parreñas, R. Salazar (2002), 'The Care Crisis in the Philippines: Children and Transnational Families in the New Global Economy,' in B. Ehrenreich and A. Hochschild (eds), *Global Woman: Nannies, Maids and Sex Workers in the New*

Economy, Granta Books, London, pp. 39-54.

Pettman, J. (1999), 'Globalisation and the Gendered Politics of Citizenship,' in N. Yuval-Davis and P. Werbner (eds), *Women, Citizenship and Difference*, Zed Books, London, pp. 207-20.

Putnam, R. (2000), *Bowling Alone: The Collapse and Revival of American Community*, Simon & Schuster, New York.

Rafael, V. (2000), *White Love and Other Events in Filipino History*, Ateneo de Manila University Press, Quezon City.

Sidel, J. (1999), *Capital, Coercion, and Crime: Bossim in the Philippines*, Stanford University Press, Stanford.

Sider, G. (2003), *Between History and Tomorrow: Making and Breaking Everyday Life in Rural Newfoundland*, Broadview Press, Peterborough.

Smith, C. L. (1999), 'Is Citizenship a Gendered Concept?,' in A. Cairns and J. Courtney et al. (eds), *Citizenship, Diversity, and Pluralism: Canadian and Comparative Perspectives*, McGill-Queens University Press, Montreal, pp. 137-61.

Taylor, C. (1999), 'Democratic Exclusion (and Its Remedies?),' in A. Cairns, J. Courtney et al. (eds), *Citizenship, Diversity and Pluralism: Canadian and Comparative Perspectives*, McGill-Queen's University Press, Montreal, pp. 265-87.

Taylor, C. (1994), 'The Politics of Recognition,' in C. Taylor (ed.), *Multiculturalism: Examining the Politics of Recognition*, Princeton University Press, Princeton, pp. 25-73.

Tolley, E. (2004), 'National Identity and the "Canadian Way:" Values, Connections and Culture,' *Canadian Diversity/Diversité Canadienne*, Vol. 3(2), pp. 11-15.

Tsuda, M. (ed.) (2003), *Filipino Diaspora: Demography, Social Networks, Empowerment and Culture*, Philippine Migration Research Network and Philippine Social Science Council, Quezon City.

Tyner, J. (2002), 'Global Cities and Circuits of Global Labor: the Case of Manila, Philippines,' in F. V. Jr. Aguilar (ed.), *Filipinos in Global Migrations: At Home in the World?*, Philippine Migration Research Network and the Philippine Social Science Council, Quezon City, pp. 60-85.

Voyer, J. (2003), 'Diversity Without Divisiveness: A Role for Social Capital?,' *Canadian Diversity/Diversité Canadienne*, Vol. 2(1), pp. 31-2.

Wilmsen, E. and McAllister, P. (1996), *The Politics of Difference: Ethnic Premises in a World of Power*, Chicago University Press, Chicago.

Yuval-Davis, N. and Werbner, P. (eds) (1999), *Women, Citizenship and Difference*, Zed Books, London.

Chapter 4

Why do Skilled Women and Men Emigrating from China to Canada get Bad Jobs?

Janet Salaff and Arent Greve

Introduction

Developed countries vie for highly educated immigrants to boost skills and population. Canada's skilled-based immigration policy attracts about 230,000 immigrants yearly, more than 46 per cent are professionals and technical workers. The point system is essentially based upon human capital theory. Underlying the point system is the idea that an import of highly skilled immigrants will contribute to economic growth and improve the welfare of the immigrants. Since 1998, the People's Republic of China (PRC) has contributed the largest number of skilled immigrants to Canada. Yet, despite being highly skilled, many of these Chinese immigrants suffer unemployment and end up working in low waged jobs. As we shall see, women fare the worst (Chard, Badets and Howatson-Leo 2000; Li 2000; McDade 1988). In this chapter, we try to understand the mechanisms that channel recently immigrated professionals, who had high status jobs in their fields in China, into mainly mediocre jobs in Toronto, Ontario, Canada. We consider two main approaches used to explain the jobs that new, skilled immigrants tend to acquire: human capital and institutionalist theories.

On the basis of human capital theory, the prediction would be that highly skilled immigrants should get good jobs. However, in practice, human capital theory falls short of its predictions. Nevertheless, Canadian employers ground their views in popularized human capital notions, asserting that despite their prior screening, new immigrants do not have the skills that are needed for the job. The presumption here is that, if women fare the worst, it must be due to their lack of skills for the jobs they aim for. What is more, human capital theorists' solutions to these problems will be highly individualized: restrict or retrain immigrants.

In contrast, institutional theory conjectures that the suitable qualities for jobholders are socially constructed. New immigrants, and especially women, fail to get jobs because they fit poorly into the institutional environment. Consequently, the institutionalist solutions do not target the individual, rather they point to the institutional system and call for restructuring institutions to ease access to skilled immigrants.

The choice of theoretical framework used has considerable implications for understanding the position of skilled immigrants, especially women, gaining full citizenship in Canada. In seeing how these theories help us understand our subjects, our paper argues that human capital arguments are logically unsound, do not fit the data, and suggest solutions that will not work. Institutional theory is more comprehensive. At the same time, fixing the problem demands considerable re-engineering of Canadian institutions.

In the following pages, we first discuss our frameworks. We turn to our study methods and the characteristics of our sample couples, studied with qualitative methods. In the section, Getting Skilled in China, we discuss the structure of professional jobs and their distribution by gender and positions; in the section Moving Careers to Canada we view these couples' experiences in Canada.

The Terms

Human capital theory evolved to explain the differences between labour and capital as inputs to production. The concept became economists' chief tools to study labour markets and earnings, as economists and policy makers sought to understand how nations could achieve economic growth and human welfare. One of the main tasks is learning why people get the jobs they do, our main concern here (Foray and Lundvall 1996; Temple 2001).

Human capital theory argues that employees' qualifications, skills, and work experiences, as exchanged in the labour market, are their human capital (Becker 1964). Employers match the human capital of an applicant to the job requirements. They pay higher wages for those with more skills. The framework assumes rationality. People freely choose education and occupations based on their ability. If their wages match their productivity, the market is in equilibrium. Some people, new immigrants and others, may in the short term earn less than they ought to based on their skills, but in the long term, the theory predicts that they will get the jobs they deserve.

However, few studies explain the mechanisms by which individuals' personal attributes contribute to a company's productivity. To begin with, now that most of the labour force has moved into knowledge jobs, measuring productivity is particularly challenging (Temple 2001). There are wide variations of productivity within educational categories (Andolfatto et al. 2000). Some contend that those with higher education are best able to take advantage of technological development. Yet, many firms do not take full advantage of their workers' human capital (Hall 1988; Pfeffer 1994). Other organizational resources come into play in a firm's adopting technology. In addition, studies have also shown weak links between education and job advancement (Blossfeld and Mayer 1988; Lin and Powers 2004).

Human capital is not a tangible capital, and measuring performance is ridden with a host of problems (March and Sutton 1994). To explain how bosses choose workers, economists have coined the concept of signalling theory. People with recognized education send signals; employers associate their education with previous hires for these jobs (Weiss 1995). This useful concept suggests that employers base their hiring decisions on comparing familiar symbols. They do not evaluate the worker's human capital to predict future productivity, thus reducing information costs (Bills 1988). Foreign job seekers send unfamiliar signals. Risk aversive employers, uncertain about unfamiliar job seekers, may not recognize their human capital. This is one explanation for the bad jobs new immigrants get (McDade 1988; Schoeni 1998). It is possible that the gatekeeper's assessment may be socially constructed, with no clear relation to the individual's qualifications. Signalling theory suggests this elusive link between human capital and employers' ability to evaluate skills.

Conversely, the second framework, institutional theory, explores the social structure of the labour force that receives workers, rather than the individual worker's fit. This model views professions as highly institutionalized (Scott 2001). We use the terms professional and semi-professional careers often in this chapter. We define a professional as one who has an intensive academic preparation within a field that is protected through legislation or certification procedures. A professional career starts with education, apprenticeship, and certification, according to the rules specific to each profession. Successive jobs with increasing responsibilities and managerial content follow. A semi-professional does not possess the higher degree required for certification, but has lower-level knowledge within the field and can work based on instructions (rules or advice) from professionals.

Professions in various countries view the stages in a professional career differently. In institutional theory, careers are socially constructed, by which is meant that career milestones are not universally valued because professions are embedded in social structures. The social structure consists of common and repeated patterns of behaviour, norms and expectations which come to appear necessary. These structures underlie the profession's own governance structure and norms of conduct (DiMaggio and Powell 1991).

Scott (2001) analyzes regulative, normative, and cognitive structures and activities of institutions that provide stability and meaning, and control behaviour. The government regulates the institutional environment through laws and statutes. Canada's common law system largely leaves regulation to the professions. The government negotiates and confirms the professions' requirements for certification, and codifies some regulations into law. Professional education adapts to these standards. The professions set and enforce standards and practice that become embedded as appropriate behaviour, to which firms have to conform (March and Olsen 1989). Organizations widely share cognitive understandings and interpretations of behaviour that assume that these standards are the way things should be. These behavioural norms are subject to professional sanctions. Since such norms are mostly taken for granted and not questioned, the state's ultimate legal power to coerce is rarely activated (Lerner and Menahem 2003; Richmond 1984).

Institutional theory does not deny the importance of talent or training in doing a job, but argues that human capital is culture specific. The cultural element beyond what it takes to do the job anchors human capital to specific contexts (Nee and

Sanders 2001). The institutional environment recognizes certain educational and career patterns as right. In this sense, human capital cannot have value outside its specific setting. The institutionalization of human capital in the professions poses two main barriers to new skilled immigrants. First, organizations assume professionals will graduate from certain familiar and approved schools. They will follow an expected career pattern to become certified and recognized in the professional community. These taken for granted assumptions of what constitutes a professional operate unconsciously as a set of internalized symbolic representations of the world. When new professionals apply for a position, if managers recognize their educational credentials and career paths, they will presume that the applicants can do the job. By conforming to professional norms, the applicants' human capital can be said to be institutionalized. In sum, work takes place in a socially constructed environment governed by rules and standard operating procedures. The productive force is embedded in institutionalized structures. It is not produced independently by human capital itself.

People having career structures that do not follow familiar patterns will be penalized. Their degrees will not be taken at face value, and they will have trouble being accepted as legitimate contenders for professional jobs. Such exclusion strikes a number of groups. For example, managers that have been laid off violate the norm of continued career mobility. Their return to the labour force is difficult (Newman 1988). Finally, in the case we are studying, it is clear that former professionals who immigrate, disrupt their career paths, and they are penalized. They left their country of origin, where they received their credentials and work experience for another. In their new country, academic institutions, occupational regulatory bodies and employers do not recognize their past careers, and are under no obligation to provide them with work opportunities at the level of their previous employment (Boyd 1985; Richmond 1984).

Furthermore, professional labour markets channel women and men into separate careers. This gendered employment system varies between countries (Boyd 1990; Hanson et al. 1996; Hughes 2001; Kofman 2000; Pedraza 1991). As a result, immigrant women run up against two institutional barriers: a career path that lacks legitimacy, and an unrecognized match between gender and occupation.

If skilled immigrants do not get good jobs, is it because their English is below standard, they lack suitable training, or in other ways are not competent? Such familiar arguments suggest that immigrants should bear the onus for their underemployment, and that they should be given advice to arrive with their eyes open. They should try harder to learn the ropes, see how work is done, even remove an accent. In effect, according to such arguments, immigrants have no right to jobs at their previous employment level until they demonstrate they meet Canadian standards. For this, the market will judge them. If most skilled workers get jobs that do not make full use of their human capital because employers lack information to assess them, it should be only a matter of time until their qualifications are recognized.

In contrast, institutional writers expect that structures will block immigrants' ability to use their talents, and newcomers may never 'break in.' We can think of these roadblocks as akin to women's demand for equal pay for the same work as men. Whereas human capital analysts call for opening jobs to all those that meet the criteria, institutional theorists' solutions call for equal pay for work of equal value. This entails the systematic evaluations of jobs and credentials, removing parochialism from professional credentials, and translation of job descriptions into a common language that cuts across gendered and institutionalized occupations. Similarly, for new immigrants to be treated equitably, we need to ask, what work does a professional do? How necessary is local experience to each particular profession? If we grant that new immigrants have the right to equal employment, we need new methods to evaluate non-Canadian credentials and training.

Despite the weak links between human capital, labour market outcomes and productivity, governments still act as if human capital will spur economic development. They pursue policies to enhance the human capital of their countries. When problems regarding new immigrants' adjustment arise, governments often respond with programs aimed at boosting human capital (Foray and Lundvall 1996). For this reason, we use several variables drawn from human capital research to test the mobility of the skilled immigrant labour force in our study.

We focus on the assessment of their credentials, the structure of careers, the organization of professional labour markets, and gendered employment systems. We ask whether human capital theory can explain past careers in the immigrants' country of origin? Can it explain their entry into the labour force in the new country? Does it provide for variation? Here, a key variation that arises is gender. Is the job search of men and women, and those in different professions divergent? It will become apparent that human capital categories have more trouble explaining these variations than does institutional theory.

Methods

The 50 PRC couples that we studied immigrated to Canada from 1996 to 2001, the majority in 1999. The husband was the chief applicant in 46 cases. He had good education, some English language ability, and a profession that equipped him for admission to Canada. Finding a job in Canada prior to landing is not required. Their median year of birth is: males, 1963; females, 1965. They averaged 35 years of age at immigration. The vast majority had Bachelor of Science degrees or higher, two-thirds in engineering, medicine, accountancy and computer science. Married couples with dependent children, they had to get jobs quickly. Most try to find jobs in their qualified profession. One, but rarely both, also might delay the job search while studying English.

We located half of our contacts through the rosters of a large immigration agency in Toronto, Canada, soon after they landed. The agency, which offers ESL classes and workshops on the job search to hundreds of newcomers yearly, is well known in the Chinese community, and is held in high regard by their clients. Those we contacted generously agreed to share their experiences, and introduced us to eligible acquaintances (termed a snowball sample).

Our longitudinal research charts the progress of these couples in finding jobs over a two and a half to five year period. This period, while short, is enough to reveal how those professionals with diverse experiences and personal characteristics adapt to the Canadian labour market (Remennick 2003). While we do not claim that our sample represents the range of Chinese immigrants to Toronto, like them, most recent emigrants from China are well educated and from urban centres (Liang 2001; CIC 1999). We wondered if the agency's rosters were predisposed to those who cannot find professional jobs through friends, agents or otherwise on their own. But we found that even those we met through personal contact also signed up for workshops, to get a window onto Canada. Further, few in our sample, whether participants in the NGO or those we met through snowballing, know established locals who tell them about good jobs.

Salaff, as principal investigator, carried out most interviews in Mandarin Chinese, aided by PRC-Chinese research assistants, also recent immigrants. We use qualitative methods to gather data. We conducted focus groups, did participant observation in job search workshops, and social outings. Our topical interview guide gathered information about husbands' and wives' family and work histories and personal networks. We analyzed the data with N-Vivo, a qualitative research software program. Follow-ups keep us current with their work and family experiences. We averaged 2.4 interviews with each respondent couple and have updated most information through mid-2003.

In the following pages, we draw on our 100 respondents' own job histories for understanding how this cluster of people experienced institutionalized careers in China and Canada. Quotations from the cases are followed by a pseudonym, the gender, degree and major.

Getting Skilled in China

Background: Opening Internal Labour Market

Until recently, China did not have an open market for education or labour. Strong state controls shaped students' skills, their choice of majors, and length of schooling. Students took national tests for university. State sector firms, prized places in which workers expected to enjoy lifetime employment, operated like an internal labour market. Workers entered a particular firm at the start of their careers, remained there, and were rewarded for their experiences in the firm. This system gave the Chinese state and the work unit power over professional hiring (Bian 1994; Walder 1986).

This system was in force when most of our respondents got their first jobs, but it began to change in the 1980s, with great consequences for their careers. The labour market opened to outside investors in the form of Joint Venture Corporations, or shared investment by the state and foreign firms. Chinese private enterprises also greatly increased their employment share (Walder 1989). The foreign sector exposes these workers to a performance-based management system, which makes great demands on workers' time and energy, but rewards their accomplishments. Employees are promoted locally, go abroad for training, return to school for further degrees, and may use English at work. Labour mobility has increased.

Aware of differences in the structuring of foreign and local occupations, our respondents eagerly try the new approach to market-based work. Minbo, an engineer described the systematic way he was recruited to a quality control position:

> It was a joint venture, but the American party held 95 per cent of the shares, so it's almost a solely-owned American company … It was more systematic than state firms [in hiring] … Further, the American company was very advanced. There were training courses. They had [the latest processing technology.] State-owned enterprises were too superficial, even though there were serious problems, nobody was punished. (M, BSc Eng)

Although many state sector firms also participate in the global economy, they gave workers fewer opportunities to broaden their experiences.

Gender and Employment: Government Policy and its Limits

China's centralized system of training and allocating professionals to jobs provided fairly equal opportunities for educated women and men. It is well known that strong state legislation can help equalize labour force disadvantages for women and other marginalized workers (Ronsen and Sundstrom 2002). The central place of the Chinese state in the careers of professionals to a certain extent, served as an egalitarian force. For most of its history, the PRC government directed employment policies to draw on women's labour power. During the Cultural Revolution, women were exhorted to work hard. After the Cultural Revolution ended, a time of scarce human resources, women and men who received higher education and experience got ahead. By 1983, high proportions of women enrolled in the key fields in demand: 27 per cent of the engineering students were women, 37 per cent of the science students were women (Chen et al. 1997:164).

Nevertheless, state oversight cannot ensure that women and men received the same education and experiences, or human capital (Andors 1983). Further, the social value placed on family roles in China channel men and women into divergent professions, especially after marriage (Stacey 1983). Moreover, women still face stereotyping and discrimination (Loscocco and Wang 1992). As a result, women and men weave their careers around what is expected of them in the Chinese setting, resulting in gendered careers.

Education and Gender

Our respondents earned high degrees and enjoyed on-the-job opportunities to upgrade their skills. Admitted into Canada based on their skill level, they concentrated in disciplines dominated by science and technology. The credentials and fields of our women and men overlapped. Nevertheless, gendered educational profiles were visible. Men earned more degrees. All but one has at least a Bachelor degree; half have higher degrees, including four PhDs. The sole man with a diploma was not without specialized training; his private sector firm provided him with courses. Men mainly studied technical subjects that qualified them for the industrial jobs in demand. Over half (28) enrolled in engineering, and many of the rest majored in chemistry, computer science, medicine, and physics. A minority (10) graduated with non scientific-technical degrees, in art and design, foreign languages or literature, law, or business.

Women comprised nearly all of those with diplomas and high school degrees; fewer have PhDs and Masters. Although more (18 women) had non-science majors, the majority pursued science and technology majors. There were 10 female engineering majors, and many in medicine, accounting, and computer science.

While state policy opened science and technology as a field to women, their parents also actively intervened. In the majority of cases, women were likely to be persuaded that engineering and other technical fields were not suitable for them. This occurred even when, as in the case like Liuma, both parents were engineers. Liuma's parents convinced her to become a doctor. Medicine, which was practised in the secure state sector, was defined as a female job.

> I took courses in science at high school, and I didn't feel like being an engineer, so I chose medicine, which was more suitable for women, and I liked this profession, so did my parents ... They didn't think [being an engineer] was suitable for girls. They suggested to me at that time: a teacher or a doctor. Because I didn't have much patience, I wouldn't make a good teacher.

> (How did you come to think of going abroad?) Liuma: I had that idea very early. And working in hospitals in China, people were promoted according to seniority ... No matter how well you do, you won't get the priority. At that time, I didn't know too much about other countries, but I thought that there might be more opportunities and it would be more equal. Working in the hospitals in China was like lining up, the promotion, retirement, there wasn't motivation. I chose to be an anesthesiologist because, to a large extent, it was easier to change to a nurse from an anesthesiologist. If I wanted to go abroad, it wouldn't be too hard. So after my graduation, I chose it on purpose, with consideration of the possibility of going abroad. (F, BSc Medicine)

Liuma even chose her specialty based on her emigration plan. Further, she was concerned about her English abilities abroad and added that *'an anesthesiologist doesn't need to communicate a lot with patients who are already asleep!'*

In the end, more women than men majored in non-technical subjects such as education, humanities, law, business, nursing, and social sciences, and this was also due to parental guidance.

There was initially considerable educational equality between husbands and wives, many of whom first met in school or on their first job. However, after they married, 30 per cent of men (women six per cent) got further training. Women took on greater responsibility for family matters. By underwriting their husbands 'further education', wives human capital and their career attainment fell behind. Nevertheless, at the time they left China, nearly half of the husbands and wives had the same educational level (21 couples). Moreover, the degrees held by 20 couples differ by only one educational level; only nine couples' degrees were two levels apart. In sum, women and men enjoyed substantial opportunity to get high levels of human capital in the educational system.

Job Status and Gender

After graduating, both men and women were likely to get good jobs. We can order their jobs as high, medium, and low status. At the top are full-fledged professionals, with a bachelor's degree or higher, whose fields require professional certification. Here examples include: architectural designer, electrical engineer, and construction site manager. Middle status workers are semi-professionals with a bachelor degree or diploma in white-collar jobs that do not require certification such as the following: computer programmer, delivery co-ordinator, sales person, and construction site supervisor. Skilled clerical workers with high school education held low status jobs. At the time of emigrating, nearly two-thirds held high status jobs, and less than ten per cent had lower status jobs.

Relatively more men held high status jobs; mainly women held low status positions. On the other hand, there was considerable job equality within couples. In half the couples (26), husbands and wives held the same status jobs, 19 couples were one status level apart and only five differed by two levels. Few women held higher status jobs than their husbands; more wives held lower status jobs than their husbands.

Gender differences in job status in our couples were more likely the result of different human capital, than discrimination. The positions of women with higher degrees were the same as men with the same education in the same profession. Since men were more likely than women to have technical education and higher degrees, they were more likely to be higher status professionals.

Gendered Managerial Positions

However, Chinese organizations do tend to discriminate against women for management positions (Chen et al. 1997; Korabik 1994). Professionals with higher education in a technical field were most likely to be managers. Nevertheless, fewer women with these attainments were managers. In sum, human capital and having technical qualifications lead to positions of higher job status. However, institutional factors and discrimination accorded men more positional authority, separating women's and men's careers.

Three Key Professions

We looked in detail at the professions of engineering, computer science, and medicine, in which 59 of our sample worked, to assess the career achievements of women compared to men in our sample. Engineers held predominantly professional positions. Although there were fewer female engineers, they were as likely as men to be full professionals. All the female doctors practised in their professions. Half the computer scientists were women, and most were full professionals. However, more male professionals in these three fields became managers. In sum, while men and women in these high status fields had nearly the same career opportunities, women had a more difficult time gaining managerial authority.

Job Sector and Gender

Nearly all of those participating in our study were allocated stable, prestigious state sector jobs after graduation, a sign of their elite standing. Both advanced professionally, although men were more likely to become managers. The chief limitation was the low pay levels.

Not all stayed in the state sector. The move to the private sector was gendered: 29 men and only 17 women transferred to joint venture or private sector jobs. The kinds of fields men entered eased their transfer to the private sector. Joint ventures especially courted those with technical backgrounds, which more men had. However, men with other skills were also in demand. For instance, a man that majored in Spanish language became a salesman representing international companies.

Technically trained women were also recruited into the private sector, as computer specialists, secretaries, saleswomen, and accountants. However, medicine and other fields in which many women worked remained in the state sector. Socialization for family roles figured in women's choices. Apart from their specialties, women with family duties preferred the predictable time demands and less travel of state sector jobs.

Ying Chun (F) entered Tianjin University in 1983 and majored in mechanical engineering, where she met Minbo, her husband to be. Upon graduation, they were assigned to the same factory and married. When Minbo entered a joint venture in an economic and technical development zone, she applied to teach college there, in order to have more time to take care of their child (F. BSc Mechanical Engineering).

Couples worked out a division of labour. Many wives stayed in the regulated state sector, while their husbands chose the risky private sector (Loscocco and Wang 1992). As a result, men not only earned more, their experiences in Western organizations and links to specific foreign firms prompted them to emigrate, and gave them advantages that helped them adapt to the Canadian labour market.

Moving Careers to Canada

These professionals and technically skilled employees had already completed their schooling, chosen their disciplines, and embarked on high status careers in China. While some have higher attainments than others, while men did better than women in some areas, in coming to Canada all aimed to build on earlier successes. The two theoretical frameworks have different explanations for why their hopes did not pan out.

Human capital theory predicts a close fit will eventually emerge between new immigrants' abilities and new careers. Notably, those with higher occupations and status in China should attain similar status jobs in Canada. In contrast, institutional theorists predict that roles cannot be clearly ranked by their human capital equivalent. Canadian careers, professional labour markets, and gendered and racialized employment systems differ considerably from those in China. Careers in China will be disconnected from careers in Canada. This is especially the case for women.

The Evidence: Jobs in Canada

Those we met are aware that they have lost standing. Whereas in China, the majority were professionals, in Canada professionals no longer predominate. Only 16 retain the job status they enjoyed in China, one of whom is doing better than she had done there. The rest, 84 of the respondents, have dropped from high to medium or low status jobs.

Women have fallen further away from their original fields than men. More men than women hold professional and semi-professional positions in Canada. No females are professionals, and a minority are semi-professionals. Most women are either in low status, skilled or unskilled labour or clerical work (34 per cent compared to 28 per cent men), or out of the labour force entirely (36 per cent compared to 12 per cent men).

The differences between women's and men's human capital they brought to Canada influences who wins and who loses the good jobs. More important, however, are Canadian institutional structures. We explore how the differing social structures in Canada and China account for who gets good jobs.

Education and Gender

Human capital arguments predict that higher education should provide people good jobs. But it does not. The fates of those with different credentials are varied and inconsistent. The PhDs are most likely to attain higher status jobs; here, human capital arguments hold best. Seen as a research degree, the PhD has the most international recognition. In China, the attainment of higher degrees was gendered. Holding four of the five PhDs, men had more of these scarce resources than women. In Canada, several are able to get research jobs. All five respondents with PhDs continued in their fields, three as professionals. However, two fell one level, and became semi-professionals. A dentist, the sole female PhD, became a dental assistant.

While the picture is mixed, those with Masters (29 people) do significantly worse than the rest. This is due to the social definition of managers. Two-fifths of the Masters degree holders had been higher-level managers in China. The majority practised professions that are closed to outsiders in Canada. They are often offered applied technical positions, and need to regain practical skills they had learned as younger practitioners.

Finally, the 53 with Bachelors degrees do significantly better than those with Masters degrees. Those in applied technical fields can easily enter production and work at skilled technical jobs. Only a few are unemployed or in school trying to requalify. The same applies to those with a diploma or high-school certificate. In sum, as seen from their credentials, with the exception of those few with PhDs, human capital does not determine professional status in our sample.

The Role of Joint Venture Experience

Canadian employers are more likely to recognize experience in foreign or joint venture firms than state sector firms in China. The foreign branch is a familiar frame of reference. Consequently, those that had worked in a joint venture, e.g. an engineer who worked in IBM, another in Caterpillar Tractor were most acceptable to Canadian counterparts. A few of our respondents got jobs through networking within the Canadian companies in which they had worked in China, testifying to the importance of local recognition of workers' paths. Twenty of the 28 that have gained professional or semi-professional status in Canada had this background.

Those working in foreign firms got more human capital (colloquial English and other knowledge). Recognition of joint venture experience is also consonant with institutional predictions. Women with joint venture and private firm experience also fare better in the Canadian labour market. However, because women were more likely to have state sector jobs, and they are under-represented in the private sector compared with men, fewer have this advantage.

Job Status in Canada and Gender

While many of our respondents had become managers in China, in Canada, they are presumed to lack the cultural skills. This taken for granted concept blocks opportunities for new immigrants (Ely and Thomas 2001). It rarely occurs to employers to hire skilled immigrants as managers, since today's managers will most likely manage new immigrants like themselves.

> I had begun job-hunting. I sent about 80 resumes and had about 10 agent interviews and 4 company interviews. The first one is Johnsons & Johnsons. Why I failed? They wanted a programmer, but my strong point is system administration, which is usually done by

white people. To compete with the white people, I have no advantage. (Xianyi, M, BSc Comp-Science)

Denying management positions to new immigrants has important consequences for women. Management jobs are seen to suit local women with university degrees, but foreign-trained women with the same degrees cannot access them. As a result, immigrant women are apt to be segmented into lower status white or blue-collar workers, where they do not manage others. (Chard et al. 2000; Shea 1994)

(So you feel you will do the same work next year and the year after?) I think it won't change for five years. I will still be a programmer. Language is a big problem. You can't be a manager. (What's the biggest problem?) Conversation. It's second language for us, you cannot speak as fluently as they can or write as well as they could. So you do the work at the back. For instance, they wouldn't let you do the presentation when there is a big client. You just do the coding in the back … It's hard to enter their society. (Yangyi, F, BSc Comp-Science)

Three Key Professions and Gender

The majority of our 100 respondents were in fields where professional bodies control the market. The structure of the profession prevents them from entering their fields. The professional labour market works like an occupation specific internal labour market (Boyd and Thomas 2001; Osterman 1984). Access is only possible at the entry level, but once inside, it is easy to change firms. Professional associations monopolize labour supply by controlling certification and licensing. Entry to some trades, such as tool and die making, is also licensed. Holders of foreign credentials need to repeat schooling, pass Canadian examinations, and have a stint of supervised employment to qualify, whether in a residency (medical doctor) or apprenticeship (architect and engineer). Without recertification, they cannot hold responsible positions in their line of work. For instance, uncertified architects and engineers may draft plans, but cannot sign them. With little support for retraining of foreign specialists, few have done so. Instead, those former professionals try to get an allied semi-professional/technical position, grateful to use some of their original training. These positions are far below the full profession in status, earnings and authority.

Further, the professional and semi-professional/technical jobs are seen as suited to different genders in Canada. For instance, male (former) engineers may train for jobs in applied technical, but few Canadian women work in these fields. Turning to three examples, engineering, medicine, and computer science, we find both men and women have trouble having their past career paths acknowledged as professional labour in Canada. However, women face even greater barriers of gendered definitions of suitable jobs.

Engineering Women and men (38) with engineering backgrounds dominate our sample. Spread from high to low job levels, the variations in their careers give insights into Canadian labour market institutions. Male engineers predominate when it comes to those who do well. Two men are in the process of recertifying as professional engineers and two have already done so. Eight people have attained full professional status in Canada, and seven of them are male ex-engineers. They have better resources than the rest. For instance, his PhD degree enabled one former nuclear waste engineer to do research and project evaluation for the Canadian public agency that oversees nuclear energy. While he has not recertified as a professional engineer, he still hopes to requalify so that he can work on projects directly.

Male ex-engineers often drop one level from professional to semi-professionals/ technicians. Several have become computer programmers or process engineers, who do not sign their designs. Although the skills they used before their promotions to management may be rusty, they learn on the job or requalify through college courses.

In contrast, no female trained engineer works in her profession, nor have any attained a high status position in another field. These female ex-engineers lack transferable resources. None have PhDs in engineering, none worked in internationally recognized joint ventures, and hence none can access the networks of these overseas firms.

Most crucial is the difference in gender stratification. Canadian women are less visible in engineering and allied technical applied fields. While the number of female students is increasing in Canadian engineering departments, they still do not hold parity with men: the percentage of women among practising engineers in Canada was less than five per cent (Zwyno et al. 1999). Tool and die and other craft jobs are even more sharply gendered. Women who had been engineers cannot easily take up skilled technical positions that are not customarily filled by women in Canada. Only one woman has entered and one is training for a job in a skilled blue-collar technical field. Most former female engineers work as unskilled factory workers, and other low status jobs.

Medical practitioners Former doctors also must recertify, which normally entails redoing exams and residency. They had practised in the state sector in China, without multinational links to comparable institutions in Canada. Whereas they took their professional training in the Chinese language, requalification exams are in English. Liuma is the only one of the five formerly practicing doctors/dentists in our sample who is requalifying in her profession.

Unable to resume their former profession, they are nevertheless often able to take up a job as a medical technician. These positions are defined as female. Two women use their skills in feminized jobs of medical research or medical technicians. Technical positions are far below the full professional fields in status, earnings and authority. An oculist who requalified as a EKG technician also does eye specialist work in her clinic, for which, of course, she is not paid.

Computer science Computer science is a new and unprotected field, where the market prevails. Former computer scientists are not blocked by professional regulations from re-entering. Although they cannot find work at a managerial status, they often find jobs nearly as good as those left behind. Their problem is accessing information about a good job, whether by personal contacts, agents, or schools. Only one of the 13 that trained in information technology and allied field attained full professional position in Canada, but six are semi-professionals. Women are less likely to be excluded from this field. The downturn of the field after the year 2000 put all in a precarious position.

A programmer and system analyst in a managerial position had specialized in disaster recovery of information. Holding a Bachelor's degree in Computer Science, he only acquired a low-level problem-shooting job on a hot line.

> Honestly, after signing the offer, I felt very sad – the position was a little low. They said you should get work experience in Canada as soon as possible, so I signed it anyway. It's very near my home. The boss is satisfied with me, because some of the other employees don't know much about IS400. The probation period is three months. (Xianyi, M, BSc, Comp-Science)

Employers will often ignore our respondents' experiences, relegating them to entry-level positions in their fields. Many suspect that employers know that they have the experience needed, but are hiring them cheaply (Basran and Zong 1999). They have to prove themselves through their work, not their resumes, to move forward.

> Even for people like me, this company hired me as entry-level programmer! (because my experience is not Canadian). Then if you do well, they raise your salary. (Yangyi, F, BSc, Comp-Science)

In contrast, when a computer scientist's former colleague attested to her abilities, she secured a job in a senior analyst position.

> The company I'm in now, Sprint, was introduced by a colleague that I got to know when I was doing a project in that Singapore company [I worked for in Shanghai]. His team was recruiting people then, and his manager told them that they could recommend their friends because it was more reliable. And I got it. I think that one of the main reasons is that my boss, who's from Hong Kong, understands the situation in China. If you talk with the native bosses here, and you tell them what you have done, sometimes they don't understanding. We are referring to different things with the same words. (Lei Hong, F, BSc, Comp-Science)

Gendered professionals Women do worse than men when it comes to professional positions, in part because they arrive with fewer transferable resources. Only one has a PhD, which wins better jobs in Canada. Few have worked in joint ventures, with which Canadian firms are more familiar. Because professions limit entry, the credentials of only a few women (and men) boost them to professional jobs. The best that women can often do is to become technicians, which are highly gendered jobs. Excluded by the engineering profession, women who were formerly engineers rarely become blue-collar technicians. Former doctors more easily enter the feminized sector of medical technicians and do better. In these two professions institutional factors override market mechanisms in hiring for higher status jobs. In sharp relief, both women and men get good positions in information sciences, which is a less institutionalized field and outside Canadian professional control.

As a result of men's greater opportunities, couples' equality has decreased. In Canada fewer husbands and wives hold the same job status. Only 13 couples have jobs at the same status level; in 12 couples they are one level apart; within 13 couples spouses are separated by two or more job levels. By moving to Canada, Chinese women have lost equality of status with their husbands.

Conclusion

International migrants have left one institutional setting which had shaped their human capital for another. It is difficult for those that grew up in one society to move their skill set effortlessly to another country. Arriving in Canada, the specialists we studied face social and institutional barriers in regaining the careers they had held. The poor match between the social structures that surround jobs in a migrant's home country and their new destination makes it hard to continue careers abroad. They lack recognition of their education, professional status, and their work experiences, and encounter a gendered labour market that does not match that of China. Chinese women and men fared differently and their occupational positions depended on the degree of control by Canadian professions.

We compared human capital and institutional theories to explain these findings. Both underscore the specific skills that professional and technical jobs require, but contest the link between educational and occupational structures. Human capital theory describes how opportunities follow credentials in those occupations where skills can be evaluated. Theorists ask whether the skills of new immigrants fit those demanded in the host country. Institutional theory argues that careers are rooted in structured labour markets. Labour markets based on human capital can be analyzed as a social construction that features perceptions of recognizable credentials and career paths.

The diverse fates of these women and men in China and Canada underscore how career achievements rest on a set of institutional understandings. Human capital better explains women's past career achievements in China, because their careers take place within a familiar institutional setting. In contrast, women did worse than men in Canada only partly due to their lag in suitable human capital. More problematic is the role of institutional fields. Women's education and credentials in the labour market are valued differently from those of men. Women are squeezed into fewer available jobs due to the gendered job profile in Canada which differs from the Chinese pattern. Their gendered experiences underscore the contentions of institutional theory. The highly institutionalized professional system in the receiving country affects women more than men. They are not judged by their human capital.

Our comparison faults the logical structure of human capital theory. When applying human capital theory, hypotheses testing on occupational achievements is usually done within one setting, where careers are institutionalized, and signalling theory explains these results. Comparing job achievements of people from different institutional settings removes institutional homogeneity from an empirical sample. Once one leaves the taken for granted setting, human capital constructs explain poorly why new job contenders are shunted away from fields in which their credentials are entrenched. Since labour markets are highly institutionalized, we question the validity of human capital theory in explaining market driven careers. Human capital cannot explain the lack of recognition and consequent drop in status of immigrants with Chinese human capital in Canada.

Institutional theory takes us further in spelling out how labour markets and choice of education and careers follow institutionalized patterns. The institutional perspective expects that those that grew up in one society cannot move their skill set effortlessly to another because their foreign education and experience is not taken for granted. Since the professions are closed to those whose past career paths and achievements do not conform to legitimate and recognizable patterns, immigrants will do poorly.

In conclusion, institutional theories are best able to outline the structural barriers to immigrants' employment in established occupations. The institutional environment is a sophisticated system for protecting the established professions and their local population from outside competition, and is a discriminator against immigrants. It is necessary to initiate major institutional changes to take advantage of the skills and motivations of new immigrants to Canada. The state should follow up by assessing immigrants' qualifications in a structured manner, analyzing who is immigrating and how to standardize recognition of their credentials to ease absorption of those who were schooled and trained elsewhere. Other nations adopt new strategies. The European Union spends considerable effort assessing how professionals may practice in member states (see position paper by Malta Financial Services Authority 2003). Israel has a Ministry of Immigrant Absorption, and Russian-educated engineers need just to register their diplomas to be eligible to work within their professions (Remennick 2001, 2003).

The state provides certain minimal civil, political, and legal rights to new immigrants, treating them like long standing citizens. The economic dimensions of citizenship are left erratically to individuals and firms. There are few easy answers, but we need to question the strategy of letting valuable immigrants with professional training flounder.

ACKNOWLEDGEMENT We acknowledge gratefully the support of this research by the Social Sciences and Humanities Council of Canada. The Centre for Urban and Community Studies, Department of Sociology, at the University of Toronto, and the Centre for Asian Studies, University of Hong Kong provided us with helpful support. We wish to thank Stephanie Tang and staff at CICS for their unstinting help, the many people who generously shared their views and experiences with us, and out talented research assistants; Lynn Xu, and Su Zhang worked with Salaff as excellent interviewers; Hoda Farahmandpour and Philipps

Wong helped with analysis, Heather Jiang with the bibliographical search. We appreciate the thoughtful suggestions made by Evangelia Tastsoglou and Alexandra Dobrowolsky.

References

Andolfatto, D., Ferrall, C. and Gomme, P. (2000), 'Human Capital Theory and the Life-Cycle Pattern of Learning and Earning, Income and Wealth,' Working paper, Simon Fraser University, Vancouver.

Andors, P. (1983), *The Unfinished Liberation of Chinese Women*, Indiana University Press, Bloomington.

Basran, G.S. and Zong, L. (1999), 'Devaluation of Foreign Credentials as Perceived by Visible Minority Immigrants in Canada,' *Canadian Ethnic Studies*, Vol. 30, pp. 6-23.

Becker, G. S. (1964), *Human Capital*, University of Chicago Press, Chicago.

Bian, Y. (1994), *Work and Inequality in Urban China*, State University of New York Press, Albany.

Bills, D. B. (1988), 'Educational Credentials and Hiring Decisions: What Employers Look for in New Employees,' in A. Kalleberg (ed.), *Research in Social Stratification and Mobility*, Vol. 7, pp. 71-97.

Blossfeld, H-P. and Mayer, K. U. (1988), 'Labor Market Segmentation in the Federal Republic of Germany: An Empirical Study of Segmentation Theories from a Life Course Perspective,' *European Sociology Review*, Vol. 4(2), pp. 123-40.

Boyd, M. (1990), 'Sex differences in Occupational Skill: Canada, 1961-1986,' *La Revue Canadienne de Sociologie et d'Anthropologie/The Canadian Review of Sociology and Anthropology*, Vol. 27, pp. 285-315.

Boyd, M. (1985), 'Immigration and Occupation Attainment in Canada,' in M. Boyd, J. Goyder, F. E. Jones, H. A. McRoberts, P. C. Pineo, and J. Porter (eds), *Ascription and Achievement: Studies in Mobility and Status Attainment in Canada*, Carleton University Press, Ottawa.

Boyd, M. and Thomas, D. (2001), 'Match or Mismatch? The Employment of Immigrant Engineers in Canada's Labor Force,' *Population Research and Policy Review*, Vol. 20, pp. 107-33.

Chard, J., Badets, J. and Howatson-Leo, L. (2000), 'Immigrant Women. Women in Canada, 2000,' *A Gender-Based Statistical Report*, Statistics Canada, Ottawa, pp. 189-218.

Chen, C. C., Yu, K. C. and Miner, J. B. (1997), 'Motivation to Manage: A Study of Women in Chinese State-Owned Enterprises,' *The Journal of Applied Behavioral Science*, Vol. 33(2), pp. 160-73.

CIC (Citizenship and Immigration Canada) (1999), 'Facts and Figures: Immigration Overview 1999,' Communications Branch, Ottawa.

DiMaggio, P. and Powell, W. W. (1991), 'The Iron Cage Revisited: Institutional Isomorphism and Collective Rationality in Organization fields,' in W. W. Powell and P. DiMaggio (eds), *The New Institutionalism in Organizational Analysis*, The

University of Chicago Press, Chicago, pp. 63-83.

Ely, R. J. and Thomas, D. A. (2001), 'Cultural Diversity at Work: The Effects of Diversity Perspectives on Work Group Processes and Outcomes,' *Administrative Science Quarterly*, Vol. 46, pp. 229-73.

Foray, D. and Lundvall, B. (1996), 'The Knowledge-Based Economy: From the Economics of Knowledge to the Learning Economy,' in *Employment and Growth in the Knowledge-based Economy*, OECD Documents, Paris.

Hall, J. (1988), *The Competence Connection: A Blueprint for Excellence*, Woodstead Press, The Woodlands, TX.

Hanson, S.L., Schaub, M. and Baker, D.P. (1996), 'Gender Stratification in the Science Pipeline: A Comparative Analysis of Seven Countries,' *Gender & Society*, Vol. 10, pp. 271-90.

Hughes, K. D. (2001), 'Restructuring Work, Restructuring Gender: The Movement of Women into Non-traditional Occupations in Canada,' in V. W. Marshall, W. R. Heinz, H. Kruger, and A. Verma (eds), *Restructuring Work and The Life Course*, University of Toronto Press, Toronto, pp. 84-106.

Kofman, E. (2000), 'The Invisibility of Skilled Female Migrants and Gender Relations in Studies of Skilled Migration in Europe,' *International Journal of Population Geography*, Vol. 6, pp. 45-59.

Korabik, K. (1994), 'Managerial Women in the People's Republic of China: The Long March Continues,' in N. J. Adler and D. N. Israeli (eds), *Competitive Frontiers: Women Managers in a Global Economy*, Blackwell, Cambridge, pp. 114-36.

Lerner, M. and Menahem, G. (2003), 'Decredentialization and Recredentialization: The Role of Governmental Intervention in Enhancing Occupational Status of Russian Immigrants in Israel in the 1990s,' *Work and Occupations*, Vol. 30(1), pp. 3-29.

Li, P. (2004), *Deconstructing Canada's Discourse of Immigrant Integration*, Working Paper WP04-03, University of Saskatchewan Working Paper Series PCERII, Alberta.

Li, P. S. (2000), 'Earning Disparities between Immigrants and Native-Born Canadians,' *La Revue Canadienne de Sociologie et d'Anthropologie/The Canadian Review of Sociology and Anthropology*, Vol. 37, pp. 289-311.

Liang, Z. (2001), 'Demography of Illicit Emigration from China: A Sending Country's Perspective,' *Sociological Forum*, Vol. 16, pp. 677-701.

Lin, Y-W. and Powers, D. A. (2004), *Occupational Mobility Within and Between Segmented Labor Markets,* Paper presented at ASA Annual Meeting, San Francisco, CA, Aug. 13-17.

Loscocco, K.A. and Wang, X. (1992), 'Gender Segregation in China,' *Sociology and Social Research*, Vol. 76, pp. 118-26.

Malta Financial Services Authority (2003), *Professional Services in the EU* (www.mfsa.com.mt/mfsa/euandinternational/specialreports/Website%20%20Professionals%20Final.pdf). Accessed 7 September 2004.

March, J. G. and Olsen, J. P. (1989), *Rediscovering Institutions: The Organizational*

Basis of Politics, Free Press, New York.

March, J. G. and Sutton, R. I. (1994), 'Organizational Performance as a Dependent Variable,' *Organization Science*, Vol. 8, pp. 698-706.

McDade, I. (1988), *Barriers to the Recognition of the Credentials of Immigration in Canada*, Institute for Research on Public Policy, Ottawa.

Nee, V. and Sanders, J. (2001), 'Understanding the Diversity of Immigrant Incorporation: A Forms of Capital Model,' *Ethnic and Racial Studies*, Vol. 24(3), pp. 386-411.

Newman, K. (1988), *Falling from Grace: The Experience of Downward Mobility of the American Middle Class*, New York, The Free Press, New York.

Osterman, P. (1984), 'Introduction: The Nature and Importance of Internal Labor Markets,' in P. Osterman (ed.), *Internal Labor Markets*, MIT Press, Cambridge, MA, pp. 1-22.

Pedraza, S. (1991), 'Women and Migration: The Social Consequences of Gender' *Annual Review of Sociology*, Vol. 17, pp. 303-25.

Pfeffer, J. (1994), *Competitive Advantage through People*, Boston, Harvard Business School Press, Boston.

Remennick, L. I. (2003), 'Career Continuity among Immigrant Professionals: Russian Engineers in Israel,' *Journal of Ethnic and Migration Studies*, Vol. 29(4), pp. 701-21.

Remennick, L. I. (2001), 'All My Life is One Big Nursing Home: Russian Immigrant Women in Israel Speak about Double Caregiver Stress,' *Women's Studies International Forum*, Vol. 24(6).

Richmond, A. H. (1984), 'Immigration and Unemployment in Canada and Australia,' *International Journal of Comparative Sociology*, Vol. 25, pp. 3-4.

Ronsen, M. and Sundstrom, M. (2002), 'Family Policy and After-Birth Employment among New Mothers – A Comparison of Finland, Norway and Sweden,' *European Journal of Population/Revue europeenne de demographie*, Vol. 18(2), pp. 121-52.

Schoeni, R. F. (1998), 'Labor Market Outcomes of Immigrant Women in the United States: 1970 to 1990,' *International Migration Review*, Vol. 32, pp. 57-77.

Scott, W. R. (2001), *Institutions and Organizations* (2nd edition), Sage Publications, Thousand Oaks, CA.

Shea, C. (1994), 'Changes in Women's Occupations,' in C. McKie (ed.), *Canadian Social Trends: A Canadian Studies Reader* (Volume 2), Thompson Educational Press, Toronto, pp. 151-54.

Stacey, J. (1983), *Patriarchy and Socialist Revolution in China*, University of California Press, Berkeley.

Temple, J. (2001), 'Growth Effects of Education and Social Capital in the OECD Countries,' *OECD Economic Studies*, No. 33, 2001/2, pp. 57-101.

Walder, A. G. (1989), 'Social Change in Post-Revolution China,' *Annual Review of Sociology*, Vol. 15, pp. 405-24.

Walder, A. G. (1986), *Communist Neo-traditionalism: Work and Authority in Chinese*

Industry, University of California Press, Berkeley.

Weiss, A. (1995), 'Human Capital vs. Signalling Explanations of Wages,' *Journal of Economic Perspectives*, Vol. 9(4), pp. 133-54.

Zwyno, M. S., Gilbride, K. A., Hiscocks, P. D., Waalen, J. K. and Kennedy, D. C. (1999), *Attracting Women into Engineering – a Case Study* (www.ee.ryerson. ca:8080/~womeng /wiec/news/wie_news/IEEE_Paper/BEGIN.HTM). Accessed 8 September 2004.

Chapter 5

Engendering Labour Migration: The Case of Foreign Workers in Canadian Agriculture

Kerry Preibisch and Luz María Hermoso Santamaría

Introduction

This chapter explores the incorporation of foreign workers under a temporary admission program in Canadian agriculture, using a gender perspective as an analytical starting point. Foreign migrant workers have been employed in Canadian agriculture under temporary visas since the 1960s, first from the Caribbean (1966) and later from Mexico (1974). To date, men have comprised the overwhelming majority. In the late 1980s, women were encouraged to apply and since their incorporation, their numbers have shown moderate growth. Despite the fact that paid agricultural work constitutes a highly gendered and racialized occupation, scholarly attention to the incorporation of foreign labour in Canadian agriculture has largely neglected to incorporate gender analysis in examinations of this phenomenon and has often used women's numerically small presence to justify male-bias in research design. It has only been very recently that the growing numbers of women and their increasing visibility in rural spaces has instigated the tabling of gender analysis in the debate (see Barndt 2000; Barrón 2000; Becerril 2003). Conversely, the use of foreign workers in domestic service, a predominantly feminized occupation, has received relatively more attention from researchers who tend to approach their work using feminist frameworks (Arat-Koc 1989; Arat-Koc and Giles 1994; Chang 2000; Macklin 1994; Pratt 1999; Stasiulis and Bakan 2003, among others). These imbalances in the literature and the case we detail below are further evidence of the need for feminist scholarship on migration to go beyond women-only focuses and situate gender and its intersectionality with other relations of power as constitutive elements of (im)migration, even in masculinized migration flows.

In this chapter we document and analyze the use of migrant labour in Canadian agriculture from a gender perspective and discuss some of the gendered experiences of transnational migrants serving global agriculture. These findings contribute to recent attempts to underscore the ways in which gender relations shape and organize migration and further engender the transnational (Hondagneu- Sotelo 2003). Further, our analysis is relevant to feminist scholarship on citizenship, as we examine how the denial of legal citizenship through temporary visa programs allow high income states to provide a disciplined and low cost labour supply domestically in order to ensure competitiveness in global markets. Furthermore, it highlights the discriminatory nature of Canadian immigration policy along multiple relations of power, based on North-South relations, class, race/ethnicity, gender, etc.

Engendering Migration Studies

Feminist scholarship has made important gains in revealing how multiple systems of oppression based on social difference – in which gender is but one relation of power – organize everyday life, including one of the most influential social processes of the contemporary world: the global movement of people. Following Morokvásic's (1984) call to temper the male bias characterizing the migration literature, feminist scholars have both infused a gender perspective into the subfield and exposed women's experience as transnational migrants (Goldring 1996; Hondagneu-Sotelo 1994; Kanaiaupuni 2000; Ong 1999; Salazar Parreñas 2001; Sassen 2000). The first wave of scholarship attempted to make women visible in the decades of research based predominantly on male subjects (Hondagneu-Sotelo 2003; Pessar 2003). This compensatory phase, however, tended to treat women as a variable to be added and to focus exclusively on women immigrants and female migration, segregating them further within the subfield and obscuring gender as a relation of power shaping the movement of people (Erel et al. 2003; Hondagneu-Sotelo 2003). By the early 1990s, however, the role of gender was at the centre of debates in feminist scholarship (Grasmuck and Pessar 1991; Hondagneu-Sotelo 1994; Pedraza 1991). More recently, scholars have gone beyond a focus on women, families and communities to inculcate gender analysis more fully within migration studies (Hondagneu-Sotelo 2003; Pessar 2003).

Feminist social relational analysis has also contributed to the conceptualizing of modern citizenship. In particular, feminists were among the first to dispel liberal notions of the universal citizen based on white, European, propertied males to the exclusion of others (Stasiulis and Bakan 1997). These initial contributions, while emphasizing the gendered nature of citizenship, often remained limited both to Western models of citizenship and a fairly homogeneous understanding of women (Yuval-Davis 1999). More recently, scholars have advocated for approaching citizenship in ways that take into account how individuals are positioned differently not only within nations but within the global political economy according to multiple dimensions of social divisions, including membership in dominant or subordinate groups, gender, ethnicity, country of origin, and urban or rural residence (Stasiulis and Bakan 1997; Yuval-Davis 1999).

These analyses have particular salience as the socio-economic polarization between the North and South deepens. Global restructuring has had enormous implications for the movement of labour, currently estimated to involve some 175 million people (Stalker 2004). One manifestation of contemporary labour movements is the growing incorporation of non-citizen migrant workers in high-income countries, particularly in geographically immobile sectors such as agriculture, construction, and domestic service. This phenomenon became particularly marked throughout the 1990s, growing at much more rapid rates than permanent immigration by foreign workers (OECD 2003). Sharma (2001) argues that Canadian immigration policy has shifted away from a policy of permanent (im)migrant settlement towards an increasing reliance upon temporary workers.[1]

As several authors have shown and we detail below, migrant workers' immigration status as non-citizens denies them the services and protections associated with legal citizenship and allows labour-importing states to circumscribe to a greater degree the conditions under which these workers labour and live within their borders. Research on migrant workers underscores how labour-importing states use temporary visa programs to create and maintain a pool of highly exploitable and socially-excluded workers (Baines and Sharma 2002; Salazar Parreñas 2001; Stasiulis and Bakan 1997; Ball and Piper 2004). In this regard, changes to immigration policy can be seen as attempts by the nation-state to restructure labour-capital relations in order to protect its position within the globalized political economy (Rai 2001).[2] Thus, as Stasiulis and Bakan (2003: 12) point out, modern citizenship plays a role 'in accessing a wide range of rights, but as importantly in creating and reproducing inequality among individuals and groups in the context of contemporary globalization'.

Migration and citizenship studies that take on gender as an analytical starting point have tended to focus on migration flows that are feminized. Particularly within the Canadian context, foreign workers in domestic service – a highly feminized occupation – have received inordinate scholarly attention relative to those employed in agriculture – a highly masculinized occupation. There is now an emergent literature on foreign workers in agriculture (Basok 2002; Binford 2002; Wall 1992). Although this literature has brought to light the previously unstudied phenomenon of foreign agricultural workers, both women and a gender perspective are missing. The empirical reality that both domestic service and agricultural work are markedly gendered (as well as racialized) is compelling evidence for applying a gender analysis equally to masculinized migration flows, such as migrant labour in agriculture, the motivation for the research presented here.

Foreign Workers in Canadian Agriculture

The principal program under which foreign workers are granted temporary employment visas in agriculture is the Seasonal Agricultural Workers Program

---

1   In 1973, 57 per cent of all people entering Canada for employment were awarded permanent resident status. By 1993, however, only 30 per cent of the total number of workers admitted to the country received this status while 70 per cent came as migrant workers on temporary employment authorizations (Sharma 2001).

2   Immigration serves other agendas as well, including racist ideological constructions of 'desirable' immigrants (Stasiulis and Bakan 2003).

(SAWP).[3] The SAWP has expanded significantly since its inception nearly four decades ago. The number of workers has increased from 264 in 1966 to over 19,000; the range of farming operations receiving foreign workers has broadened to include a wide range of agri-food operations; and the program now operates in nine of Canada's 12 provinces or territories. The overwhelming majority of workers are concentrated in Ontario and Quebec, where they have come to represent a growing share of the agricultural labour supply. Weston and Scarpa de Masellis (2004) estimated that foreign workers now account for some 45 per cent of person-hours in agriculture in these two provinces, and may soon account for a greater share of total hours than Canadians.

Industry and government fiercely defend the use of temporary workers as the 'keystone' of the horticulture industry, for providing a reliable, seasonal workforce to overcome chronic domestic labour shortfalls. Labour shortages and demographic polarization are growing trends in many high income countries (Nurse 2004). The inability to recruit and retain labour in agriculture has a long history in Ontario, however, indicating that domestic shortages in part reflect a poor labour environment that Canadians with other employment options reject. Agriculture is considered the most dangerous occupation in Ontario, with over 20 agricultural workers killed on the job every year (UFCW 2004). Agricultural workers, both domestic and foreign, earn lower salaries and enjoy fewer rights relative to other sectors. In Ontario, for example, agricultural workers are not covered under the existing occupation health and safety legislation and are legally prevented from unionizing.

Canada's agricultural sector has a long-standing reliance on socially disadvantaged groups to supply labour (Basok 2002; Wall 1992; Satzewich 1991).[4] Temporary visa programs can be seen as further attempts by the Canadian state to institutionalize the supply of cheap and vulnerable workers to unprotected labour sites. Such programs enable the state to supply industries with low-cost labour, but also a particular type of labour that through the denial of citizenship can be made more 'reliable' than even the most socially vulnerable domestic supplies. Indeed, the restrictions placed on workers and accompanying mechanisms of control built into the SAWP have led several authors to consider these workers as 'unfree' labour (Basok 2002; Satzewich 1991; Sharma 2001). Temporary workers do not enjoy labour market mobility.

---

3   Participating countries include Barbados, Jamaica, Mexico, the member states of the Organization for Eastern Caribbean States, and Trinidad and Tobago.

4   At the turn of the century, thousands of impoverished British children were sent to Canadian farms by philanthropist Thomas Barnardo as 'apprentices' in exchange, upon reaching adulthood, for citizenship (Bagnell 2001; Wall 1992). During World War II, the federal government supplied growers with Canadian internees, German prisoners of war, and conscientious objectors (Basok 2002; Satzewich 1991). In the post-war period, Polish war veterans and 'Displaced Persons' – immigrants recently arrived from war-torn Europe – were also recruited for work in agriculture. In addition, throughout the twentieth century the federal government instituted a series of labour recruiting programs involving internal migrants from economically-depressed regions in Canada, aboriginals, and youth (Basok 2002; Satzewich 1991).

Their visa is valid with a single employer, effectively reducing workers' bargaining power.

Constituting migrant workers as 'reliable' includes limiting their social commitments through mechanisms that are mutually reinforcing. Ironically, migrant workers enter the country as single applicants but must demonstrate they have families they support in their home countries. Preference in recruitment has historically favoured married workers with dependents. For immigration gatekeepers, the policy of recruiting migrants with strong social commitments is designed to deter attempts to secure permanent residency through marriage or to remain in Canada illegally. Residential arrangements under the SAWP also minimize the formation of social commitments. Workers are normally housed on their employers' property, allowing increased access to, and control over, their lives. Some of this control is institutionalized in the sanctioned use of 'farm rules' that include imposing a curfew, enforcing restrictions on workers' mobility, and prohibiting the entry of visitors (Preibisch 2004b). Workers' vulnerability is further institutionalized through a policy that allows employers to request the same workers every year. The 'naming policy' fosters a high degree of worker self-discipline, shores up worker loyalty, and ultimately reinforces paternalistic labour relations (Basok 2000; Binford 2002, 2004; Wall 1992). The most effective mechanism of labour discipline is employers' power to dismiss (and therefore deport) workers. Although repatriation rates are low, the fear of repatriation is pervasive as workers have been deported for falling ill, refusing unsafe work, or complaining about housing and working conditions (Basok 2002; Cross 2003; Preibisch 2000, 2004b; Smart 1998; UFCW 2002; Verma 2004). Workers consequently take measures to avoid repatriation and the loss of livelihood, including the non-reporting of personal injury. The gendered implications of these mechanisms to limit workers' social commitments will be expanded upon later in this chapter.

Labour-exporting country officials are charged with protecting their compatriots during their work periods in Canada, but workers' assessments of these representatives are highly critical (Basok 2002; Colby 1997; Preibisch 2000; Smart 1998; Verduzco 2004). The representation of migrant workers is mired by a significant conflict of interest: maintaining their country's market share of labour placements and the foreign exchange earnings they provide. Employers are free to choose the country that will supply them with labour, a privilege that disempowers labour-exporting states and leads to heavy competition between them to supply productive, well-behaved workers that do not complain. In the contemporary global economy, remittances have become an integral aspect of the economies of labour supply countries.[5]

Baines and Sharma argue that the category of migrant worker must be positioned historically within the entire set of Canadian state immigration laws that have helped organize a racialized and gendered 'hierarchal ordering of insiders and outsiders living and working in Canada' (Baines and Sharma 2002: 84). While this mandate is

---

5   In 2002, foreign exchange from remittances generated US$19 billion for Mexico and represented 102 per cent of Jamaica's merchandise trade (World Bank 2003).

beyond the scope of this paper, it is worth noting briefly those immigration policies geared at establishing a domestic agrarian class. In the first decades of the twentieth century the federal government recruited families from the United Kingdom (UK), the US and Eastern Europe for settlement based on their perceived potential to build a nation of farmers, while overtly discriminating against others on the basis of race, ethnicity, religion, and nationality. At the same time Canada's immigration policy removed explicitly racist restrictions on immigration from the South in 1967, policies to bring in temporary foreign workers were institutionalized in the Non-Immigrant Employment Authorization Program (NIEAP), a program that continues to move people into Canadian labour markets but that legitimizes the differentiation of rights and entitlements within the country along citizen/non-citizen lines (Sharma 2001, 2000). Critical historical analysis of Canadian government documents on the SAWP reveal how official discourse legitimized indenturing workers to agriculture through racist perceptions of Caribbean and Mexico workers' suitability for agriculture work and lesser entitlement to the rights afforded Canadian citizens (Satzewich 1991; Sharma 2001, 2000). To date, candidates are only eligible to qualify as foreign farm workers under the SAWP if they can prove they are economically destitute and that they lack assets such as education and land, precisely the inverse of the qualities needed to quality for immigrant status. Conversely, foreign farm operators can qualify for Canadian citizenship by proving they have the means to purchase and manage a farm. It is not surprising that the composition of post-war immigrant farmers reflects balances of power in the world economy, as they originate primarily from rich European countries where farmers enjoy considerable state support.[6] Undoubtedly, the Canadian state has used immigration policy to shape the social organization of agriculture according to hierarchies based on race/ethnicity, class, North-South relations and, as we discuss next, gender.

Engendering Labour Migration to Canadian Agriculture[7]

The labour migration of foreign workers to Canadian agriculture has been highly masculinized. Women did not participate in the SAWP until 1989, a full 23 years following its foundation, and today represent approximately two per cent of the

---

6   The top three countries of origin include the Netherlands, Switzerland, and the UK, (Statistics Canada 2004).

7   This chapter is based on research conducted with Mexican migrant agricultural workers and their employers in the southwestern part of the Canadian province of Ontario, funded in part by the Social Sciences and Humanities Research Council. The research design included a portfolio of ethnographic methods, with interviews serving as the principal method of inquiry. In-depth individual and group interviews were carried out with a sample of female workers (n=31), male workers (n=20), employers (n=10), and community service providers (n=5). The limited scope of this study did not permit research with Caribbean workers; future comparative research that includes the range of nationalities and ethnic groups represented in Canadian agriculture is clearly warranted.

workforce. Mexico supplies the greatest amount of female workers, sending between 200 and 300 in recent years. Tracing the masculinization of the SAWP, or gendering migration, emphasizes the utility of using a social relational focus when studying migration, highlighting the ways in which gender and other relations of power organize and shape migration. Gender operates at a number of levels, from the household to the level of the global political economy.

Beginning the analysis of gender relations at the level of the household in migrants' communities of origin reveals social norms that discourage women's participation as international migrants, such as the gender division of labour that circumscribes men as primary breadwinners and women as caregivers. In rural Mexico, women's contributions to the productive economy often go unrecognized and are considered as 'help,' even when they exceed men's earnings. Likewise, their reproductive labour in the care economy is often not recognised and/or accorded lesser social value (Arizpe 1989; González de la Rocha 1994; Marroni 1995; Preibisch 2001). In our interviews with male migrants, several admitted that it was not until they came to Canada and were forced to assume responsibility for the social reproduction carried out by the women in their lives that they realized the full extent of these contributions. The words of an interviewee, Elizardo,[8] aptly capture gendered cultural practices:

> In Canada you learn to value women more ... There is a saying that men are really macho but it's not that; what happens is we are accustomed, that is, every country has its customs that you adapt over the generations ... Sometimes you ask: 'What do women do?' But when you are alone and far away, you learn to appreciate that yes, it's true that women work, within the home that is. You learn to appreciate, as you miss your wife or girlfriend, because in Mexico we are accustomed – well they are also women's customs – that we men don't have to make any food or wash any dishes, rather the women. We have a wife that does all this type of work for us. And when we are here alone, we have to do laundry, cook, clean our room, make our bed, and all those things and that is when we realize that women do work, that our wives do have a lot of work and the truth is they never rest.[9]

As this suggests, an inequitable gender division of labour continues to operate in rural Mexico, with pervasive male breadwinner norms. Further, regardless of women's activities outside the home, they continue to be responsible for the bulk of social reproduction, an invisible and devalued activity.

The men interviewed for this study did not want their wives to migrate to Canada; they preferred that they were at home caring for their children. The public/private divide in Mexican cultural practices together with the entire set of social norms defining masculinity and femininity structure everyday life, including men's and women's mobility. Our female informants often stressed men's advantages of having the liberty to do what they want, move where they want, achieve what they want. As Silvia put it, 'in my country, the man has more rights. As a woman, I have more

---

8   All names are pseudonyms.

9   All quotes from Mexican informants have been translated from Spanish and in some cases, paraphrased for clarity. All italics are our emphasis.

obligations than rights.' Yet despite women's gendered responsibilities and their limited mobility, they have been active in migration flows throughout the twentieth century both as migrants and by sustaining migration flows. Women have formed the majority of Mexico's regional migrants throughout the latter half of the twentieth century and to date (Aranda 1993; Arizpe and Botey 1987; INEGI 2000).[10]

Historically, migration to international destinations has been a livelihood strategy exercised by men and supported by women (D'Aubeterre 1995; Kanaiaupuni 2000). Decisions regarding who will migrate and who will stay are ultimately circumscribed by patriarchal ideology; women are not able to exercise this livelihood strategy to the same degree as men, nor do they have direct control over men's remittances. Nonetheless, women's participation in transnational migration is changing. Recent estimates show that women are comprising a rapidly increasing number of the undocumented Mexicans emigrating transnationally in search of employment, numbering some 200,000 since the early 1990s (Latin American Data Base 2004). According to some estimates, women now comprise 20 of every 100 undocumented Mexicans crossing the border into the US, compared with a ratio of five to 100 during the 1980s (Latin American Data Base 2004). The growing incorporation of women into a formerly male pursuit further emphasizes the fluid and changing nature of gender identities and relations.

Interviews with our informants revealed similar beliefs and cultural practices around the role of women in international migration. Most of our male informants did not want their daughters or wives to work in Canada and female informants cited initial family resistance or astonishment at their decisions.

> My father tells me that he is surprised that I took the decision. That it wasn't possible. But he has always encouraged me, even when we talk on the telephone. He says: 'Keep it up! *Even though you're a woman*, you should succeed. Keep it up, keep it up! (Citlali).

Male resistance to female international migration was corroborated by Mexican officials, who claimed that the husbands and brothers of women in communities acted as an obstacle to expanding female recruitment in Canada in the late 1990s.

Other institutions beyond households reveal gendered practices that shape and organize migration. Our examination of the public institutions involved in the SAWP revealed how the concept of the male breadwinner or male international migrant is codified into policy in both labour-exporting and labour-importing states. Prior to 1989, Mexico's Department of Labour and Social Planning did not recruit women for agricultural work in Canada. In general, state policy in Mexico continues to cast as women secondary wage earners in the economy and, in particular, agriculture as a

---

10 Women's disproportionate participation in regional migration flows are partly owing to their invisible or secondary status in agriculture as the 'wife' of the producer, their lack of access to land, and patrilineal inheritance patterns that expelled them from their communities. Equally important factors include urban employment opportunities in domestic service and the expansion of commercial agriculture and *maquila* industry in Mexico's northern states (Arizpe 1989; González de la Rocha 1994; Velázquez 1992).

male domain. Gender analysis of Mexico's rural development planning shows how patriarchal ideology and male bias has historically disentitled women from control over land and other resources that are indispensable to agricultural production and other non-farm livelihoods; indeed, rural women are often still considered 'housewives' rather than agricultural producers on par with men (Arizpe 1989; Baitenmann 2000; Deere and Léon 1987, 2003; Marroni 1995; Preibisch 2000; Vizcarra Bordi 2002). This male-bias is clearly illustrated in the SAWP, which the Mexican state targeted at rural landless or land-poor men. When the state did begin to recruit women in 1989, the SAWP was only open to single mothers (widowed, separated or divorced), until 1998.[11] Thus while adult men with dependants could apply for work in Canada irrespective of their civil status, married women and single women without children were ineligible. Through this labour recruitment program, the Mexican state cast single mothers as more deserving of economic independence than women who had a man to provide for them (whether or not this occurred in reality). The above indicates the highly gendered nature of citizenship entitlements within the Mexican state, with men enjoying privileged access to land and labour markets. Although men's and women's requirements in the SAWP in terms of civil status are the same on paper, staff within the Department of Labour and Social Planning responsible for recruitment continue to give preference to single mothers. Thus, it is not surprising that our research found childless female applicants producing forged paperwork or 'borrowing' other people's children. The recruitment of single mothers also serves the exigencies of Canadian employers and immigration gatekeepers through the selection of candidates with strong social responsibilities who are less likely to desert and more committed to their jobs.

Until very recently, a further gendered entry requirement obliged female applicants with children to submit a letter in addition to the standard paperwork that designated a guardian in their absence. Although such measures were undoubtedly instituted to protect children, single fathers and widowers were exempt from this requirement. Micaela explained:

> They give you this letter in the Municipal Presidency; that is, if they give it you. They are very strict because the letter must have a photograph of the person that cedes the responsibilities and the person that receives them, with the stamp of the Presidency and the date, etcetera. They make a big deal of it. I think it is a little easier for men.[12]

Not only did the letter discriminate against women, it assumed that married men have wives that are looking after the children, or that single men cannot be the primary caregiver for their children, further codifying the concept of the male breadwinner into social practices.

---

11   The policy notwithstanding, some single women without children were able to negotiate their entry.

12   Municipal authorities charged up to US $20 to issue the letter and in some cases took over a week in preparing it, delaying women's departure.

Some of the women we interviewed had experienced an additional discriminatory dimension to the processing of their work placements: being lectured regarding appropriate female conduct and having to sign a letter in which they promised to behave when in Canada. Men also reported being instructed by Department of Labour staff to treat women with respect. Both men and women were discouraged from forming relationships in Canada that could lead to problems with their employers. The ways in which civil servants in labour-exporting countries are also bearers and inscribers of gender ideologies was particularly well illustrated in their references to men's and women's abilities to do agricultural work. For example, one agent involved in recruitment from a Caribbean labour supply country stated:

> I think that women are more reliable towards the whole scenario and in every walk of life, and *once the lady is capable of the job*, the employers like women to do the job. In tobacco and in some other crops like vegetables and so on they find that it is mostly the work of men, you know the kind of requirement. I must say that females cannot do strenuous work and the kind of difficult situations you find yourself in those crops … but like [in] fruits and so on women do fine, [such as] strawberries.

Gender ideologies at an institutional level thus also structure the foreign labour market serving Canadian agriculture.

The masculinization of the labour market for foreign workers also rests on gender systems prevalent in the host country. Farm work in Canada rests on a gender division of labour based in agrarian patriarchal culture (Halpern 2002; Leckie 1996). The male-bias in agriculture has been institutionalized within the agricultural bureaucracy that is dominated by men and where a masculinized culture prevails. Illustrative of this climate are the words of a Canadian official who explained why incorporating women into the SAWP was problematic:

> So that's what I mean, Kerry, you have to pretty well be a bit more selective in assigning the job duties. Because women are great if they're standing and working with their hands, which is what food processing is all about, or packing, if you're packing fruit in a basket … I want to be fair to the females, but if you put a female into a tobacco priming aid, like a loading machine, [the employers] may find they may not be as durable, or the longevity of females may not be as great over time.

Conversely, another Canadian civil servant critical of the male bias in agriculture, claimed:

> It's still that notion in the agriculture community that women don't belong in agriculture … And we're talking Agriculture Canada here so we're not talking the farm down the street, that's the thinking in *government*. Just take that and put that back in the community and you'll see that women still fight with employers everyday about picking peaches. For example, 'women shouldn't work hourly, they should get piece work.'

These quotations further indicate the differential character of citizenship rights within Canada, where gender has served to relegate women to specific types of work or deserving of lower remuneration.

Gender ideologies are undoubtedly reproduced by the agricultural bureaucracy, but employers are those who designate the gender and the country of origin of their workers. The Canadian civil servants who process employers' requests hear a litany of gendered and racialized traits that foreign men and women supposedly possess: Mexican men are better at weeding than Jamaican workers, Jamaican workers are better for picking fruit, etc. In terms of gender, one civil servant said:

> [Agriculture] has had these preconceived notions that women have always done light work so we need women to do light work, yet [the employers] find that some of these women coming in [from outside Canada] are quite able to do a lot of the heavy work too and are very hard workers. [Employers say] 'Well we wouldn't want them to break a finger nail' and they sit there and say, 'I only want men and not women, women can't pick peaches.' And I say, 'what do you mean women can't pick peaches?' 'Well they can't pick peaches, *they can sort them but they can't pick them.*' So we can't have females in the fields picking peaches, it has to be men? That's absolutely ridiculous.

In interviews, employers of male workers based their gender preferences mostly on perceived strength:

> [I don't hire women because of] the nature of the work. It is heavy work. Women wouldn't be able to do it. They might be able to do weeding, but not all of the work is weeding. (Ricky)

Further, preferences for male workers were often justified as part of the most cited disincentive to women's employment as SAWP workers: the requirement that employers provide separate housing for men and women (Basok 2002; Colby 1997). Since their participation is only recent, employers who also hire men must incur additional costs by hiring women, or switch genders entirely.

But quite apart from the expenses implied by additional housing (which can be very substantial), some employers wanted to avoid the implications of having women on their farm in a highly masculinized migrant worker population. One grower stated:

> We thought about [hiring women] but what we decided, the first year when we had our Mexicans we had a lot of physical labour, a lot of lifting and that's why we went with the Mexicans, um, the men. But now we have say 50 per cent that could be done by women, like all bunching and doing bouquets and stuff, and 50 per cent is lifting but we don't want to have [pause] ... I know Grower X has done it now he's mixed some men with girls and I don't know if that would cause problems, like women and men living in the same [pause] ... we want to keep away from that problem. (Lance)

Indeed, employers not only purposefully avoid hiring both genders to avoid relationships developing, but when they do, they combine labour supply countries, choosing one gender from each. An employer explained his decision for using this strategy: '[previously] it had just been Jamaican men but we did not want to get into a situation with Jamaican women, just for the simple fraternization aspect, so that's why we went with Mexican women.' Most employers did not want their workers to exercise a social life in Canada, including forming a (sexual) relationship, for a number of reasons: they thought it would affect productivity by wasting their workers' energy or distracting them from the job, because it went against their religious beliefs, or because they were concerned about what their neighbours might say. Employers and labour supply country officials used a variety of measures to discourage workers from forming intimate relationships, including threats of, and actual deportation.

The role of gender (and race) in organizing work is thus reflected not only in the lack of women's participation in the SAWP overall, but their specific insertion in the production process, shop-floor practices, and the gender ideologies that surround it. Unsurprisingly, the same gendered ideologies that pose obstacles to women's employment in agriculture have become the basis for their entry. The work women have been employed to undertake includes picking and packing of fruit and vegetables, planting and caring for ornamental or nursery plants, selecting wine grapes, or food processing and canning. Employers choose their workers and allocate tasks according to gender ideologies of men's and women's ability to perform agricultural work. Employers who choose women claimed they possessed a finer, lighter touch, could nurture plants better, and also that they were more patient and efficient:

> We're dealing with smaller plants and sticking, cuttings and rooting so we have no real heavy work here, but it is real hands-on work. I don't know how you would explain that you know, so feminine hands—without being chauvinistic—work a lot better than male hands for a lot of the jobs that we're doing because it's a little bit faster and they can work better. (John)

Throughout the 1990s, women's numbers have grown. In the case of Mexico, in 2001, 3.6 per cent of Mexican workers were women compared to 1.2 per cent in 1994 (FARMS 2001). In part, the incipient growth of women workers from this country can be explained by the efforts of Mexican consular staff and civil servants within the Department of Labour who promoted women among Canadian employers. For example, they 'marketed' women as particularly suited for strawberry harvesting and then selectively recruited candidates who had the skills, knowledge and experience in this crop that would live up to the gender stereotype:

> Two years ago we carried out a pilot project. We asked [the employer] to try women. [...] The employer had so much success, she was so surprised. Of course we didn't send her *any* women, but carefully chose women from Irapuato, Guanajuato, where women have work experience in strawberry production. We selected, therefore, skilled people.

As this quote demonstrates, Mexican officials utilized and fulfilled gender stereotypes held by Canadian employers to promote the employment of women workers from their country.

Gendered Experiences

There is now a considerable literature that has explored the limited rights of foreign workers and documented their working and living conditions (Basok 2002; Binford 2004; Colby 1997; Preibisch 2000, 2004a, b; Smart 1998). Although most research to date has focused on all-male samples, it has provided detailed information on these workers' migratory experiences. For the purposes of this chapter we have selected two areas on which to focus our discussion to show that, although men's and women's experiences of labour migration to Canada may be shared in the sense that they are non-citizens from the South and farm workers, they may also be very different as a result of their gender. Below we discuss issues of family separation, and sex and power. Although these two areas do not capture the full range of gendered and racialized experiences, our discussion highlights the need for greater regard for gender analysis and attention to women in future scholarship on the SAWP.

Family Separation

Both men and women workers in the SAWP spend lengthy periods of time away from their families. Mexican workers spend on average five months of the year working in Canada, almost a month longer than their Caribbean counterparts.[13] Overall, 40 per cent of all Mexican SAWP workers spend a larger part of their lives each year working abroad than in their home communities. Since most workers come to Canada year after year, some for decades, a large part of their working lives are spent outside Mexico and away from their families. Most of our informants stated economic necessity as the principal motivation for coming to Canada. While they recognized what this opportunity had afforded them, both men and women referred to engaging in transnational livelihoods as a sacrifice. One informant explain the exodus from rural Mexico in these terms:

> The economic situation in which we find ourselves make us leave our families, because if it wasn't for the situation that we are in, in Mexico, if all the families had enough to eat, there would be no reason to be here [in Canada] alone, to leave your children with your wife. More families would be together. It isn't possible for me [to stay in Mexico] … you earn very little and it is enough to just half-dress yourself or to half-eat. I can't do anything there but leave home to look for another penny, and I think that a poor man in

---

13   Just under half of all Mexico workers are employed for up to five months, 20 per cent work between five and seven months, and nearly a third are employed for seven to eight months (FARMS 2001).

Mexico will remain in poverty if he doesn't leave. If you don't leave, you will always be the same. (Aurelio)

Working for long periods outside their country takes an enormous toll on migrants and the relationships that they sustain with their families in Mexico.[14] The transnational livelihoods of most male SAWP workers, however, are supported by their female partners, who take responsibility for the family, social networks, fields, livestock and/or business in the migrant's absence. As mentioned, transnational masculine migration patterns have been made possible by nonmigrating women.

Single mothers, who compose the overwhelming majority of women in this program, do not have a partner from whom to draw support. Micaela explained her perspective of the situation for women as such:

It is more difficult for us, much more than the men I think, because we are single women. It is easier for them because they always have the pillar in their house that is their wife. They come, they work, they send money to Mexico and the wife there is the one that takes responsibility for everything. They have land, animals, or they have a store, a business, and the woman works there and they work here. But in the case of women [coming to Canada], the majority of us are single mothers who do not have this opportunity. For us, money sent is money spent because we send money only for the daily expenses of our children and there is no one that supports us economically there. We are the only source of work and the only source of wealth … For men, I don't think the responsibility is as heavy. (Micaela)

This lack of support was felt most keenly by women in terms of childcare in their absence. In general, women leave their children in the care of their parents, or more specifically, their mothers. There are cases in which they leave the children with a female neighbour, with other female relatives, or by themselves if the children are older. Leaving one's children without the care of a parent engendered significant emotional strain. The words of Antonieta capture the anxiety expressed by all the transnational mothers we interviewed: 'Well the truth is it feels very ugly, because to think that you will leave your children. And you are thinking: 'How are they? Has something happened to them? Where are my children at this moment?' It is difficult, very difficult. Transnational mothers felt that coming to Canada was their only option for providing a better life for their children, but that their livelihoods implied enormous costs. Silvia, explaining the reason she came to Canada, stated:

My children were growing up and my daughter was interested in studying in another school. And I didn't have the money to spend the 1800 pesos [US $180]. So she had to stay in another school that she didn't like because I didn't have [money] to pay. And this desire, to be able to do something for my children [is why I came to Canada] … But I

---

14   This sentiment is vividly portrayed in the National Film Board of Canada documentary, *El Contrato*, which documents the emotional strain men endure while working far from their families in Canada.

think that this is 'something' comes at a very high price, because I give them the financial means, but I am not with them.

Likewise, Olivia claimed: 'It is very difficult to be here without them. It is very hard. It is a horrible solitude and leaving them is very hard. Working here as *a mother* is very difficult.'

While for men, engaging in transnational livelihoods means fulfilling their primary gender role as breadwinners, for women, transnational migration to Canada implies deserting theirs, as it is traditionally defined. As one informant described:

> Sentimentally, sometimes I become depressed. Because I have always told myself that my first responsibility is my children, and in that sense I feel that I am not fulfilling it because I am not with them. And this depresses me. But I don't believe there is another option. In Mexico I do not believe I would find a job as well remunerated as this, and as a result, here I am. (Esther)

The women coming to Canada are redefining motherhood, adding a transnational dimension to the fulfillment of their primary gender role. Nonetheless, the anxiety that women suffer through absences from their children is enormous. Community groups and health professionals working with this migrant population reported high rates of mental health issues, particularly with women. Women worry both about their children's immediate welfare but also the long-term implications of their migratory periods on the mother-child relationship.[15] Indeed, both men and women feared their absences affected their children's emotional stability. Some felt the relationship had changed irrevocably:

> After so many years it hurts me because I have never been with my son. My child knows me, he knows who I am, he spends time with me but … I think he sees me more like a cash point because I have never been able to raise him, my mother has raised him, she has educated him, she has brought him up […] My child is very beautiful, he is the most beautiful thing I have, and unfortunately I have never enjoyed it, this is the only thing that I lament of the Program, is not having my child here with me. (Micaela)

These mothers in the SAWP, as Hondagneu-Sotelo and Avila (2003: 336) suggest, 'are improvising new mothering arrangements that are borne out of women's financial struggles, played out in a new global arena, to provide the best future for themselves and their children'. Despite the personal sacrifices, engaging in international migration has afforded women an enhanced measure of economic independence.[16] Before migrating, single mothers' occupations in their home states

---

15 These findings echo Hondagneu-Sotelo and Avila's (2003) work on Latina domestic workers in the US.

16 By highlighting women's economic independence here (rather than poor men's, for example), we do not suggest a disregard for class or ethnicity. Although the Mexican government has targeted the SAWP to the rural landless or land-poor with low levels of formal schooling, our informants came from a variety of social classes and with varying education levels. Some of the female informants thus came from much higher social classes than some

made it very difficult for them to provide for their families. In Mexico, small producers and wage workers in general have seen their livelihoods deteriorate since the adoption of a neo-liberal economic model in 1982 (Bartra, 2004) in which women in particular have born the brunt of economic restructuring. Occupations open to women are usually poorly rewarded and highly insecure in nature in both urban and rural areas (González de la Rocha 1994; Wiggins et al. 2002). Before entering the SAWP, very few of our female informants had formal employment. Most combined a variety of income-generating tasks, including small-scale commerce, preparing food, or washing clothes. Younger women often worked within their homes, caring for children and extended families, and thus freeing up the labour of other women in the household to engage in income-generation. The informants that were employed in the formal labour force prior to work in Canada were employed in office work or in maquiladoras.

All of the people that we interviewed, regardless of their civil status and gender, were the breadwinners for their families. Their earnings in Canada allowed them to provide the basic necessities for their children including food, healthcare and education, acquire or improve housing and, for some, make investments in farming or small businesses. Because most of these women are the sole breadwinners for their families and their migration was instigated by lack of local opportunities to fulfill this role, their ability to accumulate from their participation in the SAWP was highly constrained, as Micaela's reference to men's 'pillar in the home' suggested. These findings, therefore, support theoretical assertions that migrating women experience poorer outcomes than do men owing to their structured disadvantage and their lack of dependence on a secondary male wage earner (Kanaiaupuni 2000).

Notwithstanding, migration to Canada allowed women to overcome some of the obstacles presented by their economic marginalization as single mothers and women. Those women who had surpluses after providing the basic necessities and education to their children could buy land, build homes, and for some, finance small businesses. Esther explained what economic independence meant to her:

> [The father of my children] has his own house, we have always lived separately. That was good. But sometimes I say: 'What am I doing here? I think that I should return to him, we'll go to his house and with the money I have start a business or something, and that's the end of Canada.' But no, all of the sudden I say: 'And my independence? At what price?' (Esther 43)

---

of the men, and in both groups we had both indigenous and mestizo informants. Still, we focus on the notion of economic independence in terms of gendered advantage, since women are still cast as secondary wage earners in the economy and social policy. Further, female migrants in the US often have higher levels of education than their male counterparts, suggesting that men derive greater rewards from investments in education within the Mexican labour market than do women (Kanaiuapuni 2000).

Another woman, mentioned that she was not sure whether to accept a marriage proposal since her male partner would no longer permit her to continue her transnational livelihood: 'Of course he told me, "if we get married you won't go [to Canada] any more, absolutely not." I said no. I told him that I want to keep coming here because I want to finish building my house, and I am going to do it.' Women's migratory experiences and the greater economic independence that they experience as a result also allows them to engage in cultural practices of acquiring status and prestige formerly available only to men.[17] In addition, some women's migratory decisions also allowed them to escape abusive relationships with men or social stigmatization in their communities as '*fracasadas*' (failures in marriage). Although for most women social escape was not their primary motivation, Canada offered a space free from many of the social pressures of their everyday lives and the gendered constraints on their mobility and behaviour.

Sex and Power

The enormous differential in the ratio of women to men working as contract farm labour has a profound impact on experiences of migration. Women are subject to sexual harassment both within and outside the workplace, in some cases by their co-workers and in other cases, by their managers or employers. Given the enormous power differential between women and their employers, it is difficult for women to report sexual harassment carried out by management. It might be easier to report on co-workers' behaviour, but women may hesitate in reporting cases of sexual harassment, even when management responds, because they perceive reporting complaints to management as disloyal:

> All the men were cutting the peaches and I was selecting them. The men would come and say 'Eh, mamacita' or 'Eh' this or that. Then they said that they liked me, that I was very beautiful to them, and this made me feel bad because they would come up and get close to me. I had to give in and tell the *mayordomo*[18] about them. He called them on it right away, in an instant … Later it was like they held a grudge against me because I had reported them. But I felt obliged because they were grabbing my other [female] co-worker … We were just two women and at risk of something happening. (Tina)

Outside of the workplace, women are constantly proposed to. In a sea of men, female migrants are considered sexually available; those who do not have boyfriends are labelled 'nuns' or 'old maids.' Rejections are met with hostility. Regardless of their level of sexual activity, women who engage in transnational migration as breadwinners are stigmatized within both the migrant community in Canada and their own communities. Female SAWP participants are further devalued by some of

---

17 For example, women reported financing different religious events in their localities, such as the flower arrangements in the church or the garments of the town's patron saint.

18 Foreman.

their co-workers because they are assumed to be single mothers.[19] Iliana, a young migrant, claimed: 'There [in Mexico] they think that we come to Canada just to prostitute ourselves ... Here in this entire region they treat us poorly ... They say we are whores, that we are already well 'broken in,' ugly things.' One male worker shared his perspective:

> Clearly they [the Mexican Department of Labour] are not going to send *muchachas*[20] on the Program. They send people that really have a necessity for the job in order to support their children. So perhaps this is the reason, because we know this, is why our comrades try and abuse them as such. They say: 'well that woman has life experience, she was divorced, her husband left her, or she had two or three breakups. What has she got to lose?' Perhaps there are people that think in this way and try and abuse them.

Women's participation as seasonal migrants under the SAWP involves breaking strict gender norms regarding women's roles and mobility, reinventing gender relations. While in some communities in rural Mexico, women cannot leave their localities unattended or could be subject to physical abuse for talking to a man who is not their husband, women exercising transnational livelihoods in Canada get on a plane, travel thousands of kilometres, and spend eight months unattended and unsupervised. As Kanaiaupuni (2000) has argued, it is not the responsibility of children that explains women's lesser risk of migration and limits their mobility, but the expectations of what it means to be a good wife or daughter. While Mexican women working in Canada's SAWP do derive some degree of sexual power from the sheer gender differential in numbers – they have their pick of potential partners, for example – they are subject to tremendous efforts to control that power by their co-workers, their employers, and their home communities.

As this section has shown, although men's and women's experiences of labour migration to Canada may be shared in the sense that they are both non-citizens from the South and agricultural workers, they may also be very different as a result of their gender. One part of our discussion on gendered experiences focused on how men and women experienced family separation differently, most notably because of gendered responsibilities for childcare, while the other section explored women's experiences in a highly masculinized environment. Furthermore, our analysis has shown that women's participation in international labour markets may enable them to exercise, to a greater extent, the full set of citizenship rights accorded Mexican men within the nation and so set in motion negotiations that may ultimately result in greater gender justice at home.

Conclusions

This chapter has attempted to explore the highly masculinized transnational

---

19 One indication of this is the way in which single mothers are referred to as 'dejadas,' literally implying that their husbands left them, rather than their separation from their male partners being attributed to their own agency or left in doubt.

20 In this case, young (single) women.

migration of Mexican men and women to Canadian agriculture from a gender perspective, exposing the ways in which gender – along with other relations of power – organizes and shapes the movement of people. In addition, it provides some insight into how experiences of migration are gendered. Given that the literature on migrant agricultural workers has been largely based on all male samples, these initial findings contribute to the gendering of this scholarship and the literature on transnational migration in general.

A gender optic is a useful tool for laying bare the ways in which global production benefits from, and reinforces, a complex web of social relations that are played out on a number of levels, from the household to the global political economy. This chapter has analyzed the SAWP as an example of how global competitiveness of agriculture in the North is increasingly sustained through the incorporation of non-citizen migrant workers from the South, resting on a variety of axes of oppression: (neo)colonialism, racism, sexism, etc. In this temporary visa program, poor Southern workers' denial of citizenship and their abundance of need heighten their vulnerability as workers, a situation further accentuated by the limited power of semi-peripheral labour-exporting states to enforce the restricted set of *de jure* rights that migrant workers are accorded. As we know, this phenomenon occurs outside agriculture, as non-citizen workers from the South increasingly constitute a growing share of jobs in the economies of the North, jobs that citizens of those countries who enjoy labour mobility reject. This chapter has also emphasized how production processes themselves are racialized and gendered. For example, we have shown how gender is central in delineating workers' suitability to agricultural work and specific tasks therein, yet the ideal worker is a desexualized subject. As discussed, eligibility in the SAWP is based on proving familial responsibility, but participation requires the temporary capitulation of family rights and discourages new social commitments in the host country. Further, through our analysis of gendered state policy we have also emphasized the gendered aspects of citizenship *within* the nation-state, showing how women in Canada and Mexico are excluded from participating fully in social and economic life. As we have argued, gender is central to shaping labour incorporation and organizing the productive processes of capitalism, in a variety of contexts and involving a multiplicity of actors.

Studies of (im)migration and transnationalism, however, continue to be characterized by a persistent lack of attention to gender. Further, while attempts to remedy this situation have moved from a 'compensatory phase' that focused on women to situate gender as a relation of power, the unit of analysis continues to be gynocentric. In a recent volume on gender and migration, the editors criticize this trend, yet note that their contributors focus primarily on women (Morokvásic-Müller et al. 2003). It appears that highly gendered phenomena only make it onto the radar screen when flows are feminized. However, the explanatory power and theoretical applicability of gender analysis will be limited if it is used only for feminized migratory patterns. As Salzinger (2004: 43) and others (Marchand and Runyan 2000; Rai 2001) have contended, 'global restructuring is a gendered process.' She writes: 'within transnational production, the creation and allocation of labour power is organized around and in terms of tropes of gendered personhood, and this has consequences for the way production works in general, above and beyond its impact on gendered selves *per se*' (Salzinger 2004: 44). Further, Sassen (2003) calls for the further documentation and analysis of 'strategic instantiations of gendering in the global economy.' If the processes underlying global restructuring are to be properly understood, and therefore effectively contested, both masculinized and feminized instantiations of the global economy must be considered. This chapter hopes to contribute to this endeavour.

References

Aranda Bezaury, J. (1993), 'Políticas públicas y mujeres campesinas en México,' in S. González Montes (ed.), *Mujeres y Relaciones de Género en la Antropología Latinoamericano*, El Colegio de México, Mexico City, pp. 171-215.

Arat-Koc, S. (1989), 'In the Privacy of Our Home: Foreign Domestic Workers as a Solution to the Crisis in the Domestic Sphere in Canada,' *Studies in Political Economy,* Vol. 28, Spring, pp. 33-58.

Arat-Koc, S. and Giles, W. (1994), *Maid in the Market: Women's Paid Domestic Labour,* Fernwood Publishing, Halifax.

Arizpe, L. (1989), *La Mujer en el Desarrollo de Mexico y de America Latin*, Universidad Nacional Autónoma de México, Mexico City.

Arizpe L. and Botey, C. (1987), 'Mexican Agricultural Development Policy and Its Impact on Rural Women,' in C. D. Deere and M. León (eds), *Rural Women and State Policy*, Westview Press, Boulder and London, pp. 67-83.

Bagnell, K. (2001), *The Little Immigrants: The Orphans who Came to Canada,* Dundurn Press, Toronto.

Baines, D. and Sharma, N. (2002), 'Migrant Workers as Non-Citizens: The Case against Citizenship as a Social Policy Concept,' *Studies in Political Economy*, Vol. 69, pp. 75-107.

Baitenmann, H. (2000), 'Gender and Agrarian Rights in Twentieth-Century Mexico,' paper presented at the XXII meetings of the Latin American Studies Association, Miami, 16-18 March.

Ball, R. and Piper, T. (2004), 'Globalisation and Regulation of Citizenship: Filipino Migrant Workers in Japan,' *Political Geography,* Vol. 21, pp. 1013-34.

Barndt, D. (2000), *Tangled Routes: Women, Work, and Globalization on the Tomato Trail,* Rowman and Littlefield Publishers, Oxford.

Barrón, A. (2000), 'Condiciones laborales de los inmigrantes regulados en Canadá,' *Comercio Exterior,* Vol. 50(4), pp. 350-53.

Bartra, A. (2004), 'Rebellious Cornfields: Toward Food and Labour Sovereignty,' in G. Otero (ed.), *Mexico in Transition: Neoliberal Globalism, the State and Civil Society,* Zed Books, London, New York.

Basok, T. (2002), *Tortillas and Tomatoes,* McGill-Queens University Press, Montreal

& Kingston.

Basok, T. (2000), 'He Came, He Saw, He ... Stayed. Guest Worker Programmes and the Issue of Non-Return,' *International Migration*, Vol. 38(2), pp. 215-36.

Becerril, O. (2003), 'Relación de género, trabajo transnacional y migración temporal: trabajadores y trabajadoras agrícolas mexicanos en Canadá,' paper presented at the *Primer Coloquio Internacional sobre Migración y Desarrollo: Transnacionalismo y Nuevas Perspectivas de Integración*, 23-25 October, City of Zacatecas, Mexico.

Binford, L. (2004), 'Contract Labor in Canada and the United States: A Critical Appreciation of Tanya Basok's Tortillas and Tomatoes: Transmigrant Mexican Harvesters in Canada,' *Canadian Journal of Latin American and Caribbean Studies*, Vol. 29(57-58), pp. 289-308.

Binford, L. (2002), 'Social and Economic Contradictions of Rural Migrant Contract Labor between Tlaxcala, Mexico and Canada,' *Culture and Agriculture,* Vol. 24(2), pp. 1-19.

Chang, G. (2000), *Disposable Domestics: Immigrant Women Workers in the Global Economy*, South End Press, Cambridge, Mass.

Colby, C. (1997), *From Oaxaca to Ontario: Mexican Contract Labour in Canada and the Impact at Home*, The California Institute for Rural Studies, Davis, CA.

Cross, B. (2003), 'Tortuous Tunes Push Migrant Workers Over the Edge,' *Windsor Star*, 6 June.

D'Aubeterre, M. E. (1995), 'Tiempos de espera: Emigración masculina, ciclo doméstico y situación de las mujeres en San Miguel Acuexcomac. Relaciones de Género y Transformaciones Agrarias,' in S. González and V. Salles (eds), El Colegio de México, Mexico City, pp. 255-97.

Deere, C. and León, M. (2003), 'The Gender Asset Gap: Land in Latin America,' *World Development*, Vol. 31(6), pp. 925-47.

Deere, C. and León, M. (1987), 'Introduction,' in C. Deere and M. León (eds), *Rural Women and State Policy: Feminist perspectives on Latin American Agricultural Development,* Westview Press, Boulder and London, pp. 1-11.

Erel, U., Morokvásic-Müller, M. and Shinozaki, K. (2003), 'Introduction Bringing Gender into Migration,' in M. Morokvásic-Müller, U. Erel and K. Shinozaki (eds), *Crossing Borders and Shifting Boundaries, Volume 1: Gender on the Move*, Leske and Budrich, Obraden, pp. 9-22.

FARMS (2001), *Ontario Region – Caribbean/Mexican Seasonal Agricultural Workers Programs Year-to-Date Report*, FARMS, Mississauga.

Goldring, L. (1996), 'Gendered Memory: Constructions of Reality Among Mexican Transnational Migrants,' in E. M. DuPuis and P. Vandergeest (eds), *Creating the Countryside: The Politics of Rural and Environmental Discourse*, Temple University Press, Philadelphia, pp. 303-29.

González de la Rocha, M. (1994), *The Resources of Poverty,* Blackwell Publishers, Cambridge.

Grasmuck, S. and Pessar, P. (1991), *Between Two Islands: Dominican International*

Migration, University of California Press, Berkeley and Los Angeles.

Halpern, M. (2002), *And on that Farm he had a Wife: Ontario Farm Women and Feminism, 1900-1970*, McGill-Queen's University Press, Montreal.

Hondagneu-Sotelo, P. (2003), 'Gender and Immigration: A Retrospective and Introduction,' in P. Hondagneu-Sotelo (ed.), *Gender and US Immigration: Contemporary Trends.* Berkeley: University of California Press, Berkeley, pp. 3-19.

Hondagneu-Sotelo, P. (1994), *Gendered Transitions: Mexican Experiences of Immigration,* University of California Press, Berkeley and Los Angeles.

Hondagneu-Sotelo, P. and Avila, E. (2003), '"I'm Here, But I'm There:" The Meanings of Latina Transnational Motherhood,' in P. Hondagneu-Sotelo (ed.), *Gender and US Immigration: Contemporary Trends*, University of California Press, Berkeley, pp. 317-41.

INEGI (2000), 'Indicadores de migración según lugar de nacimiento,' XII Censo General de Población y Vivienda, Instituto Nacional de Estadística, Geografía e Información (INEGI), Mexico City.

Kanaiaupuni, S. M. (2000), 'Reframing the Migration Question: An Analysis of Men, Women, and Gender in Mexico,' *Social Forces*, Vol. 78(4), pp. 1311-48.

Latin American Data Base, (2004), 'Increasing Number of Rural Women Migrating to the US,' in *Sourcemex, Economic & Political News on Mexico,* Vol. 15(9), March 3.

Leckie, G. J. (1996), '"They never trusted me to drive:" Farm Girls and the Gender Relations of Agricultural Information Transfer,' *Gender, Place and Culture*, Vol. 3(3), pp. 309-25.

Macklin, A. (1994), 'On the Inside Looking In: Foreign Domestic Workers in Canada,' in W. Giles and S. Arat-Koc (eds), *Maid in the Market: Women's Paid Domestic Labour*, Fernwood, Halifax, pp. 13-39.

Marchand, M. and Runyan, A. (2000), 'Introduction. Feminist Sightings of Global Restructuring: Conceptualizations and Reconceptualizations,' in M. Marchand and A. Runyan (eds), *Gender and Global Restructuring: Sighting, Sites and Resistance*, Routledge, London and New York, pp.1-22.

Marroni, M. G. (1995), 'Trabajo rural femenino y relaciones de género,' in S. González and V. Salles (eds), *Relaciones de género y transformaciones agrarias*, El Colegio de México, Mexico City.

Morokvásic, M. (1984), 'Bird of Passage are Also Women,' *International Migration Review,* Vol. 18, pp. 886-907.

Morokvásic-Müller, M., Erel, U. and Shinozaki, K. (2003), *Crossing Borders and Shifting Boundaries. Volume 1: Gender on the Move,* Leske and Budrich, Obraden, pp. 9-22.

Nurse, K. (2004), 'Diaspora, Migration and Development in the Caribbean,' Focal Policy Paper, FPP-04-6.

OECD (2003), *Trends in International Migration*, OECD, Paris.

Ong, A. (1999), *Flexible Citizenship: the Cultural Logics of Transnationality*, Duke

University Press, London.

Pedraza, S. (1991), 'Women and Migration: The Social Consequences of Gender,' *Annual Review of Sociology,* Vol. 17, pp. 303-25.

Pessar, P. (2003), 'Engendering Migration Studies: The Case of New Immigrants in the United States,' in P. Hondagneu-Sotelo (ed.), *Gender and US Immigration: Contemporary Trends*, University of California Press, Berkeley, pp. 20-42.

Pratt, G. (1999), 'Is this Canada? Domestic workers' Experiences in Vancouver, B.C.,' in J. Momsen (ed.), *Gender, Migration and Domestic Service,* Routledge, London, pp. 23-42.

Preibisch, K. (2004a), 'Migrant Agricultural Workers and Processes of Social Inclusion in Rural Canada: Encuentros and Desencuentros,' *Canadian Journal of Latin American and Caribbean Studies,* Vol. 29(57-58), pp. 203-40.

Preibisch, K. (2004b), *Social Relations Practices Between Seasonal Agricultural Workers, Their Employers, and the Residents of Rural Ontario,* research report prepared for The North-South Institute, Ottawa.

Preibisch, K. (2001), *Rural Livelihoods, Gender and Economic Restructuring in Mexico: Lived Realities of Neoliberalism 1988-2000,* PhD Thesis, University of Reading, UK.

Preibisch, K. (2000), 'Tierra de los no-libres: Migración temporal México-Canadá y dos campos de reestructuración económica,' in L. Binford and M. D'Aubeterre (eds), *Conflictos migratorios transnacionales y respuestas comunitarias*, Benemérita Universidad Autónoma de Puebla, Puebla, pp. 45-66.

Rai, S. (2001), *Gender and the Political Economy of Development*, Polity Press, London.

Salazar Parreñas, R. (2001), *Servants of Globalization: Women, Migration and Domestic Work*, Stanford University Press, Stanford, CA.

Salzinger, L. (2004), 'From Gender as Object to Gender as Verb: Rethinking how Global Restructuring Happens,' *Critical Sociology* , Vol. 30(1), pp. 43-62.

Sassen, S. (2003), 'Strategic Instantiations of Gendering in the Global Economy,' in P. Hondagneu-Sotelo (ed.), *Gender and US Immigration: Contemporary Trends*, University of California Press, Berkeley, pp. 43-60.

Sassen, S. (2000), 'Women's Burdens: Counter-Geographies of Globalization and the Feminization of Survival,' *Journal of International Affairs*, Vol. 53(2), pp. 503-24.

Satzewich, V. (1991), *Racism and the Incorporation Foreign Labour: Farm Labour Migration to Canada Since 1945,* Routledge, London and New York.

Sharma, N. (2001), 'On being not Canadian: The Social Organization of "Migrant Workers" in Canada,' *The Canadian Review of Sociology and Anthropology*, Vol. 38(4), pp. 415-39.

Sharma, N. (2000), 'Race, Class, Gender and the Making of Difference: The Social Organization of "Migrant Workers" in Canada,' *Atlantis: A Women's Studies Journal* (Special Issue), Vol. 24(2), pp. 5-15.

Smart, J. (1998), 'Borrowed Men on Borrowed Time: Globalization, Labour Migration and Local Economies in Alberta,' *Canadian Journal of Regional*

Science, Vol. 20(12), pp. 141-56.

Stalker, P. (2004), *Stalker's Guide to International Migration* (www.pstalker.com/migration/)

Stasiulis, D. and Bakan, A. (2003), *Negotiating Citizenship: Migrant Women in Canada and the Global System*, Palgrave Macmillan, Houndmills, Basingstoke, Hampshire, New York.

Stasiulis, D. and Bakan, A. (1997), 'Negotiating Citizenship: The Case of Foreign Domestic Workers in Canada,' *Feminist Review*, Vol. 57, pp. 112-39.

Statistics Canada (2004), *Canadian Agriculture at a Glance*, Statistics Canada Agriculture Division, Ottawa, ON.

UFCW (2004), *Health and Safety Manuals to Migrant Workers*, (www.ufcw.ca/cgi-bin/full_story.cgi?story_id=93&from_page=37). Accessed 20 December 2004.

UFCW (2002), *National Report: Status of Migrant Farm Workers in Canada*, (http://www.ufcw.ca).

Velásquez, M. (1992), *Políticas Sociales, Transformación Agraria, y Participación de las Mujeres en el Campo: 1920-1988*, Centro Regional de Investigaciones Multidisciplinarias, UNAM, Cuernavaca.

Verduzco Igartua, G. (2004), *Mexican Workers' Participation in CSAWP and Development Consequences in the Workers' Rural Home Communities*, The North-South Institute, Ottawa.

Verma, V. (2004), *CSAWP Regulatory and Policy Framework, Farm Industry-level Employment Practices and the Potential Role of Unions*, research report prepared for The North-South Institute, Ottawa.

Vizcarra Bordi, I. (2002), *Entre el taco mazahua y el mundo, la comida de las relaciones de poder, resistencia e identidades*, Universidad Autonoma del Estado de Mexico, Instituto Literario, Toluca, Mexico.

Wall, E. (1992), 'Personal Labour Relations and Ethnicity in Ontario Agriculture,' in Vic Satzewich (ed.), *Deconstructing a Nation: Immigration, Multiculturalism and Racism in 90s Canada*, Fernwood Publishing, Halifax, NS, pp. 261-75.

Weston, A. and Scarpa de Masellis, L. (2004), *Hemispheric Integration and Trade Relations – Implications for Canada's Seasonal Agricultural Workers Program*, The North-South Institute, Ottawa.

Wiggins, S., Keilbach, N., Preibisch, K., Proctor, S., Rivera, G. and Rodríguez, G. (2002), 'Agricultural Policy Reform and Rural Livelihoods in Central Mexico,' *Journal of Development Studies*, Vol. 38(3), pp. 179-202.

World Bank (2003), *World Development Indicators 2003*, World Bank, Washington, DC.

Yuval-Davis, N. (1999), 'The "Multi-Layered Citizen,"' *International Feminist Journal of Politics*, Vol. 1(1), pp. 119-136.

Chapter 6

Brokering Citizenship Claims: Neo-liberalism, Biculturalism and Multiculturalism in Aotearoa New Zealand[1]

Wendy Larner

Introduction

There have been profound changes in the socio-political landscape of Aotearoa New Zealand over the last two decades. As is now well known, during the 1980s and 1990s the neo-liberal 'New Zealand Experiment' undermined the policy goals of full employment and state responsibility for social well-being with the consequence being a new emphasis on market provisioning and self-responsibility for both men and women. Economic relations were also reconfigured, with dramatic increases in the overseas ownership of major firms, infrastructure and resources underpinning the internationalization of the domestic economy. During the same period, however, there was another equally important shift based on the politics of Maori self-determination, or *tino rangatiratanga*. Retrospective recognition of Treaty claims via the Waitangi Tribunal[2] process, together with increasing recognition of the rights of Maori as indigenous people, or *tangata whenua*, saw claims based on Maori understandings and framed using Maori concepts included in mainstream political discourses. Major efforts were made to increase the responsiveness of government agencies to Maori concerns, and key functions were devolved to *iwi*[3] authorities on the grounds that Maori were best placed to deliver services to their own people. While often contested and highly contradictory, the unexpected articulation of

---

1   This is the fifth paper on New Zealand I have written for edited collections in the last decade. This opportunity to formally reflect on a particular country case at regular intervals pushes to the surface interesting similarities and differences. In this context, I draw your attention to Larner (1993), Larner and Spoonley (1995), Larner (1996) and Larner (2002), and acknowledge some overlapping content as well as some significant changes, both theoretically and substantively.

2   Established in 1975, the Waitangi Tribunal investigates Crown actions that are inconsistent with the spirit of the Treaty of Waitangi signed in 1840.

3   Tribal.

neo-liberalism and *tino rangatiratanga* during the 1980s and 1990s gave rise to a distinctive bicultural conception of citizenship based on the idea of two peoples (Maori and Pakeha)[4] in one country.

More recently, the fifth Labour government has moved decisively away from the 'more market' approaches of earlier forms of neo-liberalism, and has placed a new emphasis on sustainability, collaboration and partnership in their efforts to re-embed both economic and social activities 'after neo-liberalism.'[5] At the same time, bicultural conceptions of citizenship are being challenged by more complex patterns of cultural and ethnic difference associated with the globalizing economy and the changing composition of international migration flows. New Zealand's major cities, Auckland in particular, have begun to more closely resemble the multi-ethnic 'global cities' of the Pacific Rim rather than either the culturally homogeneous society assumed by the architects of the welfare state *or* the bicultural imaginaries that underpinned the politics of citizenship during the 1980s and 1990s. To date, however, the new partnership arrangements that characterize the political projects of 'after neo-liberalism' have continued to focus on Maori (and to a lesser extent Pacific[6]) communities. In contrast, other poor communities – which include refugee, migrant and rural Pakeha communities – are more usually defined as part of broader geographical communities.

It was in this context that the newly appointed Leader of the National Party and New Zealand Opposition, Don Brash, then struggling to register significantly in national opinion polls, gave a widely publicized speech to a group of predominantly white Rotary club members in Orewa earlier this year (Brash 2004). In the address – which he called 'Nationhood' – he castigated the fifth Labour government's record on issues of biculturalism and made an argument for 'one New Zealand.' He began by stating 'We are one country of many peoples, not simply a society of Maori and Pakeha where the minority has a birthright to the upper hand as the Labour government seems to believe.' His preamble then decried what he described as 'the dangerous drift towards racial separatism in New Zealand, and the development of the now entrenched Treaty industry,' and in the speech he pledged to speed up and complete the Treaty settlement process and remove all special provision for Maori from both central and local government legislation – including the four Maori parliamentary seats established by the Maori Representation Act of 1867. He also claimed that in the areas of social welfare, education and health, government funding was being influenced not just by need, but by the ethnicity of the recipient.

---

4   A Maori word used to describe New Zealanders who are the descendants of colonizing European (predominantly British) settlers.

5   As is argued in detail in Lewis et al. (2004), the term 'after neo-liberalism' is used to draw attention to the continued relevance of neo-liberal discourse and techniques, and because we think it premature to name the new political formation in more positive terms.

6   The well-established, multi-generational, Pacific communities in New Zealand are the legacy of post-war labour migrations from the Pacific Islands (notably Western Samoa, the Cook Islands, Niue, the Tokelau Islands, Tonga and Fiji).

The reaction to his speech took many people by surprise including, reputedly, Don Brash himself. Most immediately, his political party overtook the previously unassailable Labour government in national opinion polls, although this lead was not sustained in the short term. More significantly, in a context where it had been widely accepted that most Pakeha had – albeit somewhat reluctantly – begun to accept the legitimacy of the claims of Maori, the public backlash triggered by Brash's speech was both profound and deeply disturbing. Almost overnight, practices that were taken for granted in many settings, for example the use of *powhiri* (a Maori welcome) to open formal meetings and affirmative action programmes in tertiary education, began to be openly questioned. For many Maori based in public sector organizations – where the institutionalization of biculturalism had been most pronounced – the deterioration of their political position was both palpable and troubling. More generally, newspapers and talk back radio were flooded with the complaints of those – Pakeha and new migrants alike – who felt they could now publicly attack the politics of biculturalism and accuse the government of racial favouritism. In turn, shaken by the vehemence of the public response, the fifth Labour government ordered a review of social policy to ensure that their programmes were designed on the basis of need rather than ethnicity.

The most obvious feature of this volatile terrain, characterized by debates over neo-liberalism-after neo-liberalism, biculturalism–multiculturalism, and Auckland–non-Auckland, is a huge amount of public controversy – and considerable confusion – over the nature of contemporary citizenship claims. What is also apparent is that the changing relationships between neo-liberalism, biculturalism and multiculturalism, and the increasing economic and social diversity that has ensued, are having major implications for understandings of both state and nation in Aotearoa New Zealand. Not surprisingly, the gendered outcomes of these new socio-political configurations are, as yet, difficult to discern. What is clear, however, is that women are on the front line of this new politics of citizenship in their roles as politicians, policy makers, service providers, community members and mothers. In particular, a critical role is being played by those women who are successfully able to 'broker' between diverse cultural groups and political contexts because of their ability to build relationships in both professional and personal settings. Thus, whereas feminist citizenship literatures emphasize how in times of turmoil women are often re-constituted as the bearers of tradition in their roles as wives and mothers (Yuval-Davis and Anthias 1989; Yuval-Davis 1997), this chapter concludes that in Aotearoa New Zealand women are the 'midwives' of a new conception of citizenship in which contested claims-making on the basis of both biculturalism and multiculturalism is being centred in the efforts to re-embed economic and social relationships after neo-liberalism.

From Neo-liberalism to After Neo-liberalism

The 'New Zealand Experiment' of the last two decades is touted internationally as an exemplary case of neo-liberalism and market-oriented restructuring. In the period following the 1984 election the country saw a remarkable succession of reform minded politicians and policy makers. During the 1980s, economic reforms, initiated by a nominally social democratic Labour government, included corporatization, deregulation and the privatization of many state sector activities. Economic reform was succeeded by social reform. In the early 1990s the National government marked their return to office with severe cuts to social spending, and benefit levels were reduced substantially. These spending cuts were justified on the grounds that they would 'increase the "rewards" for moving from welfare to work' (Richardson, quoted in Kelsey 1993: 83). They were followed by the introduction of targeting and 'user pays' principles into the areas of health, housing and education. Social programme reforms were also introduced in conjunction with new industrial relations legislation designed to deregulate the labour market.

As a consequence, by the late 1990s the conceptual foundations of the post-war welfare state in Aotearoa New Zealand had been fundamentally eroded. Rather than the focus of state activity being a relatively closed national economy and the primary policy goal being the promotion of full employment, economic policies and programmes were designed to articulate domestic activities into global economic flows. Integral to this shift was the rise of the discourse of the 'knowledge based economy,' underpinned by the redefinition of New Zealanders as 'human resources' with the potential capacities of skill, ingenuity, and innovation. Moreover, in contrast to the male breadwinner model, in this new formulation participation in paid work for both men and women had come to be understood to be the primary basis for social inclusion, and a diminished welfare state responsible only for residual support. One consequence was increased economic and social polarization, manifest in increased class differences amongst women. Not surprisingly, given historically constituted labour force patterns, these experiences were highly racialized with Maori and Pacific women disproportionately represented amongst those struggling to survive on reduced and increasingly targeted benefits, and most likely to find themselves coping with the direct and indirect consequences of poverty (Larner 2002).

Today there is a new 'New Zealand Experiment.' Since the 1999 election the fifth Labour government, like its international 'third way' counter-parts, has attempted to move away from the 'more-market' approaches that characterized the 1980s and 1990s. As Newman (2001) argues more generally, this terrain is fundamentally different from both the economism of neo-liberalism and the welfarism of 'old' Labour. While the new approach builds on neo-liberal understandings of economic globalization and human capital, there are also sustained efforts to institutionally re-embed economic and social relations. One consequence has been the building of new relationships, many of which are with non-traditional economic and social actors. For example, environment and culture have entered into the domain of economic policy, and community and ethnic diversity now feature centrally in social policy. There is also a new approach to policy making and service provision. Collaboration and partnership between diverse institutions and organizations is identified at the highest possible level 'as our normal way of doing business' (Department of Prime Minister and Cabinet 2003) in the new ambition to overcome the increased economic and social polarization that characterized the 'more market' neo-liberalisms of the 1980s and 1990s.

For the purposes of this paper, a particularly important aspect of these changes has been the way in which the new efforts to address economic and social disparities have involved a continued focus on Maori and Pacific communities. On one level this emphasis is not surprising in that it is underpinned by demographic trends. People who identify as Maori now account for 15 per cent of the total New Zealand population and Pacific people an additional seven per cent. Both groups are also steadily increasing as a proportion of the overall population, with demographers estimating that by the middle of this century the Maori population will have doubled and Pacific populations tripled. At the same time, both Maori and Pacific people continue to under-perform on most economic and social indicators. However, the continued emphasis on Maori and Pacific communities in the emergent political formation is not simply a consequence of the 'browning' of New Zealand's demographic structure and social future. It also reflects the outcome of major political struggles during the last two decades.

From Biculturalism to *Tino Rangatiratanga*

Increased recognition of the political claims of Maori has been a second important influence on relationships between state, communities and citizens in Aotearoa New Zealand since the 1980s. Dispossessed of much of their land in the late nineteenth century, Maori struggled for 150 years to have their experience of social and economic injustice recognized by New Zealand governments. During the 1980s there was finally some progress. The fourth Labour government gave retrospective power to the Waitangi Tribunal, thereby opening up the land claims process and the possibility to address long standing grievances. During the same period there were significant attempts to institutionalize equity and biculturalism in major institutions and organizations. The aim was to overcome historical social and economic disparities between Maori and non-Maori, and advance *tino rangatiratanga*. These understandings differed dramatically from the monocultural assumptions that underpinned the Keynesian welfarism of the post-war period in which Maori were welcome to participate in state institutions, public life and popular culture, but on Pakeha terms. As an influential report had stressed in 1988:

> New Zealand institutions manifest a monocultural bias and the culture that shapes and directs that bias is *Pakehatanga*. The bias can be observed working in law, government, the professions, health care, land ownership, welfare practices, education, town planning, the police, finance, business and spoken language. It permeates the media and our national economic life. If one is outside it, one sees it as 'the system.' If one is cocooned within it, one sees it as the normal condition of existence. (Ministerial Advisory Committee on a Maori Perspective for the Department of Social Welfare 1988)

However, just as the discourse of neo-liberalism has shifted over the last two decades, so too has that of *tino rangatiratanga*. Rata (2003) suggests there have been two phases in negotiations between the state and Maori. During the early 1980s, attention was focused on the 'bicultural project' in which the aim was to facilitate entry of Maori into key institutional locations. She argues this process created structural sites within the state for some Maori. Certainly, by the 1990s virtually all government departments, many community organizations and some large New Zealand companies had Maori advisors and Maori policy analysts. Rata argues that attention has now shifted away from biculturalism and is now focused on re-creating an economic base that will allow the generation of tribal wealth. She calls this second stage 'tribal capitalism,' in which the emphasis is on gaining control of assets following Treaty settlements, and developing a formal political partnership with the government.

In conjunction with these changing political agendas, the discourses surrounding Maori-Crown relations have also shifted. In their analysis of Waitangi Tribunal reports, Maaka and Fleras (1998) describe this shift as that from 'contract to constitutionalism.' They show that early Tribunal reports assume Maori ceded sovereignty under the Treaty of Waitangi, and correspondingly represent *tino rangatiratanga* as involving tribal self-management along similar lines to local government. In contrast, more recent reports endorse the notion that Maori continue to have sovereignty by right of original occupancy. Claims for *tino rangatiratanga* are thus represented as 'a dialogue between sovereigns,' framed, in part, through concepts and categories derived from international law. Recent proposals for a 'new constitutionalism' between Maori and the Crown, which would clarify ambiguities around the status of the Treaty of Waitangi and establish the foundational place of Maori in the New Zealand polity, can be situated in this context.

Profound contradictions emerged from the articulation of neo-liberalism and *tino rangatiratanga* during the 1980s and 1990s. On the one hand, changes associated with market-oriented restructuring, particularly the sustained rise in levels of unemployment, disproportionately affected Maori and Pacific workers. On the other hand, as biculturalism received more attention and land claims were settled, there were improvements in educational achievement and labour market distribution for some Maori men and women. A new generation of tertiary educated Maori, armed with professional and technical qualifications, found their skills in considerable demand. However, while claims for *tino rangatiratanga* meant economic benefits for some, the legacy of historical inequalities continued. One consequence has been greater class differences amongst Maori, while an overall social and economic gap between Maori and non-Maori persists. Moreover, despite the presence of the new Maori technocrats (Durie 1998: 19), longstanding labour force patterns persisted with Maori women remaining significantly under-represented in higher public service income groups relative to Maori men. Thus it can be argued that these developments have unexpectedly exacerbated the gender-based subordination of Maori women.

These ongoing economic and social disparities help explain the emphasis on Maori – and by extension Pacific – communities that characterize the partnering efforts of the fifth Labour government. In their efforts to defeat the incumbent National government in the 1999 election, the Labour party aggressively courted

Maori voters promising economic development and jobs and attention to social issues such as housing and education. Once in power, their attempts to address issues of racialized economic and social polarization reached an apotheosis with the 'Closing the Gaps' policy programme of 2000. Heralded by the Labour government as representing a new ethos in the social policy, 'Closing the Gaps' aimed to reduce the socio-economic disparities between Maori and Pacific New Zealanders and other New Zealanders. However, even though only 39 out of 72 policies under the Closing the Gaps policy programme were explicitly targeted at Maori and Pacific people, in popular discourse the initiative became associated with exclusionary service delivery (Humpage and Fleras 2001). By the end of that year, opposition to 'Closing the Gaps' had prompted the Labour government to downplay explicit connections between their social policy initiatives and Maori, in favour of a broader programme of 'social equity' for all. But despite the shift in political discourse, social policy and service delivery arrangements continue to target Maori and Pacific communities by including ethnically specific components, and concepts such as self determination and the desirability of the cultural matching of service providers and clients remain central to understandings of social well being in New Zealand (Suaalli 2003).

The Challenge of Increasing Ethnic Diversity

The class, racial and gender formations that underpinned the politics of biculturalism are now being challenged by new patterns of ethnic difference associated with the globalization of the domestic economy and the changing composition of migration flows. It was changes initiated during the 1980s that saw the first steps towards the liberalization of immigration flows. In 1986 a business migration scheme was introduced, with the intent of attracting wealthy entrepreneurs and their capital to New Zealand. In 1991 there was a further shift in emphasis, with the introduction of a new migration policy based on a points system emphasizing educational qualifications and work experience. The traditional source bias towards Britain was removed with the assumption that new migration patterns would involve a much more diverse range of countries. The new migration policy was also premised on an overall increase in levels of migration with the intention being to achieve an annual net migration gain of 20,000 people. The rationale for the changes in migration policies and programmes was explicitly economic; new migrants would bring the capital, skills and expertise needed in New Zealand's restructured economy.

Further liberalization of both foreign investment and immigration flows took place during the 1990s. Major regional initiatives, including the active promotion of investment opportunities through the visits of politicians, trade seminars and the appointment of FDI counsellors to embassies in Japan, Singapore and Los Angeles resulted in record levels of inward investment. Likewise, immigration policies targeted people with high level technical and professional skills. By the year ended January 1995, net immigration gains were running at record levels and Auckland – New Zealand's largest city – was suffering major infrastructural problems. The composition of migration flows also changed dramatically during this period, with migration from 'non-traditional' source countries, particularly in Asia, becoming much more significant (Lidgard et al. 1998). While these flows have since fluctuated in relation to changing policy frameworks and economic conditions, high annual net migration gains have remained a feature of the last ten years.

Complex patterns of ethnic and cultural differences have emerged from the globalization of the domestic economy and the changing composition of migration flows. Despite a points-based system, which emphasizes skills, there is considerable evidence that migrants from 'non-traditional' source countries have experienced difficulties gaining access to the New Zealand labour market. Research shows that this is due to language problems, lack of recognition of overseas qualifications and racial discrimination (Ho and Lidgard 1996). Consequently, many new migrants have been forced to make alternative economic arrangements, including self-employment and undocumented work. These new patterns of employment have articulated with increased class differences amongst New Zealanders. In Auckland, in particular, households are increasingly opting for market provisioning of domestic services and childcare. High wage, dual income households increasingly eat out or rely on take away food. Nannies, house-cleaners and gardeners have also become more common. In contrast, those who cannot afford such solutions now experience heightened versions of the 'double burden,' as the new emphasis on paid work means more women are trying to cope with competing demands from employers, partners and children. These shifts have thus generated new patterns of gendered and racialized difference – most notably in the emergence of the category of 'the working poor' – at the same time as they have underwritten existing patterns of economic and social disparity.

As a consequence of the changes in migration policies during the 1980s and 1990s, Aotearoa New Zealand is a much more economically, ethnically and culturally diverse place than it has ever been historically. Auckland, in particular, has changed significantly in recent years. In Auckland City (the central of the four cities that make up greater Auckland), recent census figures show that New Zealand Europeans[7] now account for only 65 per cent of the population, Asians 18 per cent, Pacific people 13.7 per cent and Maori 8.4 per cent. Not only has the permanent population become increasingly ethnically diverse, but also the phenomenal growth in export education – in which students are recruited primarily from China and South East Asia – has literally transformed the face of the inner city (Lewis 2005). Cultural expressions of this increasing diversity are highly visible; two of the major annual events in Auckland are now the New Year Chinese Lantern Festival and Pacifica, a festival that celebrates the diverse Island cultures. Less visible, but equally significant, are political expressions of diversity. Culturally appropriate service delivery for Pacific communities is now widely accepted, and pressures for multi-lingual, multi-

---

7   Given the broader context, it is not surprising that the naming of census categories is contentious. The Department of Statistics recently decided to retain the descriptor New Zealand European to ensure consistency over time and because there was public objection to the use of the term Pakeha (Statistics New Zealand 2004).

cultural service delivery are increasing as other ethnic communities have developed their political voices. To date, however, these changes have been overwhelmingly concentrated in Auckland, thus underpinning a growing divide between this city and the rest of New Zealand.

Contested Terrains

It is in this complex and volatile context that debates about citizenship have re-emerged, most notably in the form of discussions about how the relationships between biculturalism and multiculturalism should be understood. Bicultural modes of thinking and acting entered into 'official culture' in the 1990s (King, Haas and Hill 2004: 7). Not only was the status of Maori as *tangata whenua* accepted in political discourse, this status had been institutionalized. Explicit legislative reference to the Treaty of Waitangi, the establishment of parallel processes for Maori in 'mainstream' politics, and the use of Maori concepts and protocols had all been normalized, particularly in the public sector. Indeed, Sharp (1997: 448) argues that Maori have largely set the agenda in recent years, and that successive governments have not been successful in wrestling the initiative back. Significant funding for Maori economic, social and educational initiatives, the settlement of major Treaty claims and, most recently, the heated debate over who owns the New Zealand foreshore and seabed only serve to underline his point.[8] In this context it might be argued that the politics of biculturalism have shifted from those of recognition to redistribution (Fraser 1997). Certainly, the issues involved are now fundamentally about equal access to resources and power sharing.

In strong contrast to the politics of biculturalism, Aotearoa New Zealand has never had a formal policy of multiculturalism and the debates around this topic have long been murky. During the 1970s – the early period of the so-called 'Maori Renaissance' – biculturalism was often seen as an evolutionary step towards multiculturalism, reflecting the broader influence of international civil rights discourse. The argument was that because of the pressing nature of Maori claims for justice these should be addressed before those of other minority groups. Once the concerns of Maori had been resolved, other forms of cultural injustice would then be taken into consideration. Today, it is much more likely to be argued that biculturalism and multiculturalism are different forms of politics, and that ultimately New Zealand is bicultural before it is multicultural. In this context, biculturalism is no longer

---

8   A recommendation from the Waitangi Tribunal that the Maori Land Court hear a case based on the claim of Maori customary ownership of the foreshore and seabed saw the Government move quickly to develop legislation that would vest ownership of the foreshore and seabed in the Crown, as the representative of all New Zealanders. While efforts were made to preserve the right for claims to be heard on the basis of Maori customary use, the Government's preemptive move was seen as a 'land grab' by many Maori. There has been intense debate, including a 20,000 person *hikoi* (march) to take Maori concerns to Wellington. The issue is not yet resolved.

understood as a subset of multiculturalism. Instead, it is argued that the claims of
Maori take political precedence over others because they were here first. It is in
this context that calls from high profile Maori for the right to exercise control over
immigration flows can be understood. Relatedly, those supportive of biculturalism
are often suspicious of overseas ownership because it is seen as unsympathetic to
local cultural considerations.

There are other reasons why the discourse of multiculturalism has been
downplayed. New Zealand's historically and demographically significant Pacific
communities, who were the most likely advocates for broader conceptions of
multiculturalism, have largely allied themselves with Maori on the basis of a
shared Polynesian ancestry and their common commitment to a politics based on
indigeneity. Other long-standing ethnic communities remained relatively small until
the 1980s, and they too often expressed their respect and support for the Treaty-
based claims of Maori. Finally, to complicate matters further, some of the more vocal
claims for multiculturalism have come from conservative politicians opposed to the
Treaty process, a tradition continued by the recent Brash speech. In this context,
it is not surprising that there is considerable scepticism amongst many Maori and
some Pakeha about multiculturalism, and that even those commentators supportive
of increased ethnic and cultural diversity, such as former Race Relations Conciliator
and Human Rights Commissioner Chris Laidlaw, have downplayed multiculturalism
in their public statements about New Zealand perspectives on cultural traditions and
concepts of nationhood (Kaul 2004).

However, as King et al. (2004: 19) point out, while Aotearoa New Zealand may
have become a bicultural Treaty based nation in the last twenty years, it is also
characterized by increasing multiculturalism in everyday life. As they observe,
new migrants are often bewildered by the discourse of biculturalism, and longer
established ethnic groups, such as the New Zealand Chinese, have begun to express
their frustration with the continued difficulties they face in articulating their specific
issues and concerns. Recently, calls for greater attention to multiple forms of cultural
and ethnic difference have become louder, and are now more likely to come from
ethnic communities themselves, some of whom are dealing with considerable
economic and social hardship. These calls are also receiving more sympathetic
official support. In part, a new attitude to recent migrants has been a response to a
tight labour market and severe skills shortages. Certainly Auckland employers were
forced to reconsider the often used excuse of 'no New Zealand work experience'
when research showed it to be the basis of exclusionary hiring practices, and
the Auckland Chamber of Commerce now actively assists the placement of new
migrants and sponsors initiatives to foster and support culturally diverse workplaces.
Politicians and policymakers have also begun to address the concerns of ethnic
communities, manifest in developments such as the formal apology to the New
Zealand Chinese community for the discriminatory head tax of last century, and in
the recent establishment of the Auckland Migrant Services Trust.

The politics of biculturalism have also begun to be questioned by some
Maori in a context where there are growing class differences amongst Maori,

the settlements process has advanced, and a new generation of tertiary educated Maori professionals and businesspeople has emerged. Some of the new generation of tertiary educated Maori are challenging the political formulations of their more traditional predecessors.

For example, high profile Labour politician John Tamihere, former CEO of Te Whanau o Waipareira, which provides social services to urban Maori in West Auckland but is open to all on the basis of need, is as vocal about the need for pan-tribalism[9] and multiculturalism as he is about the need for private training establishments and individual responsibility (see, for example, Tamihere 1997). He, along with others, also argues that the settlements process has served to reconstitute *iwi* as corporate organizations[10] while at the same time it has entrenched long-standing familial-based power relations. As Seuffert (2002) points out, these Treaty politics are gendered, with Maori men cast into the role of global entrepreneurs and Maori women largely excluded from the management of settlement assets. It is also argued that the emphasis on the new 'neo-tribes' (Rata 2003) is particularly problematic in a context where some 70 per cent of Maori live outside their *rohe*,[11] and an estimated 25 per cent of Maori are unable to identify their *iwi* affiliations, thereby missing out of the benefits derived from the settlements process. Consequently, there are growing tensions not only between so-called 'winner' and 'loser' *iwi*, but also between *iwi*-based organizations and pan-tribal organizations delivering social services to largely disenfranchised urban Maori communities (see Maaka 1994; Webb 1998; Meredith 2000).

Finally, while there has been a great deal of attention paid to the implications of biculturalism for Maori ambitions, and there is an emergent discussion about the roles of other ethnic groups and urban Maori, much less attention has been paid to how the processes associated with biculturalism and multiculturalism have reconstituted Pakeha identities. Leading political commentator Colin James (2004) recently described what he calls an 'indigenised majority' – Pakeha who have accepted the symbolic and material understandings that underpin Maori claims. In his analysis he stressed that, for Pakeha, biculturalism is no longer simply about tolerance and support for a minority culture, it is about the emergence of genuinely new understandings of state and nation premised on a distinctive national political system and a newly indigenized popular culture.

Although the reaction to the 'One Nation' speech suggests his may be an unduly optimistic analysis, one of the more interesting explanations for the subsequent Pakeha backlash was that they had never been acknowledged for the huge distance

---

9   One of the legacies of the 1980s was a renewed emphasis on *iwi* organizations as the means for the delivery of services. Pan-tribal organizations deliver services to Maori regardless of their *iwi* affiliations.

10   For example, the new Maori elite are often referred to as the Maori Browntable. This tongue in cheek name plays on that of the Business Roundtable, an elite right-wing business group that was influential during the 1980s and 1990s.

11   Traditional tribal area

they had travelled in efforts to recognize the claims of Maori, and had consequently begun to feel resentful. Perhaps more astutely, however, Goldsmith (2003) argues that biculturalism associated Maori with spiritual values and Pakeha with material values, and that in the new conceptions of bicultural nationhood Maori are increasingly confident of their cultural identity, whereas many New Zealand Europeans (to use his deliberately chosen label) still 'haven't a clue.'

Brokering Neo-liberalism, Biculturalism and Multiculturalism

If citizenship is a 'discussion, and a struggle over, the meaning and scope of the community in which one lives' (Hall and Held 1989: 175), then citizenship debates in Aotearoa New Zealand are at a critical juncture. The political configurations that will emerge in response to the current challenges are not pre-destined, although inevitably the claims of Maori and the politics of biculturalism will continue to shape political futures in profound ways. For ultimately it is biculturalism, not multiculturalism, that underpins the post-colonial political settlement in Aotearoa New Zealand. At the same time, the need to re-think the relationships between biculturalism and multiculturalism has become pressing in the context of increasing ethnic diversity and changing gendered patterns of socio-economic inequality. Not surprisingly, these issues are most pronounced in the public sector and are beginning to have major implications for both policy development and service delivery.

In an important argument, Yeatman (1994) suggests that if biculturalism is understood as a dialogical process involving non-exclusive cultural identities, this would permit a version of biculturalism to be linked to multicultural values and objectives. Certainly, over the last decade, an increasing number of New Zealand commentators from a range of ethnic backgrounds have begun to explore the implications of anti-essentialist conceptions of identity. In particular, these analyses have highlighted the critical role played by those with 'hybrid' identities in the processes associated with cultural re-visioning. It is argued that those interlocutors who straddle conjunctures of culture and politics can usefully act as brokers between different constituencies (Meredith 2000). It is in this context that the important role that gender is playing in the processes around citizenship formation in contemporary Aotearoa New Zealand can be most clearly seen.

Feminist citizenship literatures have argued that women are the bearers of culture (Yuval-Davis and Anthias 1989; Yuval-Davis 1997). Certainly, this argument is understood to have some relevance in the New Zealand context, particularly when considered in relation to Maori women. While historically Maori women were active participants in the formal leadership structures, their leadership roles were marginalized by the process of colonization and they were subsequently redefined as wives and mothers (Mikarae 1994; see also Seuffert 2002). While activist Maori women played an important role in the so-called 'Maori Renaissance,' the political claims of the 1970s and 1980s, which constructed Maori and Pakeha in binary opposition to each other (Mohanram 1999), also constituted Maori women as responsible for reproducing the nation through their reproductive and maternal positioning. Finally, and most recently, it has been argued that it is a gendered and racialized material/spiritual dichotomy between Maori men and women that has allowed Maori men to participate in corporate initiatives and the marketplace as neo-liberal subjects, whereas Maori women have been left to uphold the traditional Maori nation (Moeke-Maxwell 2003).

However, while Maori women may have been marginalized from meaningful roles in the Treaty settlement process, and their voices are often silenced in formal processes, they have long played an important role in brokering relationships between different cultural and political groups. In her analysis, Rata (2003) underlines the centrality of the roles played by Maori located within key institutions during the bicultural project of the 1980s and 1990s. The caring professions, including education, health, welfare and the church, saw some of the most sustained efforts to institutionalize biculturalism, exemplified by the rise of practices such as 'cultural safety' in nursing and the institutionalization of parallel structures within the Anglican church. Because the caring professions are largely feminized domains, it is not surprising that women featured centrally in the development of the politics of biculturalism in the public sector during this period. Today, this brokering role is identified as a key dimension of the post-colonial processes associated with tribal development. For example, Moeke-Maxwell (2003) identifies the rise of what she calls 'hybrid women;' those who can speak across 'bicultural hotspots.' She argues that these women use their cultural and political skills to work across the sites where the corporate *iwi* meets the Pakeha elite. Whereas earlier formulations would have cast these women as 'assimilated Maori' (see, for example, Awatere 1984), she argues these roles have become critical to the economic and social ambitions of Maori.

This new emphasis on brokering is not, however, confined to Maori women. More generally, in the context of 'after neo-liberalism' and the new emphasis on collaboration and partnership, there is an increased demand for those people who have the relational skills that allow relationships across diverse organizational, cultural and political divides to be advanced (Larner and Craig forthcoming). Observers of the new 'New Zealand Experiment' often comment on the fact that women now fill many senior positions, including those of Prime Minister, Chief Justice, Attorney General and senior cabinet posts. Drawing on feminist international relations literatures, Seuffert (2002) argues that women often act as mediator figures in times of transition and crisis, and that the New Zealand case can be usefully understood in this context. More generally, the new emphasis on relationship building is having important implications for those employed in the public sector. Both central and local government agencies are seeking out individuals who can build collaborative relationships between government, local institutions and diverse communities (Larner and Butler 2004). Recent research has demonstrated that these new positions in the public sector are overwhelmingly filled by women and/or people from Maori and Pacific communities. These women are expected to embody both organizational and traditional skills, and the new skills demanded by the collaborative moment (creating supportive environments, demonstrating cultural sensitivity, and strengthening community action). They are not only required to exercise new forms of leadership and management skills, they are also expected to introduce new cultures of working and learning into their institutions.

As the issues associated with increasing ethnic diversity have become more visible, so too have new brokers emerged in sites such as the community based Shakti Asian Women's Centre in Auckland. Initially established in the mid-1990s to provide a forum for Asian women to network in New Zealand, this organization now offers a range of services including language courses, legal assistance, counselling and support for women seeking safety from domestic violence. As with the government departments, the vast majority of these community-based roles are being filled by women (Roelvink and Craig 2005). As Schild (2000: 277) argues more generally, women in their day-to-day activities as professionals and practitioners, are the concrete, although largely overlooked, agents of the reconfiguration of state institutions and shifting notions of citizenship. Of course, the demand for constant networking that characterizes these positions also often leads to over commitment and the intensification of labour. Seen in this context, it is clear that it is New Zealand women, particularly those from Maori, Pacific and other ethnic communities, who are doing much of the 'emotional labour' associated with the current reconfiguration of citizenship.

Conclusion

So how should the national furore caused by Don Brash's Orewa speech be understood? One major New Zealand newspaper made parallels with the infamous One Nation Party of Australia, and equated his comments with notorious Pauline Hansen's anti-aboriginal, anti-immigrant stance. However, whereas Hansen had been seen as a maverick, and her party One Nation had remained on the fringes of political power, Don Brash is the leader of the opposition National party and a former Governor of the Reserve Bank. He also explicitly rejected accusations of racism, arguing that his point was that there should be no 'race-based' preferential funding based on the assumption that Maori had special status as indigenous people. Personal politics aside, the widespread nature of the reaction to his speech suggests that accusations of political expediency and racism are overly simplistic explanations for the events of the last few months.

This chapter has argued that these events underline growing tensions between biculturalism and multiculturalism as these understandings of cultural difference have been historically constituted in Aotearoa New Zealand. The political legacies of neo-liberalism and *tino rangatiratanga*, in combination with well-documented ethnically linked socio-economic disparities, which mean that Maori and Pacific people continue to be poorly represented on a range of key indicators, have given rise to a focus on ethnicity, rather than gender or class, as the major axis of difference for government policies and programmes. Maori, and by association Pacific communities, have subsequently emerged as an explicit focus for the targeted economic and social initiatives that have proliferated in Aotearoa New Zealand over the last two decades. The ambition to reduce socio-economic disparities is being achieved in two ways; via the implementation of Treaty-based and other culturally specific strategies in more general initiatives and through the allocation of funding streams specifically targeted for Maori and Pacific peoples.

These strategies are now meeting serious challenges. Most immediately, there are important questions to be asked about the relationships between individual and group rights in Aotearoa New Zealand and the basis on which those are founded (Sharp 1997). Are Maori equal with other New Zealanders before the law, or as indigenous people are they entitled to special assistance as a group to enable their full participation in the society and economy? If so, on what basis should that group be defined? By tribal affiliation or socio-economic status? If it is the former, how will the needs of urban Maori be met? Further, as economic, cultural and ethnic diversity has increased, the question of how other claims for social justice should be addressed has become more pressing. For example, should other ethnic communities also have separate political representation, funding streams and service provision? On what basis will these be allocated? How, for example, will the emergent category of 'Asian' meet the diverse needs of Chinese, Indian and Taiwanese New Zealanders? Given the ethnic diversity of Auckland, how will the needs of this city be reconciled with those of the rest of the country?[12] Or is it time to rethink the models that predominate in current models of policy making, resource allocation and service provision?

While it is very clear that claims of 'One New Zealand' or 'Why Can't We All Just Be New Zealanders' underwrite culturally conformist and assimilationist agendas (see Meredith 2000), calls for a more inclusionary and multi-faceted identity politics are raising difficult, but critically important, challenges for New Zealand and New Zealanders. Efforts to address these challenges will require sensitivity and attention to the politics of both biculturalism and multiculturalism. In these efforts women, particularly those who have had experience of diverse political and cultural contexts, which facilitate their ability to work as effective brokers, are likely to play a central role. The rise of the bicultural project in the 1980s and 1990s saw increasing numbers of Maori women positioned in this way, however as Aotearoa New Zealand has become increasingly ethnically diverse, so too have other women – particularly those from Pacific and new migrant communities – begun to occupy these roles. Rather than being simply the bearers of tradition, these women can be seen as 'midwives' of an inclusionary and multifaceted vision of citizenship appropriate for a bicultural multicultural Aotearoa New Zealand.

ACKNOWLEDGEMENTS   This research was funded by the New Zealand Foundation for Research Science and Technology Project UOAX0233. My thanks to the editors for their generous and constructive comments.

---

12   This is not a frivolous question. The current dispute over transportation funding illustrates the immense difficulties generated by per capita funding for public services.

References

Awatere, D. (1984), *Maori Sovereignty*, Broadsheet, Auckland.

Brash, D. (2004), 'Nationhood,' A Speech to the Orewa Rotary Club, (www.scoop. co.nz/ mason/stories/PA0401/S00220.htm). Accessed 24 May 2004.

Department of the Prime Minister and Cabinet (2003), *Sustainable Development for New Zealand: Programme of Action*, Wellington, Department of Prime Minister and Cabinet, January.

Durie, M. (1998), *Te Mana, Te Kawanatanga: The Politics of Maori Self Determination*, Oxford University Press, Auckland.

Fraser, N. (1997), *Justice Interruptus,* Routledge, London.

Goldsmith, M. (2003), 'Our Place' in New Zealand Culture: How the Museum of New Zealand constructs Biculturalism,' *Ethnologies Comparees* 6, (http://alor. univ-montp3. fr/cerce/r6/m.g.s.htm). Accessed 19 May 2004.

Hall, S. and Held, D. (1989), 'Citizens and Citizenship,' in S. Hall and M. Jacques (eds), *New Times: The Changing Face of Politics in the 1990s,* Lawrence, Wishart, London, pp. 173-188.

Ho, E. and Lidgard, J. (1996), 'Give us a chance: the employment experiences of new settlers from East Asia,' P. Morrison (ed.), *Labour, Employment and Work in New Zealand: Proceedings of the Seventh Conference*, Victoria University, Wellington.

Humpage, L. and Fleras, A. (2001), 'Intersecting Discourses: Closing the Gaps, Social Justice and the Treaty of Waitangi,' *Social Policy Journal of New Zealand*, Vol. 16, pp. 37-53.

James, C. (2004), 'The Indigenisation of Aotearoa-New Zealand: the politics of the Treaty of Waitangi,' Paper for the Australian Judges Conference, 27 January. (www.colinjames.co.nz/speeches_briefings/Aust_judges_04Jan27.htm.). Accessed 22 March 2004.

Kaul, M. (2004), 'Review' (http://iicdelhi.nic.in/12AprReview.htm) Accessed 19 May 2004.

Kelsey, J. (1993), *Rolling Back the State: Privatisation of Power in Aotearoa/New Zealand*, Bridget Williams Books Ltd, Wellington.

King, M.,Haas,A.and Hill,R.(2004),'ReconcilingBiculturalismandMulticulturalism in New Zealand,' (www.futurestrust.org.nz/Michael%20King%20Tribute.pdf). Accessed 19 May 2004.

Larner, W. (2002), 'Neo-liberalism and Tino Rangatiratanga: Welfare State Restructuring in Aotearoa/New Zealand,' in C. Kingfisher (ed.), *Western Welfare in Decline: Globalisation and Women's Poverty*, University of Pennsylvania Press, Philadelphia.

Larner, W. (1996), 'The "New Boys:" Restructuring in New Zealand 1984-1994,' *Social Politics: Special Edition on Gender Inequalities in Global Restructuring*, Vol. 3(1), pp. 32-56.

Larner, W. (1993), 'Changing Contexts: Globalization, Migration and Feminism,' in S. Gunew and A. Yeatman (eds), *Feminism and the Politics of Difference*, Allen and Unwin, Sydney.

Larner, W. and Butler, M. (2004), 'Governmentalities of Local Partnerships,' Paper submitted to *Studies in Political Economy*, under review.

Larner, W. and Craig, D. (forthcoming), 'After Neoliberalism? Community Activism and Local Partnerships in Aotearoa New Zealand,' in L. Bondi and N. Laurie (eds), 'Working the Spaces of Neoliberalism' *Antipode*.

Larner, W. and Spoonley, P. (1995), 'Post-colonial Politics in Aotearoa/New Zealand,' in D. Stasiulis and N. Yuval-Davis (eds), *Unsettling Settler Societies: Articulations of Gender, Race, Ethnicity and Class*, Sage, London.

Lewis, N. (2005), 'Code of practice for the pastoral care of international students: making a globalising industry in New Zealand,' in *Globalisation, Societies and Education*, Vol. 3(1), pp. 5-47.

Lewis, N., Larner, W. and Le Heron, R. (2004), '"After Neoliberalism" Political Projects: Co-constituting the New Zealand Designer Industry,' Article submitted to *Transactions of the Institute of British Geographers*.

Lidgard, J., Bedford, R. and Goodwin, J. (1998), *Transformations in New Zealand's International Migration System: 1981-1996*, Discussion Paper No. 25, Population Studies Centre, Hamilton.

Maaka R. (1994), 'The New Tribe: Conflicts and Continuities in the Social Organisation of Urban Maori,' *The Contemporary Pacific*, Vol. 6(2), pp. 311-36.

Maaka, R. and Fleras, A. (1998), *Re-Constitutionalising Treaty Work: The Waitangi Tribunal*, University of Canterbury Mimeo, Christchurch.

Meredith, P. (2000), 'Urban Maori as 'New Citizens:' The Quest for Recognition and Resources,' Paper presented to the Revisioning Citizenship in New Zealand Conference held at the University of Waikato, 22-24 February 2000.

Mikarae, A. (1994), 'Maori Women caught in the Contradictions of a Colonised Reality,' *Waikato Law Review* 125.

Ministerial Advisory Committee on a Maori Perspective for the Department of Social Welfare (1988), *Puao-te-ata-tu (Daybreak)*, Government Printer, Wellington.

Moeke-Maxwell, T. (2003), 'Bring Home the Body: Bi/multi Racial Maori Women's Hybridity in Aotearoa New Zealand,' Paper presented to the NZARE/ARRE Conference held at the University of Auckland, New Zealand, 30 November to 2 December 2003.

Mohanram, R. (1999), *Black Body: Women, Colonialism, Space,* Allen and Unwin, Australia.

Newman, J. (2001), *Modernising Governance: New Labour, Policy and Society*, Sage, London.

Rata, E. (2003), 'An Overview of Neotribal Capitalism,' *Ethnologies Comparees. Oceanie, debut de siecle*, No. 6, Spring (www.alor.univ-montp3.fr/cerce/r6/n6.htm). Accessed 19 May 2004.

Roelvink, G. and Craig, D. (2005), 'The Man in the Partnering State: Regendering the Social through Partnership,' *Studies in Political Economy*, Vol. 75, Spring, pp. 103-26.

Schild, V. (2000), 'Neoliberalism's New Gendered Market Citizens: The "civilising" dimension of social programmes,' *Citizenship Studies*, Vol. 4(3), pp. 275-305.

Seuffert, N. (2002), 'Race-ing and engendering the Nation-State in Aotearoa/New Zealand,' *American University Journal of Gender, Social Policy and Law*, pp. 597-612.

Sharp, A. (1997), 'Civil Rights, Amelioration and Reparation,' in M. Brown and S Ganguly (eds), *Government Policies and Ethnic Relations in Asia and the Pacific*, Harvard University Press, Cambridge, pp. 421-56.

Statistics New Zealand (2004) *Report of the Review of the Measurement of Ethnicity*, Statistics New Zealand, Wellington.

Suaalli, S. (2003), 'Competing Spirits of Governing Samoan Youth Offenders in New Zealand,' Paper presented at the *Social Policy Research and Evaluation Conference*, Wellington.

Tamihere, J. (1997) 'The Urban Native,' in M. O'Brien and C. Briar (eds), *Beyond Poverty: Conference Proceedings,* AUWRC, Auckland.

Webb, R. (1998), 'The Sealords Deal and Treaty Rights: What has been achieved?,' in L. Pihama and C. Waerea-I-te-rangi Smith (eds), *Fisheries and Commodifying Iwi – Economic, Politics and Colonisation Volume 3*, International Research Institute for Maori and Indigenous Education/Moko Productions, Tamaki Makaurau.

Yeatman, A. (1994) *Postmodern Revisionings of the Political*, Routledge, New York.

Yuval-Davis, N. (1997), 'Women, Citizenship and Difference,' *Feminist Studies*, Vol. 57, pp. 4-27.

Yuval-Davis, N. and Anthias, F. (1989), *Women-Nation-State*, Macmillian, London.

Chapter 7

Social Exclusion and Changes to Citizenship: Women and Children, Minorities and Migrants in Britain

Alexandra Dobrowolsky with Ruth Lister[1]

The aim of this chapter is to analyze the current state of citizenship in Britain in light of the rise of political discourses and practices that seek to remedy social exclusion. Citizenship involves relationships that encompass social, economic, and cultural positions, legal and institutional forms as well as identity and senses of belonging (Jenson and Phillips 1996; Werbner and Yuval-Davis 1999; Jenson 2001; Hobson and Lister 2002; Lister 2003a; Dobrowolsky and Jenson 2004). It consists of multiple dimensions affecting politics, broadly conceived, and policy at various levels. However, here we will limit our purview to citizenship concerns arising out of new efforts to combat 'social exclusion' on the part of the Labour government of Tony Blair. More specifically, we unpack the implications of social exclusion in light of two highly contested areas: i) recent welfare restructuring and ii) (im)migration and asylum. Herein lies the irony: while New Labour's concern with social exclusion is explicit in the former, it is less than apparent in the latter. In this respect, and in others, we expose the limited ways the Blair government deals with social exclusion and citizenship. We consider the repercussions of changing emphases, vis-à-vis social exclusion and citizenship, when it comes to women, racial and ethnic minorities, (im)migrants, refugees and asylum seekers, and their children. Indeed, we contend that broader readings of social exclusion and citizenship would embrace, and should respond to, both the plight of outsiders and insiders who do not enjoy full substantive citizenship rights. Sadly, this has not been the reality in contemporary Britain.

An Overview of the Issues

On one hand, the Blair government has adopted discourses of social exclusion and practices to counteract it. Along with these efforts, New Labour has pushed for active

1   Sincere thanks to Jane Jenson and the social cohesion research team, collaborators and discussants (SSHRC Grant 829-1999-2001) as this work stems from their analyses and efforts, and to Stephanie Fletcher for her excellent research assistance on this paper.

citizenship in different realms, including welfare and social policies. As we shall see, here citizenship becomes highly instrumentalized. Responsibilities and obligations are promoted over rights (Lister 1998; Lund 1999). Broader notions of citizenship succumb to over-arching economic objectives and increasingly narrow notions of citizenship become interlaced with moral undertones. Put simply, what makes the good citizen, becomes what produces the good worker, the good consumer, and to a certain extent, the good neighbour, as the community plays an increasingly important role (Lawson and Leighton 2004).

At the same time, the Labour government has paid an unprecedented amount of attention to 'the child' and the links between social exclusion and children are made manifest. The child is the focal point in recent pledges, policies and programmes, as well as in new spending priorities (Pinkney 2000; Ridge 2003). For instance, Prime Minister Tony Blair delivered a historic promise to eradicate child poverty by the year 2020 and the Chancellor of the Exchequer, Gordon Brown, has made achieving this goal a prime objective. For both, the child becomes a sound investment, as New Labour banks on the child as a citizen-*in-becoming*, and the future citizen-worker (Dobrowolsky 2002; Lister 2003b; Dobrowolsky and Jenson 2005).

On the other hand, the Blair government has not comprehensively applied the concept of social exclusion to racial and ethnic minorities, or to (im)migrants, refugees and asylum seekers, nor has it followed a broader, substantive citizenship agenda when it comes to these typically marginalized groups. These tendencies are exacerbated by a 'twinned strategy of developing race relations legislation in tandem with immigration legislation' (Lewis and Neal 2005: 436).

Granted, the essence of citizenship is about membership in specific communities and the boundaries which get drawn that both bestow inclusion and give rise to exclusion of non-members. And so, the likely argument here would be that, in order to promote social inclusion within nation state borders, there needs to be clear boundaries set up against 'outsiders' (Wolfe and Klausen 2000). Nevertheless, precisely because this is a government that has made social exclusion – as well as global poverty and conflict – a priority, one would expect that exclusion at nation state borders, and especially the political, economic, cultural, psychological exclusion faced by minority groups and migrants within Britain, would be addressed more concertedly and effectively. The contradictions are multiple in a context where social inclusion as well as social cohesion are championed, but where frameworks continue to be drawn up that encourage exclusion (and often racism and xenophobia) and weaken mutual solidarity (Lewis and Neal 2005: 439; Sales 2005: 459).

As a result, what becomes apparent is that new insiders have come to the fore while certain sets of outsiders are produced and perpetuated. New Labour has directed social exclusion resources primarily towards priorities like children and young people as well as to communities with the objective of 'neighbourhood renewal.' Yet some children – particularly those of asylum seekers – find themselves completely on the margins, literally and metaphorically. Moreover, while social exclusion efforts are geared towards communities, they nonetheless fail to acknowledge that British communities 'are not necessarily inclusive or tolerant of outsiders such as asylum seekers' (MacGregor 2003: 71).

Although children and youth are a focal point in the push to counter social exclusion and when it comes to recent welfare restructuring, the children that are invoked, in general, tend not to have a gender, race or ethnicity (although increasingly disability vis-à-vis the child is becoming more of an issue) (Dobrowolsky 2002; Dobrowolsky and Saint-Martin 2005). The erasure of these collective identities and their intersections, however, cannot rub out the discriminatory realities they face. In turn, this means that not all children are being *included*. Indeed, we stress the fact that the children of racial and ethnic minorities and (im)migrants, especially asylum seekers, are graphically *excluded*.

At the same time, whereas (some) children are hot, women are not. Women are more 'out' than 'in,' in the sense that gender inequality and its implications for citizenship and social exclusion are not a burning concern for New Labour. Although gender is a critical determinant of poverty, and women disproportionately rely on social services, they are not central to the Blair government's welfare reform agenda.[2] The main preoccupation for New Labour is that of 'activating' *certain* women, i.e., getting them into paid work. Thus, some women factor in when it comes to welfare reform, but only to the extent that they become part of the Labour government's 'employability' drive. Here, lone mothers have attracted significant attention (Bashevkin 2002).

The fact that children are a top priority and women are not is more than a little ironic given that women are the majority of carers of children (paid and unpaid). What is more, women's paid work patterns are often managed around their unpaid care work. Granted, there have been Blair government initiatives in relation to child care (notably stemming from the work of key Labour women Ministers) that have a positive impact on women, but still the emphasis has been on getting women into paid work. Essentially, the child care agenda has been captured by the issue of enabling women to become paid workers. Work/life balance concerns are now increasingly debated, but again, the intent is easing women into the paid work world, rather than dealing with women's growing work loads in the home and outside it. In short, the Blair government clearly shows a preference for the 'universal breadwinner model,' fostering gender equity by promoting women's employment (Fraser 1997: 43).

For (im)migrant women and racial and ethnic minority women, many of whom have engaged in paid work more (i.e., longer, historically, and more hours, i.e., more full-time work) than white women (Bhabha and Shutter 1994: 37-38; Krieger 1999: 104), their double and triple burdens continue to remain under-appreciated. Given the male breadwinner stereotypes that still prevail in the realm of (im)migration, but also due to the general exclusion of minority children and the offspring of (im)migrants and asylum seekers, (im)migrant women, especially of African-Caribbean, Pakistani

---

2   Where policies have focused on women, they deal with particular problems, such as teenage pregnancies, or, for example, due to feminist activism, respond to specific issues such as violence against women.

and Bangladeshi descent, are even more out of the picture than British born, white women.

For all women, because the good citizen becomes the good, paid worker, unpaid work mostly done by women in the home is devalued. As Becker (2003: 118) suggests:

> Labour will need to engage in a meaningful debate as to the *nature and value* of work. Labour's equating of work as being synonymous with *paid* employment, and its implicit denigration of other forms of unpaid work in the home and community ... serve to *undervalue those people engaged in unpaid work* and to downgrade their contribution to both society and the economy ... Many of the people who provide unpaid work- such as caring and childcare- are women and many are also clients (or potential clients) of social services and would be priorities for their support services.

In these ways, citizenship's roots in the private are obscured, and New Labour fails to grasp the fact that gendered citizenship bridges the public/private divide.

In sum, through the lens of social exclusion we will underscore that although the Labour government is promoting citizenship, it is doing so in limited and highly circumscribed ways. The paper consists of four parts. In Part I, we study the origins and manifestations of social exclusion, as well as its links to citizenship. We then, in Part II, examine the centrepiece of New Labour's social exclusion agenda and welfare reform strategy: the figure of 'the child' and how this new child/youth-focus suggests a changing citizenship regime.[3] Since not all children are included, we move onto an exploration of who else is excluded. In Part III we look at the repercussions for women in general, racial and ethnic minority women as well as (im)migrant women in particular. We contextualize this in Part IV by reviewing past and present developments in Britain relating to race and ethnicity, (im)migration and asylum. In Part V we conclude by underscoring the repercussions for citizenship.

Part I: The Concept of Social Exclusion, its Origins and its Manifestations in Britain

Social exclusion as a concept originated in France. The idea of *les exclus* can be found first, formally, in French social policy (Pierson 2002: 4) in the 1970s and early 1980s. From here, social exclusion 'entered both the European Community and EU policy discourse' and by 1994 'social exclusion was so important that it was to replace poverty in the nomenclature of the EU program targeted at the most disadvantaged' (Daly and Saraceno 2002: 86). While, the term was adopted by the European Commission, partly to deal with the reluctance of some member governments to use the word poverty, 'Social exclusion gradually became the keyword not only in what was previously named poverty research but in relation to

---

3   Jane Jenson developed the notion of a changing citizenship regime and has applied it extensively in the Canadian case (Jenson and Phillips 1996; Jenson 2001; Dobrowolsky and Jenson 2003).

all kinds of deprivation and inequalities' (Daly and Saraceno 2002: 86). There was one large exception here and that was gender. If addressing the notion of poverty directly was seen to be problematic, then confronting contentious, complex issues such as the feminization of poverty would be highly unlikely.

The concept of social exclusion gained notoriety in Britain with the Labour party's landslide election win in May 1997.[4] The new government lost little time in adopting a social exclusion strategy, one that was, in many ways, ambitious. For example, it came as a direct response to the inequities arising out of the previous Conservative governments of Margaret Thatcher and John Major. In his Preface to a 2001 document entitled 'Preventing Social Exclusion' Prime Minister Blair explained:

> We came into office determined to tackle a deep social crisis ... The result was sharp income inequality, a third of children growing up in poverty, a host of social problems such as homelessness and drug abuse, and divisions in society typified by deprived neighbourhoods ... All of us bore the cost of social breakdown directly. (Blair 2001: 2, in www.cabinetoffice.gov.uk/seu/2001/pse/ PSE%20HTML/foreward.htm)

Thatcher had advanced depoliticized notions of citizens and infamously would not even acknowledge the existence of 'society,' let alone poverty. Yet, under Conservative rule, Britain experienced growing levels of poverty. Child poverty, in particular, became untenable with child poverty levels trebling under Thatcher/ Major (Bradshaw 2003: 213; SEU 2004: 2). The incoming Labour government had little choice but to deal with the socio-economic repercussions.

To some extent, then, with social exclusion, the new government was attempting to respond to the inability of the worst off to achieve full citizenship. However, it did not articulate its aims in these terms. Initially, there was no talk of tackling poverty and the Prime Minister did not make his child poverty pledge until 1999.[5] Moreover, Blair's embrace of social exclusion was not without its limitations.For a start, the discourse of social exclusion/Moreover, Blair's embrace of social exclusion was not without its limitations. For a start, the discourse of social exclusion/inclusion

---

4   The term social exclusion was used earlier in the Labour Party's 1994 Commission on Social Justice (CSJ). The party commissioned this independent review as a catalyst for new ideas and policy prescriptions. The CSJ advocated a middle way between the Old Left, the more radical, left wing elements of the party, what the CSJ dubbed the 'levelers', and the those more predisposed to the Thatcher's New Right solutions, termed the 'deregulators' by the CSJ (Alcock 2002: 14). To be sure, the CSJ did contain some more traditional Labour messages, but these were largely ignored in favour of plotting a course through the middle, what would soon be famously referred to as the Third Way. This marked the ascendancy of Labour modernizers, who would re-brand the party 'New Labour.' The changes were already apparent under Labour leaders Neil Kinnock and John Smith, but they crystallized under Tony Blair.

5   Since 1999, the Labour government has done considerably more than expected, given its initial silence on these matters.

supplanted more traditional Labour goals. It steered the party away from concerns of equality and social rights, towards the priorities of an opportunity culture. New Labour's emphasis on social exclusion represented a break from the party's longstanding socialist and social democratic principles, in that the stress was on inclusion, rather than on equality (Lister 1998, 2001). While the Blair government attempted to improve the incomes of at least some groups in poverty, unlike Old Labour, New Labour became less keen on stressing the connections between social inclusion and the 'offer of a secure, guaranteed and adequate income, at a reasonable level, relative to the income of the wealthy' (Miller 2004: 39-40) for all.

The Labour government's social exclusion agenda would also echo certain Conservative takes on citizenship. For Thatcherites, 'the welfare state had engendered a "passive citizenship," entitlements having become more important than the achievement of personal independence or autonomy' (Meehan 1999: 234). This rationale was used to justify welfare state retrenchment. Prime Minister Blair identified similar problems with the welfare state and believed that meaningful citizenship came about via active citizens. The idea of 'active citizenship' had been championed under the Tories by Douglas Hurd. This type of left-right convergence on active citizenship was evident in a cross-party Commission on Citizenship that called for 'education on citizenship and voluntary service as an avenue for the practice of citizenship' (Meehan 1999: 235).

Blair departed from a purely Thatcherite rationale, however, in that he aimed to establish an 'enabling' state, one that efficiently and effectively invested in the future (Blair 1996; Dobrowolsky 2000; Dobrowolsky and Saint Martin 2005). And, while there were social conservatives who had a 'top down' view of citizenship, where those who were better off would help the less fortunate, New Labour has worked on more 'bottom up' considerations. This is evident in its concern with the active citizenship of those who live in deprived communities. Former Home Secretary, David Blunkett, for instance, promoted 'active citizenship' as a form of 'civil renewal' and set up a virtual Centre for Active Citizenship.

Active citizens are those who are responsible, and there are those in the Tory and Labour ranks who conflate being responsible with being gainfully employed. What is more, in both camps, active citizenship can also signify 'appropriate and inappropriate behaviour' which can provide 'a rationale for the exclusion from benefits and services … or the imposition of some other penalty' for those who engage in what is considered inappropriate behaviour (Miller 2004: 41). Here and elsewhere, New Labour, departs from more collectivist, Marshallian views of citizenship rights, and adopts a communitarian appeal that, at best, promotes mutual obligation and, at worst, involves compliance and compulsion (Krieger 1999: 27).

The contradictions involved in the Blair government's social exclusion strategy can be highlighted by drawing on Ruth Levitas' (1996) systematic analysis. She identifies three discourses of social exclusion with the following acronyms: RED, MUD, and SID. RED refers to a redistributionist, egalitarian discourse. Here social exclusion is concerned about extreme forms of inequality and the way to address them through redistributing wealth. It is a more egalitarian approach that includes notions of citizenship, social rights and social justice. In sharp contrast, MUD stands for a 'moral underclass discourse' which is a stigmatizing and divisive discourse reminiscent of disparaging American assessments regarding a 'dependency culture' (Bashevkin 1998, 2002). MUD stresses individual values and behaviour and considers social cohesion at risk due to a series of problematic behaviours and forms of social and moral decay epitomized by rising crime, or drug addiction, and even having children out of wedlock. SID points to a 'social integrationist discourse' which has gained ascendancy both in Europe and the UK. Here exclusion is associated with being excluded from paid work. The idea is that with paid work and enhanced employability, social inclusion and social cohesion will be achieved. Whereas RED veers to the left, with more of a social democratic approach, and MUD entails a sharp turn to the right, with a more neo-conservative orientation, SID, while alluding to a more European sense of social exclusion, in fact, epitomizes third way concerns.

When Labour came to power in 1997, although it occasionally made use of the MUD 'underclass' discourse, it was most keen on SID. Then, across its first and second terms (the Blair government was re-elected in 2001), we can see elements of all three. To illustrate, in 1999 the Department of Social Security, DSS (the DSS is now, notably reflecting SID-like concerns, called the Department for Work and Pensions, DWP) in a document entitled *Opportunity for All* made the links between social exclusion and 'insufficient work opportunities' and 'insufficient opportunities in terms of education and training' (DSS 1999; Pierson 2002: 16-17). There are hints of RED since 1999, with more of a poverty focus (DSS 1999; Pierson 2002: 16-17), especially with increased efforts at redistribution geared towards children. From the outset, New Labour also has lapsed into MUD-type approaches. Efforts to counteract 'children having children,' i.e., teenage pregnancies; the Crime and Disorder Act of 1998 (where the aim was to lower crime rates in local areas, with close attention to youth, using highly punitive measures); and more recent Anti-Social Behaviour Orders highlight its MUD-like proclivities.

Nonetheless, SID has been the over-arching third way priority, where social exclusion results from a shortfall in education and employment opportunities. The remedy becomes one of expanding opportunities to make Britain competitive in the global economy through activation: i.e., getting the citizenry into the paid labour market. The SID emphasis is evident in a series of 'New Deals' meant to enhance employability.[6] At first blush, policies that subscribe to SID may seem less harsh and directive than MUD ones, but the former can also be punitive, and used to justify a range of measures such as the abolition of lone parent benefits.

These different dimensions are apparent in the activities of the Social Exclusion Unit (SEU, established in December 1997). As one of the Blair government's first innovations, the SEU's remit was broad: to combat social exclusion; but it clearly worked on priorities set out by the Prime Minister. These revolved around groups

---

6 The first flagship New Deal, New Deal for Young People, was directed towards youth, but then the deals were extended to various others, including lone parents, long-term unemployed and people with disabilities.

considered to be most vulnerable: children and youth, especially those growing up in low income households, runaways, those who were in care, did not attend or left school, became unemployed or were teenaged parents. Thus, the SEU began coordinating policies that would deal with issues that ranged from truancy, and problems arising from deprived estates and districts, to homelessness and teenage pregnancy. In its operation, the Unit was also meant to epitomize what New Labour would call 'joined up government.' In other words, the SEU was to work across departments and ensure that they co-ordinated their efforts on social exclusion. The SEU also reflected other New Labour priorities, such as promoting partnerships between the state and both the private and third sectors, as well as encouraging the involvement of 'active citizens.'

Because social exclusion can be read as either limited or all-encompassing, it has the potential to be operationalized in wide-ranging ways. New Labour's use of the social exclusion concept is, in some respects, ambiguously deployed, but in others, used in a precise problem-oriented way. The latter tendency is reflected in the following SEU definition of social exclusion:

> a shorthand term for what can happen when people or areas suffer from a combination of linked problems such as unemployment, poor skills, low incomes, poor housing, high crime, bad health and family breakdown. (SEU 2001: Chapter 1, 1)

Soon, however, 'lifting children out of poverty' became a prime SEU objective (Blair 2001: 2). As the Prime Minister contends, 'lifting children out of poverty' is a priority not only because it addresses 'the costs to society' but also, because it serves to limit the costs 'to public finance' (Blair 2001: 2). The financial burden of social exclusion:

> came in paying for crime, school exclusions, drug misuse and unemployment, and in lost tax revenue. Business suffered too from a less skilled workforce, lost customers and markets, and ...had to pay the tax bills for social failure. It followed that it would benefit everyone in society if social exclusion could be reduced and made less likely in the future. (SEU 2001: 2)

Blair added, Britain was 'never going to have a successful economy while we continued to waste the talents of so many' (Blair 2001: 2 in http//:www.cabinet office. gov.uk/seu/2001/pse/PSE%20HTML/foreward.htm). Thus, there were progressive societal and more market-driven, economic justifications for rooting out social exclusion and investing in children.[7]

---

7   The titles of many SEU documents epitomize the strategic choices that have been made: 'A Better Education for Children in Care;' 'Bridging the Gap: New Opportunities for 16-18 year olds not in Education, Employment, or Training;' 'Consultation on Young Runaways;' 'The Impact of Government Policy on Social Exclusion Among Children Aged 0-13 and Their Families;' 'The Impact of Government Policy on Social Exclusion Among Young People;' 'Truancy and Social Exclusion Report' (see http://www. socialexclusionunit. gov.uk).

In sum, while the first response to the social exclusion problem was to provide opportunities to gain skills and enter paid work, soon innumerable policy initiatives and review documents began emphasizing how the state would reform and modernize the welfare state in general and tackle child poverty in particular. An association between social exclusion/inclusion policies and children and youth became more and more apparent. Let us turn to this issue in more detail and see the impact this has had on citizenship in Britain.

Part II: Social Exclusion, Citizenship and the Ubiquitous Child?

For Thatcher, children were a responsibility of parents not the state. While the Conservatives did establish a few child and youth focused reforms in the late 1980s to mid-1990s (e.g., Youth Training Scheme in 1988), the main objective was to get young people off the welfare rolls and limit benefit to those most in need. In contrast, for the Blair government, the child has become a central figure in a range of New Labour ideas, institutions, and policy initiatives.

As we have seen, New Labour is concerned with social exclusion, and while this goes hand in hand with poverty in general, the Blair government has focused on child poverty in particular. The social exclusion agenda is not entirely confined to children, but children and youth do become a preoccupation because they:

> are especially vulnerable to the effects of social exclusion. They may be exposed to crime as victims, or drawn into early offending. They may skip important stages of their education and face illiteracy and unemployment. And their long-term prospects may include homelessness, mental health problems and chronic debt ... Early preventative action is critical. (http://www.social exclusionunit.gov.uk/page.asp?id=2)

Thus, the SEU targets childhood deprivation, and the effects of family breakdown along with shortfalls in terms of education, training and work. Again, addressing the exclusion of children and youth now is a good investment for the future for they will be tomorrow's productive citizen-workers.[8]

Soon the SEU began reporting on its 'action to prevent social exclusion' and how it was 'delivering results' by ensuring that, for example, children were 'ready to learn by the time they reach primary school;' or by showing that 'school exclusions had fallen by 18 per cent between 1997-1999' (SEU 2001: 4). It also proudly pronounced

---

8   These connections were made in a series of reports released by the Centre for Analysis of Social Exclusion (CASE) at the LSE which stressed the 'importance of childhood circumstances for later outcomes;' 'how education affects patterns of advantage and disadvantage' as well as how 'processes of inclusion and exclusion operate in the labour market' (CASE 2003: 7). CASE studies with titles such as, 'Intergenerational and Life Course Transmission of Social Exclusion, Influences of Childhood Poverty' and 'Childhood Poverty, Early Motherhood and Adult Exclusions' (Hobcraft 1998; Hobcraft and Kiernan 1999). Research of this kind had an important influence on New Labour policy orientations (Dobrowolsky and Saint-Martin 2005).

that 'since 1997 more than 27,000 young unemployed people have moved into work' (SEU 2001: 4). By 2004, the SEU claimed: 'A reduction in child poverty has been one of the most notable achievements so far. In 2002/03 there were 700,000 fewer children living in poverty than 1996/97. It is estimated that by 2004/05, if the Government had taken no action, 1.5 million more children would be in poverty' (SEU 2004: 4).

These 'results' reflect the fact that, over the course of its two mandates, Labour increased the Child Benefit rate (once, for the first child), and established a whole host of new policies and programmes geared towards children and youth.[9] This represents significant investment with funds allocated to deal with child poverty, to educate and safeguard children, and to develop a range of children's services. The emphasis is strategic: with children the government can engage in forms of redistribution, but not call it that, and also not invoke specific identities, i.e., avoid specifically addressing gender and racial inequality and so on (Dobrowolsky 2002). As we shall see, certain collective identities do fall through the cracks. But for now, let us examine how children, in general, have fit with the agendas of key state actors in New Labour's first and second term: Tony Blair, the New Labour Prime Minister, his Chancellor of the Exchequer, Gordon Brown, and Blair's first two Home Office Secretaries, Jack Straw and David Blunkett.

Tony Blair is preoccupied with the child as the citizen-worker of the future (Lister 2003b) and has paid close attention to issues such as education, skills, training, and life-long learning. Beyond increased spending and new regulatory regimes directed towards education, the Prime Minister also pushed for educational reform to promote active citizenship. For example, in 1998, an Advisory Group on Citizenship was set up with the goal of providing 'good citizenship' education in schools, and this was followed by an Education Reform Act (Frazer 2002: 216).

Chancellor Gordon Brown is also committed to the child as citizen-worker of the future. However, Brown more than Blair has tried to engage in 'redistribution by

---

9   Beyond the New Deal for Young People, there was the Working Families Tax Credit (established October 1999 but replaced in 2003 by the Child Tax Credit and Working Tax Credit), together with the Childcare Tax Credit, plus the National Childcare Strategy. Sure Start was set up and focused on giving children from 0-3 years old a better start in life. Subsequently, Connexions was created for those over 13. By 2000, the Blair government broke ground with the establishment of a Children and Young Person's Unit (CYPU) (now part of the Department of Education and Skills). A Children's Fund was set up and administered by the CYPU to encourage local initiatives and community action to counter child poverty. While the Children's Fund supported community and organizational efforts, the 2003 Budget introduced a new Child Trust Fund to be paid to individuals. The government then proposed the creation of a Young People's Fund. Education Maintenance Allowances were provided in 15 pilot areas, and are now rolled out nationwide, to offer means tested support to youth aged 16-18 who attend school or college and take full-time courses. A new Vulnerable Children's Grant promised £252 million over 2003-06 to provide educational support for children most in need, including children in care (SEU 2003: 4), and the list continues.

stealth,' and children have provided a good cipher in this regard. The Chancellor's approach embodies the liberal and social democratic tensions in the social exclusion agenda. On one hand, there are strict work-related requirements with the New Deals, but on the other hand, innovations like the National Minimum Wage, the WFTC and the new tax credit that replaced it, as well as improvement in out of work benefits for children (especially young children), hint at a more redistributive agenda. Moreover, the Treasury is not limiting itself to the economic realm: it is making social policy. Brown has been a pivotal influence not only when it comes to the New Deals, but also programmes like Sure Start. And, of course, through various child tax credits and the upping of benefits, the Chancellor has been able to work on New Labour's pledge to eradicate child poverty. In a series of speeches Brown highlighted the problem of child poverty, even going so far as to describe child poverty as a 'scar on Britain's soul' (Brown 1999: 8), and his pre-budget report in 2001 was entitled: *Tackling child poverty: giving every child the best possible start in life*. The Chancellor also made the connection between the eradication of child poverty and the need for more and better childcare ('Brown looks ...' 2004: 14; White and Elliot 2004: 29).

The Home Office has taken a more directive and punitive approach, which is not surprising given the latter is the institutional locale (in charge of law and order) that gets to act on New Labour's 'tough on crime' message. The Home Office's take on citizenship also emphasizes both individuals' obligations to society and a more community-based ethos. Children and youth link these concerns. The Home Office under Jack Straw helped to promote families' responsibilities to their children by setting up the charity advice bureau, the National Family and Parenting Institute (NFPI) and piloting Family Advice and Information Networks. Then, it moved to make communities safe and secure by cracking down on criminal children and youth. In fact, several Home Office reforms, particularly those dealing with the youth justice system have reflected what some have described as 'knee jerk policy making and populist, short-term rhetoric' (Newburn 2003: 245). The Home Office's MUD-like agenda was all too apparent with its Crime and Disorder Act (1998) and its Youth Justice and Criminal Evidence Act (1999) that promoted surveillance, contained restrictions and sanctions. An array of new orders were put in place that ranged from detention and training, to parenting primers, curfews and efforts to limit anti-social behaviour. While Straw spearheaded punitive Home Office initiatives, his successor, David Blunkett, a social conservative on issues surrounding the family, sexuality and law and order (Driver and Martell 2002: 207-08), took them further. As one columnist quipped, Blunkett has positioned himself as the: 'hard man of the party, a home secretary who makes Jack Straw look like a softy, guitar-strumming liberal'('Hard man' 2002).

What has become increasingly apparent is that children in trouble with the law are separated out and treated differently from the totality of poor and excluded children. New measures that criminalize increasingly younger children reflect the idea that certain children apparently cease to be children when they get into trouble with the law. Now, children as young as ten years old are considered culpable and responsible for criminal behaviour (Barnardo's 2003: 2). There are worrisome civil liberties issues involved as when one considers Home Office plans to have troublesome children identified and tracked. There is also growing concern about the criminalization of young people in deprived areas by Anti-Social Behaviour Orders. Other Home Office proposals have been dropped in the face of opposition, such as removing child benefit from the parents of persistent truants/trouble makers. Such measures would appeal to Blair and Blunkett, but not sit well with Brown.

   The foregoing illustrates that, on issues of social exclusion, Blair's priorities reflect an amalgam of SID and MUD. The Prime Minister plays up the former and allows officials in the Home Office, in particular, to act on more of the MUD orientation. Brown reflects more of a SID and RED combination. Furthermore, although New Labour intended social exclusion to address the 'worst off,' particularly children and youth, some children are 'in' and some are 'out.' There are 'good' poor children deserving of assistance, but then there are 'bad' criminal children. These efforts appear to not be 'joined up' enough as there is a disjuncture between 'good' worthy children, those perceived to have genuine needs (children who are poor, in care, have health problems), and those unsalvageable 'bad' children for whom the Home Office's prescription is to throw them in jail.

   We begin to see a pattern where New Labour's social exclusion concerns have been responsive in certain respects, but are also deployed in ways that discipline individuals and groups deemed undeserving or who do not perform the requisite duties and fulfil the required obligations. Therefore, the social exclusion focus is neither comprehensive nor is its implicit citizenship dimensions criticism free. The lapses become even more apparent when we turn to those who have been, largely outside of the social exclusion agenda, such as women, and (up until very recently) racial and ethnic minorities, particularly (im)migrants, refugees and asylum seekers. While some are deemed 'deserving' of inclusion, here even 'more rigid exclusion is proposed for the "undeserving"' (Sales 2005: 445).

Part III: Who is Included and Who Is Excluded? Women

Children are in (or more accurately, some poor children are in) but women are definitely not high on the list of Blair government priorities. Gender is rarely addressed in citizenship debates. The few exceptions that occur here are with, for example, constitutional reform (Dobrowolsky and Hart 2003), particularly issues around women's representation in parliament, as with the Representation Bill (Russell 2003; Squires 2003). Yet, despite the fact that gender is a key variable in determining who is in poverty, gender inequality has not been flagged in the fight against social exclusion, or even child poverty (Lister 2005).

   The exceptions to this rule are revealing in that they tend to involve the child, but in ways that underscore the citizen-worker model. Women are implicated in SID, MUD, and RED policies, but they are most explicitly targeted in programs that deal with work–rest of life, or work–care balance. Women and girls are affected by MUD-inspired programmes with SEU campaigns to prevent youth pregnancy, and lone motherhood. RED efforts have the potential for the most positive impact on women, as evidenced by the disproportionate benefit women receive from the National Minimum Wage. Still, SID is the main preoccupation, and so here we see a strong incentive to get women into paid work. The activation thrust explains new policies like the Child Care Strategy and recent promises of more nursery spaces. Concomitantly, there have been some advancements in maternity and parental leave terms, reflecting the 'universal breadwinner' model (Fraser 1997: 43). The Blair government is primarily concerned with getting people on benefit into work and ensuring at least one (and ideally two) earner(s) per household.

However, with this paid work focus, neither the domestic division of labour, nor the sexual division of labour in the marketplace are being addressed. Some Labour women Ministers, known for their feminist sympathies try to buck this trend.[10] For instance, Patricia Hewitt has recently referred to 'career sexism' to describe gender segregation in the labour market and the Woman and Work Commission was launched to look 'at how women can get a fairer deal in the workplace' and occupational segregation (WEU 2004: 1). Still, the Labour government has not addressed the fact that because women care for others, many women take on part time work which tends to be lower paid. Given their unpaid responsibilities, many higher paid, professional and managerial jobs, which tend to be full-time commitments, are often not an option for women. Women's earnings are negatively affected now, and these shortfalls can have even more serious repercussions in the future with, for instance, low pension rates (Fitzpatrick 2004). This situation also helps to explain why women are more reliant than men on the benefit system. Many new social security rules disproportionately affect women and, as we shall see, especially minority and migrant women (Fitzpatrick 2004).

Nonetheless, women are not a primary concern for the Blair government that is loathe to address the concerns of collective identities in general. Identity politics are partly blamed for Labour's past electoral failures. The women's movement, along with the anti-racist movement and other critical social movements evoke the fractious identity struggles which engulfed Old Labour in the 1970s and 1980s. These battles led Thatcher, the dailies, and much of 'middle England' to dismiss Labour as the 'loony left' (Lovenduski and Randall 1993). For New Labour, the women's movement, like the trade union movement, is associated with yesterday's troublesome politics (Coote 2000, 2001: 128), and thus it seeks to avoid these types of associations.

---

10 The Labour government did act on its pre-election promise to create the position of a Women's Minister, and responded to women's demands by setting up a Women's Unit (which later became the Women and Equality Unit). But both remained marginal (Dobrowolsky 2003). Still, some female Labour Ministers have tried to push women's concerns forward (Childs 2001). Nonetheless, any inroads that have been made have mostly come by hitching women's issues to government's labour force attachment and/or children and youth bandwagons.

For feminists, there have been peaks and troughs since the 1997 Labour landslide.[11] On the whole, gender tends to be an oversight and women are an afterthought when it comes to welfare reform. To illustrate, when the old Family Credit was replaced by the WFTC in October 1999, it was to be distributed through the 'pay packet.' Chancellor Brown wanted to make the connection to paid work explicit, i.e., he believed 'paid people will associate the tax credit more closely with their employment if they see wage and credit on the same computerized read out, hence appreciating the final rewards of working' (Grover and Stewart 2000: 244). Women's groups had to mobilize to show how this change could be detrimental to women and children. In women's experience, assuming a male breadwinner norm and heterosexual two-parent family, if the credit went through the father's pay cheque, it was less likely that funds would actually go directly to the family than if the credit went to the mother (Lister 2003b, 2004). Thus, women's groups wanted the credit to go to 'the purse' rather than the 'wallet.' They lobbied to have the WFTC go to the main carer, typically to women (McLaughlin et al. 2001: 168). After extensive mobilization, the Labour government conceded that families would have the choice of having the WFTC paid to the mother at the post office. Subsequently, when the WFTC was replaced by the Child Tax Credit, the new credit was paid to the main carer.

While women, in general, are peripheral to the welfare reform and social exclusion project, some women are even more marginalized than others. The fact that racial and ethnic minority and (im)migrant women are not a social exclusion target is particularly surprising given the extreme dislocation faced by them. Consider writer Yasmin Alibhai-Brown's experience (coming to Britain from Uganda) as she outlines what it is like for her and other woman of colour (im)migrants to rear children in Britain:

> Black women and Asian women were and are having to bring up their children in a racist country. Rearing children in this atmosphere is so tough I sometimes wonder how we have had the courage to reproduce at all. So white mothers…understand what it is like when, added to all the moods and furies of teenage life, your child hates you for bringing him or her into this country, or regards you as inferior, or worst off turns to self-destructive acts because he/she expected to be embraced and was instead rejected, and there is no place to go? What is more, it is a thankless task, one that our men have mostly left to us. (Alibhai-Brown 2001: 192)

---

11   The elation around the unprecedented election of 101 Labour women was soon followed by despondency as Harriet Harman, in her role of Secretary of State for Social Security, cut lone parent benefits, mostly received by women. Reparations were made in what was dubbed the 'women and children budget' (Thomson 2001: 201). Harman was influential here, and she and fellow Minister Margaret Beckett helped to steer through Labour policies considered to have had the most positive impact on women: the national childcare strategy and the minimum wage. But again, both emphasize New Labour's activation thrust, and one deals with children. Few social security measures directly respond to women's needs, save for perhaps increases in maternity grants, now called the Sure Start Maternity Grant (and paid because of the presence of a new infant).

In light of the Labour government's expressed concern with the child, and given the SEU's definition of what constitutes social exclusion, i.e., the interrelation of unemployment, low skills and income, poor housing and family breakdowns (SEU 2001: Chapter 1, 1), not tackling ethnic and racial minority women, and (im)migrant women's exclusion, is paradoxical.

People from minority ethnic backgrounds in Britain are more likely to live in poor housing, be unemployed, have low incomes, die young and suffer social exclusion (Pierson 2002: 190). These probabilities are even higher for women given the sexual division of labour, the feminization of poverty, and the fact that women typically care for others at the expense of their own health and livelihood. There are also differences that do not pertain across all minority and ethnic groups, such as the fact that there are more lone mothers in Black Caribbean families than in the general population, or that Bangladeshi women tend to have larger families and larger families 'are more likely to be in poverty and are harder to support on the relatively low earnings that apply to the sectors in which these families are most likely to be concentrated' (Platt 2003: 262).

The confusion deepens in light of New Labour's preoccupation with work. In Britain, certain minority ethnic women can engage in more full time, paid work than white women:

> One of the most interesting and consistent findings about patterns of labour market participation by ethnic minority women...shows a marked divergence from the experience of white women with reference to part-time employment. Approximately half of white women work full time, but more than two-thirds of ethnic minority women work full time, with little variety in the rate of part-time work among women from different ethnic minority groups. (Krieger 1999: 104)

In this respect, many women from minority racial and ethnic backgrounds would appear to be the ideal New Labour citizens. But then, of course, there are the disparities in the conditions and type of employment most women do, compared with men. Notably, here the gap between ethnic minority and white women is far less than that between ethnic minority men and white men. Still, because they are not only women, but are racial and ethnic minority women, employment 'ghettoization' is even more of a problem:

> female labor participation from every ethnic minority group indicates a marked concentration in the service sector and thus displays a particularly acute form the characteristic pattern of female labour market participation...Women of African-Caribbean descent are especially concentrated in the hospital and health care sectors, while the women of Indian descent are represented heavily in hotels and catering services and low-end manufacturing industry. Women with West Indian and Guyanese origins are strongly over-represented in a range of relatively low paid service work. (Krieger 1999: 104)

These patterns and conditions point to some serious problems that perpetuate social exclusion. Still the Labour government directs its attention to women only intermittently. This is particularly problematic for those who are most likely to be excluded: racial and ethnic minority women and (im)migrant women. To situate and help to explain these apparent lacunae and inconsistencies, a closer examination of how 'race,' ethnicity, (Im)Migrants, refugees and asylum seekers are treated in Britain would be beneficial.

Part IV: Who is Included and Who is Excluded? Racial and Ethnic Minorities, (im)migrants, Refugees and Asylum Seekers

Britain today is a heterogeneous society. The racial and ethnic minority population has reached the eight per cent mark according to the 2001 census, with a much higher concentration of Black and ethnic minority communities, 76 per cent, in London, the West Midlands and three other localized areas (Home Office 2004: 16). Several trends point to growing diversity: from the reality that in Britain mixed race relationships are among the highest in the world; to the fact that in the UK, Islam is the fastest growing religion (Alibhai-Brown 2001: 2-3). Also of note, given the concerns of this paper, is the fact that the ethnic minority population tends to be younger than that of the white population (Krieger 1999: 100).

Despite this diversity, racial and ethnic communities continue to experience racism, discrimination and exclusion in multiple realms, including employment. There are variations here in that certain minority groups are highly represented in professions such as medicine, nursing and accountancy. There are, no doubt, 'billionaires who are brown-skinned;' nevertheless, 'unemployment among Afro-Caribbeans, Pakistanis and Bangladeshis is substantially higher than the national average' (Alibhai-Brown 2001: 3). Platt (2003: 258) elucidates:

> Employment in vulnerable sectors, alongside discrimination, concentration in poorer areas which offer fewer opportunities and some groups, notably Pakistanis, Bangladeshis and Black Caribbeans, greater difficulty in obtaining high levels of qualifications, have resulted in both high unemployment for many minority groups, especially [for] Caribbeans, Pakistanis and, particularly, Bangladeshis, and much higher rates of self-employment among certain groups, in particular Indians, Chinese and Pakistanis.

This helps to explain why, in 2001-02, the risk of being in poverty (measured as below 60 per cent of median income after housing costs) was 20 per cent for whites and 69 per cent for Pakistanis and Bangladeshis. For Indians it was 22 per cent and Afro-Caribbeans it was 32 per cent (Lister 2004: 62).

Given the government's preoccupation with work and the links made between employment and exclusion, one would think that addressing the needs of racial and ethnic minorities would be at the top of the Prime Minister's social exclusion list. There have been some policies (if inadequate) to address employment disadvantage, but these have failed to meet the mark.

Racial and ethnic minorities continue to be marginalized, in part, because immigration continues to be treated as a threat (Parekh 1991). To be perfectly clear, substantial numbers of racial and ethnic minorities are British citizens. Therefore, members of racial and ethnic minority communities, are not necessarily (im)migrants, nor are they refugees and asylum seekers. What is more, these categories are *not* one and the same.[12] However, the problem is one where they tend to run together in the public consciousness, especially on the part of the white majority, through processes of racialization. Moreover, both Conservative and Labour governments have tended to conflate race relations and immigration policies, further exacerbating these tendencies (Lewis and Neal 2005: 436). As a result, despite significant differences, there can be similar treatment involved.

Concomitantly, the most vivid example of racialization and one of the most blatant cases of exclusion in Britain occurs in relation to (im)migrants, refugees and, especially, asylum seekers. Pierson (2002: 203) details the situation for asylum seekers:

> They face many parallel experiences to that of the ethnic minorities; dislocation, powerlessness and discrimination while having few supports to call on and no concerted action from government to reconstruct public opinion. From the moment they arrive they face a volatile and often aggressively hostile local public with racist political sentiment openly engaging in intimidation and local press making accusations of 'bogus claims' and 'a drain on national resources'.

As just one example of the extent of the backlash, consider the following advertisement run by *The Sun* in 2003: 'End the asylum madness ... this sea of humanity is polluted with terrorism and disease and threatens our way of life ... Blair must say no more *now*, revoke the human rights law and lock up all the illegals *now* until they can be checked.' Hundreds of thousands of *Sun* readers signed up to this campaign (CIH 2003: 4).

This is the harsh reality, and still New Labour's social exclusion concerns have not adequately addressed ethnic and racial minority issues, nor do they extend to issues of (im)migration and asylum. In the case of the latter, exclusionary controls and punitive policies abound. To understand the nature of the inconsistencies and paradoxes involved, a brief historical overview would be beneficial.[13]

In the past, and over time, different groups have been targeted by the British state, and the rights of certain 'aliens' have been circumscribed in multiple ways. Britain did not subscribe to specific immigration controls as part of its state policy until the *Aliens Act of 1905* which was intended to control Jewish immigration

---

12 Members of racial and ethnic minorities can be longstanding British citizens with formal British citizenship rights reaching back for several generations. In contrast, refugees are persons fleeing their country to avoid persecution and who fall under the UN Convention's designation entitling them to refugee status. "'Asylum" refers to the legal status that may be granted to an individual refugee by a host country. An "asylum applicant" or "asylum seeker" is someone who applies for asylum. Though normally co-extensive, the term "refugee" and "asylum applicant/seeker" are not synonyms. A person may not fear persecution but nevertheless apply for asylum because he or she does not wish to return to the country of origin ... ' (Bhabha and Shutter 1994: 232-33).

13 For a comprehensive account see Hayter (2005).

from Russia and Europe. This was followed by an *Aliens Restriction Act* in 1914 which gave the Home Secretary extensive powers to 'ban the entry of aliens, limit their movement and restrict their stay' (Layton-Henry 2001: 127). This Act and the 1919 *Aliens Restriction (Amendment) Act* 'provided the Home Secretary with wide powers to deport anyone whose departure was considered to be "conducive to the public good"' (Bhabha and Shutter 1994: 31).

Large-scale immigration occurred in the 1940s, and patterns of immigration changed significantly with the advent of the *British Nationality Act of 1948*. It extended British citizenship to all members of the empire and dominions, allowing them to enter Britain. The theory was that this would maintain a strong and united Commonwealth. The practice was that citizenship claims from 'non-white' dominions grew, with people from India, Pakistan and the Caribbean settling in Britain. In the 1950s, a need for labour power (especially cheap, un- or semi-skilled workers), led some employers to recruit from places like the Caribbean and India. What then followed were explicit forms of racial exclusion on the part of the citizenry and the state.

Racial minorities faced blatant discrimination, open hostility, and even violence. In 1958, race riots broke out in Nottingham and Notting Hill involving 'whites' attacking 'blacks.' Both Labour and Conservative governments responded by putting into place measures, covertly then overtly, to limit 'black' migration (Carter et al. 2000: 23). Restrictive immigration acts were passed in 1962, and 1968 that limited the entry of 'black' first time immigrants and their families. The controls on Commonwealth citizens effectively 'operationalized the significance of skin colour in the definitions of group identities and "Britishness"' (Krieger 1999: 128). Calls for tighter controls on immigration, and to keep Britain 'British,' i.e., 'white,' grew; and there were those who linked immigration with violence or crime. It is in this context, in 1968, that Conservative MP, Enoch Powell made his infamous 'Rivers of Blood' speech advocating not only an end to 'black' migration, but calling for those who had settled to leave Britain (Budge et al. 2001: 650).

Race riots flared up in subsequent decades as well. Riots in Brixton led to an inquiry headed up by Lord Scarman. His 1981 Report was 'authoritative and widely welcomed' but nonetheless, 'little progress was made to remedy the deficiencies identified ... in the political climate of the 1980s (Bennett 2002: 465). History would repeat itself in the spring and summer of 2001, where riots in the north of England compelled the Labour government to act.[14]

Meanwhile immigration restrictions continued. The 1971 *Immigration Act* contained only a modicum of leeway to permit Asian refugees from Uganda to enter Britain on compassionate grounds. It also stipulated that those seeking family reunification would not have access to public funds until the applicants were granted residence status (Platt 2003: 258-59). In 1981, Margaret Thatcher's *British Nationality Act* restricted immigration to those with British parents or parents settled

---

14 We will describe and assess the nature of the Labour government's response to these 2001 'disturbances' later in the paper.

in Britain. That is, British citizens not born in the UK and with no familial link to Britain could not settle in the UK, preventing most of the Hong Kong population from re-settling there. By the mid-1980s, pre-entry visa controls were imposed on previously exempt Commonwealth countries such as Sri Lanka, Bangladesh, India, Pakistan, Ghana and Nigeria (Flynn 2005: 467).

This history is not only marked with racism but also with sexism, and the complicated interactions between the two. For example, until 1948, British women marrying men from abroad lost their citizenship, whereas 'foreign-born' women became British if they married British men. Overall, as Bhabha and Shutter (1994: 6-7) explain:

> The view of immigrant and black women, as wives and mothers responding to life choices made by men, rather than initiators of families in their own rights has pervaded official thinking and moulded the relevant immigration rules. Black and immigrant women have had severely curtailed rights to create the family of their choice in their own home country, the assumption being that this is a male prerogative. This has been true for women (particularly those of Asian origin) whose home has always been Britain but who have chosen husbands from abroad, as well as for women who have taken the initiative of traveling to Britain for work or study and have then wanted to be united here with preexisting families. Indeed there has been persistent official denial of the fact that immigrant women could have this dual role, as workers or students, when they are at the same time wives mothers.

Successive British governments made it more difficult for husbands to immigrate than wives. Beyond using the justification that this discriminatory policy simply reflected the norm in which men determine where the family should reside, they also argued that immigrant men constituted more of a threat to the British, domestic labour force than women, once again based on stereotypical male breadwinner/female dependant assumptions (Bhabha and Shutter 1994: 37-38). This alleged dependence on men resulted in women's near invisibility when it came to immigration rules, and immigration legislation in general (Bhabha and Shutter 1994: 45).

The complex interplay between sex and race was also evident in the *1981 Nationality Act* (which came into force in January 1983). Here, in the name of equality, i.e., ending the sexual discrimination that characterized previous nationality legislation, the new Act 'consolidated the discrimination against black Commonwealth citizens' (Bhabha and Shutter 1994: 49). It brought nationality law in line with immigration law with the intent of limiting immigration and with the effect of increasing restrictions. Also in the name of equality, women's rights were scaled back. Here we see a process of levelling down, as 'foreign-born' women who married British men (like 'foreign-born' men who married British women) would now no longer automatically gain British citizenship.

In spite of this less than welcoming environment, in the 1980s and 1990s, asylum applications to Britain grew. The Conservative government, in turn, imposed mandatory visas on countries such as Haiti, Turkey and Somalia, and it raised fines for carriers found with undocumented passengers with the *Carrier's Liability Act*

(1987) (Layton-Henry 2001: 130-31). Two pieces of legislation passed in the 1990s also took an uncompromising approach: the Conservative government's 1993 *Asylum and Immigration Appeals Act* and its 1996 *Asylum and Immigration Act*. They reinforced the idea that asylum seekers should not get social security and other benefits, introduced measures such as fingerprinting to address concerns about social security fraud, 'reduced obligations on local authorities to provide permanent accommodation and removed some rights of appeal' (Layton-Henry 2001: 130-31). The belief was that tough immigration and asylum policies were needed to safeguard domestic race relations.

And so, these measures developed alongside British domestic policies meant to prevent racial discrimination. *Race Relations Acts* in 1965, 1968 and 1976 were all oriented towards dealing with both direct and then indirect discrimination (the latter in 1976) in areas of education, employment and housing. A Race Relations Board, which would become the Commission for Racial Equality (CRE) was also established. Multiple forms of racism and discrimination persisted despite these efforts.

Public figures continued to play into racist, anti-immigrant hysteria. In 1978, echoing Enoch Powell-like sentiments, Thatcher stated that the 'British character' might be 'swamped' by immigrants from different cultures (Budge et al. 2001: 650). There was little formal political opposition to these views, given that since World War II (when three MPs of Indian origin were elected), and until 1986, the House of Commons contained not a single MP from a racial and ethnic minority background. Various forms of political mobilization did occur on the ground, and increasingly, in and against the state (Parekh 1991; Bhabha and Shutter 1994; Meehan 1999: 24; Hayter 2005), often instigated by British racial and ethnic minority women (Chatterjee 1995; Griffin 1995; Roy 1995; Mirza 1997).

Nevertheless, the systemic nature of the problem was tragically illustrated in the 1993 case of Stephen Lawrence. This young black teenager, while standing at a bus stop, was attacked and stabbed to death by five young white men. The police took their time in getting to the scene of the crime and then provided little support in gathering evidence that could lead to the prosecution of the identified suspects. The incident led to calls for an inquiry, but the Conservative government refused.

From 1995-1996 alone, the police recorded 12,222 racial incidents in England and Wales, a three per cent increase from the previous years (Budge et al. 2001: 651). When New Labour came to power in 1997, action was obviously necessary and thus it wasted little time in launching an official inquiry into the Lawrence scandal. The ensuing Macpherson Report of 1999, named institutional racism and identified it in all major British institutions. It also acknowledged that some of the police officers who appeared before the inquiry were '"palpably wrong" and could not have told the truth. It concluded that the police investigation had been 'marred by a combination of professional incompetence, institutional racism and failure of leadership by senior officers' (Budge et al. 2001: 531). Seventy recommendations were made.

By setting up the Macpherson Inquiry, the Blair government did try to 'engage in a national conversation about how it could tackle the racism affecting its institutions and infecting its private, public and popular culture' (Younge 2002: 11). It proceeded to introduce a new offence of racial aggravation in the 1998 *Criminal Justice Act*, and then extended the Commission on Racial Equality's (CRE's) ambit (Driver and Martell 2002: 152). Acting on the Macpherson Report's recommendations, amendments to the *Race Relations Act* in 2000 and 2003 were made, with the latter implementing EC Article 13 Race Directive outlawing discrimination on 'grounds of racial or ethnic origin in the areas of employment, vocational training, goods and services, social protection, education and housing' (Squires 2004: 6). There have also been other initiatives coming out of a Home Office that now houses a Racial Equality Unit. And yet, it was not long before 'the pendulum of racial discourse [began] swinging back to an altogether more complacent and less challenging era' (Younge 2002: 11).

This retrogression is most visible in the area of (im)migration. Despite having a population 'stemming from multiple roots and complex patterns of inward, outward and return migration through processes of conquest, colonization and decolonization,' (Platt 2003: 240), the state and the general public continue to act hostile to those deemed to be 'foreigners.' Sensational media reports stoke xenophobic and reactionary fires. Beliefs that newcomers are getting unfair priority when it comes to public services, that they take away jobs from British born citizens, or that they contribute to growing crime rates are widespread (Krieger 1999: 130). Recent polls show public opposition to further immigration and indicate that a sizable section of the British public blames (im)migrants and asylum seekers for deficiencies in public services. Still, up until recently, the numbers of people seeking asylum in Britain have continued to rise, doubling and tripling the 1990s levels of 20,000 – 40,000 asylum seekers a year (CIH 2003: 2),[15] making (im)migration, refugees and asylum seekers 'hot button issues.'

Given negative public sentiments, and in light of its efforts to disassociate itself from an earlier 'loony left' image, the Blair government has gone out of its way to show that it does not have a 'soft touch' when it comes to (im)migrants, refugees and asylum seekers. Beyond tightening entry controls, tackling illegal immigration and accelerating the application process for asylum seekers, it also has put in place various punitive measures, from restricting benefits to promoting a policy of dispersal.

Blair's first Home Secretary succumbed to 'knee jerk populism' not only in relation to children in trouble with the law, but also in terms of immigration and asylum law. With respect to the latter, Jack Straw's 'tough stance on asylum seekers' revealed 'that New Britain isn't always as compassionate and cosmopolitan as we are led to believe by New Labour' (Driver and Martell 2002: 150). The government's first White Paper on the topic was entitled 'Fairer, Faster and Firmer: A Modern Approach to Immigration' (1998). It opened with encouraging comments regarding the benefits of immigration, but then the tone rapidly deteriorated. Migration was treated as 'a dire threat to British salvation than its modernizing salvation' (Flynn

---

15 Because of the deliberate government policy to reduce numbers, which we will outline, these numbers have dropped recently.

2005: 473). With this so-called 'modern' yet 'firm' approach, appeal and legal aid rights were reduced and asylum applicants were held in detention centres when they had not committed any crimes (Layton-Henry 2001: 132). Like the Conservatives, the Blair government extended carriers' liability,[16] and its first (of several) attempts at 'reform,' with the *Immigration and Asylum Act of 1999,* raised a number of concerns. For example, one part of this Act took away means tested benefits for those who are 'subject to immigration control,' including benefits from the Jobseeker's Allowance and Income Support to Child Benefit and Disability Allowance. Asylum seekers were given subsistence in the form of vouchers instead of cash that were to be redeemed in designated supermarkets. 'They were thus removed from mainstream welfare benefits making them more visible and thus targets for stigmatization and racism' (Sales 2005: 446).[17]

The National Asylum Support Service (NASS) was established in the Home Office to provide assistance, but this was usually conditional on being dispersed from London, and only gave asylum seekers about 70 per cent of the income support level (Fitzpatrick 2004). The government's objective was to provide basic needs for asylum seekers and house them 'more evenly throughout the country' (Pierson 2002: 204), but, in effect, this meant that they were compelled to go with little recourse to challenge where they were sent (Pierson 2002: 207). One study reported that:

> Some dispersal has been successful ... Other cases were unsuccessful, most dramatically with the murder of the Kurdish asylum seeker Firsat Dag in Sighthill, Glasgow, the use of poor quality accommodation in places like North West England, and difficulty in securing sufficient 'dispersal'. (CIH 2003: 3)

Asylum seekers have been treated abysmally, and this applies to women asylum seekers and their children as well. For example, maternity payments are limited to £300 for asylum seeking women as compared to £500 for other women. Whereas women receive milk tokens for children up to age five, women asylum seekers receive these for children only up to the age of three (Fitzpatrick 2004). Furthermore, because women asylum seekers are not eligible for benefit, consider the dire circumstances they face in the case of family breakdown or violence. If they have children, they can

---

16 Levying greater fines against carriers that contained undocumented passengers.

17 Although vouchers have since been withdrawn in the face of opposition, more restrictive policies have come into force in relation to both the entry of asylum seekers and their treatment once in the country. Restrictions are placed on the help available to asylum seekers, from temporary housing to limited financial assistance. Conditions are imposed: 'intended to exclude "unpopular" groups from entitlement to social security benefits' (Fitzpatrick 2004). Most recently, the Blair government has introduced rules whereby adult asylum seekers who do not claim asylum immediately, 'as soon as reasonably practicable' are not entitled to basic assistance (CIH 2003: 2). This has left many destitute. Given their experiences in their countries of origin, and in light of their treatment once in Britain, many asylum seekers will live on an income that is below income support levels for many years.

try to get help under the *Children Act*, but this assistance is not consistently received, and when it is, it is typically directed towards the child not the mother. This means that in the context of family violence, women 'subject to immigration control' often have little choice but to stay with their abusive husbands.

In Labour's second term, Straw's successor, David Blunkett, was entrusted to revamp asylum policy. Like his predecessor, Blunkett's MUD-inspired approach extended from children in trouble with the law to (im)migrants and asylum seekers, and their children. In Blunkett's view, 'the only way Britain will accept further decades of immigration, and a fully multi-ethnic future, is on the basis of tough rules and "order and stability"' ('Hard Man' 2002). Labour's 2002 White Paper on immigration (with the paradoxical and exclusionary title, *Secure Borders, Safe Haven*) reflected his 'monoculturalist thinking' with 'its emphasis on national allegiance, citizenship testing and concerns about traditional marriage' (Lewis and Neal 2005: 436). Blunkett, for instance, referred disapprovingly to 'arranged marriages to foreigners' as though they were 'something alien to British culture' when one columnist reminded readers 'of the six British monarchs of the last century five married foreigners and most of these unions were arranged' (Younge 2002: 11). Labour's subsequent *Nationality, Immigration and Asylum Bill* (2002), homed in on asylum seekers and contained a new measure – the proposal to remove the children of asylum seekers from mainstream education. Although this sparked MP revolts, Blunkett justified this proposal in language reminiscent of Thatcher claiming that 'asylum-seeking children were "swamping" local schools' (Sales 2005: 447).

Paradoxically, the Labour Home Office also strove for social cohesion. This social integration strategy's assimilationist undercurrent was exposed under Blunkett with his efforts to prop up 'core British values' and institutionalize selective versions of Britishness. For example, *Secure Borders, Safe Haven*, recommended that all new immigrants would require a working knowledge of English as well as a basic knowledge of UK culture and history, and envisaged new citizens swearing an oath of allegiance to Queen and Country (Coxall et al. 2003: 394). Acting against the advice from a panel of experts, the Home Office decided to introduce 'tougher than expected' English tests for new immigrants: 'People wanting to become British citizens will have to demonstrate a defined minimum standard of English or take a compulsory course of language and citizenship classes for which those who can afford will be expected to pay' (de Lotbiniere 2004: 1). Sales (2005: 452) explains the nature of the problem here:

> While language is central to the enjoyment of the rights of citizenship and to participation, the acquisition of language is particularly difficult for some groups, particularly the elderly and those suffering trauma. To impose duties to acquire language, rather than the opportunity to learn, can exclude some people for possibilities of gaining citizenship rights.

These requirements were clearly attempts to 'reconfigure the contours of belonging through the frame of integration' (Lewis and Neal 2005: 451) and in so doing promote a limited, common citizenship.

The post 9/11 climate and 'war on terror' added fuel to the fire. In the public mind, and fed by outrageous reports in the tabloid press, asylum seekers (and also Muslims) are sometimes linked to terrorists. This perception in people's minds was effectively cemented by the fact that a number of terrorist suspects arrested in January 2003 proved to be asylum seekers. As Coxall et al. (2003: 394) recount:

> The events of 11 September 2001 and the war against terror not only raised suspicions over asylum seekers, but caused massive problems for members of ethnic communities long settled in Britain. Britain's now substantial Muslim population have been victims of irrational panic reactions in what has been termed 'Islamophobia'.

Consequently, Home Office White Paper, *Secure Borders, and Safe Haven* also suggested that citizens could be stripped of their citizenship if they concealed any involvement with terrorism (Coxall et al. 2003: 394).

Recent developments further emphasize the hard line taken, especially when it comes to asylum seekers and illegal migrants. *The Asylum and Immigration (Treatment of Claimants, etc.) Act 2004*, passed in July 2004, 'removes all support from asylum-seeking families who have lost their claim for asylum, and substantially reduces the rights of appeal' (Sales 2005: 447). Akin to the disciplinary/criminalization tack taken with wayward youth, the Home Office plans the introduction of biometric identity cards, equipping the state 'with potentially powerful tools to allow the migrant to be tracked through all the stages of his/her residence in the UK, and for discipline to be inflicted on those who infringe the rules' (Flynn 2005: 485). Furthermore, 2004 Home Office figures indicate over 1,000 illegal migrants have been arrested after 'random swoops on Underground passengers and pedestrians in London.' This practice has become 'a regular weekday event in the capital, with 235 operations in the past 15 months' on the part of police and immigration service officials. Home office information suggests that 717 of those who were arrested constituted failed asylum seekers ('More than 1,000 … ' 2004: 15).

All this has come to pass, and yet the plight of refugees and asylum seekers in Britain remains deplorable. As just one example, consider the case of the young, Kurdish man with a disability, who had been granted refugee status. In September 2004, he left the apartment he shared with his brothers and friends, to buy a pizza and:

> Within the hour he was dead, clubbed from behind in a single devastating blow. Police say he was killed because of the colour of his skin, but believed it was an isolated incident. Others from the 200-strong Kurdish community disagree. They talked of constant abuse and harassment. 'In this society, when you are foreign you have to look behind you all the time to see who is there,' said one. (Brown 2004: 13)

This incident is suggestive of a wider pattern. A study released by the Institute of Race Relations in late 2004 reported that 180 asylum seekers died trying to reach Britain illegally. Many expired as stowaways on planes, trucks and boats, but 34 killed themselves 'when faced with deportation, four died accidentally as they tried to avoid immigration officials ... Fifteen were killed in race-related attacks and others died while working illegally or in prison, policy or psychiatric custody.' What is more, the author of the report, Harmit Athwal, suggested that these numbers represent a '"huge underestimate of the true death toll" as most of these deaths go unrecognized' (see 'Death Toll highlighted' 2004: 14).

Despite such tragic realities, making the link between social exclusion and (im)migrants, refugees, asylum seekers has not been a prime consideration for the Blair government. Instead it invokes 'draconian measures' meant to 'stamp out the spontaneous component of global migration' (Flynn 2005: 484). Yet, as Ruud Lubbers, former UN High Commissioner for Refugees concluded – 'A policy built on exclusion is not only morally reprehensible, it is also impractical: it will simply push all forms of migration, including refugees, further underground' (Lubbers 2004).

What is even more disconcerting, given New Labour's concern with children, is that this inattention extends to migrant children. Since the 1990s especially, large numbers of unaccompanied children have arrived in Britain, mostly London:

> At first they came from countries such as Ethiopia and Somalia and subsequently from Kosovo, Algeria, China and Afghanistan. Children are especially vulnerable to violence, have no voice and no independent access to services. Many of the unaccompanied were young people able to demonstrate sufficient independence skills to survive in supported accommodation with the equivalent of Income Support in cash payments from local authority social service departments through Section 17 of the Children Act. That support system terminated by statute in 1999. (Pierson 2002: 205)

While this issue of unaccompanied children was touched upon in the 2003 Green paper, *Every Child Matters,* the children who accompany asylum seekers continue to be disregarded. In the rare instance when the government has turned its attention to these children, the reaction is awkward to say the least. Consider here the proposal to take into care the children of failed asylum seekers who face deportation because of their refusal to leave the UK!

The Labour government has also failed to address its predecessor's actions that worked to limit the scope and effect of the UN Convention on the Rights of the Child having to do with refugee children. Consequently, refugee children do not fall under Britain's 1989 Children Act. This means that the welfare of children of refugees is not held in great regard leading to censure by the UN Committee on the Rights of the Child in 2002 (Lister 2003b: 435).

Furthermore, recall that many of the targets of racially-based crimes are children and youth, and often the offspring of (im)migrants. Beyond Stephen Lawrence, in the 1990s alone, we can refer to a shockingly long list of racially-based murders of young people:

> Rohit Duggal (15), Rolan Adams (15), Navid Sadiq (15), Liam Harrison (14), Manish Patel (15), Rikki Reel (18), Imran Khan (15), Michael Menson (29), Ali Ibrahim (21), Ashiq Hussain (21), Ruhullah Aramesh (24), Panchadcharam Sathiharan (28), Donna

O'Dwyer (26) ... Thousands more have been maimed by racists – often young white malcontents. (Alibhai-Brown 2001: 104-05)

The incident recounted above, involving the young Kurdish man, shows racially-based violence causing death continued to occur in 2004.

What are women, the mothers of these children and young people, left to think? Here, Yasmin Alibhai-Brown reflects on the feelings of one such mother:

> You watch Doreen Lawrence's face displaying at once tenacity and impossible pain as she seeks justice for the killers of her son, Stephen, and you see what hopes were killed on that day at the bus stop – the hopes that drive immigration, the hopes of a young black woman who felt strong enough to risk procreation in a racist society, and the hopes of a mother who felt that the future was worth all the troubles and sacrifices that motherhood brings. Motherhood here cannot only be examined through the white, gender perspective because such an analysis fails to explain or understand what a woman like Doreen Lawrence has gone through. (Alibhai-Brown 2001: 219)

Stemming from the Stephen Lawrence inquiry, partly as a reaction to developments post 9/11, but mostly as a direct response to race riots (involving young British men of white English and Asian descent) that occurred in several northern towns (Bradford, Burnley, Oldham) in the spring and summer of 2001, an independent review committee under the auspices of the Home Office was set up and a report written, the *Cantle Report on Community Cohesion* (2001). It constructed 'cultural diversity as a direct result of migration' and then linked it both to the need to contain migration and to 'the need to train migrants in English and civic values.' Racism is hardly mentioned, 'and then only as an obstacle to social cohesion' (Yuval-Davis, Anthias and Kofman 2005: 525).

The government then came up with its own report, *Building Cohesive Communities: A Report of the Ministerial Group on Public Order and Community Cohesion* (December 2001). This, in turn, sparked several measures including a Community Cohesion Unit in the Home Office, new grants, and a consultation process, *Strength in Diversity: Towards a Community Cohesion and Race Equality Strategy* (Home Office 2004: 3). Again, however, these efforts focus on cohesion and not exclusion. Part of the former does address citizenship concerns, but the emphasis is on shared values and integration rather than tackling deeply rooted inequalities. Citizenship ceremonies, education and activities are promoted so that 'All citizens, whether by birth or naturalized, White or from a Black and minority ethnic (BME) group ... need to be able to see themselves as "British" whether or not they add their cultural identity to the term' (Home Office 2004: 8). Finally, here it is evident that the Blair government's initiatives are insufficiently 'joined up' as the Home Office even admits that while it has been 'pursuing a cross departmental agenda, there is not yet ownership within other departments and most have failed to integrate community cohesion and equality' (Home Office 2004: 18). Ultimately, as social cohesion is embraced, it is more apt to produce, at best, common aims and objectives, and at worse assimilation and control, rather than tackle exclusion, let alone racism and other forms of oppression.

Part V: Conclusions: Challenging the Statuses and Practices of Citizenship, A Case in Point: Women, Children Minorities and Migrants

When such discrimination, racial hatred, 'deliberate and unconscious exclusion are the reality' (Alibhai-Brown 2001: 105), it becomes all too apparent that the Blair government is not casting its net wide enough as it promises to deal with the worst off. Despite the prevalence of discourses of social exclusion and citizenship, then, the Labour government's actual responses have been both insufficient and contradictory, especially when collective identities like those of gender, race, and ethnicity are factored in.

As we have seen, some children are included, but others are excluded. For the most part, women are only included if their concerns are linked to certain children, or are a part of measures that promote a universal breadwinner model. Active citizenship, in the sense of being active in the labour market, is equated with good citizenship. The complicated relationship between public and private when it comes to citizenship is obscured. This negatively affects women as the contributions of the private sphere to citizenship, primarily women's contributions, are not valorized in this good paid worker/good citizen nexus. At the same time, this citizen-worker ideal does not even apply consistently to all women, as the needs of racial and ethnic minorities and (im)migrants and asylum seekers, are overlooked.

These complex, intersecting identities need to be written back in, along with more expansive views of social exclusion and citizenship. This would bring to light the plight of outsiders such as women, racial and ethnic minorities, (im)migrants, refugees and asylum seekers, and their children. This would also mean that the British government would not only deal with poverty, but lack of power, discrimination and prejudice, that it would push for full participation and the forging of meaningful solidarities. A truly comprehensive definition of social exclusion, then, would highlight the interconnections between collective identity and poverty, access to goods and services from housing to health, to physical safety and well being, would incorporate broader, more substantive citizen rights, and foster a wider array of socio-political networks and deeper senses of belonging. Then, social cohesion could potentially be about more than superficial commonalities.

According to Stuart Hall, race and ethnicity 'Is a blanked out space as far as the language of New Labour is concerned, written out of the imagined post-Millennium New Britain which the government is struggling to construct' (Hall cited in Margetts 2002: 193). More optimistically, recent documents from the SEU have begun to hint that racial discrimination will become more of an emphasis. For instance, in a September 2004 report, *Breaking the Cycle* the SEU has added 'discrimination' to its definition of social exclusion, something that was notably absent in its 2001 definition cited at the start of this paper. The 2004 definition suggests:

Social exclusion is about more than income poverty. It is a shorthand term for what can happen when people or areas face a combination of linked problems such as unemployment, *discrimination*, poor skills, low incomes, poor housing, high crime, bad health and family breakdown. These problems are linked and mutually reinforcing so that they can create a vicious cycle in people's lives. (SEU 2004: 3, our emphasis)

What is more, this same document also identifies groups 'with complex needs' and 'three main broad and overlapping groups of people for whom policies consistently seem less effective' with one of these categories being: 'People from some ethnic minority groups, including asylum seekers and refugees' (SEU 2004: 7). This is precisely where we argue the Labour government has been remiss. Indeed it should vigorously pursue the priorities that it has only just begun to acknowledge. But of course, now we have to wait and see if these words lead to deeds.

Realistically, the future is not bright, given distressing, recent developments. Two journalists in a September 2005 *Guardian Weekly* article give the following account:

A mother and her four year-old child have become the first family to be evicted from their home under a pilot scheme that takes away all benefits from failed asylum seekers who do not leave Britain voluntarily ... Loss of benefits, denounced as blackmail by refugee support groups, is being piloted in the north and London before ministers decide whether to implement the sanction across the country ... Some councils complain of being forced to do the Home Office's dirty work and say section 9 [of the 2004 *Asylum and Immigration Act* which at the end of a five stage process cuts off benefits from failed asylum seekers] can conflict with their policy of keeping children with their parents. It also much more expensive for councils to take children into care than to leave them with their parents in a council house, even if no rent is paid.

'We are now seeing the devastating effect this legislation is having on families,' said Julia Ravenscroft, press officer for Refugee Action in Manchester. 'Parents are having to choose between homelessness and separation from their children in the UK or returning to a country where they fear for their lives' (Ward and Bowcroft 2005: 14).

References

Alcock, D. (2002), 'Welfare Policy,' in P. Dunleavy et al. (eds), *Developments in British Politics 6* (revised edition), Palgrave, Houndmills, pp. 238-56.

Alibhai-Brown, Y. (2001), *Imagining the New Britain*, Routledge, New York.

Barnardo's (2003), 'Response to the Green Paper on Children *Every Child Matters*, on behalf of Barnardo's UK,' Barnardo's, Runcorn, December.

Bashevkin, S. (2002), *Welfare Hot Buttons: Women, Work and Social Policy Reform*, University of Toronto Press, Toronto.

Bashevkin, S. (1998), *Women on the Defensive: Living Through Conservative Times*,

University of Toronto Press, Toronto.

Becker, S. (2003), '"Security for those who cannot:" Labour's neglected welfare principle,' in J. Millar (eds), *Understanding Social Security: Issues for Policy and Practice*, The Policy Press, Bristol, pp. 103-22.

Bennett, H. (2002), *Britain Unwrapped: Government and Constitution Explained*, Penguin Books, London.

Bhabha, J. and Shutter, S. (1994), *Women's Movement: Women Under Immigration, Nationality and Refugee Law*, Trentham Books, London.

Blair, T. (1996), *New Britain: My Vision of A Young Country*, Fourth Estate, London.

Blair, T. (2001), 'Foreword,' to *Preventing Social Exclusion*, Report by the Social Exclusion Unit (www.cabinet-office.gov.uk/seu/2001/pse/PSE%20HTML/default.htm.)

Bradshaw, J. (2003), 'Child Poverty and health in International Perspective,' in C. Hallett and A. Prout (eds), *Hearing the Voices of Children: Social Policy for a New Century* Routledge, London, pp. 213-36.

'Brown looks to golden future,' (2004), *Guardian Weekly*, 16-22 July, p. 14.

Brown, D. (2004), 'Kurdish refugee clubbed to death,' *Guardian Weekly*, 17-23 September, p. 13.

Brown, G. (1999), 'A Scar on the Nation's Soul,' *Poverty*, No. 104.

Budge, I., Crewe, I., McKay, D. and Newton, K. (2001), *The New British Politics* (2nd Edition), Pearson, Harlow.

Carter, B., Harris, C. and Joshi, S. (2000), 'The 1951-1955 Conservative government and the racialization of Black immigration,' in K. Owusu (ed.), *Black British Culture and Society*, Routledge, London, pp. 21-36.

CASE (Centre for the Analysis of Social Exclusion) (2003), *Annual Report 2002*, Case Report 20, ESRC Research Centre for the Analysis of Social Exclusion, London.

Chatterjee, D. (1995), 'Harnessing Shakti: The Work of the Bengali Women's Support Group,' in G. Griffin (ed.), *Feminist Activism in the 1990s*, Taylor and Francis, Bristol, pp. 90-100.

Childs, S. (2001), 'Attitudinal Feminists? The New Labour women and the substantive representation of women,' *Politics*, Vol. 21(3), pp. 178-85.

CIH (Chartered Institute of Housing) (2003), 'Providing a Safe Haven- Housing Asylum Seekers and Refugees,' A CIH Policy Paper.

Coote, A. (2001), 'Feminism and the Third Way: A Call for Dialogue,' in S. White (ed.), *New Labour: The Progressive Future?*, Palgrave, Houndmills, pp. 126-33.

Coote, A. (2000), 'Women and the Third Way,' in J. Klausen and C. S. Maier (eds), *Has Liberalism Failed Women?*, Palgrave, Houndmills, pp. 111-21.

Coxall, B., Robins, L. and Leach, R. (2003), *Contemporary British Politics* (4th edition), Palgrave Macmillan, Houndmills.

Daly, M. and Saraceno, C. (2002), 'Social Exclusion and Gender Relations,' in B. Hobson, J. Lewis and B. Siim (eds), *Contested Concepts in Gender and Social*

Politics, Edward Elgar, Cheltenham, pp. 84-104.

'Death Toll highlighted' (2004), *Guardian Weekly*, 8-14 October, p. 14.

DSS (Department of Social Security) (1999), *Opportunity for All: Tackling Poverty and Social Exclusion*, Stationery Office, London.

de Lotbiniere, M. (2004), 'New Citizens tested,' *Guardian Weekly*, 23-29 July, Learning English Supplement, p. 1.

Dobrowolsky, A. (2003), 'Shifting States: Women's Constitutional Organizing Across Space and Time,' in L. A. Banaszak, K. Beckwith and D. Rucht (eds), *Women's Movements Facing the Reconfigured State*, Cambridge University Press, Cambridge, pp. 114-40.

Dobrowolsky, A. (2002), 'Rhetoric Versus Reality: The Figure of the Child and New Labour's Strategic "Social Investment State,"' *Studies in Political Economy*, No. 69, pp. 43-73.

Dobrowolsky, A. (2000), *The Politics of Pragmatism: Women, Representation and Constitutionalism in Canada*, Oxford University Press, Toronto.

Dobrowolsky, A. and Hart, V. (2003), *Women Making Constitutions: New Politics and Comparative Perspectives*, Palgrave Macmillan, Houndmills.

Dobrowolsky, A. and Jenson, J. (2005), 'Social investment perspectives and practices: a decade in British politics,' in M. Powell, L. Bauld and K. Clarke (eds), *Social Policy Review 17: Analysis and Debate in Social Policy 2005*, Bristol, The Policy Press, pp. 203-30.

Dobrowolsky, A. and Jenson, J. (2004), 'Shifting Representations of Citizenship: Canadian Politics of "Women" and "Children,"' *Social Politics*, Vol. 11(2), pp.154-80.

Dobrowolsky, A. and Saint-Martin, D. (2005), 'Agency, Actors and Change in A Child-Focused Future: Problematising Path Dependency,' *Journal of Commonwealth and Comparative Politics*, Vol. 43(1), pp. 1-33.

Driver, S. and Martell, L. (2002), *Blair's Britain*, Polity, Cambridge.

Fitzpatrick, P. (2004), 'Factors linking child and women's poverty,' Briefing notes for the Women's Budget Group. On file with author.

Flynn, D. (2005), 'New borders, new management: The dilemmas of modern immigration policies,' *Ethnic and Racial Studies*, Special Issue *Migration and Citizenship*, Vol. 28(3), pp. 463-90.

Fraser, N. (1997), *Justice Interruptus: Critical Reflections on the 'Postsocialist' Condition*, Routledge, New York.

Frazer, E. (2002), 'Citizenship and Culture,' in P. Dunleavy et al. (eds), *Developments in British Politics 6* (revised edition), Palgrave, Houndmills, pp. 203-18.

Griffin, G. (1995), 'The Struggle Continues – An Interview with Hannana Siddiqui of Southall Black Sisters,' in G. Griffin (ed.), *Feminist Activism in the 1990s*, Taylor, Francis, Bristol, pp. 79-89.

Grover, C. and Stewart, J. (2000), 'Modernizing Social Security? Labour and Its Welfare to Work Strategy,' *Social Policy and Administration*, Vol. 34(3), pp. 235-

52.

'Hard man embarks on mission impossible,' (2002), *The Guardian*, 30 September.

Hayter, T. (2005), *Open Borders: The Case Against Immigration Controls* (2nd edition), Pluto, London.

Hobcraft, J. (1998), 'Intergeneration and Life-Course Transmission of Social Exclusion: Influences of Childhood Poverty, Family Disruption and Contact with the Police,' CASE Paper 15, London School of Economics, London.

Hobcraft, J. and Kiernan, K. (1999), 'Childhood Poverty, Early Motherhood and Social Exclusion,' CASE Paper 28, London School of Economics, London.

Hobson, B. and Lister, R. (2002), 'Citizenship,' in B. Hobson and B. Siim (eds), *Contested Concepts in Gender and Social Politics*, Edward Elgar, Cheltenham, pp. 23-53.

Home Office (2004), 'The End of Parallel Lives? Report of the Social Cohesion Panel,' The Home Office Communication Directorate, London.

Jenson, J. (2001), 'Canada's Shifting Citizenship Regime, Investing in Children,' in T.C. Salmon and M. Keating (eds), *The Dynamics of Decentralization*, McGill-Queen's University Press, Montréal, Kingston, pp.107-24.

Jenson, J. and Phillips, S. (1996), 'Regime Shift: New Citizenship Practices in Canada,' *International Journal of Canadian Studies*, Vol. 14 (Fall), pp.111-35.

Krieger, J. (1999), *British Politics in the Global Age: Can Social Democracy Survive?* Oxford University Press, New York.

Lawson, N. and Leighton, D. (2004), 'Blairism's Agoraphobia. Active citizenship and the Public Domain,' *Renewal*, Vol. 12(1), pp. 1-12.

Layton-Henry, Z. (2001), 'Patterns of Privilege: Citizenship Rights in Britain,' in A. Kondo (ed.), *Citizenship in a Global World: Comparing Citizenship Rights for Aliens*, Palgrave, Houndmills, pp. 116-35.

Levitas, R. (1996), 'The Concept of Social Exclusion and the New Durkheimian Hegemony,' *Critical Social Policy*, Vol. 16(1), pp. 5-20.

Lewis, G. and Neal, S. (2005), 'Introduction: Contemporary political contexts, changing terrains and revisited discourses,' *Ethnic and Racial Studies*, Special Issue Migration and Citizenship, Vol. 28(3), pp. 423-44.

Lister, R. (2005), 'The Links between Child Poverty and Women's Poverty,' in *Women's and Children's Poverty: Making the Links*, Women's Budget Group, London.

Lister, R. (2004), *Poverty,* Polity, Cambridge.

Lister, R. (2003a), *Citizenship: Feminist Perspectives* (2nd edition), New York University Press, New York.

Lister, R. (2003b), 'Investing in the citizen-workers of the future: transformations in citizenship and the state under New Labour,' *Social Policy and Administration*, Vol. 37(5), pp. 427-43.

Lister, R. (2001), 'New Labour: a study in ambiguity from a position of ambivalence,' *Critical Social Policy,* Vol. 21(4), pp. 425-47.

Lister, R. (1998), 'From equality to social inclusion: New Labour and the welfare state,' *Critical Social Policy*, Vol. (18)2, pp. 215-26.

Lovenduski, J. and Randall, V. (1993), *Contemporary Feminist Politics: Women and Power in Britain*, Oxford University Press, Oxford.

Lubbers, R. (2004), 'Make asylum fair, not fast,' *Guardian*, (www://society.guardian. co.uk/ asylumseekers/comment/0,8005,1342143,00.html).

Lund, B. (1999) '"Ask not what your community can do for you:" Obligations, New Labour and Welfare Reform,' *Critical Social Policy*, No. 61, pp. 447-62.

MacGregor, S. (2003), 'Social Exclusion,' in N. Ellison and C. Pierson (eds), *Developments in British Social Policy 2*, Palgrave MacMillan, Houndmills, pp. 56-74.

Margetts, H. (2002), 'Political Participation and Protest,' in P. Dunleavy et al. (eds), *Developments in British Politics 6* (revised edition), Palgrave, Houndmills.

McLaughlin, E., Trewsdale, J. and McCay, N. (2001), 'The Rise and Fall of the UK's First Tax Credit: The Working Families Tax Credit 1998-2000,' *Social Policy and Administration*, Vol. 23(2), pp. 163-80.

Meehan, E. (1999), 'Citizenship and Identity,' in I. Holliday, A. Gamble and G. Parry (eds), *Fundamentals in British Politics*, St. Martin's Press, New York, pp. 231-50.

Miller, C. (2004), *Producing Welfare: A Modern Agenda*, Palgrave MacMillan, Houndmills.

Mirza, H. S. (1997), *Black British Feminism: A Reader*, Routledge, London.

'More than 1,000 held in swoops' (2004), *Guardian Weekly*, 17-23 September, p. 15.

Newburn, T. (2003), 'Criminal Justice Policy,' in N. Ellison and C. Pierson (eds), *Developments in British Social Policy 2*, Palgrave, Houndmills, pp. 229-46.

Parekh, B. (1991), 'British Citizenship and Cultural Difference,' in G. Andrews (ed.), *Citizenship,* Lawrence, Wishart, London, pp. 183-204.

Pierson, J. (2002), *Tackling Social Exclusion*, Routledge, London.

Pinkney, S. (2000), 'Children as Welfare Subjects in Restructured Social Policy,' in G. Lewis, S. Gewirtz and J. Clarke (eds), *Rethinking Social Policy*, Sage, London, pp. 111-26.

Platt, L. (2003), 'Social security in a multi-ethnic society,' in J. Millar (eds), *Understanding Social Security: Issues for Policy and Practice*, The Policy Press, Bristol, pp. 255-76.

Ridge, T. (2003), 'Benefiting children? The challenge of social security support for children,' in Jane Millar (ed.), *Understanding Social Security: Issues for Policy and Practice,* The Policy Press, Bristol, pp. 167-99.

Roy, A. (1995), 'Asian Women's Activism in Northamptonshire,' in G. Griffin (ed.), *Feminist Activism in the 1990s*, Taylor, Francis, Bristol, pp. 101-12.

Russell, M. (2003), 'Women in Elected Office in the UK, 1992-2002: Struggles, Achievements and Possible Sea Change,' in A. Dobrowolsky and V. Hart (eds), *Women Making Constitutions: New Politics and Comparative Perspectives*, Palgrave Macmillan, Houndmills, pp. 68-83.

Sales, R. (2005), 'Secure Borders, Safe Haven: A contradiction in terms?,' *Ethnic and Racial Studies*, Special Issue Migration and Citizenship, Vol. 28(3), pp. 445-62.

SEU (Social Exclusion Unit) (www.socialexclusionunit.gov.uk).

SEU (Social Exclusion Unit) (2004*), Breaking the Cycle: Taking Stock of Progress and Priorities for the Future. A Report by the Social Exclusion Unit* (September), Office of the Deputy Prime Minister, London.

SEU (Social Exclusion Unit) (2003), *A Better Education for Children in Care: Summary*, Office of the Deputy Prime Minister, London.

SEU (Social Exclusion Unit) (2001), 'Preventing Social Exclusion,' Report by the Social Exclusion Unit (www.cabeint-office.gov.uk/seu/2001/pse/PSE%20HTML/default. htm).

Squires, J. (2004), 'Equality and Diversity: A New Equality Framework for Britain,' (www.bath.ac.uk/esml/library/pdf-files/squires.pdf.)

Squires, J. (2003), 'Reviewing UK Equality Agenda in the Context of Constitutional change,' in A. Dobrowolsky and V. Hart (eds), *Women Making Constitutions: New Politics and Comparative Perspectives,* Palgrave Macmillan, Houndmills, pp. 200-15.

Thomson, M. (2001), 'Femocrats and Babes: Women and Power,' *Australian Feminist Studies*, Vol. 5(16), pp. 193-209.

Ward, D. and Bowcott, O. (2005), 'Failed asylum seeker evicted under pilot project,' *Guardian Weekly*, 2-8 September, p. 14.

Werbner, P. and Yuval-Davis, N. (1999), 'Introduction: Women and the New Discourse of Citizenship,' in N. Yuval-Davis and P. Werbner (eds), *Women, Citizenship and Difference*, Zed Books, London, New York, pp. 1-38.

WEU (Women and Equality Unit) (2004), *Equality, Opportunity and Choice: Tackling Occupational Segregation*, Department of Trade and Industry (DTI), London.

White, M. and Elliot, L. (2004), 'Brown defies gloom mongers,' *Guardian Weekly*, 10-16 December, p. 29.

Wolfe, A. and Klausen, J. (2000), 'Other people,' *Prospect*, December, pp. 29-33.

Younge, G. (2002), 'Colour-coded citizenship.' *Guardian Weekly*, 21-27 February, p.11.

Yuval-Davis, N., Anthias, F. and Kofman, E. (2005), 'Secure Borders and safe haven and the gendered politics of belonging: Beyond social cohesion," *Ethnic and Racial Studies*, Special Issue Migration and Citizenship, Vol. 28(3), pp. 513-35.

Chapter 8

Citizenship, Identity, Agency and Resistance among Canadian and Australian Women of South Asian Origin

Helen Ralston

This chapter explores citizenship, identity construction, agency and resistance among Canadian and Australian immigrant women of South Asian origin. It examines specifically the interconnections of these concepts in women's organizational activities.

The term 'South Asian' is a social construction. It encompasses distinctly different categories of people who trace their origins either directly to the Indian subcontinent (India, Pakistan, Sri Lanka, Bangladesh), or else indirectly through their ancestors who migrated to East and South Africa, Fiji, East Asia, the Caribbean and elsewhere. The term is used in Canada in immigration and census data but rarely in Australia and seldom by the women themselves. Being South Asian refers to social characteristics and identities that have been constructed in specific historical, social, economic and political contexts. 'South Asian' connotes heterogeneity and hybridity, rather than homogeneity, in intersecting race, ethnicity, language, class, caste and sub-caste, religion and national origin in the construction of identity.

'Immigrant woman' refers not so much to legal status as to processes of social construction in everyday life which describe some women, who are visibly and audibly different in characteristics such as skin colour, language or accent, religion, dress, food customs and so on, as 'immigrants.' From a legal standpoint, a South Asian immigrant woman who enters Canada or Australia is not an alien visitor from a foreign country, but in both Canada and Australia, a permanent resident. She can legally apply for citizenship status within a few years (three years in Canada, two years in Australia). Unlike many European countries, both Canada and Australia encourage international migrants who enter as permanent settlers to become naturalized citizens and are renowned for being 'immigrant countries' (Castles and Davidson 2000). In fact, Australia identified post-World War Two migrants as 'New Australians.' Nevertheless, immigrant women's experience in everyday life is often that of discrimination and exclusion. Others construct boundaries that identify them as alien.

Citizenship, however, includes more than legal status of nationality, whether by birth or naturalization. Marshall's (1950) classic analysis of citizenship included full membership of the community, a progression from civic to political to social citizenship, with rights and responsibilities. Feminist scholars Lister (1997), Hobson and Lister (2002) and Rubenstein (2001) conceived citizenship as involving interconnected social and political participation as well as individual and community rights. Rubenstein noted that citizenship includes social and political belonging to the community. She commented further that even among its legal citizens Australia has not created a framework for full and equal participation. Lister (1997: 42) stressed the conception of citizenship as both a status and a practice that 'recognizes the structural constraints which still diminish and undermine that citizenship while not reducing women to passive victims.' Nira Yuval-Davis (2001) called for a differentiation between the notion of citizenship and that of belonging. She argued that 'if citizenship signifies the participatory dimension of belonging, identification relates to the more emotive dimension of association. Feeling that one is part of a collectivity, a community, a social category, or yearning to be so, is not the same as actually taking part in a political community.' A broader definition of citizenship is particularly important when considering citizenship of immigrant women. Following Yuval-Davis, in my studies I am concerned with citizenship as civic, social and political participation of all the immigrant women, whether naturalized citizens or not, in other collectivities besides the nation-state.

While recognizing the exclusion, discrimination, oppression and victimization experienced by immigrant women of colour, the emphasis in my studies is on their agency, their resistance to such experiences, their exercise of citizenship in everyday life, particularly through organizational activities. By agency I mean that immigrant women are conscious actors, not passive subjects in the various situations in which they find themselves. They act intentionally. They resist identification as aliens. They claim the right to belong to their country of settlement.

With respect to identity construction, much research has suggested a fixed identity of oppressed South Asian immigrant women. There has been a tendency to overlook their agency in the reconstruction of a creative and dynamic identity. I follow those (Agnew 1996; Bannerji 1993; Bottomley 1991; Brah 1996; hooks 1990) that conceptualize immigrant women and women of colour as dynamic and creative agents in constructing identity and shaping experience. I explore how women identify themselves with communities, construct a space for themselves, challenge and resist representations by others in the settlement country (Bannerji 1993; Pettman 1992), how they claim marginality as 'a site of radical possibility, a space of resistance' (hooks 1990: 149-50) – a site to organize as civic, social and political citizens. Elsewhere (Ralston 1998), I have discussed the alienating experience of migration for a South Asian woman. Migration involves a rupture in her worldview and consciousness of cultural identity. She crosses not only territorial borders but also cultural, social and psychic boundaries and enters into new relationships in new spaces. In those new spaces, many South Asian women have reconstructed a positive personal and social identity and have become active participants in organizations that express their multidimensional citizenship.

Nira Yuval-Davis (1994, 1997: 204) has referred to a process of 'transversal politics' with reference to citizenship participation. Using terms coined by the Bologna Women's Resource Centre, she has described transversal politics as 'rooting' and 'shifting:'

> The idea is that each participant in the dialogue brings with her the rooting in her own grouping, but tries at the same time to shift in order to put herself in a situation of exchange with women who have different groupings and identities.

Immigrant women remain rooted in their own identities, values and beliefs but my research has indicated that they are often willing to shift in dialogue with others. Of course, a true dialogical relationship implies a similar rooting and shifting on the part of 'those who are constructed and represented as indigenous' (Brah 1996).

Avtar Brah's (1996) conception of 'diaspora space' is helpful in furthering analysis of citizenship, agency and identity construction among South Asian immigrant women. For Brah (1996: 208), 'Diaspora space is the point at which boundaries of inclusion and exclusion, of belonging and otherness, of "us" and "them," are contested … (It refers to) a space that is "inhabited" not only by those who have migrated and their descendants but equally by those who are constructed and represented as indigenous.' In diaspora space, both immigrant women and non-migrants encounter new and different values, attitudes, meaning systems and codes of conduct. South Asians struggle to reconstruct their identity, values, and codes of conduct. Many also experience race and gender discrimination. Nevertheless, I argue that immigrant women are agents, rather than passive victims, in the situations and social spaces that they enter. In practical activities of everyday life, they reawaken and reconstruct their ethnocultural and ethnoreligious consciousness. In relations with their community, other immigrants and native-born people, they define and redefine their identity and their self-representation to others. Through organizational activities, above all, they resist negative representations, discrimination and oppression and exercise their rights as civic, social and political citizens of the new settlement country. I contend that South Asian immigrant women's collective organization can raise identity, gender and race consciousness, and clarify their sense of citizenship and belonging in the settlement society. While some organizations are spaces that establish their citizenship as members of specific communities and provide them with needed services, other organizations are spaces for advocacy and active resistance to the marginalization, discrimination and exclusion they experience in family, community and civil society. Through organizational activities, the women become conscious agents in their movement towards empowerment and full citizenship in its widest social definition.

Research Samples of South Asians in Canada and Australia

The research focuses on South Asian women in two Commonwealth countries that share a British colonial heritage with India, the former jewel in the imperial crown. Both Canada and Australia are Commonwealth federal states – Canada since 1867, Australia since 1901. Both had racially discriminatory immigration policies – Canada until the 1960s, Australia until the 1970s. Both have a poor record of relations with indigenous peoples. Multicultural and settlement policies and practices in Canada and Australia differ in that there has been much greater involvement of the federal government in Australia than in Canada in the provision and delivery of services (Jupp 1992; Lanphier and Lukomskyj 1994). The research is based on the assumption that, in the study of immigrants' experience, identity construction, agency, citizenship and resistance, it is necessary to consider *where migrants have settled* as well as their origins (Careless 1987). When I began this study in the late 1980s, rarely had this been done in previous research with South Asian immigrants. Canadian publications with titles such as 'South Asians in Canada' usually referred to residents of Toronto or Ontario. It was often assumed that cultural origins accounted for the lived experience and identity construction among immigrants, no matter where they settled. South Asians have settled unevenly throughout Canada and Australia – in Canada predominantly in Ontario, in Australia in the two major metropolises, Sydney and Melbourne. I therefore decided to explore South Asian immigrant women's experiences in two different settlement centres in Canada and Australia, namely centres that were less and more densely populated and centres with larger and smaller concentrations of South Asians. Since the fieldwork for this research was conducted in the late 1980s and the first half of the 1990s, I used 1991 census data (Statistics Canada 1993; BIMPR 1995).

Atlantic Canada is isolated from the densely populated central and western regions of Canada. It is very different from the Pacific maritime Province of British Columbia – demographically, historically, and socially. The total population of British Columbia was more than twenty times that of Atlantic Canada. Whereas, South Asians comprised 3.2 per cent of the British Columbia population, they represented only 0.2 per cent of the Atlantic Canada population. In British Columbia, 74 per cent of the South Asian population resided in Vancouver metropolis. In Atlantic Canada, only 44 per cent of South Asians were settled in Halifax, the major metropolis. Historically, British Columbia was the port of entry for the initial South Asian immigrants at the turn of the twentieth century. South Asians migrated to Atlantic Canada only after World War II when racially discriminatory policies were beginning to relax (Ralston 1994). Socially, British Columbia, especially Vancouver, has a large population of diverse Asian ethnic origins. Atlantic Canada has relatively few people of Asian origin. Moreover, South Asians who migrated to British Columbia a century ago were mainly male Punjabi Jat Sikhs (farmers). South Asian immigrants to Canada of recent decades have comprised a heterogeneous population in terms of regional, linguistic, religious and national origins.

As in Canada, the Australian metropolises, Sydney, Melbourne and Perth differ demographically, historically and socially. All are coastal cities. Sydney, which was settled by Europeans in 1788, is the oldest European settlement of Australia. Europeans first settled Melbourne in 1835. Britain established a colony in Perth in 1829. In the post-World War Two influxes of migrants to Australia, Sydney and Melbourne have been the prime destinations. In 1991 over 30 per cent of the population in these metropolises was overseas-born and three-quarters of these people were born in non-English speaking countries. Today, Australia is the tenth most urbanized country in the world – 91 per cent, as compared to Canada, which is in 40th place with 79 per cent urbanized.[1] The large metropolises of Sydney and Melbourne comprise about 40 per cent of the population of the country, Perth metropolis about five per cent. Of Perth's overseas-born population, 45 per cent were born in non-English speaking countries. Perth, on the southwest coast bordering the Indian Ocean, is distinguished by its isolation from the densely populated eastern region of Australia. It is the most isolated capital city in the world.[2] Although Perth is closer to the Indian sub-continent than Sydney and Melbourne, fewer South Asians are settled in Perth.

It was with the demographic, historical and social factors in mind, together with the different methods of census data collection in each country, that I chose to explore the experience of South Asian immigrant women in different settlements of the respective countries: in Canada, sparsely populated Atlantic Canada with relatively few, dispersed South Asians, and relatively densely populated and highly urbanized South Asians in British Columbia; in Australia, South Asian women in the largest Pacific metropolises of Sydney and Melbourne, compared with those in the smaller, isolated metropolis of Perth. I have drawn on data gathered in face-to-face, semi-structured interviews: with South Asian immigrant women in Atlantic Canada between 1988 and 1990, in British Columbia, Canada, between 1993 and 1995, and in Australia in 1995. The focus of the interviews was on actual experiences of everyday life in migration and settlement. The women were not asked directly about their sense of identity and belonging. I also participated in ethnoreligious and ethnocultural organization events in the various research contexts.

Atlantic Canada women of my studies entered Canada between 1956 and 1988, the modal year being 1967; British Columbia women between 1949 and 1994, the modal year being 1973. Australian women migrated there between 1961 and 1995, the modal year being 1990. The women in all samples were of diverse national, linguistic and religious backgrounds. Atlantic Canada women identified with six different religions (Hindu, Sikh, Christian, Muslim, Zoroastrian, Jewish), with over half Hindu. British Columbia women identified with five different religions (Sikh, Hindu, Muslim, Christian, and Zoroastrian), with Sikhs and Hindus each comprising 40 per cent of the sample. Australian women identified themselves as Hindu Sikh, Muslim, Christian and Buddhist. Punjabi and Hindi were the dominant mother tongues of the women in both Canadian samples, while a diversity of Indian languages was represented, particularly in the Atlantic Canada sample. Like the Canadian women, Australian women had a diversity of 13 different mother tongues, with Hindi (20 per cent) being dominant. In other words, heterogeneity rather than homogeneity characterized these women of South Asian origin. Despite significant diversity, there

---

1   http://www.nationmaster.com. Accessed 30 May 2004.
2   http://www.nationmaster.com. Accessed 30 May 2004.

were, however, some points of commonality among the women. For instance, 90 per cent of them were married. Among the married women, 75 per cent of the Atlantic Canada sample, 69 per cent of the British Columbia sample, and 64 per cent of the Australia sample had arranged (or what some called 'semi-arranged') marriages. Many migrated as dependants of an arranged marriage contract. Approximately 80 per cent had an educational level beyond high school at the time of their entrance to Canada or Australia.

Citizenship and Organizational Activities

Citizenship can be a useful device for bringing immigrant communities together and for binding them in common enterprises. At the same time, community organizations serve to establish boundaries not only between themselves, other immigrants and other Canadians or Australians, but also among South Asian immigrants of specific regional, cultural, linguistic and religious backgrounds. Concentration and diversity of South Asian immigrants at the time and place of settlement determine organization formation, participation and activities. Through membership in such organizations women affirmed their right as citizens to belong to the community. Through active civil, social and political participation they pursued their collective interests, common enterprises and goals in the new settlement space.

Community organizational goals can be loosely categorized as service-oriented and advocacy-oriented (Agnew 1993). Community organizations are service-oriented in that they provide a forum for recreational, social, cultural and religious exchanges and celebrations. They establish children's right to belong to the community, transmit cultural heritage, and facilitate heterosexual relations within the group. Such organizations can empower people by creating a self-conscious awareness of ethnic identity, solidarity and a sense of belonging to the community. They are spaces for social and civic citizenship. Most ethnoreligious and ethnocultural organizations are service-oriented. Advocacy-oriented community organizations, on the other hand, are proactive responses to an oppressive reality. They seek to translate awareness and articulation of concerns about racist and sexist discrimination into active resistance, legislation, policies, programmes and actions that transform unequal and unjust structures and relations of ruling in community and society (Agnew 1996). Some advocacy groups may be *gender*-specific groups that are organized to address the interests of women *within the ethnocultural group itself* as well as within society as a whole. Feminists organizing to combat the many forms of violence against women and children constitute such gender-specific advocacy-oriented groups. In both service-oriented and advocacy-oriented organizations South Asian immigrant women engage in practices of civic, social and political citizenship.

Eighty per cent or more of women in each sample participated in various types of ethnoreligious and ethnocultural community organizations. For South Asian immigrants, ethnoreligious and ethnocultural identity are primary boundary markers. High or low concentrations of South Asians who belonged to particular ethnic, religious and linguistic identities in a specific time and space directly influenced organization formation, participation and activities.

Ethnoreligious and Ethnocultural Organization in Canada

The initial 1956 immigrant to Atlantic Canada, a Hindu woman, came as a dependant of her professional husband. Her unfamiliar Indian sari and Indian-English accent confused the overwhelmingly dominant White Anglo-Celtic residents to whom brown South Asians were strangers, whereas Canadian-born 'coloured people' were familiar. In the absence of a South Asian community, the Indian woman resisted racist marginalization by claiming identity, membership and social citizenship with families of her husband's supportive collegial community.

For Atlantic Canada South Asian Hindu women, the absence or presence of regional and linguistic variations in temple rituals and style of worship was a key factor in determining participation in organized temple activities. Where few Hindu families were settled, they met monthly in private homes. The worship was described as 'a mixture in celebration' to accommodate the variety of members' identities. The gathering sacralized a generalized Hindu identity and provided a space for social support. Even in metropolitan Halifax, regional religious, linguistic and cultural differences created an experience of alienation. For example, one woman who migrated in 1979 complained:

> None of them at the temple are Sindhi. They speak Hindi. In Toronto, there are so many people of my own language.

Other Halifax Hindu women of South Indian origin described temple celebrations as being North Indian: 'We're lost ... (it's) almost like another religion.' Consequently, they formed the South Indian Cultural Association of the Maritimes (SICAM) in the late 1980s. South Indians who identified with many religious, linguistic and regional origins held informal social gatherings. Being *South* Indian was their salient marker of identity. Belonging to that region moved them to participate together in cultural and social citizenship activities despite religious differences.

By contrast, in British Columbia, where there is a high concentration of Hindu families, there are many Hindu temples of varying regional and linguistic identities. British Columbia Hindu South Asian women belonged to ethnospecific temples and organizations. For example, Indo-Fijian migrants in Vancouver formed an ethnocultural group that was distinct from other Indian Hindu migrant categories. Fijian origin and culture rather than religion were the salient markers of their identity. An Indo-Fijian interviewee belonged to an Arya Samaj Hindu community, the Fiji-Canadian Association, a multicultural association at her workplace and served as a volunteer at her children's school. She had reconstructed an Indo-Fijian Canadian identity. She criticized Canadian and British Columbia multicultural policies and some immigrants' use of government funds:

It's great to practice your own religion and culture but sometimes it separates people. The Government shouldn't be promoting (multiculturalism) on the scale it has been. Women's groups should get some (funding), but not religious groups. That should come from the community. Funding for English language classes is fine, but not to form our own schools. It's a waste of money to fund everything.

As an active civic and social citizen in various organizational activities, this woman expected other immigrants to be similarly committed citizens.

For Atlantic Canada Sikhs, there was one *gurdwara* (temple) in Halifax for the entire region. Sikh families living outside metropolitan Halifax travelled long distances to visit the *gurdwara* occasionally. Because South Asians had settled in British Columbia early in the twentieth century, post-World War II Sikh immigrants to British Columbia became members of a long-established Punjabi Sikh community with many active *gurdwaras*. They had choices for organizational participation as citizens of their new settlement country. Sikh women visited *gurdwara* – for prayer, peace of mind, celebration of feasts of the ten Gurus, but also for social events, such as marriages, birthdays, anniversaries and secular holidays. However, politicization of *gurdwaras* led some Vancouver women to visit them rarely. They took a pro-active citizenship stance of resistance to the internal and external Indian politicization of *gurdwara* management committees.

Although there were relatively few Muslim families in the Atlantic region, Muslims of diverse national origins established mosques in the three metropolises: Halifax, Nova Scotia, St. John's, Newfoundland, and Saint John, New Brunswick. The population base of South Asian Muslim families is not sufficient to support an independent mosque in any one of these metropolises. The Atlantic Canada Muslim women were of diverse national origins: Pakistani, Bangladeshi, Indian and Ugandan. Women regularly visited the mosque with husbands and children. The mosque was the space for reconstruction of *Muslim* consciousness and identity and for educating children in the Qu'ran and Islamic studies. Islamic religion, rather than national or regional origin, was the most salient marker of identity. Members of the New Brunswick mosque, by inviting non-Muslims to their religious and social gatherings, created a diasporic space for exchange and civic and social participation across ethnic boundaries. The community thus signified its collective Canadian citizenship.

British Columbia Muslim women were also of diverse national origins: East Africa, Fiji, Pakistan, India and Bangladesh. They visited Sunni or Ismaili mosques, usually only for big festivals. In secular service-oriented organizations (such as the Pakistan-Canadian Friendship Society and multicultural societies) and advocacy-oriented organizations (such as the Vancouver Society for Immigrant and Visible Minority Women), they engaged in collective social and political citizenship by facilitating teacher certification programmes for newcomers and anti-racist activism

Atlantic Canada and British Columbia South Asian Christian women reconstructed their identity with the least discontinuity. They were affiliated with various Christian denominations whose organization, traditions, rituals, values, beliefs and sentiments were most akin to those of their religion in the source country. They felt that they belonged in such groups. An Atlantic Canada Christian woman summed up her migration experience:

> I didn't find anything a trouble, because the religion was there and the language. We were always brought up with missionaries—white people, Americans and Canadians and English and Scottish people. So we were used to all their rules and regulations, their religious practices and all those things.

However, some Halifax Christian women also belonged to the Allied Christian Association, a social organization that comprised Christians of Indian or Pakistani origin. For these women, a specific ethnocultural organization was an important space for reconstructing their cultural hybridity and for social citizenship. Some British Columbia South Asian Christian women were active advocates and political citizens on behalf of visible minority and abused women.

Perhaps because of the relative lack of ethnospecific organizations in Atlantic Canada, over half of the interviewees were affiliated with the Indo-Canadian Association of Nova Scotia (INCA). INCA provided services such as social, cultural and entertainment events, public relations, orientation and settlement of newcomers. A human rights committee addressed advocacy-related issues, such as job discrimination, but not women's rights in family and society.

Ethnoreligious and Ethnocultural Organizations in Australia

As in Canada, Australian South Asian migrant women, together with their husbands, in Melbourne and Sydney in the 1960s, were founders and active members of ethnoreligious and ethnocultural service organizations. For example, a South Indian Melbourne woman who migrated at age 21 in 1961, was a founder and life member of several organizations: the Hindu Society, the Australia-India Society, the latter's women's auxiliary, and the ethnocultural Kannada Society. She acknowledged her hybrid identity and was an active civic and social Australian citizen in diasporic settlement spaces:

> When you marry and migrate, it's two-ways. You also have to go forward and meet people. I like Australia. I take what I like in the Australian way of life and combine it with mine to make a better life for us.

This woman practised transversal politics (Yuval-Davis 1997) in her everyday life. Rooted in Indian culture, she shifted to engage in dialogue and exchange with native-born Australians. A Sydney woman who also migrated from South India to Australia in 1970 at age 22 played a similar role. Both women married professional husbands who gained admission to Australia when the Australian government, despite its racially discriminatory policies, recognized that the country needed highly skilled professionals for the exploding metropolises of Sydney and Melbourne (Ralston

1994). Their identification with neighbours, colleagues at work and other Australians, and their organizational initiatives affirmed that citizenship implies more than legal status; it includes a sense of belonging, solidarity and commitment to civic and social participation in the settlement community (Rubenstein 2001; Yuval-Davis 2001). Such women also created spaces for future South Asian settlers to reconstruction of identity and citizenship.

Like the wives of professionals described above, a Christian Malaysian Sri Lankan Tamil migrated in 1968 at age 46 as wife of a founding professor at a Melbourne university. Her primary role in life was advocacy and political citizenship. She was a founder of the Tamil Association, became its secretary for immigration, then founded an international Tamil Federation. Interviewed long after retirement from teaching, she was 'working for justice and human rights' on the Board of the Australian Foundation for Human Rights, and as producer of a newsletter advocating for Sri Lankan Tamils. Her friends were: 'People of any kind of group that is actively concerned about social rights.'

This extraordinarily active woman was a civic, social and political citizen who resisted and advocated against oppression and discrimination wherever she saw them. She summed up her experience of Australian institutional racism as follows:

> I find that belonging to a minority is a problem. I work closely with Multicultural and Ethnic Affairs. I find that, for voting purposes, we are a minority. Government keeps our numbers down for various reasons, even though they say there is no White Australia policy. In Ethnic Community Council, unless you are really pushy, little minority groups from Asia don't get a say-so. I find that minority groups even if Christian, get pushed aside.

Nevertheless, she identified Australia and Melbourne as home and took every opportunity to proactively resist and change policies and practices she considered unjust. Sri Lanka was an imagined home community that she could not visit while Tamils were suppressed.

As in British Columbia, South Asian Hindu women who migrated to Sydney and Melbourne from the latter 1970s onwards had many specific ethnoreligious and ethnocultural service organizations available for membership and participation. For example, another Melbourne Malaysian-born Sri Lankan Tamil woman, who migrated in 1981, actively participated in an established Tamil temple, in the Sri Lankan Tamil Association, the Hindu Society and the Australia-India Society. She was a dynamic agent in education and communication of Tamil culture in these diasporic spaces. She too was an advocate and practical organizer on behalf of oppressed Sri Lanka Tamils:

> My third 'job' right now is an autumn carnival in March, a Food and Fun Fair. I am getting the Tamil community to work together to raise $50,000 to reconstruct north and east Sri Lanka through events, sale of crafts and food.

A legal Australian citizen, this woman constructed a hybrid Malaysian/Tamil/ Australian social identity. She presented Tamil social and cultural identity to a wider community. At the same time, she was a proactive social, cultural and political Sri Lanka citizen resisting oppression.

By contrast with Melbourne and Sydney women, Perth Hindu women had fewer choices for participation in ethnoreligious and ethnocultural community organizations. A Perth Hindu interviewee who migrated in 1970 had lived initially in remote Western Australian mining towns for eleven years, and thereafter in Sydney for four years. She was quite sure that she would stay permanently in Perth. She visited the temple 'to meet people' and belonged to the India Society of Western Australia. For her, Australian citizenship meant active social, cultural and civic commitment to Australian people and the country's national celebrations. She criticized the India Society of Western Australia that celebrated only one big festival day: India Independence Day. Her wry comment was:

> It's kind of funny! We all came from our country and now we celebrate India independence here. It's sheer hypocrisy when you've left India and are now Australian. They should do something for Australia, not be celebrating Indian Independence Day. It was *our* decision to come to this country. We had to compromise more than people who were already living here. I had to be friends with everyone. So I started calling them for dinner, whether they were reciprocating or not. I invited them. I didn't wait to be invited.

This interviewee also engaged in transversal politics as an Australian citizen. Rooted in her Indian culture, she shifted to initiate dialogue and exchange with women from different groupings (Yuval-Davis 1997). She expected other migrants to do the same.

Like Hindu women, Australian Sikh women living in Sydney and Melbourne in the 1990s had many choices for participation in *gurdwaras* and in ethnocultural community organizations. Earlier migrants had created these cultural spaces for themselves and to serve later newcomers. Two Sydney Sikh interviewees who migrated in the early 1960s were founding members of their respective *gurdwaras*. One of them, with her husband, also initiated the Indo-Australian Cultural Society. Others belonged to the Sikh Australian Association. Such organizations encouraged dialogue and exchange with other Australians. Melbourne Sikh interviewees were younger and more recent migrants to Australia. They were successful independent business and professional people—transnational migrants. They and their relatives lived or travelled throughout the world. In Melbourne they participated in *gurdwaras* and belonged to ethnocultural organizations: the Australia-India Society and its sub-group, the Punjabi Club, and the Hindi-Niketan cultural committee. The majority of the women became Australian citizens soon after they completed two years as permanent residents. Their organizational activities established them as civic and social Australian citizens long before their legal citizenship.

In contrast to Sydney and Melbourne, Perth (like Halifax) had only one *gurdwara* that was an open community for all Sikhs. According to one interviewee, there were relatively few Punjabi Sikhs in Perth. A Malaysian-born Punjabi Sikh woman, aged

46, married with two children, had a history of transnational migration. Her story highlighted the significance of life stage in organization participation. She had studied in New Zealand, joined relatives in Australia, become an Australian citizen in 1976, gone to England and married there in 1984, then lived in London until 1987. Her Malaysian-born Punjabi Sikh husband entered Australia as her dependant. They settled in Perth. She observed:

> We found Perth small after London. We tried Sydney for two months. We came back to Perth. Now we are settled here and could not live anywhere else. Sydney is too busy for us. This is home now. This is my country, where I belong. I don't find discrimination. I seem to get on well with everyone. I don't separate myself. I came young. I could not live in Malaysia now. I find people strange there.

As a married woman with two young children in Perth, she reported that she had no time for a Perth Punjabi women's group or a Khalsa club for families. However, as a young single woman in Sydney in the early 1970s, she had formed a group for single Punjabi Indian-origin men and women to meet partners and belonged to a folkloric Sikh group that performed in multicultural festivals. At that stage in her life, she had time and opportunity to initiate an ethnospecific group that fulfilled the purpose of many ethnic community organizations in large cities. In Perth, at a later stage in her life, her friends and Australian citizenship activities were multicultural.

Nine of the eleven Australia Muslim women normally visited mosques only for celebration of major festivals. Muslims in the large metropolises of Sydney and Melbourne had several possible mosques to visit – more than 12 in Melbourne. Mosque membership was multicultural and included Anglo-Celtic Australian-born Muslims. The multicultural mosque was the principal space for reconstructing Muslim religious identity and solidarity. Sydney Muslim interviewees, all of Bangladesh origin, belonged to the religious Bangladesh Islamic Centre of New South Wales, and to ethnocultural and secular organizations: the Bangladesh Association of Australia and the Australia-Bangladesh Friendship Society. Secular ethnocultural organizations created spaces for reconstructing ethnic identity, dialogue and participation with other migrants and native-born Australians as civic and social Australian citizens.

A multilingual Muslim Perth woman of Bangladesh origin told a different story of her experience in that city. As a married woman aged 20, she had migrated first to New Zealand, then in 1984 to Sydney, where she lived for six years before moving to Perth. She described her negotiation of religious and cultural identity as a teacher at a Perth university. She belonged to an ethnocultural organization 'to maintain my cultural identity.' At the same time, she socialized not only with her extended family and members of her own cultural group, but also with university colleagues. She described how she chose to present herself in academic space:

> Back home I followed *purdah*. I don't do that now. If people want to maintain their culture, I think that they should stay (in their home country) instead of trying to migrate to a western country. It's a very different situation. They have to accept compromises.

Because I was working, I could not maintain *purdah*. I wasn't sure what might happen to my career as a teacher. If I wear a scarf or a veil I am not sure whether my contract will be renewed or not. They wouldn't say that. They would give other reasons. I had to abandon it because of my work. I do not want to jeopardize my work. I do wear the veil and long skirts, but at work no. There are many women here from Malaysia and Singapore. But I can't take the risk without their support. I need the women's support. It's hard for women to get jobs – especially in accounting.

This Australian Muslim woman feared racist discrimination in her academic career. At the same time, she recognized the power of women's collective political anti-racist citizenship. She compared responses to cultural and racial differences in a smaller city, Perth, to that in the very large Sydney metropolis:

One of the most difficult things for a migrant woman is the attitude of people towards migrant people. In Perth people are not open. They sometimes even look at you with suspicion, sometimes amounting to unfriendliness. I didn't find that in Sydney. I find people in Perth more conservative. Even at work, when I came here first, I felt that people seemed to think, 'They are taking our jobs.' When I went to University, colleagues would ask, 'What sort of a degree do you have? Where did you get it?' If I were not qualified, I wouldn't have been given the job. [The reason] could be that there are fewer migrants in Perth. Even in five years time, there are more people here than in 1990. It's changing here.

In this Muslim woman's opinion, greater concentration of Asian migrant women of colour who engage in exchange and activities in various spaces with native-born Australians, together with anti-racist and anti-sexist collective action, are likely to reduce discrimination.

Women's Advocacy Organization

In the majority of ethnoreligious, ethnocultural and secular community organizations, patriarchal gender roles and structures prevailed. Men, not women, were in positions of power and prestige as leaders and office-bearers in worship and organization. The Maritime Sikh Society at Halifax was exceptional. After the interviews were completed, it elected an all-woman executive that was responsible for all temple-related activities and management. Many feminist critics argue that women are disempowered in most South Asian ethnocultural organizations. Members of the Maritime Sikh Society who settled in Halifax in the early 1970s disagreed. Interviewees claimed that holding executive positions was related more to willingness to work than power. While proclaiming strong Sikh identity and community, members also identify and participate with the larger Atlantic Canada society. The Halifax *gurdwara* is open to visitors of all faiths and to students who come to learn about Sikhism – and to enjoy a free meal after the service.

The impact of differences in density of population and concentration of South Asians on women's lives, identity construction, and citizenship participation is nowhere more evident than in the women's advocacy organization. Forty per cent of British Columbia interviewees and 16 per cent of Australian interviewees belonged to women's organizations. In Atlantic Canada, I found only one autonomous South Asian women's organization in a small town outside metropolitan Halifax. The association was a secular service-oriented organization that crossed religious and cultural boundaries by celebrating festivals of its various members. Over the years, the association's activities expanded beyond cultural education of children to include financial donations to support a battered women's society and educational toys for children in Nova Scotia hospitals, and education of poor Indian children or Mother Teresa's care of destitute Indians. The members thus acknowledged their hybrid Canadian and Indian identity and at the same time practised civic and social citizenship as Nova Scotians and as women of South Asian origins.

Although women's organizational activities in all regions were mainly service-oriented, there was evidence of women's advocacy-oriented organizations in Melbourne (for instance, the Sri Lanka Tamil advocates) and Sydney, and, especially in British Columbia. One might speculate as to why Atlantic Canada women and British Columbia women were so different in organizational activities. The most obvious reason is the lack of a critical mass for collective organization in Atlantic Canada. South Asian immigrant women in Atlantic Canada are very isolated from each other, especially in the long, hard winter months. Moreover, as I have described above, even in the largest metropolis, Halifax, there are few South Asian women of a specific cultural group.

By contrast with Atlantic Canada, there is a high level of gender and race awareness in British Columbia, especially in Vancouver, a city with a large population of ethnically and racially diverse immigrant people, as well as a high concentration of women of South Asian origins. Furthermore, British Columbia South Asians have historical memory of Sikh organizations and resistance against rampant racism and sexism in government policies and among white British Columbia settlers in the early twentieth century (Johnston 1979). Social and political participation among South Asian women is high in Vancouver. Creative and competent women have attracted other women to collective activity and resistance around race and gender justice issues. Middle-class South Asian immigrant women organized advocacy groups to promote awareness, education, and change among men and among working-class grass roots women. Areas of specific concern are violence against women, reproductive technology and amniocentesis clinics, English-language training, and recognition of foreign credentials and experience, race discrimination in housing and paid work experience.

The India Mahila Association (IMA) is an outstanding example of a Vancouver women's advocacy organization. IMA has engaged in both service-oriented and advocacy-oriented activities with no government funding over its 30-year history. Its goal is stated as follows,

> The objective of the organization is to fight racism and sexism in society and in particular address issues affecting South Asian women living in Canada. Violence against women

is of major concern to us and we are committed to eliminating it. The guiding principles of IMA are to empower women and promote the unifying aspects of our culture while challenging those that devalue women. (IMA 1994: 10)

IMA has conducted educational and advocacy work. It has produced and participated in proactive radio and television programmes dealing with issues of particular concern to South Asian Canadian women: arranged marriages, dowry, prenatal sex selection, violence against women, and challenges faced by young women of South Asian origin. It conducted a study of spousal abuse with a view to proactive response to violence, transformative action, egalitarian family relations and greater empowerment of women of South Asian origin.

British Columbia South Asian women's organizations have conducted protest marches in South Asian markets, criticized South Asian newspapers for publishing advertisements for sex-selection clinics and gender-discriminatory articles, produced television and radio programmes, lobbied provincial and federal members of parliament, and sought active support from mainstream women's organizations. They have also used social situations like banquets, festival celebrations and temple gatherings for weddings and birthdays to enlist the support of gender-conscious husbands in presenting skits that raise consciousness to specific aspects of violence against women. In these spaces, whole families are educated to awareness that such abuses against women are reprehensible. In sum, many British Columbia South Asian Canadian women are highly organized proactive civic, social and political citizens who resist racism and sexism in family, community and society.

In Melbourne and Sydney, some women's advocacy organizations actively lobbied governments for appropriate services for women; other groups had proactive anti-sexist and anti-racist goals; others took steps to raise consciousness among women and men through dialogue and media presentations. I found no evidence of such organization or activities in Perth.

In Sydney, 12 women who recognized that women did not have adequate support services started an organization called Shakti in 1991. The group expanded to 23 members and lasted for about three years. My informant described its activities and life history as follows,

We offered referral services; for example, what to do if they needed housing or dole (welfare) payments, where to go for a crisis centre if there was domestic violence. (Shakti) was not well received by women as well as men. There was a lot of flack, especially from men. Indian women don't 'hang their washing out.' The standard is 'What do the neighbours think?' That's what they are concerned about. For the Indian community 'social standing' is very important. Our greatest achievement was that we raised awareness about the needs of people rather than saying, 'Indians always support other Indians, so we don't need an organization like that.' As a result, two Indian welfare organizations were formed later. There were few willing to accept that we started stirring the pot. We came from the women's perspective rather than the Indian perspective. We offered them options. 'What do *you* want to do?' Men were upset that women were actually getting up, making a noise and saying what they wanted. Women were frightened by the change that would occur in their families. Men felt threatened by our existence. Sometimes I still get calls from women in abusive situations. We advise them to access mainstream services.

The description of Shakti's short life illustrates several important points besides proactive, anti-sexist civic and social citizenship of a small advocacy organization. It highlights the steps taken to raise consciousness through dialogue and media activities. It describes the value-system of at least some Indian migrant families. It suggests that any challenge or change to family relations, structures and values is threatening, not only to men but also to women who may lose family status and security. It also raises an important question that is beyond the scope of this chapter, namely, whether abused women are better served by ethnospecific organizations or by mainstream organizations.

Conclusion

Citizenship is a key concept for understanding South Asian immigrant women's agency in identity reconstruction, resistance to discrimination and oppression, and organizational participation. Through participation in community organizations South Asian immigrant women raise their collective consciousness of racism, sexism and other forms of oppression, reconstruct their identity in positive terms and practise their multidimensional citizenship. By doing all of the above they demonstrate their agency. The research has indicated that population density and concentration of South Asians of specific ethnic, religious and linguistic identities in settlement spaces facilitated the formation and activities of organizations, both service and advocacy-oriented. On the other hand, where there were few South Asians of specific ethnic and religious identities, overarching secular organizations such as the Indo-Canadian Association of Nova Scotia (INCA), the Fiji-Canadian Organization of British Columbia, and the Australia Indian Society, served to unite South Asians of diverse cultural origins. Such organizations provided diasporic spaces for transversal dialogue and citizenship practice among these diverse South Asians, other immigrants and native-born Canadians or Australians. Moreover, women's collective consciousness of racism, sexism and other forms of oppression, formed in part through organizing, impelled them to resistance, advocacy and transformative action. Through organized collective agency South Asian women engaged in civic, social and political citizenship for empowerment and justice in family, community and society.

References

Agnew, V. (1996), *Resisting Discrimination: Women from Asia, Africa, and the Caribbean and the Women's Movement in Canada*, University of Toronto Press, Toronto, Buffalo, London.
Agnew, V. (1993), 'Community Groups: an Overview,' Paper presentation, Biennial

Canadian Ethnic Studies Association Conference, Vancouver, 27-30 November.

Bannerji, H. (ed.) (1993), *Returning the Gaze: Essays on Racism, Feminism and Politics*, Sister Vision Press, Toronto.

Bottomley, G. (1991), 'Culture, ethnicity, and the politics/poetics of representation,' *Diaspora*, Vol. 1(3), pp. 303-320.

Brah, A. (1996), *Cartographies of Diaspora: ContestingIidentities*, Routledge London, New York.

BIMPR (Bureau of Immigration, Multicultural and Population Research) (1995), *Community Profiles 1991 Census*, Government Publishing Service, Canberra, Australia.

Careless, J.M.S. (1987), '"Limited identities" in Canada,' in C. Berger (ed.), *Contemporary Approaches to Canadian History*, Copp Clark Pitman Ltd., Toronto, pp. 5-12.

Castles, S. and Davidson, A. (2000), *Citizenship and Migration: Globalization and the Politics of Belonging*, Routledge, New York.

Hobson, B. and Lister, R. (2002), 'Citizenship,' in B. Hobson, J. Wilson and B. Siim (eds), *Contested Concepts in Gender and Social Politics*, Edward Elgar, Cheltenham UK, Northampton, MA, USA, pp. 23-54.

hooks, b. (1990), *Yearning: Race, Gender and Cultural Politics*, Between the Lines, Toronto.

IMA (India Mahila Association) (1994), *Spousal Abuse: Experiences of 15 Canadian South Asian Women*, A Report by India Mahila Association, authors: Raminder Dosanjh, Surinder Deo, Surjeet Sidhu, Vancouver.

Johnston, H. J. M. (1979), *The Voyage of the Komagata Maru: the Sikh Challenge to Canada's Colour Bar*, Oxford University Press, Delhi.

Jupp, J. (1992), 'Immigrant settlement policy in Australia,' in G. P. Freeman and J. Jupp (eds), *Nations of Immigrants: Australia, the United States, and International Migration*, Oxford University Press, Melbourne, pp. 130-44.

Lanphier, M. and Lukomskyj, O. (1994), 'Settlement policy in Australia and Canada,' in H. Adelman, A. Borowski, M. Burstein and L. Foster (eds), *Immigration and Refugee Policy: Australia and Canada Compared*, Melbourne University Press, Carlton, Victoria, Vol. II., pp. 337-71.

Lister, R. (1997), 'Citizenship: towards a feminist synthesis,' *Feminist Review*, Vol. 57, pp. 28-48.

Marshall, T. H. (1950), *Citizenship and Social Class*, Cambridge University Press, Cambridge.

Pettman, J. (1992), *Living in the Margins: Racism, Sexism and Feminism in Australia*, Allen and Unwin, North Sydney.

Ralston, H. (1998), '"Crossing the Black Water:" Alienation and Identity among South Asian Immigrant Women,' in D. Kalekin-Fishman (ed.), *Designs for Alienation: Exploring Diverse Realities*, SoPhi Press, University of Jyväskyla, Finland, pp. 152-70.

Ralston, H. (1994), 'Immigration policies and practices: their impact on South Asian women in Canada and Australia,' *Australian-Canadian Studies*, Vol. 12(1), pp.

1-4.

Rubenstein, K. (2001), 'Citizenship in Australia' in J. Jupp (ed.), The Australian People: An Encyclopedia of the Nation, its People and their Origins, Cambridge University Press, Cambridge, pp. 762-64.

Statistics Canada (1993), Ethnic Origin: The Nation. 1991 Census of Canada, (Catalogue 93-315), Industry, Science and Technology Canada, Ottawa.

Yuval-Davis, N. (2001), 'World Conference Against Racism (WCAR) and the Politics of Belonging,' Paper presentation, BSA conference, SOAS, London, 14 September 2001.

Yuval-Davis, N. (1997), 'Ethnicity, gender relations and multiculturalism,' in P. Werbner and T. Modood (eds), Debating Cultural Hybridity: Multi-cultural Identities and the Politics of Racism, Zed Books, London, New Jersey, pp. 193-208.

Yuval-Davis, N. (1994), 'Women, ethnicity and empowerment,' in K. Bhavnani and A. Phoenix (eds), Special issue on 'Shifting Identities, Shifting Racisms,' Feminism and Psychology, Vol. 4(1), pp. 179-97.

Chapter 9

Gender, Migration and Citizenship: Immigrant Women and the Politics of Belonging in the Canadian Maritimes

Evangelia Tastsoglou

Introduction and Conceptual Framework

And you? Did you change your name somewhere along the way? Does a part of you live hundreds or thousands of kilometres away? Do you have two countries, two memories? Do you have a border zone? (Verdecchia 1993: 77)

Migration is not just a geographical move from one country to another. It involves more than crossing geographical borders, settling in a new land or even acquiring citizenship in the technical sense. As Mexican writer and intellectual Carlos Fuentes (1985) reminds us, a border is more than just the division between two countries; it is also the division between two cultures and two memories. Above all, migration involves crossing cultural boundaries, experiencing another culture, and making a new home in a new country, with all the internal transformations on the self that such processes entail. Unlike spatial borders that are relatively static and fixed, at least over a period of time, cultural borders are fluid and shifting. As another Latin American writer, Guillermo Verdecchia, exclaims, 'On all sides [of the border] I have been asked: How long have you been ...? How old were you when ... ? When did you leave? When did you arrive? As if it were somehow possible to locate on a map, on an airline schedule, on a blueprint, the precise coordinates of the spirit, of the psyche, of memory' (Verdecchia 1993: 51).

In this chapter, the term borderlands is used to encompass an entire cultural and mental area cutting across territorial boundaries and often extending over multiple physical locations (nationally and transnationally). Avtar Brah's (1996) concept of the 'diaspora' is very similar. Brah defines the term as networks of transnational identification encompassing 'imagined' and 'encountered' communities or as 'multi-locationality within and across territorial, cultural and psychic boundaries' (1996: 196-97).[1] In the same vein, Appadurai (1991) uses the term 'ethnoscapes' to refer to

---

1   Brah's definition of diaspora as 'multi-locationality' is different from Soysal's definition of the same term as based on the nation-state model and level of analysis and involving bi-directional economic, political, and cultural transactions (2000: 3). Both Shuval

social formations connecting people, actually or potentially, living in different parts of the world, regardless of the actual location of 'home.' Immigrants in Canada live for the most part on a fluid cultural and mental borderland between Canada's politically dominant culture,[2] their socially constructed ethnic communities, other socially constructed immigrant and ethnic communities as well as various transnational 'encountered' and 'imagined' communities. Making contact and working politically with others as allies from such a position is a possibility, not a certainty, because, as Brah argues, 'diasporic or border positionality does not in itself assure a vantage point of privileged insight into and understanding of relations of power, although it does create a space in which experiential mediations may intersect in ways that render such understandings more readily accessible. It is essentially a question of politics' (Brah 1996: 207). This special fluid and liminal zone, this cultural and mental borderland, is 'home' for many of Canada's immigrants.

In this chapter the point of departure is that Canada as a country of immigrants, of multiple and overlapping diasporas, is a borderland, a space where cultural affinities are being negotiated in an ongoing way. Furthermore, following Gloria Anzaldua's (1987) theorization of border as a metaphor for psychological, sexual, spiritual, cultural, class and racialized boundaries,[3] Canada can be conceptualized as a borderland and a 'diasporic space' (Brah) not only for its immigrants but for its native-born as well. In a diasporic space 'the native is as much a diasporian as the diasporian is a native' and a native can become terrorized, alienated and dislocated within her own home (Brah 1996). Both inhabit positions of 'multi-axial locationality' defined as a 'simultaneous situatedness within gendered spaces of class, racism, ethnicity, sexuality, age' (Brah 1996: 204). How each group/individual moves across shifting cultural, religious and linguistic boundaries depends on their 'politics of location,' their politics of belonging. Yet, multi-axial locationality does not predetermine the subject position nor the direction of the movement (Brah 1996: 205).

More specifically, this chapter empirically explores the ongoing negotiation of cultural affinities, that is the cultural border crossings of immigrant women[4] in the Maritime region of Canada, multi-axially located within and across imagined and encountered state communities and gendered spaces of class, racism, ethnicity, sexuality and age. Ultimately this ongoing negotiation of cultural affinities, this politics of belonging, though influenced by the multi-axial locationality of the subject

---

(2000) and Bhatia and Ram (2001) also base their notions of diaspora on commitments to and transactions with a historic homeland.

2   In Kymlicka's (1995: 76) definition of 'societal culture' of which there are actually two in Canada, the English and the French.

3   For a critical review of the sociological literature on the concepts of 'borders' and 'boundaries' see Tastsoglou (2000: 98-121).

4   The term immigrant women combines legal and social criteria in this study and refers to women who 1) have permanent resident status (or acquired citizenship) and 2) belong to a racialized minority group or do not speak English well or have English as a second language (Miedema and Tastsoglou 2000: 83; Tastsoglou and Miedema 2003: 206).

is not determined by it, as the subject position is not pre-determined either. Avtar Brah (1996: 193) makes a distinction between 'feeling at home' and staking a claim to a place as one's own. It is possible to feel 'at home' in a place and, yet, not to claim it as one's own as a result of social exclusion but to claim, instead, another place and identity as one's own, though one may have never been in the place one claims or know very little about it. The immigrant women represented in this study may assert that they feel 'at home' in Canada (and feel quite connected to this country), though Canada is not their 'home' (or only home) nor their primary identity (or their identity), i.e., they can also stake a claim to another country as their 'home,' or immigrant women may also declare Canada as their 'home.' Moreover, the same women may embody both of these positions at different moments, depending on the politics at play under given sets of circumstances. In any case, for migrants or members of a diaspora 'home' is often multi-placed, 'multi-locational' (Brah 1996: 197).

Anthias uses the concept of 'translocational positionality' to refer to a complex 'positionality' faced by those at the intersection of multiple locations in relation to class, gender, racialization[5] and national belonging mainly. 'Positionality' in turn is an intermediate term between structure and agency, involving not just locations but also how individuals intersubjectively organize and represent or perform identification (Anthias 2002: 501-02). As such, the term 'translocational positionality' is close but not identical to multi-axial locationality and the politics of belonging. The latter refers first to what subjects do as a result of belonging and, second to what subjects do in order to foster belonging. This active component of 'politics' may be organization and representation or performance of identification (i.e. 'positionality') but it may involve civic engagement and political action well beyond performance of identification. It is this broader meaning of 'politics' that is being deployed here.

The aim of this chapter[6] is threefold:[7] 1) To examine the meaning of 'home' for immigrant women in the Maritime region of Canada, or the experience of living

---

5   Racialization is being broadly defined as the process of socially constructed 'otherness' and social exclusion based thereupon. Racialization intersects with other forms of social division (see especially, Bolaria and Li 1988; Li 1999; Satzewich 1990, 1992; Stasiulis 1999; Jakubowski 1997).

6   This chapter is based on data collected in a larger study about immigrant women's organizing and integration in the Maritimes (Tastsoglou and Miedema 2000, 'Immigrant Women Organizing for Change: Integration and Community Development by Immigrant Women in the Maritimes') funded by the Prairie Centre of Excellence for Research on Immigration and Integration (PCERII). Special thanks to my research assistant on this paper, Jill Murphy.

7   The empirical research on which this chapter is based was carried out during the winter and spring of 1998 in two Maritime cities. Semi-structured interviews with 40 immigrant women were conducted, transcribed and analyzed using QSR NU*DIST. Participants were identified through a snowball sampling method. They were immigrant women (as defined in the project) who had been in Canada for at least five years and had arrived after the age of 16. The researchers aimed at geographical and ethno-cultural heterogeneity as much as

between cultures (the experience of the cultural and mental space of the borderlands located in the Maritimes) that is, border crossings as experience. Such experiences, sometimes but not always, lead to claiming the Maritimes and/or Canada as 'home.' Part of the experience of living in a diaspora located in Canada, is how the immigrant women imagine/have learnt to think about Canada. Border crossings as experience refers then to the structure of belonging. 2) To examine the social processes and practices by which immigrant women come to feel comfortable and 'at home' in the Maritimes, especially the social relations and networks they create and engage for that purpose as well as what they do as a result of their particular sense of belonging, that is border crossings as processes and practices. Both exist in a dialectical relationship, mutually reinforcing each other, and both refer to their politics of belonging. 3) To examine the effect of cultural border crossings on self and identity, i.e. border crossings as individual identity shifts. More specifically, in this case I examine identity shifts as and through immigrant women's perceptions and narratives of self-change. By doing so, I assume identity not as a possessive property of individuals but as a process that is actively and intersubjectively performed through their narratives of change (Anthias 2002: 498-501). Gender, race, ethnicity, class, age are the most important locational axes and identity markers that are being utilized to interpret particular practices and actions, i.e. the politics of belonging for the immigrant women of this study.

By focusing on these questions, this chapter addresses the psychological dimension of citizenship, i.e. citizenship as a sense of belonging, emotional attachment and identification (Carens 2000: 166). To what geo-political community do immigrant women feel they belong? Is it Canada, is it their countries of birth, is it their ancestral and imagined homelands? What does 'home' mean for immigrant women beyond geo-political communities or independently of them? Is belonging an either/or question, or is a new topography of belonging required, one that is based on a multi-locational conception of 'home?' What are the consequences of belonging in each case? What does 'belonging' mean to the immigrant women in this study? What are their politics of belonging and how are they affected by (and, in turn, impact on) their multi-axial location? What are the implications of immigrant women's politics of belonging for Canadian citizenship specifically? What are the directions for citizenship theory that multi-axial locationality and the politics of belonging imply?

Carens (2000: 168) makes it clear that, as (legal) citizenship is a 'threshold concept,' psychological affiliation should have no bearing on rights, as there might be native Canadians who do not feel any emotional attachment to Canada. However,

---

possible and ensured inclusion of racialized women as well. Owing to the qualitative nature of this study no attempt is made to generalize from these findings to all immigrant women in the Maritimes, much less so to all immigrant women in Canada. Overall the immigrant women who participated in this study were highly educated, with highly educated spouses and with higher than average family incomes (Miedema and Tastsoglou 2000; Tastsoglou and Miedema 2000, 2003, 2005).

the conception of citizenship focused on here is about the feelings of belonging and politics based thereupon of individuals vis-à-vis the state and not the latter's recognition of individuals as citizens. On a normative level, Taylor and Laforest (1993: 182-83) argue for a 'deep diversity' model of citizenship in Canada, a form of differentiated citizenship, compatible with multiple, largely overlapping and yet distinct, emotional and political attachments and practices and 'simultaneous situatedness' of Canada's citizens on different levels of collectivities. Although Taylor refers to the Quebecois and Aboriginal peoples, his model has broader implications for various ethnic collectivities. Over and above the nation state, Soysal points to a similar model based on simultaneous situatedness through her 'postnational membership' (1994), another form of differentiated citizenship. In the case of Muslim migrants in the European Union, she argues, the logic of the 'national order of things,' the level of the nation-state as a unit of analysis, has been superseded by the very practice and geography of citizenship and belonging (Soysal 2000: 1-3). Such practice operates at both local and postnational (EU) levels for Muslim migrants.

Beyond the national and postnational levels, feminist theorists have introduced other models of differentiated citizenship aimed at overcoming not only nation-state bounded notions of citizenship but also gender-based binaries such as the private versus public dichotomy; taking into account diversity and difference; as well as reconciling individual and collective rights. Lister's (1997: 28) 'differentiated universalism' and Yuval-Davis' (1997: 88) 'transversal dialogue,' 'transversal politics' and 'dialogical transversal citizenship' (Yuval-Davis 2002: 45) are based on the assumption of simultaneous situatedness of women in various levels of collectivities. Werbner and Yuval-Davis (1999: 5) have re-interpreted Marshall's citizenship theory by arguing that it provides a framework for allowing for multicultural citizenship (i.e., collective rights) and even interlocking citizenship at different levels of collectivities of which the nation-state is only one.

As other research (Goldring 2000; Jones-Correa 2000) has underlined the transnational and gendered dimensions of citizenship practices in the social and political arenas, this research points to the direction of transnational and gendered citizenship for migrant women in the psychological and cultural spheres. As the 'deep diversity' and 'postnational' and feminist citizenship models are based on and legitimating 'simultaneous situatedness' of legal, civic, political and social rights and practices, evidence provided by this research suggests that a similar articulation of belonging, of the psychological dimension of citizenship, is based on and legitimating multi-axial locationality and 'simultaneous situatedness' within and across imagined and encountered communities, state and otherwise. This research indicates that multiple and overlapping spatial and symbolic attachments of various degrees of complexity are the rule among immigrant women who demonstrate multi-dimensional geographies of belonging and citizenship, involving political and cultural practices, at the local, national and transnational levels. Such attachments and practices are eclectic, synthetic, syncretic, hybrid and multi-directional (as opposed to bi-directional ethnic transactions).

As feminist theory, migration theory and transnational theories have demonstrated, gender plays a major role in both the migration process (Kelson and DeLaet 1999; Anthias and Lazaridis 2000; Kofman et al. 2000; Willis and Yeoh 2000) and the practice of citizenship (Stolcke 1997; Yuval-Davis 1997; Ackers 1998; Isin and Wood 1999; Werbner and Yuval-Davis 1999; Goldring 2000; Jones-Correa 2000; Hobson and Lister 2002). I argue in this chapter that gender plays a major role in identification and the politics of belonging, and that the psychological dimension of citizenship is as deeply gendered as the legal, political, civic, social and economic ones. Overall, as DeLaet (1999: 2) asserts, 'female migration is neither driven exactly by the same determinants as male migration nor do women experience migration in precisely the same way as men.' More specifically, the sense of belonging is a unique one for women because of their gender-based roles in families and the so-called private sphere: as care-givers for the younger and older generations they tend to come more in contact with extended families, locally, nationally and transnationally (Salaff 1997; Alicea 1997). In addition, they tend to interface more with school boards and social service providers with very different consequences than men in terms of involvement, political participation and longer-term commitment to the society where they have settled (Jones-Correa 2000). Furthermore, in their role as guardians of ethnic cultures, they are more involved with heritage language instruction and thus responsible for the construction, maintenance and transmission of ethnic identity (Tastsoglou 1997). These gender-based differences make it likely that immigrant women will sustain stronger forms of identification with both families overseas and local communities – ethnic and otherwise – in Canada. In addition, another consequence of gender roles and practices has been for immigrant women to be less employed than immigrant men and more underemployed or unemployed, making it more likely for women to be economically and professionally marginalized and non-integrated (Tastsoglou and Preston forthcoming). Both economic and professional integration especially are important venues for successful integration and feeling 'at home' in Canada (Miedema and Tastsoglou 2000). Although I focus on the experiences of women specifically in this research, I consider experiences, practices and politics of belonging as outcomes of distinct gender roles in the migration process.

A final note as far as the significance and possible impact of the Maritime region of Canada on immigrant women's sense of belonging. Owing to its low rates of immigration compared with other Western and Central Canadian provinces, less diversity characterizes the Maritime region and especially its urban centres, compared with major metropolitan centres in Canada. As a result, Maritime cities generally do not have 'institutionally complete' (Breton 1964) communities. The lack of such communities increases the likelihood for immigrants and women in particular to feel isolated and under more pressure to conform. In addition, lower income and economic prosperity levels, coupled with higher rates of unemployment historically, are more likely to reinforce feelings of alienation, and lower levels of commitment, as those manifested by the high rates of immigrants who leave the Maritimes shortly after their arrival.[8] In short, without multi-locationality of 'home' and the sense of belonging being in any way unique issues of immigrants in the Maritime region of Canada, they are expected to appear in a sharper and more polarized form. However, comparative analysis only can confirm this plausible hypothesis.

The Findings

Living in the Borderlands

For the most part, the immigrant women of this study lead comfortable lives in Canada, though they feel caught between two (and, occasionally, several) cultures and communities on the local, national and transnational levels. This 'in-between' space makes for an uneasy habitat, one that is often fraught with conflict. It renders these immigrant women outsiders in both places, their country of residence which they highly appreciate but cannot feel they fully belong to (even if they try), and their country(ies) of origin from where they feel increasingly, though not guiltlessly, alienated, yet in strange ways perceive as 'home,' as the place where they belong. Many immigrant women in this study are aware that they occupy this space where they are pushed and pulled between cultures and have accepted it as a fact of life. Canadian-educated and of European background, Irene has found it hard to adjust to life in Canada. Part of the problem has been her lack of success in finding full-time employment, but the cultural differences loom much larger:

> Well, in a way I've adjusted, I can say I have a family and we have a house and we have work and we live our lives somehow. But I don't think I will ever adjust fully... into Canadian society. I don't think it will ever happen. Maybe if I immigrated to Canada when I was a child and I spent my childhood and teenage years and I had friends and I spoke the language properly. But I will always feel like a foreigner and I don't think it's something to do with me. Because many people, many friends that I talk to they feel the same way.

---

8   Based on the percentage of immigrants as a total of the population, the Maritime provinces of Canada, i.e. Nova Scotia (with a total population of 932,400), New Brunswick (with 749,900), and Prince Edward Island (with 136,700), are not a preferred destination (Statistics Canada 2003a). In 2001, 4.6 per cent of Nova Scotia, 3.1 per cent of New Brunswick and 3.1 of Prince Edward Island populations indicated that they were foreign born; the rate for Canada was 18.4 per cent (Statistics Canada 2003b). Of Canada's 229,091 immigrants in 2002, Nova Scotia's total share was 0.62 per cent, New Brunswick's 0.31 per cent and P.E.I. 0.05 per cent, while Ontario received 58.34 per cent, British Columbia 14.84 per cent and Quebec 16.43 per cent (Citizenship and Immigration Canada 2003). The Maritime provinces have been among the poorest regions of Canada, with higher unemployment rates than the Canadian average. For example, in May 2004 (Statistics Canada 2004) while the latter stood at 7.2 per cent, Nova Scotia had an unemployment rate of 8.9 per cent, New Brunswick a rate of 10.00 per cent and P.E.I. a rate of 12.6 per cent.

And I think it's natural. I don't think we can ever get rid of it because we, I mean, we left, you know, so much luggage behind us... it's just impossible (laugh).[9]

The women are aware that going back to their countries of origin will not resolve the conflict they experience knowing so well two cultures, only one of which is really legitimated as the 'right' way to be, know and feel. Ingrid immigrated to Canada many years ago and holds a Canadian University degree. Ingrid, factually and rationally, describes the transition from the emotional turmoil of nostalgia for her native country to a peculiar process of shifting allegiances, mentally going back and forth between her country of origin and Canada and starting to feel less critical towards Canada and more sceptical about the realities of her native Norway. Interestingly, this transition took effect the moment that she and her husband decided to 'go back home' in the near future upon his early retirement. It is this shifting that, paradoxically, proves that Ingrid belongs to both 'homes' and yet to no one in particular.

> As soon as that had been decided that we are going to do it, I feel I have been starting to look at Norway in a different, a little bit different light, and a much more relaxed light. It is like I now have the option and I'm starting to appreciate Canada even more, you know ... I am finding now I am mainly more and more concerned about how I will be in Norway because there are things there that I don't like and how am I going to be able to live with that?

Regardless of whether these immigrant women state they have 'adjusted' to living in Canada or not – and adjustment has obviously different meanings for different women – their descriptions of the mental space they inhabit 'in-between' reflect some systematic patterns. Some women even construct their own mental balance sheet where they list and assess the advantages and disadvantages of living in Canada versus living in their country of origin. This balance sheet demonstrates how aware they are of the unique ways of living and being in different cultures. They aim at a minimum level of pragmatic 'adjustment,' just enough to allow themselves to live in Canada while at the same time sustaining and reproducing in the Maritimes ethno-cultural identities inspired from their countries of origin. Often, as 'cultural entrepreneurs' (Bhachu 1996: 300), they select the values and practices they appreciate most from cultures they have experienced, thereby creating new cultural syncretisms[10] (Papastergiadis 2000: 125-27) or hybrid states of mind and living (Hall 1992: 310-14; Papastergiadis 2000: 168-95).[11] By doing so, they at the same time (i) reaffirm possibly suppressed heritages; (ii) challenge

---

9   Interviews have been minimally edited for clarity.

10   Although its literal meaning may have been different, the term syncretism historically refers to the union of communities and religions *(Catholic Encyclopedia on CD- ROM)*. The most frequent use of the term has been in the sociological analysis of religion.

11   Papastergiadis emphasizes the difference between S. Hall's and H. Bhabha's notion of 'hybridity' from that of G. C. Spivak. For the latter hybridity does not and should not refer to the subaltern in the Third World but only to diasporic communities in the First World

the hegemony of the dominant culture; (iii) reaffirm allegiance and belonging to multiple countries thus transgressing the boundaries of the nation-state; and (iv) engage in citizenship practices locally that derive however from transnational levels. Isadora, with a Canadian university degree, married to a Canadian-born, and living in comfortable material circumstances, vividly describes her experience of living in the borderlands:

Isadora: The sense of community here is different. Than it is in my home country ... There are things like the family. You know, I love to have my boy sleeping in my bed (pause). You know, there are those are things that I don't want to give up. I don't want to put my, my baby in a different room (pause). You know in my country, kids sleep with the parents (pause). In my country, children go to bed when their parents go to bed. And here, you know, children go to bed at a certain age and at a certain time, and that's, you know, a rule ... I like to be able to give a hug to my friends. I like to touch, you know. And here people are more (pause) distant, you know, it's something that unless you're family, you probably do [not do] that ... And those are things that, you know, I like. About my culture (pause). But there are things like machismo, for instance. That's something I had such a hard time in my own country, you know, that I rebelled against. When I was there. And here is (pause) women, I don't know, they have (pause) advanced in that sense. And so that's what I like about it (laugh). That men work in the kitchen with the women. You know, that's something I like (pause) and so I think, I would like to always have that combination. I mean adjusting to some sort of degree in terms of (pause) that I'm able to live here. You know, but (pause) not to forget my roots and not to (pause) to forget who I am. That I am an indigenous woman from Guatemala.

Some of the women who have successfully 'adjusted,' according to their own set of definitions of life in Canada admit feeling guilty about 'losing' their ethnicity, an interpretation based on a zero-sum conception of ethnicity, but justify themselves by arguing that Canada is ranked as one of the best places in the world to live, despite some pressure to assimilate. Eva is a white, European, university-educated in her home country and was pursuing a second university degree in Canada at the time of the interview. She is middle-class and married:

Eva: And on the other hand I feel like guilty, maybe I'm losing my ethnicity and all, like I should stick with who I am, I'm Slovak basically, but I feel very fortunate to be in Canada, because I have many friends in Europe where they push you to join, to be a part. And, here, they take you as you are. So. It's just my feeling, you know, like it's maybe different for visible minorities or like different for people with different backgrounds. I feel very comfortable here ... from my experience I had all around the world I find it's the best you can have in the world today.

Regardless of their level of 'adjustment,' immigrant women feel that 'adjusting' is a process that unfolds over time and can go on forever. Ingrid, a white European, who has lived for a long time in Canada, describes the processual character of

(Papastergiadis 2000: 188-95). These theoretical debates are beyond the scope of this paper which, in addition, refers to transnational diasporas specifically in Canada.

'adjustment,' as a move from getting used to practical things, such as shopping in supermarkets, getting around in the city, going to school and finding a job, to subtler changes in mentality and ways of thinking and perceiving oneself, a feeling of being more 'at ease' with oneself in Canada. Feeling more at ease with oneself, in some women this translates into increasingly perceiving Canada as 'home.' Another participant, Gurinder, a visible minority[12] woman, describes this shifting meaning of 'home' for her. Her personal process of identification, as that of many other immigrant women's, has been one of gradually shifting attachments, of shifting 'ethnoscapes' (Appadurai 1991).

> Gurinder: I have never ever regretted coming here. I never said oh, it would be nice to go back to India and maybe live there for a few years. But on I go for a two month holiday or something, I am glad to come back. And, there was time in the early years when I would talk, when I would say, we are going home to India. And I don't do that anymore. I find the last few times I've been there I am saying I have this feeling that I'm coming home to Canada, I'm coming home to Fredericton. And I think that shows you how you change.

Alongside those who consider themselves to have 'adjusted' and walk the borderlands with relative ease, there are women who consider themselves not to have 'adjusted' either for lack of time or lack of opportunity in Canada brought about by racialization, the process of social construction of 'otherness' and social exclusion based thereupon. Menen, a visible minority with a Canadian university degree and a community activist who has been fighting racism throughout her life in Canada, lives mentally in her own culture and considers residence in Canada a temporary stage. 'Ethnicity' or ethnic hybridity for visible minority immigrants is not an option, like it might be for white immigrants (Waters 1990), but to a large extent a forced path. Despite a pragmatic political and civic engagement in order to improve circumstances in the 'here and now,' this path is not conducive to feelings of belonging to Canada.

---

12   Members of 'visible minorities' in Canada are defined as 'persons, other than Aboriginal peoples, who are non-Caucasian in race or non-white in color' (*Employment Equity Act of 1995*, Department of Justice Canada http://laws.justice.gc.ca/en/E-5.401/49886.html#rid-49897). According to the guidelines established by the Interdepartmental Working Group on Equity Employment, ten visible minority subgroups are identified: black, South Asian, Chinese, Korean, Japanese, Southeast Asian, Filipino, Other Pacific Islanders, West Asian and Arab, and Latin American (Boyd 1999). Although not many of this study's participants did actually use this technical term 'visible minority,' many had in fact an acute sense of being racialized and discriminated against on various grounds, despite not falling under any of the legal categories. This analysis considers how participants were implicated in ethnic and race relations based on their accounts, over and above the categories recognized in the legal definition of 'visible minorities.' Yet, the analysis retains this category as potentially useful for comparisons with the general population and a general descriptor to refer to those identified by the law (Tastsoglou and Miedema 2005).

Although I'm Canadian in terms of documentation (phone rings) I'll never be Canadian. I never introduce myself as a Canadian, not once. I live here temporarily. Hopefully after I accomplish what I want to accomplish in terms of my education and experience, I'll be going back home (pause). This is not my home (laugh).

While German classical sociologist Georg Simmel introduced the concept of the 'stranger' (Simmel 1950: 402-08) and applied it specifically to migrants, it was American sociologist Robert E. Park (1950: 354) who came up with an explanation for the condition of 'marginality' (the 'marginal man' is his term for Simmel's 'stranger'), the condition of the person who 'lives in two worlds but is not quite at home in either' (Park 1950: 51). For Park, marginality is the result of exclusion, subordination and racism, and, ultimately, of imperialism, economic, political and cultural. More contemporary writers have demonstrated the processes and effects of social exclusion and 'incomplete' or 'lessened' or 'partial' citizenship based on intersecting gender, race, immigrant status and class differences (for example, Ball 2004; Maher 2004; Man 2004; Creese and Kambere 2003; Ehrenreich and Hochschild 2002; Parreñas 2001, 2000; Calliste 2000; Sassen 2000; Pratt 1999; Agnew 1996; Das Gupta 1996; Stasiulis and Yuval-Davis 1995). The case of Cecilia illustrates the relevance of such analyses. As in the case of Menen, social exclusion and racialization greatly interfere and mediate the sense of belonging and home. Cecilia is middle-class, a feminist and political activist. She has not 'adjusted' to life in Canada in part because she has not been allowed to; she is always reminded of her differences from Canadians and is socially excluded because of socially constructed racial difference. Despite that, and unlike Menen, she is accepting of and grateful for many things Canadian. Furthermore, she is capable of using her 'double consciousness' (Werbner 1997: 21) and double vision in assessing Canada as well as her country of origin. Hers is yet another variation of living in the borderlands, encompassing exclusion but also resistance, appreciation of positive elements in the new country but also selective retaining / construction of original cultural identity.

Cecilia: Yeah, name calling simply because we look different... because racism exists in this society. It's also so hard to adjust because I will always be, I mean, I have different thought patterns than I think the white Canadians. Because sometimes when I speak it's different from the way they [would]. I don't know how to adjust here... but it's a move that I have chosen. I mean now, as a single parent I am grateful for it, for what Canada stands for. Like, I know that if my daughter or myself get sick I don't have to worry about where do I get the money to see a doctor, that really hit me when she was sick and I didn't have to think whether I had money in my pocket or not...Her schooling is free which is unheard of where I come from.

Yet another approach to living in the borderlands is expressed by Farzaneh, a well-educated, well-travelled woman from the Middle East, who has not 'adjusted' to life in Canada well but attributes her lack of adjustment to the short time she has been in Canada. In this case, it is her culture and religion that encourage Farzaneh to practice tolerance and to positively value diversity while she is holding fast to her own cultural and religious values. At the same time, she acknowledges that she sees herself as having been 'invited' to 'their country:'

> Farzaneh: For example, (pause) according to our religious idea, we should have, for example, only sexual relations when we are married. Not out of marriage. And here many people have boyfriends and girlfriends. But, (pause) that is a difference of culture. We believe in [our values] ... but, we are not blaming other people for what they are doing. This is their culture or belief and their way of life ... This is their own country (pause). We impose our own [beliefs] on ourselves. They didn't invite us to come.

No matter what their specific experiences of living in Canada, their degree of nostalgia for their countries of origin, and whether or not Canada has fulfilled their expectations, the immigrant women of this study overall think and speak highly about their adopted home. Their ways of seeing and speaking about Canada reflect popular hegemonic ideologies about Canadian values and the role Canada plays in the world, centring on the difference between Canada and the United States. Canada is a 'fantastic country' for Pui Leng, a successful middle-class, multi-lingual and multi-cultural businesswoman, with a post-graduate Canadian university degree, who, despite the obstacles she has had to overcome, considers herself 'very lucky' to be 'here.' Other immigrant women are more specific about the reasons why they appreciate living in Canada. Having come from developing countries or war zones where personal safety and security might be non-existent, many immigrants give Canada high marks for its lawfulness, predictability of life and security. Such views resonate with Canada's traditionally high rank on the United Nations' index of development, which indicates that Canada is one of the best countries in the world in which to live, a primary source of pride for immigrant and non-immigrant Canadians alike (Parkin and Mendelsohn 2003: 10).

Farzaneh, coming from the political turbulence of the Middle East, offers a broader definition of security, as peace and absence of interethnic conflict, and cites the availability of health insurance, public education and protection from poverty that she experienced in her country of origin. The fact, especially, that people from different cultural groups in Canada get along and live in peace, along with state policies on multiculturalism, tolerance, rights and freedoms, are ranked highly among the reasons of pride at being Canadian for immigrant and non-immigrant Canadians alike (Parkin and Mendelsohn 2003: 11). Farzaneh and other women in this study emphasize how they learnt – by positive experience – to be Canadian.

> Farzaneh: Because when you compare the conditions of life in all other places, here is the best place. It has (pause) security (sigh), (pause) better than many other places. And from (pause) health insurance, from education and the way that the people are living with each other, they don't have grudges in their heart of, you know, different, other religious [groups] nationalities and other races. But, here people live in peace with each other and here is a safe country. All the things that are happening in other parts of the world, thank God, they are not happening here, yet. Yeah. Yes I would do it again, yeah. I was not Canadian (laugh). I learned to be Canadian.

For Mei Feng, of middle-class background, a professional with Canadian post-graduate degrees and a community activist, Canada is unique because it attracts some very talented people through a process of self-selection and then offers them opportunities to hone their skills even further. As has often been the case historically, many such individuals may feel confined by social relations in their country of origin that block their social mobility and freedom, and emigrate to Canada because of the opportunities they perceive for upward mobility and forging new social relations. Furthermore, this selective blend of people who live peacefully makes Canada an ideal place to promote world peace:

> I never had any expectations. I think Canada is a good country for immigrants to learn how to fight. I mean, Canada's, besides Native people, the population is still very young. Lots of people come here, with a little bit of an idea about not being satisfied with their old country. And those people are usually more interesting people. So you've got a lot of a potential, interested and capable people as a population... I find it's a good place to develop the idea of world peace. Develop the idea about the genuine peace, how to live in peace in the world, how to get along with neighbours and respect each other.

Politically-minded immigrant women appreciate Canada's role as a peace-keeping, non-interventionist country. Canada's participation in peacekeeping activities around the world is yet another source of pride in being Canadian for both immigrant and non-immigrant Canadians (Parkin and Mendelsohn 2003: 11). Isadora as a political activist is outspoken in her critique of the US politics, which she contrasts with Canadian politics, another aspect of the prevailing Canadian ideology focusing on differences between Canada and the US:

> I think it's a humanitarian, sort of, country ... I don't have as much strong feelings towards (pause) Canadian foreign policies. I'm not saying they're great, by any means, you know (pause), and I'm against a lot, a lot of their policies. But I always compare them with the United States and ... I don't, I don't like the, the Yankee way of (laugh) treatin' other, other communities and other countries. My country has suffered so much because of their foreign policies.

Creating a New Home in Canada

Claiming a 'Voice' for Ethnic Community While the immigrant women of this study may live in the cultural borderlands of Canada and her diverse ethnic cultures, not fully belonging anywhere, they actively participate for the most part in processes and social relations that are intended to secure a measure of comfort for them in Canada, i.e. to make Canada into a new 'home' for them. One of the first steps the immigrant women of this study have taken in order to re-establish the familiar in their adopted home is to make contacts with other immigrants from their country/ culture or origin and, together, to claim their (cultural) voice by organizing cultural activities, setting up a space where they can get together and raising their visibility within the larger community. Following Soysal (2000: 8, 10-11), I argue here that claiming an ethno-cultural 'voice' is not the enactment of an 'ethnicity project' but a citizenship one, since the claim and, perhaps, the funding for this type of organizing often comes from the Canadian state and is couched in a language of Canadian multiculturalism and, ultimately, universal human rights (that include the right to one's cultural identity). Tarvinder has a University degree and is of a professional, middle-class background, though she herself has never worked for pay:

> And so in those days, I think, we started first with education. Working with the teachers. Going to the schools, and talking about our own Indian culture. And I was very busy, I mean, then some of the people were organizing these workshops in multicultural education, especially [Ms. X]. I started working with her in the late 60s. And so, I was going school to school. And so that was a priority and, then, of course, [the second] priority became [to be] organized as a group. Then that's how the Indian Association came and those days, again, the priority was education. Mainly, who we are, what we are contributing. We are going to stay here, we are not going to go ... So those were, I think, very important and exciting days. We started having an India night, and there were six, five, six, seven hundred people coming in the playhouse we used to have once a year, this India night, and, then, they came to know who we are and what we have to share with them, and they appreciated it ... The focus was in those days, in the 60s and 70s cultural, because we had to introduce ourselves.

Community Involvement and Fighting for Social Justice   Getting involved in organizations that fight against racism and for equality and social justice but also in all kinds of voluntary social service organizations is one of the ways by which immigrant women in this study come to gradually feel at home in Canada (Agnew 1996; Bristow 1994; Miedema and Tastsoglou 2000; Tastsoglou and Miedema 2003). A highly educated, middle-class, professional, Mei Feng underlines the importance of doing 'community work,' of getting involved in various causes and organizations in Canadian society and contributing to them in order to improve the life of the community at large. She feels that it was this type of involvement that helped her become a 'real' Canadian citizen:

> One woman who was in my class said, Mrs. [X], can we stop this, can you teach me how to drive? I said no, no I can't teach you to drive. Why don't you go to drivers' school? She said I don't understand them. What's right and left and red light and everything ... I said this is impossible. She said, this class is useless, say John and Mary go to church and get married in the church and all this kind of j- What has this got to do with me? I've got to learn how to drive. Then I realized, that's right, this is a ridiculous textbook. Then I started changing the content of my teaching, I started to teach them how to open bank accounts, how to sign your cheques...I can't teach driving, so I said, I got a driving book, the right, left, amber light and red light and green light, I am gonna teach that sort of thing, okay? Finally, many years later – I didn't teach there anymore – I met her on the street. She ran to me... She said, you remember me? I said of course I remember you (pause). She said, see my car? (laugh) She drove, she said, I have a car! So, I mean, if it's like this, the thing that you have to know is what communities need ... So I became a Canadian citizen by doing community work. A real Canadian citizen by doing community work.

Networking and Friendships The importance of friendship in the process of adjusting to life in a new society is shared by most immigrant women of this study. Friends can be women of the same ethnic origin or other immigrant women whom they often meet in ESL classes or multicultural organizations. Leopoldina, an activist, of middle-class background, pursuing an undergraduate degree in Canada and working in a multi-cultural organization, vividly expresses her joy at meeting people from diverse cultures and getting to know more about their cultures as well as the comfort she finds in meeting other immigrants like herself. Creating networks of friends, who include not only other immigrants from ESL classes and multicultural organizations, but individuals from every environment one comes in contact with, has been a common strategy of survival for many immigrant women in this study and the key to making Canada into a new home. Grace, a visible minority activist, with a Canadian-university degree and a professional certificate from her country of origin, has friends from 'all walks of life,' who can support her in case of need. These are diverse people with whom she has different things in common, including language, geographical origin, minority status, and so forth.

> Grace: So yeah, I've got friends from all from all different walks of life and ... from all different communities ... I have enjoyed it, and I also have the church that I go to, so they are sort of like, more family kind of thing. If I need support or things like that, I'll go there. And I have the Ethiopian Association here in Halifax ... I go there sometimes for different activities and I'm also actively involved there and with my friends who speak my language ... I've diversified myself and so I have friends from all different cultures and different walks of life. I have my academia friends, I have my, you know, all sorts of friends.

Some women stress that they know different people from many different cultures. They feel that they need a variety of people in their lives, but that they are not really friends with all of them. Migration and consequent hybridity appear to heighten reflexivity and facilitate a 'double consciousness' in these women (Werbner 1997: 21), an awareness that one can see things in more than one way, from multiple cultural perspectives, with multiple cultural 'lenses.' Many of the women in this study are aware that they are using multiple cultural lenses and various cultural 'selves.' They suggest that it is impossible to share all of what they are with a single individual. Nevertheless, they need to be able to give a voice to their various selves through these associations with different individuals. Esther, a multi-lingual, multiple migrant of diverse cultural background, who is a professional and a political activist with a Canadian post-graduate degree, seems such a post-modern 'de-centred subject' well aware of her multiple cultural selves (Hall 1992: 285-91):

> Just because I feel I understand their life, and uh, really appreciate who they are. And I really understand the Nova Scotian culture, or the Canadian culture. But I feel that they only know a part of me. My Canadian part. And, not my [other country] part, not my [yet another country] part. Not my American part. So (pause) in that sense, I don't really feel like they really know me completely. But I have a lot of different friends, some of my friends relate to me in certain aspects of my life. While others, to others. So I'm really

lucky I've been blessed with (pause) wonderful friends. And not just here in Canada but, all over the world really.

Sharing and Exchanges across Cultures   Getting involved in multicultural organizations and events, sharing and cultural exchanges across cultures is a fulfilling way of becoming a part of Canadian society, of feeling 'at home' in Canada for many an immigrant woman. Sharing and exchanging across cultures implies a process of negotiation, a give-and-take, where individuals, being exposed to different sets of values and practices, unavoidably assess them and make personal choices as 'cultural entrepreneurs' who choose cultural forms and create new ones (Bhachu 1996: 300). These 'personal' choices are of course contextualized products of time and space occupied by the women of this study in the migration process, where their migration histories and those of their families, as well as codes of peer culture(s), class, and regional location(s) in national and global economies are at play (Bhachu 1996: 300). At the same time, these 'personal' choices are unique syntheses, and, as such, are expressions of human agency and individuality. The end result is new cultural syncretisms or hybridities. The process of negotiating different sets of values and practices is reflected upon by the immigrant women of this study. Connie is a multi-lingual and multi-cultural, a visible minority activist and a professional with a Canadian University degree:

So I think it's that whole ability to juggle and I still do it now. You know, I mean, even after all those years, I think it's a lot of time at one point, trying to figure out, well how much, if you know what I mean, which part of me is Chinese and which part of me has Western (laugh) influences. Because it is that kind of juggling and deciding what you keep and what you decide to change. About yourself and your values and how you do things.

In her 'juggling' of diverse cultural practices Connie becomes a 'translated' person, in the original meaning of the word, which, as Salman Rushdie (1991) notes comes etymologically from Latin for 'bearing across.' Connie inhabits at least two identities and constantly translates and negotiates them.

Exchanges across cultures happen for many women naturally, in the course of everyday life. Immigrant parents, for example, are often exposed to mainstream Canadian beliefs and values through their children. They learn to listen to them, and, in the process, modify their own beliefs and practices, as they make choices about what they think is best for their children. Some of these choices may be very different from what is expected in the countries of origin and reflect the very eclectic and unique amalgams or hybrid behaviours created at the intersections of new and old values and practices. As parents go about making choices that include Canadian values and practices, their sense of belonging to Canada is mediated through parenting. Angela has immigrated to Canada a long-time ago. She is an active volunteer in her ethnic community as well as an activist for various social causes:

Angela: We got the kids, the kids are better here. They got better manners, they got better everything. Than back home. When they go home, they're a little bit different. You can see the difference. But because we're outside here, and we try to keep the culture, we try to keep everythin' and that's how the kids are (pounds surface for emphasis) a little bit different so, even me, I have different ideas. I got now the Canadian mentality, the American how you gonna put it. When I go there, (pause) I don't agree with what they do [back in the country of origin].

Int: For example?

Angela: How I raise my kids. Why don't let your kid go outside all the time? Let's say, or why don't you let your kids smoke? Stuff like that. And we didn't do that here because we were overprotective (pause). Because I was always afraid, you know.

At the same time, in their desire to keep some of the cultural practices and beliefs of their own childhoods intact, the immigrant parents of this study sometimes adhere to them more diligently than their compatriots in the country of origin. The latter are not particularly concerned with keeping their cultural and ethnic identities because where they live such identities are culturally hegemonic:

Angela: Yes. More, yes. Because I have to, I had to teach my kids which is their background, obviously they didn't see it, they were only going to visit Cyprus … The kids back home don't go to church. We go every second Sunday. I don't say every Sunday, but every second Sunday (laugh). You know … we try to keep the culture because we are here. If I was in Greece, it would be different, but because we're here, we try to keep the culture.

Family Ties Another way by which the immigrant women of this study come to feel 'at home' in Canada is, paradoxically, by meticulously sustaining close connections with their families of origin and extended families transnationally no matter what the geographical distance between them. Caring for far away family members is a way of asserting that the immigrant is still connected, still a part of the same yet now multi-local family, and that geographical distance does not imply real, emotional separation. Keeping in close touch is a way by which the immigrant woman restores continuity between her old and new homes, between her old and new selves. In an era of globalization involving rapidly increasing mobility of people across national borders (Castles and Davidson 2000: 7-8) and 'time-space compression' (Harvey 1992) this is not only desirable but also practically more feasible than ever before.[13] It is these extended family networks, in addition to the local friendship and ethnic networks, that make the diasporic identities of this study's immigrant women at once global and local (Brah 1996: 196). The immigrant women of this study all have strong links with their immediate and extended families regardless of where

---

13 This study is based on immigrant women in Canada as defined in the beginning of this chapter (i.e. permanent residents and citizens in terms of legal status) and not on temporary migrants on work visas, including live-in caregivers. The latter are often forced to leave families behind, i.e. to create transnational families, in the new international division of labour in social reproduction (Maher 2004; Parreñas 2002, 2001, 2000; Yeates 2004a and 2004b; Sassen 2002, 2000; Hondagneu-Sotelo and Avila 2000).

the latter are located. They will try to keep in touch with and visit their families of origin, no matter what the distance and economic sacrifice. Immigrant women will try to provide transnational care 'from away,' and even on site by visiting, when care is needed. Kiran, who runs a business with her husband, could not go home to India when her father passed away but sent her sister instead. She was going to visit her family in India, soon after this interview to take care of her mother on site for a while.

> Because if it was winter, business had to be taken care of, children had to be taken care of … I send my sister. She went for six months. She came back, now I'm going because I've got to settle my mom … what they're doing with the house. And look after her too, for awhile.

Links with extended family or families of origin persist over the life-time for the women in this study. Working-class, community volunteer, Angela describes her connection with her country of origin and family:

> So I'm here, 30 some years. You know, actually I lived more years here than back home. But I was always going back home, I never cut the ties from there. You know, all the rest of my family's back there, and my husband's too. So uh, every time I could, every time I had time or had somebody to work at the business … I went back home. That was in the summers when the kids were off school. Take the kids and go. At least every second summer. I was going home.

The links among siblings and the sense of the family members belonging together continue to be strong after migration to Canada for many women in this study, and the material and emotional support are significant factors easing the adjustment process of immigrant women in Canada. Siblings will go out of their way to help the immigrant women with settlement as well as other plans and aspirations. Links between family members persist independently of how dispersed extended families are and how remote the biological affinity.

Under certain circumstances, extended family may even include people who have no biological relation with the immigrant woman. As Cecilia explains:

> An old woman who took care of us, and who was with us for like 45 years. I mean, like (pause) we called her Nanai which is the Filipino word for mother. And she basically raised us up. All eight of us. So my mother could afford to do that. So we called her our heart mother as opposed to our biological mother. If she wasn't around, I think we would all be like (laugh) young offenders (laugh). I mean we all turned out as best as we turned out because, I think, of her. Because when she died in 1993, she was senile and she had her memory gone. But we took care of her. She required 24 hour care. We all went home, I was unemployed. I said I'm going home, I don't care where I am going to get the money I'm going home (laugh). So all of us went home and people were saying, but she was just your maid. She wasn't our maid. She was our mother. And we were all there and they all thought, who is your mother? Because my mother was there as well. I said both of them are (laugh).

The importance of an immediately available family-based support network to immigrant women is underscored by how the immigrant women in this study feel in its absence. In a new country where most of the extended family are often far away, the lack of present extended family and relatives is sorely felt. Angela, for example, has acutely felt the lack of such a family-based support network:

> That's very hard, for us and for the kids later on. Because every time it was something like, you know, they would have friends and they would say, okay, we're going to my aunt's or we're going to my cousin's. We never had anybody. And that was the hardest part of all (pause). You know, coming to Canada, otherwise (pause) nothing else bothered but the family thing. You know.

Labour Market Integration Economic and labour market integration, or the ability to earn a living based on one's own work, especially work that is commensurate with one's qualifications and experience, goes a long way toward helping immigrant women adjust and make a home in Canada (Tastsoglou and Miedema 2005). Family income is not an accurate measure of immigrant women's economic integration (Miedema and Tastsoglou 2000). Volunteer work and community organizing are sometimes seen as means to achieve economic independence (Tastsoglou and Miedema 2003). Volunteer work and even paid employment in community organizations however, despite credentials, is often limited to short-term contracts in the 'multicultural industry.' Those immigrant women who desire to achieve labour market integration resort to a number of strategies, some collective and some individual, including, in their assessment, 'working much harder than Canadian co-workers and always having to prove yourself' (Tastsoglou and Miedema 2005). Ralston's analyses of immigrant women's labour force experiences in both British Columbia and Atlantic Canada support similar conclusions (Ralston 1998: 160-62). In the present study, Cecilia, a successful professional, explains eloquently the reason, mentality and necessity behind immigrant women's need to 'always prove yourself.'

> I also know that, like other minority women in the profession, you tend to work more than you expected to. And you always try to be better than all the rest of them, or even better than what you can do. It's not because you're looking for a promotion, but it's because you're opening other doors for other immigrant women to come in. Or other women of colour. Because if you make a good impression, and they know that you can work as hard, and as good, as anybody else that creates a good impression or will tend to erase stereotypes and make it easier for other women to come into this profession.

Time spent in Canada and professional success with a single employer does not alleviate the burden of having to prove oneself again when one's place of residence or work changes. At the same time, 'proving oneself' is vitally important in terms of feeling 'a part of this society.' Eugenia, Canadian educated, with a professional degree and a visible minority makes this clear: 'Over here [in Canada] you're constantly proving yourself, and unless you stay in a particular place long enough; each place I've gone, I have had to prove that I am good stuff.' In this woman's experience, even finding a job requires more effort from immigrant women than from Canadian-born women. The visible minorities' plight is a more complex and acute one: 'I find that as immigrants we have to work hard. Harder. You know, twice as much as any other woman. To get a job, to be and feel a part of this society.' This woman has no illusions as to why this is the case:

> Eugenia: I think it's the Canadian laws for a multicultural society, and so many things that have developed in order to sort of respond to the needs of people that have been marginalized, are good, but that doesn't mean it's changing a lot. Because I think that people are more afraid to really show ... overt discrimination. It's more hidden.

Religion Either in the form of a community of people or in the form of spirituality and faith sustained by ritual and symbol, religion provides a very important factor in the process of adjustment for some immigrants. Classical sociologist Emile Durkheim (1965) was the first to emphasize the role of religion to social integration within the group sharing the same faith. In a global world, the community of co-religionists who are not necessarily co-ethnics may serve to ease the transition to a new society. People who share the same faith are important in welcoming immigrants at a time when they are most vulnerable and most lonely:

> Farzaneh: We have many friends, as a matter of fact we have a party room down the stairs. And when we arrived here, uh we did one or two weeks and the Bahias came to see us. All of them, we didn't know anyone else at that time. And all the neighbours just wondered... They arrived two weeks before. How do they know all these people? But, later after that, we have beautiful, very good, (pause) Christian friends and Jewish friends, or friends from all the other religions. Because they are no different [than us] and we have many friends from Africa, from Europe from Asia uh, our house is open to the face of whoever who wants to come, everyone is welcome.

Assessing the Immigrant Experience

In this section I examine border crossings as identity shifts or the effects of cultural border crossings on immigrant women's identities based on their own perceptions and narratives of self-change. The immigrant women interviewed in this study assess their experience of migrating to and settling in Canada in very positive terms. Had they been given a second chance, they overwhelmingly assert that they would not hesitate to repeat their decision about migrating to Canada. Their responses are unequivocal, even for those women who experienced hardship in the settlement process.

> Awa: I would. I would. I wouldn't go to any other country (pause). Because of the immigration policy, and because I lived for two years (pause) as a refugee in one country, and over there, I was really [treated as good for] manual labour. Under fire (laugh) from an amazing [number of] people from that country telling us go back where you came from and things like that. So you're sick of it (laugh). So I still think that Canada is the country that has a great future. Built of people with the ideas, healthy ideas to work and have something. And it's uh, for me, for my eyes, quite the, (pause) it's a part of the formula for success.

The women who were experiencing difficulties such as unemployment at the time they were interviewed, who were not as enthusiastic about repeating the decision about migrating to Canada, were quick to add information to qualify their hesitation and to explain that they felt ambivalent due to the temporary difficulties in their lives. Even the women who were more ambivalent about repeating the experience of migrating to Canada were still positive about coming, yet, had they been given a second chance, they would have planned their move much more carefully and they would have given this option a lot more thought. Menen has suffered a lot from racism and prejudice in Canada and has often been frustrated in her ambitions:

> Menen: I would come, I think, maybe I would, but under different circumstances. I'd come with having maybe worked for a few years, with money saved, and having made contacts from home. Like people establishing something for me. Prior to [coming] and knowing that I would be here temporarily, [that] I would come back. But the way I came I wouldn't, I, hopefully, wouldn't have to do so again (laugh). Yeah.

The major reasons why immigrant women, despite the hardships they experienced in the migration process, would be willing to repeat the experience of migration to Canada, were not only their positive appreciation of Canada, but their sense that they had grown immensely since they left their homelands and because they left. That sense of growth, of really knowing oneself, of exploring one's potential, the 'eye-opening' experience, is repeated by most immigrant women, and, I believe, constitutes the most important reason why even women with the least positive feelings about Canada and those experiencing the worst hardship would still take the same decision about migrating, if given a second chance. Women know deep inside that this 'double consciousness' (Werbner 1997: 21) can only be gained by shifting grounds, by adopting a different optic, by deploying different lenses than those used in the country of origin. Grace captures the essence of what many are saying in different ways as well.

> Int: Okay so if you, if you had to do it again, would you come to Canada?

> Grace: Ohh, that's a good question. It's very hard to answer that ... Sometimes (laugh) and I mean there are times when I would have said oh, why, why go through all the struggle. And I wish I was just home you know, nice, peaceful, work, school, get married, have children. Now I'm settled and I'm not peaceful. I mean, that would, I think sometimes you wish that, maybe, that could have been, you wish that were your life. But then, I mean that's just that ... the reality of it is (pause) that I've learned a lot. My mind has, like, opened up. Big time. I cannot, I cannot you know, use ignorance as an excuse. And my mind has become a very intuitive and I, you know, like, I've become as curious now, I wanna know more, I wanna know more, I wanna go, I wanna go learning more, constantly. So because of that, now, I mean, I cannot go back. I mean I cannot, I cannot say I wish I had a different life ... You know I've never lacked food or anything on my table, so my family are still alive. You know, my immediate family. But, I'm grateful for the experience that I've gone though. I've learned, I mean I've accumulated knowledge that I wouldn't

have accumulated by staying home. So because of the knowledge that I've gained, I guess I'm grateful and I don't have any regrets.

Some women value that eye-opening experience so much that, in retrospect, even though they may have developed ambivalent feelings about Canada since they chose to migrate, they say they would leave their country of origin just to acquire such an experience. It is the borderlands here, rather than any specific migration, that is the desired location. Esperanza, from Latin America, is a professional with a Canadian post-graduate degree, and a political activist:

Esperanza: Oh, yeah, I don't like English. I would have liked to have learnt or spoken any other language. But English. And I'm not sure I would have come to Canada, no. But I would have left my homeland yes. Because I feel that leaving your homeland makes us, gives us a much broader view of the world.

Contemporary feminist scholar, bell hooks, refers to that shifting of ground or move to the borderlands or the 'margin' as a positive choice and 'a radical standpoint, perspective, position ... where we begin the process of re-vision' (hooks 1990: 145). For some women the borderlands or 'marginality' is the desired space because it is from that location that they can bring about change (hooks 1984; 1990; 1992). The same woman, Esperanza, stresses the 'magic' of working with others, and even taking the initiative of reaching out to others as one of the ways and perhaps the first step to overcome the isolation and disempowerment of migration to Canada, i.e. activism as a means of empowerment for immigrant women:

Esperanza: But I think it is a process we have to make for ourselves, it doesn't come to us, we have to go to it. We have to make it. And I have known many people, and especially women, who are so isolated in new Canadian communities specially. Who feel so disempowered, who haven't discovered the magic of coming together and working together. And uh, (pause) and that's what I want to work with and for. I want to work to bring (pause) out to other women, you know, some of that strength and some of those things that I have developed in myself.

The immigrant women of this study are also specific in describing what exactly they have learned and how exactly they have changed based on their migration experience. Esperanza eloquently describes how she overcame the confines of her culture, and how, in the process of border crossings, being discriminated as an immigrant and working together with other women, she became more aware of gender equality issues as well:

Yeah, I think that living in a new culture makes you really think about who you are ... And your own prejudice and your own (pause) racism, bigotry, and all the narrow-mindedness of your own culture and of yourself. So it does help you, I think. And it has done that for me to a big extent (pause) ... I think it makes a big difference being a woman. You know, sometimes I think if I had stayed home, I probably would have married and you know, had seven kids and spent the rest of my life working to keep them alive. And my husband probably would have been, you know, had three other women on the side, it would have been just a nightmare. And I don't think [I could have escaped that fate], even though I had a very (pause) [good upbringing] … I think that's a kind of a universal fact. But, the women were much stronger in my family, and I did learn a lot from my grandmother, who was a very active Communist party member … But I still think that I would have not had the clarity about myself as a woman, and you know, awareness of (pause) of the gendered issues that I have here.

Some immigrant women have become more self-sufficient, more self-centred and pay less attention to others' opinions as a result of the migration experience. Long-time, working class immigrant Kiran describes the process of ceasing to care as much about other people's opinions of herself:

> Kiran: Because now it's different than what I was before. Before, I used to sort of worry about it. And care about it too, you know. And try my hardest to be extra nice to somebody else, okay. Now, I don't really care whether that person has an opinion about foreigners and doesn't like foreigners, I don't care, it doesn't really bother me, you know. I am what I am, whether you like it or not (laugh).

Finally, the change for some women involves discovering aspects of themselves they never knew were there. As a result, they are grateful for the ingratiating experience, though they might have experienced all sorts of hardships in Canada. Eloise has found it hard to adjust her engineering and teaching credentials from her native Nigeria to the Canadian job market, as a result of systemic and racialized professional gate-keeping in Canada beyond her immediate control. Yet, she has not stayed idle but has explored different options:

> In Nigeria I taught in a university, and I, you know, I got up every day and it was a rat race, you know, you just, you went and you taught one more class and you went and you taught one more class and you know, like it was just … and there were times you just wondered, you know, I'm just doing this for the pay cheque or I'm just, you know, you didn't really have the time to stop and (sniffle) think about yourself and who you are and then, you know. Since coming here, I've found skills that I didn't believe that I had, you know. I never, I would never have thought about myself as an artist, for example. But, you know, a friend taught me to paint a few months ago and I've loved it and just found that this is beautiful, you know, artistic talent in me that you know, I would never have discovered if I just was on that treadmill of life. You know, just going till, you know, what next. So (sniffles) in a sense, I was forced into the role that I am but it's one in which I have found lots of contentment.

Conclusions

The plight of this study's immigrant women crossing cultural borders in the Canadian Maritimes is a universal one. The anguish and guilt of leaving ancestral homes and well defined selves, the fear and stress that comes from building new homes and selves in a new country where one is not always welcome, the lack of 'precise coordinates' for spirit and memory that travel back and forth in time and space, the tension of the search for belonging and desire to leave, the willing and yet conflictual letting go of parts of self that do not fit in the new environment, critically gazing at one's own culture and feeling guilty for doing so, carving new mental spaces that do not require choosing are all dimensions and stages of a universal quest and the historical experience of migration. Furthermore, the hardships and suffering that individuals and groups go through as a result of socially necessitated migration (Ehrenreich and Hochschild 2002: 6; Parreñas 2002; Sassen 2000, 2002; Ball 2004) and socially constructed 'otherness,' racialization and social exclusion are also part and parcel of the historical experiences of migration in class-divided societies and conditions of global inequality.

Nevertheless, living in the Canadian borderlands is not a single and uniform experience. Although the tension between cultures, the 'pull-and-push' dynamic, is always present, the time that has passed since the original migration, the systemic economic and political context of departure and reception, and the availability of support mechanisms, i.e. immigrant women's unique and specific multi-axial locationality, greatly differentiates their experiences. Some of this study's women trod with relative ease and material comfort in this liminal zone. Others, more recent immigrants, and especially visible minority women, have experienced more discrimination and relative economic and social marginalization, as a result of which they appear more reluctant to make emotional long-term commitments to Canada. Most maintain a rational mental 'balance sheet' where they register the advantages and disadvantages of their stay in Canada. To the extent that they have options, if the balance is overall positive, they will stay, but do not consider themselves either Canadian or fully 'adjusted.' Many develop a critical 'double consciousness' that allows them to keep a certain distance from either side of the border and prepares the way for syncretic cultural expressions and practices.

The social processes and practices by which immigrant women make a 'new home' for themselves in Canada include, most importantly, community involvement and organizing; securing that the 'voice' of their ethno-cultural communities is being heard in Canada; actively seeking and striking friendships with people from diverse walks of life and cultures they come into contact with in Canada while, at the same time, sustaining transnational contacts and emotional connections with extended multi-local families despite geographical distance and travel costs as a way of restoring continuity in their lives after migration; integration into the Canadian labour market or, in the very least, making a decent living financially in Canada; sharing and exchanges across cultures leading to blending and molding cultural values and practices to create unique and original syncretisms or hybridities; and the ongoing spiritual support of organized faith communities. All of the above occur in a context where immigrant women learn ideologically to appreciate Canada, even if the country has not met their expectations or their initial reason for migrating. Immigrant women engage in these processes and practices out of the desire to make themselves feel 'at home' in Canada, i.e. live comfortably but by doing so they also negotiate cultural values, and re-define the very meaning of 'home' as multi-local and the experience of living in an ethnic diaspora in Canada as a borderland, a translocal space.

To be sure, the borderlands that the immigrant women of this study inhabit do not involve clear cut choices between 'pure' forms but, for the most part, positive (though agonizing) new syntheses, cultural syncretisms, hybridities, 'intermingling, the transformation that comes of new and unexpected combinations of human beings, cultures, ideas, politics, movies, songs... It is change-by-fusion, change-by-conjoining' (Rushdie 1991: 394). By making connections across cultures and borders and constructing 'home' as multi-local, the immigrant women of this study indirectly yet firmly challenge existing nation-state based notions of membership and make identity-based claims aiming at a more plural and multi-layered citizenship.

Furthermore, the social processes and practices by which immigrant women make a 'new home' for themselves in the Maritimes are interestingly characterized by: 1) cutting across the private-public sphere division and 2) cutting across local, national and transnational levels. Practices at the local or national levels are often inspired and informed by the transnational and vice versa. Both features of immigrant women's politics of belonging are very significant in terms of their implications for citizenship theory. Undermining the divide of private-public means disrupting the divide's gendered meaning, which is crucial for a feminist understanding of citizenship as challenging women's exclusion from full membership in society on the basis of limited or non-participation in the public sphere (Werbner and Yuval-Davis 1999: 6). Demonstrating empirically the links between local, national and transnational supports a multi-layered citizenship theory that goes beyond the nation-state system.

Finally, the immigrant women of this study overwhelmingly assess their experience of migrating and settling in Canada in positive terms. Had they been given a second chance to re-live their lives, most of them would not hesitate to repeat their decision. Even those who had experienced hardship would still act in the same way, though many would have prepared themselves better in terms of education or building networks from their home country before migrating. Several women who appeared less positive about Canada were quick to add that their feelings should be seen in the context of their present hardship. The most important reason why women would overwhelmingly repeat their decision to migrate was the 'growth' they experienced internally, primarily in terms of their ability to develop a 'double consciousness' and to construct and engage in syncretic and hybrid cultural expressions and practices. They assess such growth to be the direct result of leaving their countries of origin and immersing themselves in a new culture and country; of getting to know new people and experiencing new situations; of getting to discover aspects of themselves they never knew were there before.

Belonging, the psychological dimension of citizenship, for the immigrant women of this study is simultaneously local, national and transnational. Although they engage in practices that are mostly local and transnational, such practices are inspired and informed by transnational, national (Canadian) and local ethnic identifications. Like the 'deep diversity,' 'postnational membership' and feminist

226 *Women, Migration and Citizenship*

models of citizenship establish and legitimate overlapping and simultaneously situated rights on various levels, similarly multi-axial locationality within the nation state and across national spaces and simultaneous cultural situatedness establish and legitimate multi-locationality of 'home' and belonging.

References

Ackers, L. (1998), *Shifting Spaces: Women, Citizenship and Migration Within the European Union*, The Policy Press, Bristol.

Agnew, V. (1996), *Resisting Discrimination: Women from Asia, Africa, and the Caribbean and the Women's Movement in Canada*, University of Toronto Press, Toronto.

Alicea, M. (1997), '"A Chambered Nautilus:" The Contradictory Nature of Puerto Rican Women's Role in the Social Construction of a Transnational Community,' *Gender and Society*, Vol. 11(5), October, pp. 597-626.

Anthias, F. (2002), 'Where Do I Belong? Narrative Collective Identity and Transnational Positionality,' *Ethnicities*, Vol. 2(4), pp. 481-514.

Anthias, F. and Lazaridis, G. (eds) (2000), *Gender and Migration in Southern Europe*, Berg, Oxford, New York.

Anzaldua, G. (1987), *Borderlands/La Frontera: The New Mestiza*, Spinsters/Aunt Lute, San Francisco.

Appadurai, A. (1991), 'Global Ethnoscapes: Notes and Queries for a Transnational Anthropology,' in R. G. Fox (ed.), *Recapturing Anthropology: Working in the Present*, School of American Research Press, Santa Fe, pp. 191-210.

Ball, R. E. (2004), 'Divergent Development, Racialized Rights: Globalised Labour Markets and the Trade of Nurses – The Case of the Philippines,' *Women's Studies International Forum*, Vol. 27, pp. 119-33.

Bhachu, P. (1996), 'The Multiple Landscapes of Transnational Asian Women in the Diaspora,' in V. Amit-Talai and C. Knowles (eds), *Re-situating Identities: The Politics of Race, Ethnicity and Culture*, Broadview Press, Orchard Park, NY, pp. 282-303.

Bhatia, S. and Ram, A. (2001), 'Rethinking "Acculturation" in Relation to Diasporic Cultures and Postcolonial Identities,' *Human Development*, Vol. 44(1), pp. 1-18.

Bolaria, B. S. and Li, P.S. (1988), *Racial Oppression in Canada* (2nd edition), Garamond, Toronto.

Boyd, M. (1999), 'Integrating Gender, Language, and Race,' in S. Halli and L. Driedger (eds), *Immigrant Canada: Demographic, Economic, and Social Challenges*, University of Toronto Press, Toronto, pp. 282-306.

Brah, A. (1996), *Cartographies of Diaspora: Contesting Identities*, Routledge, London, New York.

Breton, R. (1964), 'Institutional Completeness of Ethnic Communities and the Personal Relations of Immigrants,' *American Journal of Sociology*, Vol. 70, pp.

193-205.

Bristow, P. (ed.) (1994), *'We're Rooted Here and They Can't Pull Us Up' Essays in African Canadian Women's History*, University of Toronto Press, Toronto.

Calliste, A. (2000), 'Nurses and Porters: Racism, Sexism and Resistance in Segmented Labour Markets,' in A. Calliste and G. S. Dei (eds), *Anti-Racist Feminism*, Fernwood Publishing, Halifax, pp. 143-64.

Carens, J. (2000), *Culture, Citizenship, and Community: A Contextual Exploration of Justice as Evenhandedness*, Oxford University Press, Oxford.

Castles, S. and Davidson, A. (2000), *Citizenship and Migration: Globalization and the Politics of Belonging*, Routledge, New York.

Catholic Encyclopedia on CD-ROM (http://www.newadvent.org/cathen/14383c. htm). Accessed 24 October 2005.

Citizenship and Immigration Canada (2003), *Facts and Figures 2002: Immigration Overview*, Cat No. MP43-333/2003E, Minister of Public Works and Government Services Canada, Ottawa.

Creese, G. and Kambere, E. N. (2003), 'What Colour is Your English?' *Canadian Review of Sociology and Anthropology*, Vol. 50(5), pp. 565-73.

Das Gupta, T. (1996), *Racism and Paid Work*, Garamond Press, Toronto.

DeLaet, D. L. (1999), 'Introduction: The Invisibility of Women in Scholarship on International Migration,' in G. A. Kelson and D. L. DeLaet (eds), *Gender and Immigration*, New York University Press, New York, pp. 1-17.

Durkheim, E. (1965), *The Elementary Forms of Religious Life.* The Free Press, New York (original in English 1915).

Ehrenreich, B. and Hochschild, A. R. eds. (2002), *Global Woman*, Metropolitan Books, Henry Holt and Company, New York.

Fuentes, C. (1985), *Latin America: At War with the Past*, CBC Enterprises, Toronto.

Goldring, L. (2000), 'The Gender and Geography of Citizenship in Mexico-U.S. Transnational Spaces,' *Identities*, Vol. 1(1), pp. 1-37.

Hall, S. (1992), 'The Question of Cultural Identity,' in S. Hall, D. Held and T. McGrew (eds), *Modernity and Its Futures*, Polity Press and Open University, Cambridge, pp. 274-325.

Harvey, D. (1992), *The Condition of Postmodernity*, Basil Blackwell, Cambridge, Mass., (original publication date: 1998).

Hondagneu-Sotelo, P. and Avila, E. (2000), '"I'm Here, But I'm There:" The Meanings of Latina Transnational Motherhood,' in K. Willis and B. Yeoh (eds), *Gender and Migration*, An Elgar Reference Collection, Cheltenham, UK, Northampton, MA, USA, pp. 331-54.

Hobson, B. and Lister, R. (2002), 'Citizenship,' in B. Hobson, J. Lewis, and B. Siim (eds), *Contested Concepts in Gendered Social Politics*, Edward Elgar, Cheltenham, pp. 23-54.

hooks, b. (1992), *Black Looks: Race and Representation*, South End Press, Boston, MA.

hooks, b. (1990), *Yearning: Race, Gender and Cultural Politics*, Between the Lines,

Toronto.

hooks, b. (1984), *Feminist Theory: From Margin to Center*, South End Press, Boston, MA.

Isin, E. and Wood, P. (1999), *Citizenship and Identity*, Sage, London.

Jakubowski, L. M. (1997), *Immigration and the Legalization of Racism*, Fernwood, Halifax.

Jones-Correa, M. (2000), 'Different Paths: Gender, Immigration and Political Participation,' in K. Willis and B. Yeoh (eds), *Gender and Migration*, An Elgar Reference Collection, Cheltenham, UK., pp. 357-80.

Kelson, G. A. and DeLaet, D. L. (eds) (1999), *Gender and Immigration*, New York University Press, New York.

Kofman, E., Phizacklea, A., Raghuram, P. and Sales, R. (2000), *Gender and International Migration in Europe*, Routledge, London, New York.

Kymlicka, W. (1995), *Multicultural Citizenship: A Liberal Theory of Minority Rights*, Oxford University Press, Oxford.

Li, P. S. (1999), 'Race and Ethnicity,' in P. S. Li (ed.), *Race and Ethnic Relations in Canada* (2nd edition), Oxford University Press, Toronto, pp. 3-20.

Lister, R. (1997), 'Citizenship: Towards a Feminist Synthesis,' *Feminist Review*, Vol. 57, Autumn, pp. 28-48.

Maher, K. H. (2004), 'Globalized Social Reproduction,' in A. Brysk and G. Shafir (eds), *People Out of Place*, Routledge, New York and London, pp. 131-51.

Man, G. (2004), 'Gender, Work and Migration: Deskilling Chinese Immigrant Women in Canada,' *Women's Studies International Forum,* Vol. 27, pp. 135-48.

Miedema, B. and Tastsoglou, E. (2000), '"But Where Are You From, Originally?" Immigrant Women and Integration in the Maritimes,' *Atlantis*, Vol. 24(2), Spring/Summer, pp. 82-91.

Papastergiadis, N. (2000), *The Turbulence of Migration: Globalization, Deterritorialization and Hybridity*, Polity Press, Cambridge, UK.

Park, R. E. (1950), *Race and Culture*, The Free Press, New York.

Parkin, A. and Mendelsohn, M. (2003), 'A New Canada: An Identity Shaped by Diversity,' The CRIC Papers, Centre for Research and Information on Canada, No. 11, October.

Parreñas, R. S. (2002), 'The Care Crisis in the Philippines: Children and Transnational Families in the New Global Economy,' in B. Ehrenreich and A. R. Hochschild (eds), *Global Woman*, A Metropolitan/Owl Book, Henry Holt and Company, New York, pp. 39-54.

Parreñas, R. S. (2001), 'Transgressing the Nation-State: The Partial Citizenship and "Imagined (Global) Community" of Migrant Filipina Domestic Workers,' *Signs,* Vol. 26(4), pp. 1129-54.

Parreñas, R. S. (2000), 'Migrant Filipina Domestic Workers and the International Division of Reproductive Labor,' *Gender and Society*, Vol. 14(4), pp. 560-80.

Pratt, G. (1999), 'From Registered Nurse to Registered Nanny: Discursive Geographies of Filipina Domestic Workers in Vancouver, B.C.,' *Economic*

Geography, Vol. 75(3), pp. 215-36.

Ralston, H. (1998), '"Crossing the Black Water:" Alienation and Identity Among South Asian Immigrant Women,' in D. Kalekin-Fishman (ed.), *Designs for Alienation: Exploring Diverse Realities*, Sophi, University of Jyvaskyla, Finland, pp. 152-74.

Rushdie, S. (1991), *Imaginary Homelands*, Granta Books, London.

Salaff, J. (1997), 'The Gendered Social Organization of Migration as Work,' *Asian and Pacific Migration Journal*, Vol. 6(3-4), pp. 295-306.

Sassen, S. (2002), 'Global Cities and Survival Circuits,' in B. Ehrenreich and A. R. Hochschild (eds), *Global Woman*, A Metropolitan/Owl Book, Henry Holt and Company, New York, pp. 254-74.

Sassen, S. (2000), 'Women's Burden: Counter-geographies of Globalization and the Feminization of Survival,' *Journal of International Affairs,* Vol. 53(2), Spring, pp. 503-24.

Satzewich, V. (ed.) (1992), *Deconstructing a Nation: Immigration, Multiculturalism and Racism in '90s Canada*, Fernwood, Halifax.

Satzewich, V. (1990), 'The Political Economy of Race and Ethnicity,' in P. S. Li (ed.), *Race and Ethnic Relations in Canada*, Oxford University Press, Toronto, pp. 251-68.

Shuval, J. T. (2000), 'Diaspora Migration: Definitional Ambiguities and a Theoretical Paradigm,' *International Migration*, Vol. 38(5), pp. 41-57.

Simmel, G. (1950), 'The Stranger,' in K. H. Wolff (ed.), *The Sociology of Georg Simmel*, The Free Press of Glencoe, New York, pp. 402-08.

Soysal, Y. N. (2000), 'Citizenship and Identity: Living in Diasporas in Post War Europe?,' *Ethnic and Racial Studies*, Vol. 23(1), pp. 1-15.

Soysal, Y. N. (1994), *The Limits of Citizenship: Migrants and Post-National Membership in Europe*, University of Chicago Press, Chicago, London.

Stasiulis, D. (1999), 'Feminist Intersectional Theorizing,' in P. S. Li (ed.), *Race and Ethnic Relations in Canada* (2nd edition), Oxford University Press, Toronto, pp. 347-97.

Stasiulis, D. and Yuval-Davis, N. (1995), *Unsettling Settler Societies: Articulations of Gender, Race, Ethnicity and Class*, Sage Publications, London.

Statistics Canada (2004), *Labour Force Characteristics For Both Sexes, Aged 15 and Older. Latest Release From the Labour Force Survey, June 4*, (http://www.statcan.ca/english/ Subjects/Labour/LFS/lfs-en.htm). Accessed 18 June 2004.

Statistics Canada (2003a), *Population, provinces and territories*, CANSIM, table 0510001, (http://www.statcan.ca/english/Pgdb/demo02.htm). Accessed 18 June 2004.

Statistics Canada (2003b), *Proportion of Foreign-Born Population, Provinces and Territories: 2001 Census of Population*, (http://www.statcan.ca/english/Pgdb/demo46a. htm). Accessed 18 June 2004.

Stolcke, V. (1997), 'The "Nature" of Nationality,' in V. Bader (ed.), *Citizenship and Exclusion*, MacMillan Press, Houndmills, London, pp. 61-80.

Tastsoglou, E. (2000), 'Mapping the Unknowable: The Challenges and Rewards of Cultural, Political, and Pedagogical Border Crossing,' in G. Sefa Dei and A. Calliste (eds), *Power, Knowledge, and Anti-Racism Education*, Fernwood Publishing, Halifax, pp. 98-121.

Tastsoglou, E. (1997), 'Immigrant Women and the Social Construction of Ethnicity: Three Generations of Greek Immigrant Women in Ontario,' in M. Texler Segal and V. Demos (eds), *Advances in Gender Research*, Vol. II, JAI Press, pp. 227-53.

Tastsoglou, E. and Miedema, B. (2005), '"Working Much Harder and Always Having to Prove Yourself:" Immigrant Women's Labour Force Experiences in the Canadian Maritimes,' in M. Texler Segal and V. Demos (eds) *Gender Realities: Local and Global, Advances in Gender Research*, Vol. 9, Elsevier / JAI Press, pp. 201-33.

Tastsoglou, E. and Miedema, B. (2003), 'Immigrant Women and Community Development in the Canadian Maritimes: Outsiders Within?,' *Canadian Journal of Sociology*, Vol. 28(2), June, pp. 202-34.

Tastsoglou, E. and Miedema, B. (2000), *Immigrant Women Organizing for Change: Integration and Community Development by Immigrant Women in the Maritimes*, A Report to the Prairie Centre of Excellence for Research on Immigration and Integration (PCERII). http://pcerii.metropolis.net/frameset_e.html

Tastsoglou, E. and Preston, V. (forthcoming), 'Gender, Immigration and Labour Market Integration: Where We Are and What We Still Need to Know,' *Atlantis*.

Taylor, C. and Laforest, G. (1993), *Reconciling the Solitudes: Essays on Canadian Federalism and Nationalism*, McGill-Queen's University Press, Kingston and Montreal.

Verdecchia, G. (1993), *Fronteras Americanas (American Borders)*, Coach House Press, Toronto.

Waters, M. (1990), *Ethnic Options. Choosing Identities in America,* University of California Press, Berkeley and Los Angeles, California.

Werbner, P. (1997), 'Introduction: The Dialectics of Cultural Hybridity,' in P. Werbner and T. Modood (eds), *Debating Cultural Hybridity: Multi-Cultural Identities and the Politics of Anti-Racism*, Zed Books, Atlantic Heights, NJ., pp. 1-25.

Werbner, P. and Yuval-Davis, N. (1999), 'Introduction: Women and the New Discourse on Citizenship,' in N. Yuval-Davis and P. Werbner (eds), *Women, Citizenship and Difference*, Zed Press, New York, pp. 1-38.

Willis, K. and Yeoh, B. (eds) (2000), *Gender and Migration*, An Elgar Reference Collection, Cheltenham, UK, Northampton, MA, USA.

Yeates, N. (2004a), 'A Dialogue with "Global Care Chain" Analysis: Nurse Migration in the Irish Context,' *Feminist Review*, Vol. 77, pp. 79-95.

Yeates, N. (2004b), 'Global Care Chains,' *International Feminist Journal of Politics*, Vol. 63, pp. 369-91.

Yuval-Davis, N. (2002), 'Some Reflections on the Questions of Citizenship and Anti-Racism,' in F. Anthias and C. Lloyd (eds), *Rethinking Anti-Racism: From Theory to Practice*, Routledge, London, pp. 44-59.

Yuval-Davis, N. (1997), *Gender and Nation*, Sage, London.

Chapter 10

Refugees, Gender-based Violence and Resistance: A Case Study of Somali Refugee Women in Kenya

Awa Mohamed Abdi[1]

Introduction

In the last two decades of the twentieth century, the world had witnessed natural and human-made disasters, such as the 1984 Ethiopian famine, the 1991 collapse of the Somali state, the 1991 American attacks on Iraq, the 1994 Rwandan genocide, and the 1995 Balkan wars. Similarly, the present century began with the 11 September 2001 attacks against the United States, the invasion of Afghanistan and the continuing Iraqi occupation. Other less publicized crises also transpired during these periods, namely those in Sudan, Sierra Leone and Liberia. All these 'disasters' caused humanitarian catastrophes resulting in the forced displacement of hundreds of thousands of people. Conflicts such as the American attacks on Afghanistan and Iraq drew much international media attention, whereas others, such as those in Somalia and Sudan, disappeared into oblivion after five minutes in the limelight. Amid competing catastrophic discourses in this 'age of terrorism,' silence surrounds the condition of millions of refugees around the world.

Somali refugee women in Dadaab camps in Kenya are not immune to this silence, as illustrated by this excerpt:

> You [refugees][2] are closed in a trunk [camp]. The journalists don't come to see us; we are not put in the airwaves of the world; nobody takes news from us; and we are not even visible. So what exactly are we? Aren't we human beings? We are not human beings! No, we are not: since the government under whose jurisdiction we have been living for the last ten years has denied us any legal standing, not even simple ID cards which, when needed, we could use to travel, maybe to Nairobi, to try to plead with our people, or to make a phone call. We don't have that. (Timiro Sugulle)[3]

The struggle to articulate and resist violence against women in war zones remains imperative. This article is a small step in this resistance. By centralizing affected

---

1 This author is the copyright holder.
2 All explanatory brackets are the author's.
3 To protect participant anonymity, pseudonyms are used throughout the article.

refugee women's self-representation, this chapter has four core objectives: first, it examines if and how women's (in)security in Dadaab has changed since 1993, when a Human Rights report first publicized the plight of refugee women in these camps. Second, women's personal narratives about life in Dadaab will be analyzed in terms of the intersectionality of forced displacement, gender, and citizenship. Third, I will argue that the insecurity refugee women experience is intrinsically tied to their non-citizen outsider position, which locates them in the margins within the host nation-state. Fourth, the chapter explores women's agency in refugee camp environments. This last objective highlights the double-edged nature of what we refer to as 'women's agency,' which, in spite of myriad obstacles existing in refugee camps, remains vibrant and real.

The findings reveal that violence against women in the form of rape is still very widespread in Dadaab camps. Despite attempts by the humanitarian organizations to curb this violence, women's narratives testify to a fear of rape that is deeply embedded. An effort by the international organizations to surround refugee residents with live fencing – similar to wire fencing but utilizing thorn bushes – had the unintended consequence of increasing women's sense of vulnerability as they now feel 'fenced in' for the enemy. I argue that these fences epitomize the citizenship exclusionary measures demarcating the boundaries for citizens and non-citizens, thus the marginal position refugees in general, and refugee women in particular, occupy within a world divided into nation-states. Despite such phenomenal constraints, however, I will argue in this chapter that women's victimization in environments where they are treated as 'subcitizens' does not annul their agency. Refugee women demonstrate agency in action by having survived the atrocities of the previous conflict that first uprooted them and by also surviving, articulating, and condemning both in narrative and in poetry the constant threat of violence and rape that confronts them in Dadaab. Still, this remarkable agency aside, the findings of this research conclude that barricading refugees in a closed, remote, and intrinsically insecure region reproduces conditions much resembling those from which refugees fled in the first place. Thus, the failure of the international humanitarian organizations and the Kenyan government to curb this violence will be underscored.

Precursors to the Creation of Dadaab Camps

The overthrow of Siad Barre's regime in January 1991 culminated in a Hobbesian 'State of war of all against all' in Somalia. At the height of this war, between 1991 and mid 1993, it is estimated that close to 400,000 people died from violence and famine (Samatar 1994). In addition, over a million Somalis fled to neighbouring countries, seeking shelter from this atrocity. The proximity of camps initially established at the Kenya/Somali border to conflict areas rendered refugees, as well as the physical and material security of international organizations posted here, under constant threat. This necessitated refugee transfer into Kenyan territory. Dadaab refugee camps, located about 100 km from the Somali/Kenya border were created in September 1991

(Ifo), March 1992 (Dagahaley), and June 1992 (Hagadera). About 130,000 of the original 400,000 Somali refugees in Kenyan refugee camps in early 1990s currently remain in Dadaab. Refugees in these camps are prohibited from leaving the area without special permits from the United Nations High Commissioner for Refugees (UNHCR), the main organization administering the camps. CARE, working under UNHCR, is responsible for social service provisions, Word Food Program (WFP), for food distribution and Medecins Sans Frontieres (MSF), for health.[4]

Kenyan Reaction to Refugee Influx

While producing the majority of world refugees, African countries also host almost all of these refugees, with dismal numbers of Africans resettled in countries in the first world.[5] African refugees of the 1960s and 1970s often integrated within host populations, with very little assistance from international agencies. Most of these refugees were fleeing from independence-related conflicts, and African states, which supported the decolonization process, opened their doors to demonstrate their solidarity. With independence, some countries such as Tanzania and Botswana continued more lenient refugee policies, and even granted permanent residence and citizenship rights to some refugees (Rogge 1994: 20). However, this has been the exception rather than the rule. Most states relegated refugees to either camps or settlements designated for them. One explanation for this heightened restriction is the economic and political turmoil host countries themselves were/are experiencing. Large refugee flows are perceived as potentially exacerbating the situation for citizens of the host country, resulting in a hostile attitude towards the refugees.

The Kenyan state behaved differently towards refugees before and after the 1990s. In the 1980s, Kenya had hosted and successfully integrated a small number of Ugandans, Rwandans and Burundians who were absorbed into the mainstream community. Encampment was not perceived to be a solution to this small flow of refugees. In contrast, the culmination of Somali and Sudanese civil wars and the civil strive in Ethiopia resulted in refugees in the hundreds of thousands coming to Kenya at the end of the 1980s and early 1990s. The Kenyan government was unprepared for this mass inflow and, was unable to control it. The scale of the refugee population coming to Kenya during this period subsequently led to the complete collapse of the system of individual refugee status determination that the Kenyan government employed up to this point (Verdirame 1999: 56). Unable to assume the financial and political implications of managing close to 500,000 refugees fleeing from countries such as Somalia, a hostile-neighbour, the Kenyan government took the conservative approach of creating refugee camps. In fact, this trend epitomizes the whole 1980s and 1990s dealings with refugees in Africa (Crisp 2000: 6). By creating these camps,

---

4   MSF pulled out of Dadaab at the end of 2003 and GTZ (German Technical Cooperation) is currently running the health services of these camps.

5   For 2002, 55,500 out of just over 20 million refugees worldwide, or less than 1 per cent of all refugees, resettled in a third country (UNHCR 2003b).

the Kenyan authorities transferred all responsibility for refugee determination and care and maintenance to UNHCR.

Dadaab camps are situated in a disputed region formerly known as Northern Frontier District (NFD), a semiarid area with predominantly Somali inhabitants. The division of Africa by European powers at the end of the nineteenth century left one large Somali inhabited region as part of Kenya, and another as part of Ethiopia. Subsequent to independence, Somalia continued irredentist claims to these regions until its collapse in 1991. This claim led to tense, at times hostile,[6] relations between Somalia and its neighbouring countries. Due to this tension, Kenya has kept NFD, now known as North eastern Province of Kenya (NEP), and its population under a permanent state of emergency from independence until 1992 (Issa-Salwe 1996), crushing viciously any aspirations to join Somalia. Presently, this region remains neglected and peripheral in its socio-economic status within the country, and Somali-Kenyans themselves marginally enjoy their citizenship rights. In addition to the loss of citizenship rights ensuing from the collapse of Somalia as a nation state, Somali refugees in Kenyan camps also suffer the consequences of policies informed by historical animosities between Somalia and Kenya. The Kenyan government has still not granted Somali refugees legal refugee status, despite their presence in Kenyan territory for over a decade, and categorizes them as 'aliens in transit,' thereby denying them legal status as stipulated in international refugee covenants, which Kenya has ratified The economic, social and psychological costs of this denial for Somali refugee women in particular are very high, as this chapter will demonstrate.

Citizenship, Gender, and Forced Displacement

The scant literature on Dadaab discusses the insecurity inherent in being a refugee in these closed camps (Crisp 2000; Verdirame 1999). However, there exists very little analysis of the gendered nature of this violence and the modes of resistance women utilize. An exception is the 1993 Human Rights report, which first documented and publicized the pervasive nature of insecurity in Dadaab. It has been over ten years since the release of this report, and academic research following up on the condition of the refugee women is dismal. In addition, there is a paucity of research centring on linkages between gender, migration and citizenship, the three core themes of this book.

Adelman characterizes the refugee as the 'Achilles heel' of the nation state system (Adelman, 1999: 93 cited in Turton 2002: 25). 'Refugees flee from their homeland because the basic bond between citizen and government has been broken, fear has replaced trust. Refugees gain this status because they fled from their state territory, "'the father- or the motherland" persecuting and rejecting some of its own,' (Stein 1986: 269) and find themselves in another state committed to upholding only the rights of its members, by definition excluding all others. By the mere fact of

---

6   There was a war between Somalia and Ethiopia in 1977 regarding the Ogaden region.

being beyond the borders of his/her country, the refugee occupies 'no man's land' or as Turton puts it, is out of place, relegated to the domain of the excluded or the abject … (Hyndman 2000: xxii). The protection guaranteed for citizens, albeit limited in many regions of the world, and always gendered (Lister 1997; Yuval-Davis 1997; Pettman 1999), is denied them. Their existence is often clandestine in urban centres or marginally managed in closed refugee camps. The state hosting the refugees may persecute or, at best, tolerate them and sometimes use them as pawns for international aid and legitimacy (Harrell-Bond 1986; Benard 1986). Depending on the historical relations between nations tied by territorial disputes, colonial relationships or East-West alliances in the cold war era, refugees become entangled in global politics and turn into victims of a history not always of their making. For example, Benard (1986) cogently argues that the reception granted by the host population to refugees can vary, with the least hostility towards groups that are entirely foreign, and the most antagonism towards those coming from groups with ethnic or other types of affinity with the host state; such examples include the Algerians in France, Afghan Pathans fleeing to ethnically similar regions to Pakistan (Benard 1986: 622). The Somali refugee in Kenya is another such example.

In a discussion of the locations occupied by citizens and expatriates working with humanitarian organizations versus refugee women enclosed in camps, Hyndman (2000) also highlights the contrasting peripheral status occupied by the latter. Lack of protection for refugee women relegates them to 'subcitizen' status vis-à-vis the protection and emergency evacuation procedures bestowed on citizens and 'supracitizens' or expatriates. Referring to the design of UNHCR housing compound in Dadaab, Hyndman contends, 'to the extent that violent confrontation is anticipated, the design represents a geography of fear' (Hyndman 2000: 98), in its multiple layers of wire fencing, its round the clock armed guards, and the armed convoys all traveling in camps require. Contrary to these stringent security measures to protect 'citizens' and 'supracitizens,' refugee women, who remain the most vulnerable group in the camp population, reside in unsafe and unprotected spaces. Akin to Goffman's (1961) contrast in the locations occupied by inmates and staff within total institutions, Hyndman highlights the discursive and material sites of power people occupy depending on their inclusion/exclusion of the powers in place, whether it is the state or the humanitarian organizations administering the camps. In these sites of power, refugee women become mere recipients of care and maintenance from humanitarian organizations who work in a circumscribed environment with laws dictated by a sovereign state. This state deliberately denies refugees any social, economic, or political rights. Containment becomes the supra-policy of many host states, concerned more with the destabilizing effect large number of refugees can create. Thus, bare minimum protection in the enclosures is provided and this results in refugees falling through the cracks, which underscores the 'contradiction between citizenship as a universal source of all individual rights, and nationhood as an identity ascribed at birth and based on a sentimental attachment to a specific community and territory' (Turton 2002: 25). The refugee out of her 'nation' thus becomes outside the international system divided into states, and thus often falls prey to myriad human rights abuses.

'[C]itizen-based claims which do not attend to the many people in the state who are not citizens easily become complicit with exclusivist or racist politics' (Pettman 1999: 215). Although the citizenship rights enjoyed by women in many parts of the world are themselves questionable, it is nevertheless paramount to question the exclusivist policies many states enact towards refugees, both in the North and in the South. Denial of basic rights to non-citizen refugees/aliens often results in human rights abuses. Struggling against these human rights abuses, feminists have been engaged in a project of engendering forced displacement for the last few decades (Lentin 1997; Martin 1992; Callamard 1999; Niarchos 1995; Indra 1999). While the first victims of gender-based violence in times of crisis are women, it needs to be acknowledged that wars, natural disasters and other forms of catastrophes intrinsically disrupt both men's and women's lives. Denying the drastic impact these types of upheavals have on both genders (El-Bushra and Kukabubuga 1995; Moser and Clark 2001) results in the representation of women as 'eternal victims' thus monopolizing the 'victimization' discourse. This denial does in fact damage women's cause. First this denial undermines the multiple manifestations of women's agency, even in times of crisis. Second, it ignores women's ability to partake in violence. Available literature documents the bifurcated nature of women in conflict situations: for instance, in discussing women's role in communal conflict in India, Butalia (1997) shows how women's collective resistance to patriarchy consolidates their power and agency, whereas the religious and ethnic divisions lead to disengagement from women's causes. The division between victim and agent, as two distinct spheres where men monopolize power and women are designated perpetual victims, is very problematic. Rather, both men and women have the power 'to be either powerful-dominant-or powerless-dominated' (hooks 1989, cited in Lentin 1997).

Alternatively, I argue that acknowledging the shared hardship of both genders in times of crisis, however, should not blind us to the gender specific experience of women. Political and religious crises are almost always gendered: it is normally men who instigate these conflicts, whereas oftentimes women suffer the consequences. Women's sexuality becomes their biggest burden in times of war. Women are often targeted as bearers of future generations and violence inflicted on them takes myriad forms: rape (often gang rape), sterilization, killings, and slavery (see Niarchos 1995; Askin 1997, 1999; Butalia 1997; Bennoune 1995; Ringelheim 1997; El-Bushra and Kukabubuga 1995; Vickers 1993; Haeri 1995). Recent cases documented by international human rights organizations include the rapes perpetrated on Rwandan women in the 1994 genocide and those committed in the ethnic cleansing against Muslim Bosnians in the former Yugoslavia (Human Rights Watch 1996; 2000)[7]. In cases where the nation state fails as legitimate central power, protection for citizens – especially women whose political, social and economic position is subordinate to

---

7   Men are also targeted in times of conflict, and this violence can on occasion take a sexual nature (Zarkov 2001).

that of men – is marginal at most (Yuval-Davis 1997; Pettman 1999). Women's bodies become the terrain through which men inscribe the humiliation and annihilation of the 'other,' the enemy. Violence on women unfortunately does not end with the crisis in the home country. It is often reproduced in exile when refugees seek shelter and security in neighbouring countries where they occupy the outsider non-citizen status of 'refugee.'

Methodology

This research was conducted in summer 2001 in Dadaab refugee camps. Data collection comprised 20 in-depth interviews with refugee women in Hagadera camp. In addition, research included focus groups with refugees of both sexes working with NGOs in the social services sector. Even though no formal interviews were conducted in the two other refugee camps in Dadaab, the researcher spent ample time in both camps, and had discussions with refugee women and NGO workers on the issue of gender and security.

Narrative analysis as a form of research tool involves a mediation of interpretations of interviewees and researcher: participant's account of her situation and her interpretation of it, coupled with the researcher's interpretation, produces a doubly mediated text.[8] Questioning the narratives researchers re-present in the final text and the control we have over the text remains essential (Borland 1991; Stacey 1991). As Borland (1991) discovered, the researcher's final product may be very different from that intended by the narrator. Nevertheless, relinquishing impartial research as having been a one time feminist delusion, this researcher concurs with Stacey (1991: 117) who asserts '[t]here also can be and should be feminist research that is rigorously self-aware and therefore humble about the partiality of its ethnographic vision and its capacity to represent self and other ... I believe the potential benefits of "partially" feminist ethnography seem worth the serious moral cost involved'.

---

8   My positionality as a Somali-Canadian researcher with Somali refugee women deserves a few words. Literature on insider/outsider dilemma in feminist research often presents an essentialization of these positions (Lal 1996). I won't go as far as to claim that my insider position has bestowed on me a 'double vision' or 'double consciousness' (Collins 1990 in DeVault 1999: 40). However, my being a Somali who speaks the language fluently and my knowledge of the social, political, economic and geographical situation of Somalia all greatly facilitated the rapport with research participants. On the other hand, I left Somalia for Canada in 1988, a few years prior to the collapse of the Somali state, and have lived in the Diaspora since; I am educated and trained in Canadian universities. Hence, the experiences of refugees are close, as many of my family members were uprooted in the civil war, yet distant, since I myself do not have a first hand experience of the chaotic turmoil ensuing from civil unrest, treacherous flight displaced individuals undergo, and life in a refugee camp. This latter fact therefore makes me an outsider of some sort. Most importantly, I believe that representing others, whether from an insider or an outsider position, is filled with pitfalls, and power disparities. I therefore remain cognizant that the representation of others I present here is a mere interpretation.

Narratives of Fear

At night, the *shiftas*[9] just enter your house. You are sitting among your children and a gunman enters. There is nothing you can do. He will kill you if he wants to, he will rape you if he pleases, he will rob you of the rations you collected that day, if he pleases. And the children are without food the next day. We are even robbed of the plastic bags that are distributed. Every time anything decent and useful is distributed, someone comes in and robs you. They beat you and take the few shillings you might have saved. They beat you up and take the money. You are in pain, forced to reveal everything; you give up everything you have, even the clothes you are wearing, and they take them. There is no one to tell or complain to. (Anab Ali)

Intruders come to your house in the middle of night. They know the door to your dwelling, search the house, and when they don't find anything, they take you away and rape you. You come back to your house and then tomorrow you are raped again. There is no security (*nabad*) whatsoever here. How many times have we been raped now? We have become grateful that it is only rape. Being only raped by this stranger becomes a luxury (*caano iyo biyo*). When you have to choose between being raped and being killed, you think that it is better to be raped. We go in search of wood in the bushes, since we have no wood. Again, in the outskirts of the camp, we are raped, and we still go fetch firewood. And if you don't go fetch firewood, how will you feed your children? How do you cook the grains for them? If you have no wood, you have nothing. They say they distribute firewood now at this place. It is once in a blue moon that they distribute these. You can do nothing. And if you go to the outskirts, there is an enemy waiting for you there. The enemy might as well rape you over and over; all that matters is getting firewood to cook for your children. (Khadija Ma'alin)

Rape became a key weapon in the Somali civil war. Raping the women of a clan enemy is interpreted as tantamount to winning the psychological war and humiliating the other clan. Women (as well as men and children) escaped from pervasive violence prevailing in Somalia at the onset of the civil war and sought refuge in Kenyan camps. However, *shiftas* perpetuate violence against refugee women in and around the camps. Rape, intrinsically a hideous crime, is exacerbated in myriad ways for Somali women, most of whom have undergone female circumcision, a procedure of sewing the opening of the vagina, leaving a small space for urine and menstrual blood to pass. Men, both in the Somali civil war and in the camps, often employ weapons such as knives, cans and other sharp instruments to open up the women thus inflicting excruciating physical and mental pain. The use of unsterilized instruments leads to tetanus infections and many other health complications including death.

Refugee women's narratives clearly testify to the intrinsic insecurity in Dadaab camps. With only dispersed pastoral nomadic families traditionally inhabiting this

---

9   The term *shifta*, which means bandit, was originally used by the Kenyan government to criminalize and undermine the independence movement in the Northern Frontier District (now North Eastern Province). It is now widely used by everyone to refer all those who commit crimes around the North Eastern Province.

area, the refugees became the biggest settled community in the surroundings, sharing the land and the resources with the local Somali Kenyans. Despite the widespread assumption that co-ethnics in border territories extend hospitality to each other – what Kibreab (1985: 68) calls 'myth of the African hospitality' – there is often competition and conflict between refugees and host communities. In the case of Dadaab region, this conflict stems in part from competition over scarce resources such as water and firewood. Availability of food and other donations destined only for refugees in the area further exacerbate matters, resulting in an increased resentment of the local population towards refugees who are viewed as outsiders not only depleting the scarce environmental resources, but also living better off than the Kenyan citizens in the area.

At the height of this violence, 200 rape cases were reported in 1993. In the next four years, this dropped to between 70 and 105, but again increased to 164 in 1998, dropping back to 71 in 1999, and rose again to 108 in 2000, 72 in 2001 (UNHCR 2003a). UNHCR documented over 100 rapes from February to August 2002 (US Department of State 2003: 6). Given the stigma attached to rape in the Somali culture, these statistics fall short of the actual number of rapes in Dadaab. Furthermore, these numbers alone cannot and do not convey the immensity of the violence inflicted on women. Women constantly refer to the precariousness of their physical safety, with the certainly that any bandit or man who sets his mind to commit rape is able to do so with impunity. The unpredictability of when violence will strike further reinforced women's vulnerability: something akin to Goffman's (1961) discussion of the loss of all sense of security inmates in total institutions experience occurs here. Goffman argues that this loss includes 'anxieties about disfigurement. Beating, shock therapy, or, in mental hospitals, surgery – whatever the intent of staff in providing these services for some inmates – may lead many inmates to feel that they are in an environment that does not guarantee their physical integrity' (Goffman 1961: 21).

A widely held belief in the camps is how Kenyan police stationed in the camps, responsible for keeping the peace and security in the area, fear these *shiftas*. Many argue that because of this fear the police never venture into the camps at night, and therefore do not provide protection to refugee women. Moreover refugees allege that they are not only terrorized by *shiftas*, but also greatly mistrust and fear Kenyan police, who are notorious for their corruption and brutality (Waldron and Hasci 1995; Goldsmith 1997), especially against marginalized and excluded groups such as refugees. Accusations of Kenyan police perpetrating rapes and violence against women refugees, and refugees in general, are not uncommon (Human Rights Watch 1997). Distrust and fear of those responsible for keeping law and order in the camps leaves refugee women little recourse to escape their precarious situation of outsider non-citizen in peripheral closed camps.

Repeatedly women emphasize the difficulties of protecting them from Somali men, 'their own people,' who wear masks to conceal their identity. 'Shadows' is a term one woman used to depict these perpetrators' elusiveness from justice. Many of the rapes were and are still committed in the outskirts of the camps where women fetch firewood for cooking. Rapid depletion of already scarce firewood resulted in women traveling further and further to collect wood. Moreover, rapes committed during *shifta* raids of the camp abound. During this fieldwork, such rapes occurred where the perpetrators went to specific houses, demanded jewellery, money, and even usurped the food, sugar, and flour that were in the house. There exist many other accounts where refugee women were forced to carry the rations that were donated that week, and subsequently raped, and at times, killed by the *shifta*.

In the absence of court of law, perpetrators rarely pay for their crimes. Refugee women argue that they had not only lost protection as citizens of a country, but have also lost the protection of their families and of their communities. The protection male relatives previously may have provided (Callamard 1999; Williams 1990) are lost in the camp setting. Even for those whose husbands/fathers are present, the protection these male relatives can provide in the camp setting is limited. The shiftas are armed whereas the refugees are not.[10] With no guaranteed protection in the camps due to the loss of their membership to a 'state,' women claim that their sense of security has drastically changed from what it was in prewar Somalia. Although the rights they enjoyed as women was marginal to those of men, similar to women in other regions of the world (Lister 1997; Yuval-Davis 1997; Pettman 1999), they nevertheless enjoyed some state protection as citizens of a functioning state body. Furthermore an erosion of systems of mitigation that traditionally supported these women further increases their vulnerability. The fragility of refugee dwellings, which are built with porous dry sticks, is another factor reducing women's sense of protection and security. Research participants claimed that rape has now become such a normal occurrence that husbands are no longer abandoning their wives once they are raped, which was traditionally the case in Somalia. Rape brings shame both to the family and to the husband of the raped victim, a trend observed in other conflict zones (Turshen 2001). One participant who herself experienced this abandonment described how her husband deserted her and their children at the beginning of the civil war once he found out about the rape.

A question many ask is why Somali men are not protecting the women? For example, why do men not go out to fetch the firewood themselves instead of allowing women to face rape? Crisp (2000) discusses how Ethiopian and Sudanese men perform these tasks. One explanation provided is that the *shiftas* mainly target Somali refugees and rarely other ethnic groups. Somali men thus confront the possibility of being killed if they venture to the outskirts of the camps. When the researcher asked the above question to focus group participants, refugees recounted how at the height of *shifta* violence, the bandits lined up refugee women to load them with the plunder, and shot any husband/male member of community who dared protest. They also discussed the high number of men who perished in the hands of *shiftas*. Hence, they argued, for a man to protect his wife, the result is his death. Informants argue that this has had great impact on the community's outlook on the

---

10   There have been allegations that Dadaab is an arms centre (Austin 2002). A few refugees may have guns, but as far as this research could ascertain, most refugees are unarmed, and probably would have utilized their arms to protect themselves if they had that option.

issue of rape. In Somalia, one of the participants said, two men could never share a woman, but in this environment of rape and insecurity, men are 'tamed' to accept living with this reality and 'humiliation,' accounting for one more blow to the male refugee ego.

Accounts of camp security provided by refugee women were almost uniform irrespective of social status. For instance, women who can afford to buy firewood in the camp market articulated exactly the same fears as those who have to travel to collect firewood. This is an illustration that all refugee women[11] in Dadaab experience the fear of being a potential rape victim. Thomas's famous statement of the importance of the subjective in human life illustrates the reality of these women: '... if men [women] define situations as real, they are real in their consequences' (quoted in Stryker 1980: 31). The narratives testify to the damage that is far reaching in its deep-rooted psychological impact. The women's fear is also much tied to their flight history in the height of the Somali crisis, which, with the collapse of the nation-state, constituted terror in the killings, maiming and raping that characterized the civil war. One could argue here that refugee women around the world are denied both 'national and transnational citizenship' (Yuval-Davis and Werbner 1999: 3), since their countries of birth and host states where they sought refuge both deny them their humanity. 'Humanity without frontiers' (Levi-Strauss 1996: 177, cited in Yuval-Davis and Werbner 1999: 3) potentially intrinsic in citizenship remains a desired yet distant objective in the current 'nation state' system. And this particularly holds true for refugee women whose 'sex' is an extra burden in times of conflict and forced displacement.

Finally while the narratives explicitly illustrate how all the women are affected by camp insecurity, slight group differences may be identified. During this fieldwork, the researcher observed that many of the firewood carriers belonged to the Somali Bantu group who are the most marginalized group in the camp, a continuation of hierarchies that prevail/ed in Somalia. Also, some of the rapes are committed within the camp by refugee men on minority groups who lack the clan protection some other Somalis might enjoy. For example, a Somali Bantu teenage servant was raped by the father of the family she was working for during this fieldwork, highlighting the multiple layers of the insecurity minority women within the refugee population confront.

---

11 The representation of refugee women as a homogeneous group is somewhat erroneous. The day-to-day life of those with close family members in the Diaspora, those with business or connections, and those who have no links and survive on the bare minimum distributed by the international aid regime who account for most refugees in Dadaab, drastically differ. Many better-off refugees opt to settle in Nairobi as they can afford to rent housing and buy national identity cards.

Bush Fire: Reproduction of Violence in Camps

We fled from a conflict yesterday and the UN organizations assisted us, assisted us well. We thank them for it; we thank Allah for it. When we got settled, when our children started schools, when we would have done something for ourselves, an enemy was born (*cadow baa dhulkii oo dhan ka dhaqaaqay*). The other [the Somali conflict] might even have been better; at least you could get out, you could move around even if a bullet hits you. And now we miss that. In that one, we could run. During the conflict, we had freedom of movement! Now, we cannot escape. You just sit around waiting. (Najma Jama)

I would have liked that we return to our country and that we get peace. When I say 'our country,' we previously fled from our country. Why did we flee? Not because we could not find what to eat or what to drink; we fled because of the insecurity. And today, the insecurity still persists. We also don't have security here … When I want to go collect firewood, I cannot do it. Even if this man [any passer-by] means no harm to me, I am apprehensive. I feel great apprehension. As soon as he moves, it is guaranteed that I will get scared because of the situation in the camp, because of what the women like me have been subjected to. And there are plenty of these. (Hawa Gurey)

Refugee women used the metaphor of 'an uncontrolled bushfire' and draw myriad parallels of their experiences in the chaotic environment following the collapse of law and order in Somalia at the onset of the civil war, resulting in loss of state protection, and their in-limbo legal status and camp experiences. Women discuss how the violence they first fled has followed them to the camps. 'For nearly one half of the women who reported being raped, rape was a factor in causing them to become refugees in the first place. 85 out of the 192 reported cases involved women who were raped in Somalia before fleeing to Kenya…' (Africa Watch 1993: 8). Many wonder why they ever left, as they previously fled from rape in the chaotic environment ensuring from the civil war, but still confront rape in the camps.

Live Fencing: To Protect or to Control?

There is no security whatsoever at this place. The twin of the problem that drove us from there [Somalia] is here. This is even worst since there is nowhere to escape to at night. We are fenced in a place where there is heat, where there is suffering, where there is hardships, where there are killings and robberies. (Khadija Ma'alin)

Similar to livestock in a fenced space where a hyena enters, we run in every direction. Life is precious, you know; we run around, run around. (Timiro)

We are surrounded by fences (*oodd baa nagu eedaaran*) and any man, whether he is carrying a knife or a gun, who wishes to do so, can penetrate through this fence to your residence. (Kaaha Bihi)

International organizations surrounded the blocks where refugees reside with 'live fencing,' transplanted thorn bushes used as a substitute for razor-wire fencing. Fencing the camps with thorn bushes is intended to impede intruders accessing refugee living quarters. 'UNHCR and the German agency GTZ have assisted the refugees in Dadaab to plant more than 150 kilometres of live thornbush fencing around the blocks ...' (Crisp 2000: 614). However, in my observations in Dadaab and from women's accounts, the thorn bushes were providing very little protection, if any at all. In fact, these are easily penetrable even by children who create multiple entries to the residential blocks, and will not hinder any intruders from accessing refugee dwellings. Thus, the conditions women refugees confront in these camps very much resemble those they fled when militias constantly threatened their and their families' security back in the civil war in Somalia.

In the nomadic Somali culture, livestock are always fenced at night so as to protect them from wild animals. In fact, originating from a nomadic culture, the Somali language is full of livestock allegories. Using the simile of the fences surrounding the camps, refugees equate their situation to that of domestic animals, with the full control of whether to open the entrance to the fenced space to let the animals out resting with the animal owner.[12] This owner, in the camp context, is the camp administration and the Kenyan government, both of whom are perceived to restrict refugee freedom of movement. This can be tied to the widespread curtailment of the freedom of movements of those 'outside' of the nation-state (Stolcke 1997; Lister 1997; Yuval-Davis 1997). The camp's spatial enclosure with transplanted thorn bushes originally intended to attenuate the violence against women contributes to refugee women's heightened sense of vulnerability. The women as beings entitled and deserving protection are negated by the camp setting and by the barriers to the outside world. The international NGOs' commitments or ability to curb the terror in the camps are very limited. The women are literally robbed of any sense of security, which is replaced with one of permanent fear of victimization. Lack of concerted effort by the Kenyan State to resolve the limbo state of these refugees exacerbates these situations (Abdi 2004), condemning refugees to permanent 'statuslessness,' both beyond their country of birth, Somalia, and their country of refuge, Kenya.

Worthy of mention are commendable, albeit limited, efforts by humanitarian organizations working with refugees in Dadaab. These organizations implemented a program to assist women – the Vulnerable Women and Children (VWC) Program – that provides them with counselling, accompaniment and support. This program also provided women deemed 'at risk' with opportunities for transfer to other camps,

---

12   UNHCR provides travel documents to refugees who for health/emergency-related reasons need to travel. But these passes are difficult to obtain, and waiting times are often lengthy. Despite this constraint on freedom of movement, refugees with economic means to pay bribes travel within Kenya and to and from Somalia. I observed this as I took the bus from Dadaab to Nairobi, which cost me 800 Kshillings, whereas refugees with no documentation paid 1600 Kshillings (this was in August 2001). The extra 800 Kshillings paid by refugees serves as bribe to government agents who stopped the bus 8 times during this trip.

or even resettlement through the Canadian and Australian Women-at-Risk programs. Efforts such as the VWC meet women's basic needs after they report rapes, but do little to prevent the rapes. However, a contact with a CARE staff informed the author that a mobile court was brought to Dadaab and two rapists were given harsh sentences at the end of 2001. This surely is a great progress, but more efforts are necessary in order to end the barricading of over 100,000 people in closed spaces for over ten years and to break the cycle of violence.

Agency: in Spite of all Odds

The representation of women victims of violence as solely victims is problematic. This is particularly so for women from the south, who are often portrayed as needing salvaging from permanent victimization (Mohanty et al. 1991). Presenting the challenges women from the south confront without obliterating their agency, their multiple subjectivities, and their power remains fundamental. As discussed earlier, I prefer to 'conceptualize victim and agent as alternatives within a framework of multiple, shifting subject positions' (Julian 1997: 208).

The structure and the location of Dadaab camps place a severe limitation on women's capacity to resist, while at the same time women's narratives and practices represent a protest denouncing both *shiftas* and the international community. Kelly (2000: 46), critiquing the interpretation of the focus of women as victims as a denial of their agency, argues

> [A]gency appears to reside solely in the actions of the violator; thus, the position of agent for women is confined to perpetration of, or support for, violence. The agency which women exhibit (and feminist research has documented) not only in resisting and coping with personal victimization but also through collective opposition to interpersonal violence and/or war is disavowed.

She further asserts that women's agency is recognized only when women's behaviour is consistent with male behaviour, thus undermining women's agency in surviving violence, which should count as resistance in itself.

As stated above, the main focus of this article is women's interpretation of their situation regarding security. Highlighting this point is paramount to avoiding viewing Somali refugee women as only victims. The day-to-day survival mechanisms utilized by these women in mitigating the harsh material and physical insecurities in Dadaab is a testimony to these women's agency. The interviewees were diverse in their occupations (homemakers, petty traders, community outreach workers, etc.) and diverse in their socio-economic backgrounds. Nevertheless, all shared the responsibility of caring and mediating the difficult reality of camp life for their families. These women fled a war zone and brought their families to these camps. They survived despite insidious physical and economic insecurities both during the flight and in the camps, again testifying to their agency. The central role women in Dadaab play in the economic well-being of their families cannot be emphasized enough.

Women sell merchandize: from clothing to the smallest grams of sugar or spices in the market. Most of these women make a bare minimum, which, nevertheless, supplements the inadequate food rations provided by the international organizations. Thus, refugee women devise ways of resisting and working around some of the limitations inherent in camp life. Their daily routine as caretakers provides them with a sense of purpose aiding them to cope under difficult conditions (Martin 1992; DeVoe 1993). These women manage their families' needs and affairs regardless of whether they are raped or not. In fact, one can argue that women's efforts are the underpinning of refugee families' survival in these harsh conditions.

Another form of resistance that refugee women utilize is composing songs and poetry denouncing and articulating their daily reality. Two such poems that this researcher collected were broadcasted on BBC Somali Service for the occasion of International Women's Day, 8 March 2004. These poems, with powerful lyricism, described the constraints of life in Dadaab camps, with appeals to Somali leaders, the United Nations and to the international community. Furthermore, the woman composing these poems used her voice to condemn the Kenyan government for turning a blind eye to the plight of 'status-less' refugees under its jurisdiction, while at the same time acknowledging and appreciating this same government's willingness to settle the refugees, even if in closed refugee camps. Refugee women's narratives presented here are further articulation of memories of violence, turning 'private memories of victimization into articulated political acts of resistance' (Lentin 1997: 14).

One last phenomenon exemplifying the agency and resourcefulness of these women, but also the permanent fear of rape in the camps, is the addition of pants to women's attire. Pants were garments that were exclusively worn by men in Somalia. Prior to the civil war, woman's clothing consisted of an underskirt, a long dress, and a shawl worn over the dress. When the author inquired about this topic, she was informed that this trend commenced with the civil war: because of indiscriminate rapes at the beginning of the Somali civil war, women started wearing pants under their usual clothing with the hope of prolonging the time necessary for the attacker to disrobe her, and with the hope of being rescued in time. Women continue to wear these pants in the camps for the same reasons that they wore them in Somalia.[13]

All these examples are illustrative of women's agency in practice, in an environment of scarcity and insecurity, and contradict refugee women's representation as passive victims.

---

13 Some women also mentioned that wearing pants under their dresses is an Islamic practice that was previously absent from the Somali culture. This increases their modesty. For example, they argue that in case of an accident in the market, their private parts won't be revealed in public.

Conclusion

Refugee camps designated and theorized as temporary emergency shelters often turn into long-term 'living environments' (Harrell-Bond 1999: 137). Also what refugee women first considered as a safe haven turns for many into 'a site of gendered violence' (Giles 1999), as the conditions encountered in the new setting much resemble those from which women fled in the first place. The analysis provided in this chapter therefore requires a questioning of the dichotomization of origin and destination as differing for women. Women's integrity remains precarious both at home in times of crisis, when the relation between citizens and state is disrupted, and in the so-called safe haven where all social, economic, and political rights are curtailed. This chapter demonstrates the process of the individual refugee woman's descent from a citizen with a certain amount of guaranteed security from family, community, and government, to a 'subcitizen' in an enclosed refugee camp. While refugee women in Dadaab live in circumscribed insecure camps, where violence and rape reign, it was argued that this reality should not obscure women's agency in resisting this violence. Examples provided in this chapter testify to women's agency in resisting and denouncing the insecurities in these camps.

Somali refugee women in Kenya are confronted with multiple betrayals. First and foremost their countrymen, who are ultimately responsible for their geographical and social location, have betrayed them. The warlords engaged in the civil war have to this day failed to resolve peacefully their political and clan differences. These warlords are in great part responsible for the 'status-less' state of these refugees. Second, the Kenyan government, under whose jurisdiction the refugees find themselves, has betrayed these women by denying them freedom of movement and other basic rights enshrined in refugee law for over ten years. Although Kenya is a signatory to both the UN convention on human rights and on refugees, and the OAU convention on refugees, it has in actuality thus far taken a hands-off approach to its refugee population. Even after ten years in Kenya, the government still maintains that Somali refugees are aliens in transit thereby refusing to extend legal rights to them. About nine years ago, Waldron and Hasci (1995: 14) wrote:

> [T]he literature we have examined shows very little follow-up by either the United Nations or individual countries who have important bilateral agreements with Kenya. This raises some serious questions about the present state of international human rights covenants, which are designed to protect refugees such as those in Kenya. It further calls into question both the ability of the international community to enforce them and the willingness of host countries like Kenya to adhere to them.

Not much has changed from what the above authors concluded: the outcry about the plight of refugee women in Kenya from the early 1990s fell on deaf ears. There are minimal attempts to curtail this persecution and to find alternative solutions to encampment. 'There is little doubt that many refugee women's experiences in refugee camps amount to persecution according to the accepted definition' (Callamard 1999: 210). The location of Dadaab camps, the physical construction of refugee shelters, and the absence of adequate state protection to non-citizens all contribute to the increased vulnerability experienced and articulated by these women. The situation of refugee women in camps epitomizes the culmination of forced displacement, lack of citizenship rights, and gender vulnerability in remote closed camps, a situation many women who migrate, both voluntarily and involuntarily, confront in different parts of the world.

Addressing the situation of refugees in Sudan, Harrell-Bond has argued that 'UNHCR's power to influence through discourse, diplomacy, or the use of the media has hardly been exploited. Nor has it apparently been recognized that the use of its economic power, the aid programme itself, has enormous potential for preventing many of the situations which give rise to breaches of the human rights of refugees' (Harrell-Bond 1986: 162). Similarly, more pressure on the Kenyan government to respect its obligations towards refugees is paramount. Provision of adequate night security to the blocks where the refugees reside remains necessary to protect refugee women from rape and to assuage the ten years of psychological and physical terror *shiftas* have inflicted on them. Increasing the firewood donated to refugees would also reduce women going in search of fuel for cooking, and would thus decrease the number of rapes committed in the outskirts of the camps. In addition, more research is necessary to assess the extent of violence against women in Dadaab camps. It was apparent from this author's discussions with both refugee women and NGO workers that other types of violence, such as domestic abuse, are widespread and are intensified by the frustration and disempowerment men feel under camp administration and in the camp environment. Thus, assessing the types and the extent of violence against women in the camps would contribute to ascertaining the types of interventions necessary to assist women victims of violence.

To conclude, many have already cogently demonstrated how citizenship is gendered and the link between gender, citizenship and the nation state (Yuval-Davis 1997; Yuval-Davis and Werbner 1999; Lister 1997). In addition to denouncing violence against refugee women, this chapter attempted to demonstrate the 'non-citizen' position refugee women in many parts of the world occupy, and the vulnerabilities intrinsic in being outside of the nation-state. This 'outsidedness' demonstrates that refugees represent a rupture to the nation-state-based notions of citizenship. In fact not belonging to the 'imagined community' positions refugee women outside the citizenship debate. It is paramount to question the basis for this exclusion and to advocate for more universalistic rights that all individuals, men, women, and children, within any state, should be guaranteed regardless of their ethnicity, race, religion, and immigration status. And this should go beyond conventions ratified by all, yet respected by few.

References

Abdi, A. M. (2004), 'In Limbo: Dependency, Insecurity and Identity amongst Somali Refugees in Dadaab Camps,' *Refuge: Canadian Periodical on Refugee Issues*,

Vol. 22(2).

Africa Watch and Women's Rights Project (1993), 'Seeking Refuge, Finding Terror: The Widespread Rape of Somali Women Refugees in North Eastern Kenya,' Vol. 4(14).

Askin, K. D. (1999), 'Sexual Violence in Decisions and Indictments of the Yugoslav and Rwandan Tribunals: Current Status,' *The American Journal of International Law*, Vol. 93(1), January, pp. 97-123.

Askin, K. D. (1997), *War Crimes Against Women:Prosecution in International War Crimes Tribunal*, Martinus Nijhoff, The Hague.

Austin, K. (2002), 'Letter to Sadako Ogata,' *The Fund for Peace*, 13 November.

Benard, C. (1986), 'Politics and the Refugee Experience,' *Political Science Quarterly*, Vol. 101(4), pp. 617-36.

Bennoune, K. (1995), 'S.O.S. Algeria: Women's Human Rights Under Siege,' in M. Afkhami (ed.), *Faith and Freedom: Women's Human Rights in the Muslim World*, Syracuse University Press, London.

Borland, K. (1991), '"That is not what I said:" Interpretive Conflict in Oral Narrative Research,' in S. Berger Gluck and D. Patai (eds), *Women's Words: The Feminist Practice of Oral History*, Routledge, London, pp. 59-75.

Butalia, U. (1997), 'A Question of Silence: Partition, Women and the State,' in R. Lentin (ed.), *Gender and Catastrophe*, Zed Books, London, New York.

Callamard, A. (1999), 'Refugee Women: A Gendered and Political Analysis of the Refugee Experience,' in A. Ager (ed.), *Refugees: Perspectives on the Experience of Forced Migration,* Pinter, New York, pp. 196-214.

Crisp, J. (2000), 'A State of Insecurity: The Political Economy of Violence in Kenya's Refugee Camps,' *African Affairs*, Vol. 99, pp. 601-32.

DeVault, M. L. (1999), *Liberating Method: Feminism and Social Research,* Temple University Press, Philadelphia.

DeVoe, P. (1993), 'The Silent Majority: Women as Refugees,' in R. S. Gallin, A. Ferguson and J. Harper (eds), *Women and International Development Annual*, Vol. 3, Westview Press, San Francisco, pp. 605-29.

El-Bushra, J. and Mukarubuga, C. (1995), 'Women, war and transition,' in C. Sweetman (ed.), *Societies in Transition*, Oxfam, Oxford.

Giles, W. (1999), 'Gendered Violence in War: Reflections on Transnationalist and Comparative Frameworks in Militarized Conflict Zones,' in D. Indra, (ed.), *Engendering Forced Migration: Theory and Practise,* Berghahn Books, New York, pp. 83-93.

Goffman, E. (1961), *Asylums: Essays on the Social Situation of Mental Patients and Other Inmates*, Doubleday Anchor Books, Garden City, NY.

Goldsmith, P. (1997), 'The Somali Impact on Kenya, 1990-1993: The View From Outside the Camps,' in H. M. Adam and R. Ford, *Mending Rips in the Sky*, The Red Sea Press Inc, Lawrenceville, pp. 461-83.

Haeri, S. (1995), 'The Politics of Dishonor: Rape and Power in Pakistan,' in M. Afkhami (ed.), *Faith and Freedom: Women's Human Rights in the Muslim World*,

Syracuse University Press, London, pp. 161-74.

Harrell-Bond, B. (1999), 'The Experience of Refugees as Recipients of Aid,' in A. Ager (ed.), *Refugees: Perspectives on the Experience of Forced Migration*, Pinter, New York, pp. 137-68.

Harrell-Bond, B. E. (1986), *Imposing Aid: Emergency Assistance to Refugees*, Oxford Publishing Press, New York.

Human Rights Watch (2000), 'Federal Republic of Yugoslavia, Kosovo: Rape as a Weapon of "Ethnic Cleansing,"' (www.hrw.org/reports/2000/fry).

Human Rights Watch (1997), 'International Failures to Protect Refugees: Protection of the Rights of Refugee Women,' (www.hrw.org/reports/1997/gen3/general. htm).

Human Rights Watch (1996), 'Rwanda's Genocide: Human Rights Abuses Against Women,' HRW Documents on Women, New York, 24 September, (www.hrw.org/press/1996/09/rwandagenocide.htm).

Human Rights Watch (1993), 'Somalia: Beyond the Warlords: The Need for a Verdict on Human Rights Abuses,' 7 March, Vol. 5(2), (www.hrw.org/reports/1993/somalia).

Hyndman, J. (2000), *Managing Displacement: Refugees and the Politics of Humanitarianism,* University of Minnesota Press, Minneapolis.

Indra, D. (ed.) (1999), *Engendering Forced Migration: Theory and Practise*, Berghahn Books, New York.

Issa-Salwe, A. M. (1996), *The Collapse of the Somali State: The Impact of the Colonial Legacy*, Haan Publishing, London.

Julian, R. (1997), 'Invisible Subjects and the Victimized Self: Settlement Experiences of Refugee Women in Australia,' in R. Lentin (ed.), *Gender and Catastrophe*, Zed Books, London, New York.

Kelly, L. (2000), 'Wars Against Women: Sexual Violence, Sexual Politics and the Militarised State,' in S. Jacobs, R. Jacobson and J. Marchbank (eds), *States of Conflict: Gender, Violence and Resistance*, Zed Books, London, pp. 45-65.

Kibreab, G. (1985), *Reflections on the African Refugee Problem: African Refugees*, Africa World Press, New Jersey.

Lal, J. (1996), 'Situating Locations: The Politics of Self, Identity and "Other" in Living and Writing the Text,' in D. L. Wolf (ed.), *Feminist Dilemmas in Fieldwork*, Westview Press, Boulder, Colorado, pp. 185-214.

Lentin, R. (ed.) (1997), *Gender and Catastrophe*, Zed Books, London, New York.

Lister, R. (1997), *Citizenship: Feminist Perspectives,* Macmillan, Basingstoke.

Martin, S. F. (1992), *Refugee Women*, Zed Books, London.

Mohanty, C. T., Russo, A. and Torres, L. (eds) (1991), *Third World Women and The Politics of Feminism*, Indiana University Press, Indianapolis.

Moser, C. O. N. and Clark, F. C. (2001), 'Introduction,' in C. O. N. Moser and F. C. Clark (eds), *Victims, Perpetrators or Actors? Gender, Armed Conflict and Political Violence,* Zed Books, London, New York, pp. 3-12.

Niarchos, C. N. (1995), 'Women, War, and Rape: Challenges Facing the International Tribunal for the Former Yugoslavia,' *Human Rights Quarterly*, Vol. 17, pp. 649-

90.

Pettman, J. J. (1999), 'Globalization and the Gendered Politics of Citizenship,' in N. Yuval-Davis and P. Werbner (eds), *Women, Citizenship and Difference*, Zed Books, London.

Ringelheim, J. (1997), 'Genocide and Gender: A Split Memory,' in *Gender and Catastrophe*, R. Lentin (ed.), Zed Books, London, New York.

Rogge, J. R. (1994). 'Repatriation of Refugees,' in T. Allen and H. Morsink (eds), *When Refugees Go Home: African Experiences*, Africa World Press, New Jersey, pp. 14-49.

Samatar, A. I. (ed.) (1994), *The Somali Challenge: From Catastrophe to Renewal?* Lynne Rienner Publishers, London.

Stacey, J. (1991), 'Can there be a Feminist Ethnography?,' in S. Berger Gluck and D. Patai, *Women's Words: The Feminist Practice of Oral History*, Routledge, London, pp. 111-19.

Stein, B. (1986), 'Durable Solutions for Developing Country Refugees,' *International Migration Review*, Vol. 20(2), Special Issue: Refugees, Issues and Direction, Summer, pp. 264-82.

Stolcke, V. (1997), 'The "Nature" of Nationality,' in V. Bader (ed.), *Citizenship and Exclusion*, Macmillan Press, Houndmills, London, pp. 61-80.

Stryker, S. (1980), *Symbolic Interactionism,* The Benjamin/Cummings, California.

Turshen, M. (2001), 'The Political Economy of Rape: An Analysis of Systematic Rape and Sexual Abuse of Women during Armed Conflict in Africa,' in C. O. N. Moser and F. C. Clark (eds), *Victims, Perpetrators or Actors? Gender, Armed Conflict and Political Violence*, Zed Books, London, New York, pp. 55-68.

Turton, D. (2002), 'Forced Displacement and the Nation-State,' in J. Robinson (ed.), *Development and Displacement*, Oxford University Press, Oxford, pp. 19-75.

UNHCR (2003a), 'Security Analysis,' Sub-Office, Dadaab.

UNHCR (2003b), 'Refugees by Numbers,' (http://www.unhcr.org/). Accessed 24 October 2003.

Yuval-Davis, N. (1997), *Gender and Nation,* London: Sage.

Yuval-Davis, N. and Werbner, P. (eds) (1999), *Women, Citizenship and Difference*, Zed Books, London.

US Department of State Bureau of Democracy, Human Rights and Labour (2003), 'Somalia: 2002 Country Report on Human Rights Practices,' released 31 March.

Verdirame, G. (1999), 'Human Rights and Refugees: The Case of Kenya,' *Journal of Refugee Studies*, Vol. 12(1), pp. 55-77.

Vickers, J. (1993), *Women and War*, Zed Books, London.

Waldron, S. and Hasci, N. A. (1995), 'Somali Refugees in the Horn of Africa: State of the Art Literature Review,' *Studies on Emergencies and Disaster Relief*, No. 3, Nordiska Afrikainstitutet, Uppsala.

Williams, H. A. (1990), 'Families in Refugee Camps,' *Human Organization*, Vol. 49(2), pp. 100-09.

Zarkov, D. (2001), 'The Body of the Other Man: Sexual Violence and the Construction of Masculinity, Sexuality and Ethnicity in the Croatian Media,' in C. O. N. Moser and F. C. Clark (eds), *Victims, Perpetrators or Actors? Gender, Armed Conflict and Political Violence*, Zed Books, London, New York, pp. 69-82.

Index